Manuel Wörsdörfer

AI Ethics and Governance

Also of interest

Artificial Intelligence in Higher Education.
Generative AI, Personalized Learning, Digital Transformation
Stamatios Papadakis, Georgios Lampropoulos (eds.), 2026
ISBN 978-3-11-914829-0, e-ISBN 978-3-11-222672-8

Intelligent Educational Robots.
Toward Personalized Learning Environments
Stamatios Papadakis, Georgios Lampropoulos (eds.), 2025
ISBN 978-3-11-135206-0, e-ISBN 978-3-11-135269-5

Demystifying Artificial Intelligence.
Symbolic, Data-Driven, Statistical and Ethical AI
Emmanuel Gillain (ed.), 2024
ISBN 978-3-11-142567-2, e-ISBN 978-3-11-142614-3

Digital Trust.
Online Safety, Identification Models, Ethical Digital Environments
Pascal Muam Mah, Mahmoud Ahmed Nasr, 2026
ISBN 978-3-11-222974-3, e-ISBN 978-3-11-222975-0

Deepfake and Image Forgery Detection.
Cybersecurity, Multimedia Forensics, Image Manipulation
Chad Johnson, 2026
ISBN 978-3-11-914827-6, e-ISBN 978-3-11-173436-1

Manuel Wörsdörfer

AI Ethics and Governance

Historical, Cultural, and Regulatory Perspectives

DE GRUYTER

Author
Prof. Dr. Manuel Wörsdörfer
School of Computing and Information Science
Maine Business School
University of Maine
5723 DP Corbett Business Building
Orono, ME 04469
USA
manuel.woersdoerfer@maine.edu

ISBN 978-3-11-224594-1
ISBN 978-3-11-224595-8 (PDF)
ISBN 978-3-11-224596-5 (EPUB)
DOI https://doi.org/10.1515/9783112245958

Library of Congress Control Number: 2026938138

Bibliographic information published by the Deutsche Nationalbibliothek
The Deutsche Nationalbibliothek lists this publication in the Deutsche Nationalbibliografie; detailed bibliographic data are available on the Internet at http://dnb.dnb.de.

De Gruyter and Walter de Gruyter GmbH are part of De Gruyter Brill.
www.degruyterbrill.com

Questions about General Product Safety Regulation:
productsafety@degruyterbrill.com

Cover illustration: Monsitj/iStock/Getty Images Plus

Foreword

This volume presents six essays that examine the ethical, cultural, regulatory, and sociopolitical dimensions of artificial intelligence (AI), drawing on historical, philosophical, business and computer ethics, and policy perspectives. It begins with a historical analysis of AI's origins and early debates, tracing lessons on hype, institutional influence, and the limits of replicating human intelligence. Subsequent chapters explore AI in popular culture, analyzing recurring motifs such as autonomy, surveillance, and techno-authoritarianism to reveal ethical insights and critique dystopian narratives. The volume then addresses governance challenges, evaluating the need for stronger AI regulation, the implications of U.S. policy shifts, and the strengths and limitations of the E.U.'s AI Act and California's Transparency in Frontier AI Act. Finally, it examines antitrust concerns and the ethical, economic, and societal rationale for interventions, including breaking up dominant tech firms. Collectively, the essays provide a multidimensional and interdisciplinary framework for understanding AI's promises, perils, and governance in an evolving technological landscape.

Keywords
AI ethics, AI history, AI in pop culture, AI governance, Trump administration, California's Transparency in Frontier AI Act, E.U.'s AI Act, antitrust, competition policy, ordoliberalism 2.0

 | https://doi.org/10.1515/9783112245958-202

Dedicated to my parents, whose belief in education shaped my path, and to my wife, whose partnership made this work possible.

Acknowledgments

I am grateful to the anonymous reviewers whose thoughtful comments and careful readings significantly strengthened the clarity and rigor of this work. My sincere thanks also go to the editorial and production team at De Gruyter for their professionalism, guidance, and unwavering support throughout the development of this book. I would like to acknowledge the support provided by the Maine Business School, UMaine's School of Computing and Information Science, and the College of Liberal Arts and Sciences, whose sabbatical and research funding made it possible for me to devote the necessary time and attention to this project. I am indebted to my colleagues for their encouragement, insightful conversations, and generosity in sharing ideas that helped shape the arguments presented in this work. Any remaining shortcomings, of course, are my own.

 | https://doi.org/10.1515/9783112245958-203

Contents

Introductory remarks

1 Aims and scope

The past few years have witnessed what commentators frequently describe as the *(generative) AI revolution* – a period of extraordinary technological acceleration accompanied by equally intense public debate. The rapid proliferation of large language models (LLMs) and image-generation systems has sparked both optimism and anxiety: enthusiasm about innovation, productivity, and creativity on one hand, and apprehension about (algorithmic) bias and discrimination, mis-/disinformation, and existential risk (e.g., due to the automation of blue and white-collar jobs) on the other. While some observers have warned of an AI bubble driven by speculative investment and inflated expectations (i.e., AI hype and hubris), others have adopted a markedly dystopian outlook, invoking Frankenstein or Terminator-like imagery to describe a looming crisis of human control (i.e., AI doomerism).

These contrasting narratives have unfolded amid a broader reconfiguration of AI governance. Following the 2024 U.S. presidential election, the second Trump administration adopted a distinctly laissez-faire and hands-off orientation, emphasizing deregulation and market-driven innovation as strategic imperatives for U.S. technological leadership. Executive Order 14179, *Removing Barriers to American Leadership in AI,* revoked earlier federal oversight measures and relaxed safety, transparency, and accountability requirements in the name of competitiveness. By mid-2025, this deregulatory approach had consolidated into a comprehensive framework, including additional executive orders and an *AI Action Plan,* aimed at accelerating domestic innovation while minimizing federal intervention. The accompanying rhetoric on 'ideological bias' in AI systems further exemplified the politicization of AI governance and ethics, reframing normative concerns over fairness and accountability as issues of market freedom and national strategy (Trump White House, 2025a, 2025b, 2025c, 2025d).

In contrast, the E.U. has pursued a more precautionary and institutionalized regulatory trajectory. The *AI Act,* in conjunction with a *Code of Practice* for general-purpose AI providers, aims to strike a balance between innovation and legal accountability through mechanisms of transparency, copyright protection, and public safety (European Commission, 2025). Although non-binding, the Code functions as an instrument of soft law, prefiguring the compliance expectations of the forthcoming E.U. framework. At the subnational level, jurisdictions such as California have advanced parallel initiatives – notably the *Transparency in Frontier Artificial Intelligence Act* (TFAIA) – further illustrating the increasing diversification and fragmentation of global AI governance (California State Legislature, 2025).

These developments provide the broader context and serve as the starting point for the present volume, which comprises six essays examining key challenges at the

 | https://doi.org/10.1515/9783112245958-001

intersection of AI, philosophy, society, politics, and law. Conceived in recognition of the fact that contemporary debates around AI are often fragmented, reactive, or dominated by hype, dystopian fears, and technical speculation – and frequently lack historical context, ethical depth, and a nuanced understanding of societal and regulatory dimensions – the book brings together multi- and interdisciplinary perspectives, including historical, pop-cultural, socio-political, business-ethical, computer-ethical, regulatory, and economic (including antitrust and competition policy). The contributions explore how AI technologies both reflect and reshape human values, institutions, and power structures, inviting readers to consider not only the promises and perils of (generative and frontier) AI but also the normative frameworks and governance models needed to ensure its responsible development in an era of rapid change. To address the conceptual and ethical gaps in current discourse, the volume adopts ordoliberalism – both in its classical formulation and its contemporary extension, ordoliberalism 2.0[1] – as a unifying theoretical framework. Initially rooted in the German and European tradition of the social market economy, ordoliberalism seeks to balance individual freedom, human dignity, and social justice with fair competition, market freedom, and the rule of law; its updated form extends this vision to the digi-

1 *Ordoliberalism* constitutes a foundational business-ethical framework underpinning Germany's and the E.U.'s post-World War II social market economy. It aims to reconcile moral imperatives, such as social justice, human rights, and human dignity, with economic objectives of market freedom, fair competition, and efficiency. Classical ordoliberalism developed along two principal intellectual strands: the Freiburg School of Law and Economics (notably Eucken, Böhm, and Großmann-Doerth) and the sociological neoliberalism of Röpke and Rüstow. A central tenet of ordoliberal thought is the distinction between *Ordnungspolitik* (regulatory policy) and *Prozesspolitik* (process policy), which delineates the proper role of the state as a neutral 'market police,' 'ordering power,' and 'guardian of the competitive (socio-economic) order.' In this capacity, the state establishes, monitors, and enforces the rules of market order without engaging in direct economic intervention. Eucken's principles further advocate market-conforming regulation, the curtailment of lobbying power, and the protection of competition, individual freedom, and citizen sovereignty. Collectively, these ideas chart a middle course between laissez-faire capitalism and totalitarian collectivism, envisioning an efficient yet humane socio-economic order grounded in the rule of law and fairness. *Ordoliberalism 2.0* represents a contemporary evolution of this tradition, reinterpreting classical ordoliberal principles to meet the challenges of the digital economy, platform capitalism, and AI-driven markets. Building on the foundational vision of a socially responsible and competitive market order, this updated framework calls for regulatory structures that preserve competition while safeguarding individual liberties and collective welfare in highly digitized environments. Its core commitments include promoting open and competitive markets, freedom of contract and liability, preventing the abuse of market power, and limiting rent-seeking behavior. Additionally, it emphasizes coherent regulatory and competition policies, adherence to the rule of law, non-discrimination, subsidiarity in governance, and mechanisms for addressing negative externalities, such as environmental pollution. By integrating classical ordoliberal ethics with the governance demands of the digital era, ordoliberalism 2.0 provides a normative foundation for promoting innovation while ensuring accountability, fairness, and the sustainability of the socio-economic order (Biebricher et al., 2022; Goldschmidt & Wohlgemuth, 2008; Wörsdörfer, 2020, 2022a, 2022b, 2023, 2024, 2025a, 2025b).

tal age, offering normative tools for governing platform capitalism, AI-driven markets, and the concentration of technological power.

2 Research questions

Building on this framework, the book offers a comprehensive, interdisciplinary examination of AI that integrates historical, philosophical, cultural, socio-political, economic, and regulatory perspectives. The analysis is organized around six interconnected research questions.
- *First,* it considers what the history of AI can teach us about the present and (likely) future of the field, combining historical analysis with insights from computer philosophy and AI ethics.
- *Second,* it examines recurring themes in influential books, films, and TV series, exploring the ethical lessons they offer and their relation to contemporary narratives of hype, competition, and (existential) risk.
- *Third,* it assesses the adequacy of current AI governance mechanisms, evaluating ten key areas of concern – from labor markets and algorithmic bias to environmental impacts, political power, and military applications – and exploring potential reforms, including soft versus hard law approaches and emerging models such as constitutional AI and AI guardrails.
- *Fourth,* the study analyzes recent U.S. policy shifts, particularly under the second Trump administration, highlighting their implications for academia, science funding, diversity, equity, and inclusion (DEI) initiatives, industry regulation, social media oversight, privacy/data protection, surveillance, and emerging technologies/industries, such as cryptocurrencies and deep-sea mining.
- *Fifth,* it provides a systematic evaluation of the E.U.'s AI Act and California's TFAIA, assessing their strengths, limitations, and potential reforms from a computer- and business-ethics perspective informed by ordoliberal 2.0 principles.
- *Finally,* it examines ongoing lawsuits, legal investigations, and antitrust concerns in the United States and the E.U., evaluating the ethical and economic rationale for structural remedies, such as breaking up dominant tech firms, to safeguard consumer welfare, innovation, and competition.

3 Methodology

To address these questions, the volume adopts a normative-analytical and qualitative research methodology. It draws extensively on primary sources, including the writings of AI pioneers (e.g., McCarthy, Minsky, Simon, Turing), researchers (e.g., Bender, Bradford, Buolamwini, Eubanks, Muldoon, Narayanan, O'Neil, Zuboff), ethicists (e.g., Bostrom, Coeckelbergh, Edmonds, Floridi, Vallor, Wallach), and policymakers (e.g.,

Khan, Wu),[2] as well as legal and policy documents (e.g., executive orders, laws and legislations, regulatory frameworks, [inter-]national and best practice guidelines). Ongoing lawsuits and current investigations (e.g., against Apple, Facebook, and Google) are examined to capture real-world applications, enforcement dynamics, and emerging governance challenges. These sources are complemented by a comprehensive review of relevant scholarly and policy literature. By linking each research question to this rigorous methodological foundation, the study offers an in-depth, multidimensional, and interdisciplinary examination of AI governance, ethical implications, and societal impact, thereby fostering conceptual clarity, critical reflection, and practical insight for navigating contemporary technological challenges.

4 Contributions

The volume's contribution lies in its capacity to link theory and practice. It offers a fresh synthesis that connects ordoliberal 2.0 ethics with AI philosophy, governance, competition policy, and antitrust analysis. It further introduces technological realism as a constructive perspective for interpreting cultural narratives and policy debates. Case studies – including Trump-era policy changes (e.g., the revocation of Biden's AI Executive Order and Blueprint for AI Bill of Rights), California's TFAIA, and major antitrust actions – illustrate how abstract principles translate into real-world decisions and institutional challenges. As a result, the volume becomes not only a theoretical exploration but also a practical guide for policymakers, researchers, and industry leaders.

By integrating history, culture, ethics, law, and economics around a coherent ordoliberal 2.0 foundation and a unified set of research questions, the book provides a multidimensional and deeply contextual understanding of AI. It equips readers with the analytical tools and practical insights needed to engage thoughtfully with an evolving technological and regulatory landscape – one that demands fairness, accountability, innovation, and the long-term sustainability of the socio-economic order. This broad, integrative framework also shapes the book's intended audience, extending its relevance beyond disciplinary boundaries.

Due to its interdisciplinary approach, the book is designed for a broad readership, including scholars in business, computer science, law, political science, and the social sciences, as well as policymakers, technology developers, and informed readers seek-

2 See, for example, Bender and Hanna's *The AI Con* (2025), Bostrom's *Superintelligence* (2014), Bradford's *The Brussels Effect* (2020) and *Digital Empires* (2023), Buolamwini's *Unmasking AI* (2023), Eubanks' *Automating Inequality* (2018), Dachwitz and Hilbig's *Digitaler Kolonialismus* (2025), Muldoon et al.'s *Feeding the Machine* (2025), Narayanan and Kapoor's *AI Snake Oil* (2024), O'Neil's *Weapons of Math Destruction* (2016), Wallach's *Moral Machines* (2010), Wu's *The Age of Extraction* (2025), and Zuboff's *The Age of Surveillance Capitalism* (2019).

ing a rigorous yet accessible understanding of AI. By situating generative and frontier AI within their historical and philosophical contexts, the volume demonstrates how technological systems intersect with human values, institutional structures, and evolving power dynamics. In doing so, it offers readers conceptual clarity as well as practical tools for navigating AI's promises and pitfalls.

5 Chapter synopses

This essay compilation offers a comprehensive examination of the ethical, cultural, regulatory, and socio-political aspects of AI, drawing on historical, philosophical, and policy perspectives. It opens with "We Propose That a 2-Month, 10-Man Study of Artificial Intelligence Be Carried Out During the Summer of 1956 at Dartmouth College" – *A (Different Kind of) History of AI,* which revisits the origins of AI to provide context for contemporary debates. Amid recent advances in generative and frontier AI, as well as discussions around artificial general intelligence (AGI), much of today's discourse lacks a historical perspective. This chapter traces key moments in AI history, presenting lessons chronologically, including reflections on early philosophical and political debates, the persistence of hype and hubris, funding dynamics, institutional influences, and the limits of replicating human intelligence. By critically engaging with historical trajectories, it challenges dominant narratives and highlights the ethical and practical lessons that can inform current AI research and development (R&D), policy, and governance.

Next, *From HAL to Her: AI Philosophy Through the Lens of Pop Culture* examines how AI is represented in literature, film, and TV, analyzing recurring motifs such as autonomy, emotional intelligence, techno-authoritarianism, and surveillance. Through a thematic analysis of selected cultural works, it explores the ethical insights these portrayals offer and their connection to contemporary narratives of hype, competition, and existential risk. The chapter critiques dominant dystopian narratives, such as the Terminator or Frankenstein trope, arguing that they conceal grounded understandings of technological change. It advances a framework of technological realism, situated between optimism, pessimism, determinism, and somnambulism, to foster more constructive and critically reflective discourse.

Why AI Requires Better Regulation: Ten Compelling Arguments addresses the need for stronger AI governance amidst trends of deregulation in the United States and soft-law initiatives in the E.U. It presents ten key reasons for robust regulation, covering labor market impacts, algorithmic biases and discrimination, privacy concerns, the amplification of harmful content (e.g., dangerous and hate speech), business and human rights issues, environmental consequences, the power of big tech, threats to democracy, and military applications. The chapter evaluates pathways for future AI regulation, considering both soft and hard law approaches, as well as emerging frameworks such as constitutional AI and AI guardrails. It also proposes strategies to enhance existing frameworks, including the E.U.'s AI Act.

Computer Ethics in the Age of Trump: The Politics of AI and Tech Governance analyzes key policy shifts during the second Trump administration, contrasting them with previous leadership approaches. It focuses on areas such as changes in academia and science (funding), DEI initiatives affecting big data ethics, industry regulation, including the repeal of Biden-era AI guidelines, social media oversight, surveillance and privacy involving government and private actors, cryptocurrency deregulation, and legislation on deep-sea mining and conflict minerals. This chapter illustrates how political shifts intersect with AI ethics, highlighting the broader ethical implications of policymaking for digital governance.

California's AI Act vs. the E.U.'s AI Act – A Comparative Ordoliberal Analysis compares the TFAIA and the E.U.'s AI Act, assessing their scope, governance mechanisms, and ethical safeguards. By situating California's precautionary approach against a deregulatory federal backdrop, the chapter highlights global challenges in balancing innovation, safety, accountability, and ethics. It identifies potential measures to 'harden' AI governance frameworks and draws lessons for policymakers, researchers, and industry stakeholders seeking to manage AI risks responsibly.

Finally, *The Case for Breaking Up Tech Conglomerates* explores ongoing lawsuits, regulatory investigations, and anti-competitive business practices across the E.U. and the United States, assessing their ethical, economic, and societal implications in the context of concentrated corporate power. Using an AI ethics and antitrust perspective, the chapter evaluates how dominance by firms such as Alphabet, Apple, and Meta affects consumer welfare, innovation, market competition, and small and medium-sized enterprises. Drawing on ordoliberal (2.0) principles, it assesses policy instruments ranging from automatic sanctions to structured enforcement pyramids, and ultimately considers corporate breakups as a measure of last resort to restore competitive balance, linking ethical concerns with practical regulatory strategies.

Together, these chapters provide a multidimensional and interdisciplinary understanding of AI, bridging historical, cultural, ethical, regulatory, and business perspectives. They highlight the promises and risks of AI while offering insights into governance strategies, normative frameworks, and policy innovations necessary to ensure responsible technological development in a rapidly changing world.

6 Originality and new research

A careful examination of AI's historical development underscores the importance of grounding contemporary technological innovation in historical awareness and ethical responsibility. While historical surveys of AI exist, this book makes an original contribution by *integrating historical analysis directly into a normative governance framework*, demonstrating how past intellectual traditions, research practices, and philosophical debates inform current regulatory challenges. Rather than treating history as background material, the book uses it as an analytical tool for identifying recurring misconceptions, governance failures, and ethical blind spots. This historically informed approach highlights enduring lessons – managing expectations, anticipating ethical risks, and recognizing that technology evolves within the context of political, social, and cultural factors – thereby offering a distinctive and conceptually rich foundation for contemporary AI policy and ethics.

Cultural representations of AI in literature, film, and television deepen this perspective, adding another layer to the book's interdisciplinary approach. Although cultural commentary on AI is common, the book makes a unique contribution by systematically integrating *cultural narratives* into a broader regulatory and ethical framework. It reveals how cultural imaginaries expose societal anxieties about autonomy, surveillance, labor, and corporate power, and how these narratives can serve as early-warning signals for real-world challenges. Rather than simply cataloging depictions of AI, the book develops *technological realism* as an original interpretive lens – one that avoids hype-driven extremes and instead foregrounds democratic accountability, moral responsibility, and the social embeddedness of AI systems. This synthesis of cultural analysis with policy-relevant ethics is rare in the literature and offers a new perspective on how public imagination and governance debates mutually shape one another.

Insights from history and culture, taken together, inform a subsequent analysis of governance frameworks across ten key areas – from labor markets and systemic bias to environmental impacts, democratic vulnerabilities, and military applications. These domains illustrate why AI requires strong and anticipatory regulation, combining enforceable hard law with adaptable soft law, including constitutional AI and guardrails. This discussion sets the stage for one of the book's core original contributions: the introduction of *ordoliberalism 2.0* as a comprehensive, interdisciplinary framework for AI governance. While ordoliberal thought has shaped European economic policy, it has not been systematically applied to digital markets, algorithmic power, or contemporary AI regulation. By integrating business ethics, computer ethics, legal theory, and historical analysis, the book presents a comprehensive framework for assessing market structures, accountability mechanisms, and the rule of law in the digital era.

Political developments further illustrate the need for this approach. The book provides one of the first *systematic ethical and governance-oriented assessments of Trump-era AI and digital policies*, examining shifts in science funding, DEI programs, surveillance practices, social media governance, and cryptocurrency regulation. Because these developments have received (almost) no academic scrutiny, the book fills a significant gap in understanding how political contexts shape AI ecosystems and societal risk.

The book offers an *early and detailed analysis of California's TFAIA*, a landmark frontier-AI law that has received limited scholarly commentary. It evaluates the Act's strengths, such as its transparency requirements, whistleblower protections, and public infrastructure provisions, alongside its weaknesses, including definitional ambiguity, insufficient environmental safeguards, and underfunded enforcement. This assessment provides a foundation for future scholarly and policy debate. A *comparative analysis of the TFAIA and the E.U.'s AI Act* highlights how different jurisdictions operationalize similar principles. While both emphasize transparency, accountability, and adaptive governance, each exhibits notable gaps that necessitate reform. Framed through the lens of ordoliberalism 2.0, these comparisons make an original, normative, and analytical contribution to the rapidly developing field of AI governance, where rigorous cross-jurisdictional studies remain scarce.

Finally, the book applies ordoliberal 2.0 principles to the ethical and economic dimensions of corporate concentration in the AI sector. By linking AI ethics with competition policy and antitrust enforcement – illustrated through contemporary E.U. and U.S. cases involving Apple, Google, and Meta – the analysis demonstrates how unchecked platform power affects consumer welfare, innovation, and democratic resilience. This integration, still rarely explored in current scholarship, provides a novel conceptual and policy-oriented contribution to debates on market structure and the future of the AI ecosystem.

References

Biebricher, T., Nedergaard, P., & Bonefeld, W. (eds.) (2022). The Oxford Handbook of Ordoliberalism. Oxford, Oxford University Press.

California State Legislature. (2025). Senate Bill 53 (Transparency in Frontier Artificial Intelligence Act). https://legiscan.com/CA/text/SB53/2025 (last accessed: December 30, 2025).

European Commission. (2025). The General-Purpose AI Code of Practice. https://digital-strategy.ec.europa.eu/en/policies/contents-code-gpai (last accessed: December 30, 2025).

Goldschmidt, N. & Wohlgemuth, M. (eds.) (2008). Grundtexte zur Freiburger Tradition der Ordnungsökonomik. Tübingen, Mohr Siebeck.

Trump White House. (2025a). Removing Barriers to American Leadership in Artificial Intelligence. https://www.whitehouse.gov/presidential-actions/2025/01/removing-barriers-to-american-leadership-in-artificial-intelligence/ (last accessed: December 30, 2025).

Trump White House. (2025b). White House Unveils America's AI Action Plan. https://www.whitehouse.gov/articles/2025/07/white-house-unveils-americas-ai-action-plan/ (last accessed: December 30, 2025).

Trump White House. (2025c). Winning the Race. America's AI Action Plan. https://www.whitehouse.gov/wp-content/uploads/2025/07/Americas-AI-Action-Plan.pdf.

Trump White House. (2025d). AI.Gov. https://www.ai.gov/#home-services-anchor (last accessed: December 30, 2025).

Wörsdörfer, M. (2020). Ordoliberalism 2.0: Towards a New Regulatory Policy for the Digital Age. Philosophy of Management 19(2). 191–215.

Wörsdörfer, M. (2022a). Big Tech and Antitrust: An Ordoliberal Analysis. Philosophy & Technology 35. Article 85.

Wörsdörfer, M. (2022b). Walter Eucken: Foundations of Economics. In: Biebricher, T., Nedergaard, P., & Bonefeld, W. (eds.). The Oxford Handbook of Ordoliberalism. Oxford, Oxford University Press. 91–107.

Wörsdörfer, M. (2023). The Digital Markets Act and E.U. Competition Policy: A Critical Ordoliberal Evaluation. Philosophy of Management 22(1). 149–171.

Wörsdörfer, M. (2024). Biden's Executive Order on AI and the E.U.'s AI Act – A Comparative Computer- and Business-Ethical Analysis. Philosophy & Technology 37. Article 74.

Wörsdörfer, M. (2025a). The E.U.'s Artificial Intelligence Act – An Ordoliberal Assessment. AI and Ethics 5 (1). 263–278.

Wörsdörfer, M. (2025b). AI Ethics and Ordoliberalism 2.0: Towards a 'Digital Bill of Rights.' AI and Ethics 5 (1). 507–525.

Chapter 1
"We propose that a 2-month, 10-man study of artificial intelligence be carried out during the summer of 1956 at Dartmouth College" – A (different kind of) history of AI

Abstract: Recent advances in AI – particularly in generative AI and the growing discourse around artificial general intelligence – have intensified debates about the ethical and socio-political implications of intelligent systems. Yet much of today's discussion lacks historical perspective. This chapter revisits key moments in AI history to explore how past debates, expectations, and ethical concerns can inform current developments. Adopting an interdisciplinary approach that draws on primary sources and insights from AI ethics and computer philosophy, the chapter presents a series of lessons structured chronologically. These include reflections on early philosophical and political discussions, the persistence of hype (and hubris), the role of funding and institutions, and the limits of replicating human intelligence. By critically engaging with the historical trajectory of AI, the chapter challenges dominant narratives and calls for a more context-aware and ethically grounded framework for shaping the future of AI research, development, and policy.

Keywords: AI history, Alan Turing, symbolic reasoning, artificial neural networks, chatbots, artificial general intelligence, AI hype

1.1 Introduction

The rapid evolution of AI in recent years – marked by unprecedented advances in generative AI, growing discussions around artificial general intelligence (AGI), and a shift toward deregulation, privatization, or soft law frameworks[1] – has reinvigorated debates around the societal, ethical, and philosophical implications of intelligent sys-

1 In early 2025, Biden's AI Executive Order (EO) was revoked and replaced with EO 14179, *Removing Barriers to American Leadership in AI* (Trump White House, 2025a). This new directive reversed the previous safety regulations, reflecting the current administration's broader policy shift toward deregulation and 'free-market' principles. It eliminated key requirements related to AI safety standards, content watermarking, and national security risk assessments, aiming instead to boost innovation, entrepreneurial activity, and U.S. leadership in AI R&D. By summer 2025, Trump unveiled a sweeping initiative to accelerate AI development in the United States, centered on market liberalization, reduced federal oversight, and efforts to eliminate what he described as 'partisan bias' in AI systems. This initiative included three additional EOs and the release of a comprehensive *AI Action Plan*. Key

 | https://doi.org/10.1515/9783112245958-002

tems. These developments are not occurring in a vacuum: they are shaped by political dynamics, such as those during the Trump administration, and driven by significant public and commercial hype. Yet amid this flurry of activity, a critical question remains underexplored: What can the history of AI teach us about the present and future of the field?

This chapter revisits the early – and not-so-distant – stages of AI history to explore how past debates, expectations, and ethical concerns can illuminate current trends. From early warnings about superhuman intelligence and overinflated predictions to foundational discussions about the regulation of intelligent machines and their philosophical implications, the past offers a rich archive of insights. However, these insights have been largely overlooked in today's dominant AI discourse, which often lacks historical awareness and tends to isolate technical progress from broader ethical and societal concerns.

In contrast to the existing literature,[2] which often presents AI history as a sequence of milestones or technological achievements, this chapter adopts an interdisciplinary approach that integrates historical analysis with perspectives from computer philosophy and AI ethics. Drawing extensively on primary sources – original writings by AI pioneers and ethicists – it offers a structured narrative through a series of key lessons, arranged (largely) chronologically (see also Appendix I). These lessons not only contextualize historical developments but also extract their relevance for contemporary AI research, development, and policy. Given the scarcity of comprehensive and critically engaged work in this space, this chapter aims to fill a crucial gap. Rather than simply recounting events, it evaluates them – highlighting overlooked implications, challenging prevailing narratives, and advocating for a historically informed framework in addressing today's AI challenges.

---

measures included banning federal procurement of AI tools deemed ideologically biased, fast-tracking permits for AI data center construction, promoting AI exports, and reducing environmental and DEI-related regulations. The administration also pledged to prioritize government contracts for companies aligned with its stance on free speech. In his public remarks, Trump reiterated Republican concerns about perceived 'woke' influences in AI models and framed the plan as a strategic effort to outpace China in AI development (Trump White House, 2025b, 2025c, 2025d). Meanwhile, in Europe, debates continue over the future of the E.U.'s AI Act – often regarded as the gold standard for AI regulation (Wörsdörfer, 2024a, 2025a). Amid growing industry pressure, policymakers are considering a potential pause, enforcement delay, or even fundamental reform of the legislation (EU AI Champions Initiative, 2025; FAZ, 2025; IAPP, 2025). In parallel, the Commission has introduced a voluntary code of practice for general-purpose AI providers, addressing transparency, copyright protection, and public safety. Though non-binding, these guidelines are intended to help industry players align with forthcoming AI Act requirements and are viewed as a form of soft law (European Commission, 2025; Wörsdörfer, 2025e).

2 See, for example, Al-Amin et al. (2024), Bennett (2023), Buchanan (2005), Haenlein and Kaplan (2019), Kaplan (2016, 2024), Muthukrishnan et al. (2020), Rasheed et al. (2024), Toosi et al. (2022), and Wooldridge (2021).

The chapter is structured around a series of key lessons drawn from different moments in AI's history. Each section introduces one such lesson, supported by examples and ending with a takeaway message. Topics explored include the long trajectory of AI research, the role of interdisciplinary collaboration, foundational philosophical debates, the often slow and incremental nature of progress, the diversity of research methodologies, the importance of funding and institutional infrastructure, and the persistent gap between hype and reality. Other sections focus on the rediscovery of past ideas, the centrality of data, the challenge of scalability and commercialization, the ethical and governance frameworks surrounding AI, the unintended consequences of increasing system complexity, and the continuing limitations in efforts to replicate human-like intelligence (i.e., AGI). The chapter ends with a summary of its main findings and an outlook on future research questions.

1.2 Lessons learned

1.2.1 AI through the ages: A (surprisingly) long history

Lesson: While the formal establishment of AI as a scientific discipline began in 1956, its conceptual roots extend much further – drawing from ancient mythology, medieval philosophy, religious thought, literature, and early mechanical inventions. Understanding this long and layered history provides essential context for interpreting the capabilities and limitations of modern AI systems.[3]

Examples: The formal inception of AI as an academic discipline is widely marked by the 1956 Dartmouth Workshop, often referred to as the birth or 'constitutional convention' of modern AI. Organized by McCarthy and Minsky, with the support of Shannon and Rochester of IBM, the workshop was outlined in their proposal, *A Proposal for the Dartmouth Summer Research Project on Artificial Intelligence*. The aim was to test the provocative assertion that "every aspect of learning or any other feature of intelligence can be so precisely described that a machine can be made to simulate it" (McCarthy et al., 1955). It was during this event that McCarthy first coined the term 'artificial intelligence' and that Newell and Simon presented their groundbreaking program, the *Logic Theorist*, considered one of the earliest AI programs.[4]

3 Bennett (2023), Buchanan (2005), Kaplan (2016, 2024), and Wooldridge (2021).

4 In 1955, Newell and Simon, in collaboration with Shaw, developed the computer program *Logic Theorist* (also referred to as the *Logic Theory Machine*). Designed to perform automated reasoning, the program was engineered to prove mathematical theorems and could demonstrate most of the theorems found in Whitehead and Russell's *Principia Mathematica*. Newell and Simon even claimed that the program had, in a sense, addressed aspects of the mind-body problem by showing that reasoning could be mechanized. Shortly thereafter, Newell, Simon, and Shaw developed the *General Problem Solver*, a computer program designed to function as a universal problem-solving machine. This pro-

The Dartmouth Workshop brought together several pioneering researchers, including Ashby, Bigelow, Holland, MacKay, McCulloch, More, Nash, Newell, Robinson, Samuel, Sayre, Selfridge, Shoulders, Simon, and Solomonoff (Solomonoff, 1956). Among them, McCarthy, Minsky, Samuel, Newell, and Simon emerged as central figures in the formation of the field and are now widely regarded as the founders of AI. Their influence extended well beyond the workshop itself. In 1959, Minsky and McCarthy co-founded the AI Lab at MIT, laying the foundational groundwork for the discipline. McCarthy later left MIT to establish the AI Lab at Stanford University in 1963, where Samuel joined him in 1966. Meanwhile, Newell and Simon[5] continued their influential research at Carnegie Mellon University, beginning in 1965. The Dartmouth Workshop thus marked the beginning of what is now known as the 'golden age of AI' (1956–1974) – a period characterized by rapid theoretical advances and growing optimism about the potential of intelligent machines.

While the formal inception of AI as an academic discipline dates back to 1956, the idea of AI has deep roots in ancient and medieval mythology, religion, literature, and early mechanical inventions. Ancient myths already envisioned lifelike machines and artificially created beings – for example, Talos, a bronze guardian from Greek mythology, and Pygmalion, the sculptor whose statue came to life in Ovid's *Metamorphoses*. Similarly, medieval legends include tales of artificial beings, such as the Golem, created by Jewish mystics like Eleazar, or the works of Islamic alchemists, including Jabir, who speculated about the *takwin*, the artificial creation of life. Goethe's *Faust Part II* also features the creation of an alchemically fabricated homunculus, a small artificial human being. Across centuries, (humanoid) automata – self-operating machines or mechanical (i.e., automated) puppets – were built by skilled craftsmen in various civilizations, laying the groundwork for later robotics.[6] The term 'automaton' itself dates back to Homer's *Iliad*. In modern fiction, the word 'robot' was first introduced in Čapek's 1921 play *R.U.R. (Rossum's Universal Robots)*, which explored themes of artificial life and labor. The term derives from the Czech word 'robota,' meaning forced, repetitive, or drudge work. Building on early imaginative foundations – most notably Shelley's *Frankenstein*, which explored the moral consequences of creating artificial life – Asimov introduced a more structured approach to robotic ethics with his influential *Three Laws of Robotics*. First published in 1942 and later expanded in his 1950 collection *I, Robot*, these laws prohibit robots from harming humans, require obedience to human orders, and mandate self-preservation without violating the first two rules. Asi-

gram was built upon Simon and colleagues' earlier work on logic machines, aiming to emulate human problem-solving processes across a wide range of tasks (Newell, 1963; Newell et al., 1959).

5 Simon's later contributions to theories of bounded rationality and the 'satisficing man' earned him both the Turing Award (1975) and the Nobel Prize in Economics (1978).

6 Note that robot-like automata were mechanical creatures that were made possible by advances in clock and watch making (see, e.g., the automata duck by de Vaucanson or 'The Turk' by von Kempelen).

mov's framework has profoundly shaped our understanding of the responsibilities and risks associated with intelligent machines (Wörsdörfer, 2025f).

The early history of mathematics (and computer science) is deeply rooted in the tradition of formal or mechanical reasoning, which dates back to ancient thinkers such as Aristotle and Euclid, whose *Elements* became one of the most influential works in the history of mathematics. During the Islamic Golden Age, al-Khwarizmi developed algebra and gave his name to the modern term 'algorithm.' In the medieval period, figures such as William of Ockham, Duns Scotus, and Llull, who are known for their development of logical machines, further advanced the formalization of reasoning. In the seventeenth century, Leibniz envisioned a universal language of reasoning, known as the *characteristica universalis,* which laid the groundwork for symbolic logic and computation. The emergence of mathematical logic in the nineteenth and early twentieth centuries provided a crucial foundation for AI, with key contributions from Boole (*The Laws of Thought* [1854]), Frege (*Begriffsschrift* [1879]), Whitehead and Russell (*Principia Mathematica* [1910–1913], Gödel (famous for his incompleteness theorems [1931]), Church (Lambda calculus [1935] and the Church-Turing thesis), and Turing (Turing machine [1936/1937]).

The origins of computer science were marked by the design and construction of early calculating machines. Leibniz himself built one of the first mechanical calculators. Later developments included Jacquard's programmable loom (1800), Babbage's (and Lovelace's) designs for the Difference Engine and Analytical Engine (1822/1843/1859), often considered the first computer programs (i.e., programmable mechanical calculating machines). Other pioneers, such as Ludgate (1909), Torres Quevedo (see his 1914 *Essays on Automatics*), and (Hazen and) Bush (1928–1931), contributed important early concepts. The first modern computers appeared in the twentieth century, with key advances by Zuse (1936/1941), Turing (1936/1937), and the team of Atanasoff and Berry (1942). The Electronic Numerical Integrator and Computer (ENIAC), completed in 1945, is widely considered the first programmable, electronic, general-purpose digital computer. It was based on Turing's theoretical work and developed by von Neumann, with design contributions from Mauchly and Eckert (Copeland, 2020).

The beginnings of modern AI, in turn, can be traced back to a series of groundbreaking contributions by early pioneers, including Turing, McCulloch and Pitts, and Walter (discussed in this section), as well as Wiener, Shannon, and Hebb (discussed in the next section). Between 1936 and 1938, Turing developed the concept of the Turing Machine, as detailed in his 1936/1937 papers *On Computable Numbers, with an Application to the Entscheidungsproblem* (Turing, 1936/1937; see also Turing,1938a and Appendix III), as well as his 1938 doctoral thesis *Systems of Logic Based on Ordinals* (Turing, 1938b) completed under the supervision of Church at Princeton University. Turing's work provided a proof that effectively negated Hilbert's Entscheidungsproblem, which had conjectured that certain yes-no mathematical questions could never be resolved through computation. Central to his proof was the invention of a typewriter-like universal or general-purpose computing machine governed by a simple set of rules.[7]

In 1943, McCulloch and Pitts published *A Logical Calculus of the Ideas Immanent in Nervous Activity* (McCulloch & Pitts, 1943), which laid the groundwork for artificial neural networks (ANNs). In this seminal work, they analyzed networks of idealized artificial neurons and demonstrated how such networks could perform basic logical functions. Their model proposed the nervous system as a network of simple logical units – later known as McCulloch-Pitts neurons – and demonstrated that, in principle, such networks could compute any function that a Turing machine could, establishing a deep connection between logic, computation, and brain function.

Between 1948 and 1949, Walter developed some of the first electronic autonomous robots, famously known as 'turtle robots.' These cybernetic robots exhibited simple self-regulating behaviors, such as phototaxis, and are considered early examples of embodied intelligence. Similar efforts, such as the Johns Hopkins Beast in the 1950s, used analog circuitry to control robot behavior (Watson & Scheidt, 2005). Walter further explored these ideas in his 1953 book, *The Living Brain*, drawing connections between machine behavior and biological brain function (Walter, 1953).

Takeaway: The history of AI stretches back much further than many realize, shaped by recurring cycles of bold ideas and early breakthroughs. Recognizing this long and evolving journey reveals that today's innovations are deeply rooted in decades of exploration and ambition.

1.2.2 Interdisciplinary research

Lesson: The history of AI shows it is inherently interdisciplinary, drawing on fields like mathematics, cognitive science, psychology, linguistics, engineering, and philosophy (see below), and requiring more than coding skills – demanding a deep understanding of theory, cognition, problem-solving, and societal impact.

---

7 During World War II, Turing served as a mathematician and cryptanalyst at Bletchley Park, the center of Britain's secret code-breaking efforts. He played a pivotal role in deciphering the German Enigma and Lorenz cipher machines, which the Axis Powers used to encrypt military communications. This groundbreaking work in decoding intercepted messages was instrumental to the Allied victory. Turing was part of a remarkable team that included figures such as Alexander, Cairncross, Golombek, Hilton, Knox, Michie, Milner-Barry, Tiltman, Tutte, Welchman, and Joan Clarke, who was briefly engaged to Turing in 1942. The team operated under the leadership of Commander Denniston, a Scottish codebreaker and deputy head of the Government Code and Cypher School. Notably, women made up approximately 75% of the Bletchley Park workforce, and their often-overlooked contributions were vital to the program's success (Copeland, 2004; Hodges, 2012, 2019).

Examples: The early development of AI was profoundly shaped by interdisciplinary contributions from fields such as mathematics, neuroscience, and engineering – reflected in the foundational work of pioneers like Wiener in cybernetics, Shannon in information theory, and Hebb in neuropsychology. Early AI research was also showcased at the interdisciplinary 'Special Interest Group in Information Theory' conference held at MIT in 1956 – a crucial event that brought together experts from psychology, computer science, and neuroscience, and helped spark the cognitive revolution in understanding human intelligence and artificial systems.

In 1943, Wiener (together with Rosenblueth and Bigelow) coined the term 'cybernetics,' defining it as the science of communication related to living things, such as animals, and machines. Cybernetics introduced the concept of self-regulating machines, focusing on how control and stability could be achieved in electrical networks. Wiener's influential book, *Cybernetics: Or Control and Communication in the Animal and the Machine* (Wiener, 1948/2019), framed cybernetics as a mixture of engineering, mathematics, and brain sciences to understand how behavior is generated and how information is processed in the brain, and how these mechanisms could be replicated in machines. In this sense, cybernetics became a forerunner of both AI and cognitive science.

Meanwhile, in 1948, Shannon published *A Mathematical Theory of Communication,* which established information theory as a new scientific discipline. This theory describes the mathematical principles underlying the quantification, storage, and communication of information, with a particular focus on digital 'all-or-nothing' signals (Shannon, 1948). Shannon's work provided a formal framework for understanding how information could be encoded and transmitted efficiently, which proved essential for both telecommunications and computing. The close relationship between the ideas of Shannon, Wiener, and Turing supported the emerging belief that constructing an 'electronic brain' was within reach, inspiring early research into machine intelligence and self-regulating systems.

In 1949, Hebb published *The Organization of Behavior: A Neuropsychological Theory,* a foundational text in modern neuroscience that introduced a groundbreaking view of how learning occurs in the brain. Central to Hebb's theory was the idea that 'cells that fire together wire together,' meaning that neural networks and synapses strengthen or weaken over time based on patterns of activity (Hebb, 1949). This concept of neural plasticity, later known as Hebbian theory, provided critical insights into the biological mechanisms of learning and memory. Importantly, Hebb's work not only advanced neuroscience but also laid the theoretical foundation for the development of learning algorithms in AI, influencing later models of ANNs and connectionist approaches to cognition.

In 1956, Newell and Simon presented the *Logic Theorist* program (see above) at a meeting of the Special Interest Group in Information Theory at MIT – a gathering that also featured Chomsky's discussion of generative grammar[8] (Chomsky, 1965) and Miller's presentation of his influential paper *The Magical Number Seven, Plus or Minus Two*[9] (Miller, 1956). This meeting is often regarded as a pivotal moment in the so-called cognitive revolution, a significant interdisciplinary paradigm shift that reshaped psychology, philosophy, computer science, and neuroscience. It also inspired the creation of numerous subfields, including symbolic AI, generative linguistics, cognitive science, cognitive psychology, cognitive neuroscience, and the philosophical schools of computationalism and functionalism.

Takeaway: Since its inception, AI has drawn on a diverse range of fields, encompassing both the natural and social sciences, with neuroscience being a key contributor among them (Bennett, 2023). Today, cross-disciplinary expertise remains essential, especially as AI's influence expands across society. Building effective, ethical, and human-centered systems depends on insights from multiple domains.

1.2.3 (Early) philosophical considerations

Lesson: From the start, AI research has engaged with key philosophical questions about intelligence and consciousness. These debates began with Turing's influential 1950 paper, which introduced the Turing Test to explore the concept of machine intelligence (see Appendix III).

Examples: The Turing Test, also known as the 'imitation game,' was introduced by Turing in his 1950 essay *Computing Machinery and Intelligence* as a way to evaluate a machine's ability to exhibit intelligent behavior indistinguishable from that of a human. In this test, a human evaluator communicates via written messages with two participants – a human and a machine – without knowing which is which. If the evaluator cannot reliably distinguish the machine from the human based on their responses, the machine is said to have passed the test, demonstrating its ability to imitate human behavior (Turing, 1950; see also Turing, 1948). Philosophically, the Turing Test challenges traditional notions of intelligence and consciousness by shifting the focus from internal states or intentions to observable behavior. It raises fundamental questions about what it means to think or be intelligent and whether these qualities

8 *Generative grammar* is a theory of syntax that aims to describe the implicit knowledge humans have about the structure of their language. It proposes a set of formal rules that can generate all and only the grammatical sentences in a language, capturing the deep structure underlying surface expressions. This approach revolutionized linguistics by treating language as a system governed by universal principles rather than just a collection of learned habits.

9 In this influential 1956 paper, psychologist Miller explored the limitations of human short-term memory. He argued that people can hold about 7 (plus or minus 2) discrete items or 'chunks' of information in their immediate memory at one time. This finding highlighted constraints on cognitive processing and had broad implications for psychology, communication, and information theory.

can be attributed to machines purely based on external performance. The test also sparked extensive debate on the limits of behavioral criteria for intelligence and the nature of the mind, influencing fields such as philosophy of mind, cognitive science, and AI ethics (Saygin et al., 2000).

While the Turing Test offered a behavioral criterion for assessing machine intelligence, it did not address the deeper philosophical question of whether machines genuinely understand or merely simulate understanding. This notion was challenged by Searle through his famous *Chinese Room* thought experiment. Searle argued that computers do not truly think; instead, they execute deterministic sequences of mathematical or logical operations (Searle, 1980; see also Searle,1982, 1997, 2014). According to this view, machines simulate thinking and appear to possess cognitive abilities – what is known as weak AI – but they do not replicate genuine human thought processes, or strong AI.[10] Key aspects of human cognition, such as consciousness, self-awareness, subjective experience (also known as *qualia*), sentience, and empathy, are seen as uniquely human (Nagel, 1974). Searle contended that computer programs lack intentionality – the capacity to have thoughts about something – and therefore, genuine understanding cannot arise from formal computation alone. This, he argued, marks a fundamental difference between human thinking and machine processing (McCarthy & Hayes, 1969; Saygin et al., 2000).[11]

In contrast, Kaplan (2016) poses an intriguing counterpoint: Are human brains truly so different from computers? Both biological and computational systems consist of physical material that processes sensory inputs and signals. Thus, Kaplan suggests, either both humans and machines can think, or neither can. This ongoing debate addresses fundamental philosophical questions about the nature of thought, consciousness, and the limitations of AI.

Closely related is the question of free will, which is a complex and multifaceted concept tied to autonomy and unpredictability. While computers and robots can make decisions that appear autonomous or non-deterministic, these choices remain governed by algorithms and pre-programmed rules, meaning they lack true free will as humans understand it. That said, the concept of 'black boxes' in machine learning (ML) – where decision-making processes are opaque and not fully understood – introduces an element of unpredictability.

---

10 *Weak AI* suggests that robots can only mimic human-like intelligence and consciousness without truly replicating them (in other words, they may appear intelligent, but they will not actually possess true intelligence), while *strong AI* suggests that robots could possess their own minds and consciousness.

11 A similar argument is Dreyfus' 'humans are special' perspective, which emphasizes that human intuition sets us apart from computers. This viewpoint can be seen as a critique of the concept of strong AI, suggesting that machines can never truly replicate the depth of human cognition and intuition (Dreyfus, 1965, 1972; Dreyfus & Dreyfus, 1986).

Yet, even the concept of human free will is a contentious issue. Neuroscientist Libet's experiments (Libet, 1981, 1985; Libet et al., 1979, 1983) suggest that unconscious brain processes precede our conscious decisions and actions, implying that our brains may initiate decisions before our conscious minds are aware of them. This challenges traditional notions of free will, suggesting that human decisions may be governed by deterministic natural laws, much like those of other animals and machines. Such findings raise a deeper question: If humans operate similarly to machines under physical laws, what does free will truly mean in the context of consciousness and decision-making?

The issue of whether computers can be conscious or possess feelings remains a deeply philosophical and contentious topic. While it is challenging to definitively comprehend human consciousness or its precise nature, it seems unlikely that machines will ever attain genuine subjective experience. At best, AI might become quasi-conscious, but authentic consciousness appears beyond reach. Similarly, human-like emotions are improbable in AI systems. This debate extends to current (generative) AI platforms such as ChatGPT: Are they early steps toward AGI – the ability for machines to understand meaningfully – or are they merely 'stochastic parrots,' as Bender et al. (2021) describe, or 'AI mirrors,' as Vallor (2024) argues? Fundamentally, these systems use statistical models to identify patterns in vast amounts of human-generated data and make predictions or generate outputs based on those patterns. However, they lack a proper understanding of the world. This raises important questions about moral agency: Should AI be considered moral agents or granted rights? Vallor's concept of the AI (silicon) mirror emphasizes how these systems reflect not only human thoughts and desires but also entrenched biases, such as racism, sexism, ableism, and classism, which can perpetuate harmful feedback loops (see also Bender & Hanna, 2025). Thus, while AI can mimic human behavior and cognition, its role in society carries complex and unresolved moral implications.

Takeaway: Philosophical inquiry remains central to AI, raising questions about what it means for machines to 'think' and the ethical implications of intelligent systems. While AI can mimic human behavior, debates surrounding consciousness, free will, and moral agency highlight the gap between simulation and genuine understanding – reminding us that responsible development must extend beyond technical capability.

1.2.4 Incremental progress

Lesson: The development of AI is not a straightforward, linear journey but rather a series of incremental advances built upon the foundational work of pioneering figures. Researchers have stood on the shoulders of giants, such as Turing and von Neumann, whose groundbreaking contributions across mathematics, neuroscience, computing, and social sciences have collectively propelled the field forward over many decades.

Examples: The early development of AI was shaped by thinkers from a wide range of disciplines, including mathematics, logic, neuroscience, psychology, and engineering. Turing's foundational work provided both philosophical and scientific grounding for the field, significantly influencing later pioneers such as McCarthy and Minsky by helping to frame enduring questions about the nature of machine intelligence. At the same time, Wiener's development of cybernetics in the 1940s introduced the concept of feedback systems, which became central to control theory and would later inform early ML models. In parallel, Shannon – widely regarded as the father of information theory – formalized key concepts in data transmission and communication. His mathematical models of information processing had a significant impact on computer science and AI, particularly in the domains of logic, pattern recognition, and learning. On the biological side, the conceptual link between brain function and computation was first established by McCulloch and Pitts in their 1943 model of the artificial neuron. Their work laid the groundwork for understanding the brain as a logical system and directly influenced psychologist Hebb, who proposed a theory of learning based on neural adaptation and activity-dependent synaptic strengthening. These ideas laid the foundation for the development of early neural networks and later deep learning (DL) systems. The trajectory of this research was also shaped by Turing's 1936 paper, *On Computable Numbers*, which introduced the theoretical framework for computation and inspired subsequent work on machine intelligence. Building on these ideas, Minsky, along with Edmonds, created SNARC[12] in 1951 – the first neural network machine – paving the way for further innovations such as Rosenblatt's perceptron (see below).

Of particular importance was von Neumann, who influenced early AI research through his foundational work in computing, mathematics, and biological modeling. His development of the stored-program computer – now known as the von Neumann architecture – revolutionized computing by allowing instructions and data to be stored in the same memory. This became the standard model for digital computers, enabling the flexibility required for developing early AI programs (von Neumann, 1945). Beyond hardware, von Neumann's work on automata theory and self-

12 In 1951, Minsky and Edmonds constructed the first neural network machine, known as SNARC (Stochastic Neural Analog Reinforcement Calculator) (Minsky, 1952). This early device was significantly influenced by the 1943 work of McCulloch and Pitts on artificial neurons, as well as by principles of Skinnerian reinforcement learning. It was also inspired by Shannon's earlier experiment known as 'Shannon's maze,' in which an electromechanical mouse named Theseus attempted to solve a maze – one of the first demonstrations of ML behavior. SNARC simulated a network of roughly 40 artificial neurons (i.e., Hebb synapses) and was designed to mimic probabilistic learning through reinforcement, using analog components. Although primitive by today's standards, SNARC represented an important milestone in the development of neural networks and laid early groundwork for reinforcement learning in AI.

replicating systems inspired researchers to think of machines not just as tools, but as entities capable of simulating life-like processes such as adaptation, autonomy, and learning – ideas that would later shape fields like ML and artificial life (von Neumann, 1966). His co-authorship of *Theory of Games and Economic Behavior* introduced game theory, offering a formal framework for strategic decision-making that remains central to AI disciplines, such as multi-agent systems and reinforcement learning (von Neumann & Morgenstern, 1944). Moreover, von Neumann was among the first to draw explicit parallels between computers and the human brain, exploring how neural activity might be modeled computationally. This early interest in cognitive processes laid the groundwork for later developments in neural networks and brain-inspired AI. Altogether, his interdisciplinary research – combining logic, biology, computation, and economics – helped establish AI as a serious scientific field and provided many of its conceptual and technical foundations.

In the 1950s and 1960s, a new generation of AI pioneers emerged. McCarthy, who coined the term AI and organized the seminal Dartmouth Workshop, helped formalize AI as an academic discipline (he also invented the Lisp programming language family in 1958, among others). Working alongside him at MIT was Minsky, who also drew from cybernetics and neuroscience to develop models of cognition and symbolic reasoning. Meanwhile, Newell and Simon approached AI from the perspective of human problem-solving and cognitive psychology, producing the first AI program, *Logic Theorist*, which simulated human reasoning in mathematics. On another front, Rosenblatt developed the perceptron in 1958, a model inspired by the brain's neural structure that marked one of the earliest implementations of ML in hardware. His work built on the theories of McCulloch, Pitts, and Hebb, and although it faced criticism – most notably from Minsky and Papert (see below) – it laid critical groundwork for the neural networks that would later power DL (see, in this context, also the work of Ivakhnenko, Lapa, and Amari). The interdisciplinary nature of early AI also extended to linguistics and psychology. Chomsky's theory of generative grammar, discussed above, provided a computational approach to language that challenged the behaviorist paradigm and profoundly influenced early work in NLP. His emphasis on structured, rule-based representations resonated with symbolic AI approaches, fueling broader interest in modeling cognition through computational systems. In sum, early AI research was not the product of a single discipline or thinker, but rather a convergence of ideas from logic, cybernetics, neuroscience, information theory, and cognitive science. Each of these fields contributed critical insights, and the dialogue between them laid the foundations for the complex and multifaceted discipline that AI is today.

Takeaway: The development of AI is a series of incremental advances built on the foundational work of pioneering figures. Modern researchers continue to build on these groundbreaking contributions, which have collectively propelled the field forward over many decades. This long, evolving history shows that today's advancements are not sudden revolutions but the result of steady, cumulative progress spanning decades – if not centuries.

1.2.5 Diverse research methodologies

Lesson: The field's history highlights the importance of methodological open-mindedness, exemplified by Rosenblatt's exploratory approach to neural networks in contrast to Minsky's more rigid commitment to symbolic reasoning. Over time, AI has undergone significant paradigm shifts – moving from the early coexistence of competing research traditions to the dominance of symbolic AI, and eventually to today's prevailing focus on ML, DL, and ANNs.

Examples: Initially, AI developed along two distinct but coexisting paradigms: rule-based symbolic reasoning and data-driven learning through ANNs. These approaches represented fundamentally different methodologies for modeling intelligence.

Symbolic or classical AI – often referred to as 'Good Old-Fashioned AI' – followed a top-down, rule-based approach centered on logic, symbols, and explicit reasoning. In this paradigm, human experts manually encoded domain knowledge into systems using structured rules, often in the form of decision trees and 'if . . . then' statements. These so-called expert systems (see below) performed well in structured and predictable environments, where the range of possible scenarios was limited and outcomes could be reliably anticipated. While such systems offered transparency and interpretability, they were constrained by the cognitive and epistemic limitations of their human designers.

In contrast, the ML paradigm[13] followed a bottom-up, data-driven methodology inspired by biological neural systems. Instead of relying on predefined rules, ML systems learn patterns from large datasets and adapt to new information autonomously.

13 In 1959, Samuel developed a checkers-playing program that became one of the first successful applications of ML. His landmark paper, *Some Studies in Machine Learning Using the Game of Checkers*, detailed how the program could improve its performance over time by learning from experience rather than relying on a fixed set of rules. Samuel's work built on earlier efforts by Strachey, who developed a checkers program, and Prinz, who created one of the first chess programs – together laying the groundwork for what would become the field of game-playing AI. Unlike rule-based or symbolic AI systems of the time, Samuel's approach was data-driven, marking a shift toward learning-based methods and establishing his program as one of the earliest examples of ML in action (Samuel, 1959).

Techniques like DL[14] and ANNs[15] exemplify this approach. Unlike symbolic AI, ML is particularly well-suited to unstructured or dynamic environments where all possible outcomes cannot be anticipated in advance. Its flexibility allows it to handle high-dimensional data and infinite state spaces, although it may struggle in scenarios with sparse data or single-shot decision-making.

At its core, this divergence reflects a broader epistemological divide in AI: knowledge engineering versus ML. Knowledge engineering prioritizes human-crafted models that are interpretable but rigid, while ML emphasizes adaptability through data, often at the cost of transparency. Although both paradigms (Kuhn, 1957, 1962/1990, 1963; Lakatos, 1976, 1978; Lakatos & Musgrave, 1972) developed in parallel throughout the 1940s, 1950s, and 1960s, symbolic AI, rooted in the knowledge engineering tradition, eventually became the dominant approach (from the early 1960s to the late 1980s). This dominance sidelined neural network research for nearly two decades, a

---

14 DL is a central subfield of ML, closely connected to the architecture of ANNs. The term 'deep' refers to the presence of multiple layers of processing units, typically involving millions of artificial neurons and thousands of interconnections – often more than 10,000 per neuron – forming what are known as deep neural networks. DL has been significantly shaped by the work of Hinton (see below), a leading figure in the parallel distributed processing movement and a pioneer in the development of backpropagation and unsupervised learning techniques. One of the key strengths of DL lies in its ability to accurately classify and categorize (random) objects in images or videos based on visual features, making it fundamental to artificial perception systems such as those used in autonomous vehicles. Notable applications include image recognition and automated language translation, as demonstrated by Li's ImageNet project (see below). DL models typically require vast amounts of raw visual training data and can be trained through either supervised learning – where the algorithm learns to predict a specific target variable from labeled data – or unsupervised learning, which involves detecting patterns in unlabeled data without predefined outcomes (i.e., without supervised training). Another approach is reinforcement learning, in which the algorithm learns through trial and error, guided by feedback in the form of rewards or punishments. Unlike rule-based or top-down systems, DL algorithms are well-suited to highly unstructured, chaotic, or unpredictable environments. However, a notable drawback of DL is its 'black box' nature: despite their high performance, the internal decision-making processes of these models remain largely opaque and difficult to interpret.

15 One important type of ML algorithm is ANN, which is inspired by the organizational principles of biological neural networks. In the brain, biological neurons transmit signals to other neurons through connections known as synapses or synaptic interfaces. When a neuron reaches its activation threshold, it fires and releases neurotransmitters into the synapse, enabling communication between neurons. ANNs are composed of interconnected units called artificial neurons, which function analogously to biological neurons. These networks are typically structured into multiple layers, with each layer responsible for processing and transmitting different types of inputs and signals. This layered architecture forms what is known as a multi-layer perceptron, a concept developed in the work of Rosenblatt and others (see below). Through learning and repeated exposure to data, the strength of connections – analogous to synapses – increases, reflecting the principle of synaptic plasticity. ANNs form the technological backbone of modern DL software. They are also widely used in the field of computational neuroscience, where they help researchers analyze the structure and simulate the function of the human brain through computational modeling. The goal of this research is to gain a deeper understanding of how the human brain works.

shift that many critics argue stifled methodological diversity and led to a narrow, overly rigid research agenda.

The foundations of neural networks were laid as early as 1943, when McCulloch and Pitts introduced a model of the nervous system as a network of idealized neurons capable of performing logical operations (McCulloch & Pitts, 1943). This model – later known as the McCulloch-Pitts neuron – established a crucial link between computation and brain function. Building on this foundation, Rosenblatt developed the perceptron, one of the first ANNs capable of basic pattern recognition (Rosenblatt, 1958, 1962).[16] Around the same time, Widrow and Hoff introduced ADALINE (1960) and MADALINE (1962), while Rosen and Brain developed the MINOS I and II machines (1961, 1963), all of which expanded the range of early ANN architectures.

Despite these early innovations, interest in neural networks declined sharply following the publication of *Perceptrons: An Introduction to Computational Geometry* by Minsky and Papert (1969/1987). In this influential critique, the authors argued that single-layer perceptrons, such as Rosenblatt's,[17] had fundamental limitations, including their inability to solve non-linearly separable problems like XOR, and highlighted the lack of effective training methods for multilayer networks. Their assessment led to a significant reduction in funding and interest/enthusiasm for neural network research for over a decade. During this time, symbolic AI, championed by figures like Minsky, became the intellectual and institutional center of the field, further consolidating the dominance of rule-based approaches (Minsky, 1988).

Nevertheless, the symbolic paradigm was not without its limitations. While Newell and Simon's *Logic Theorist* (1955–1956) helped establish reasoning as symbolic manipulation,[18,19] symbolic systems generally struggled with ambiguity, uncertainty,

---

16 Constructed as an electronic device modeled on biological learning principles, the perceptron functioned as a single-layer neural network capable of basic pattern recognition.

17 Noteworthy is that Rosenblatt and Minsky were high school classmates – an ironic twist, considering that their intellectual paths would later diverge so sharply and shape opposing sides of one of AI's most defining debates. While both shared early exposure to science and mathematics, they ultimately championed very different visions for AI: Rosenblatt pursued a biologically inspired, data-driven approach through neural networks, whereas Minsky became a staunch advocate of symbolic, rule-based reasoning. Their personal connection makes the later ideological divide – especially Minsky's harsh critique of Rosenblatt's perceptron – even more striking in retrospect.

18 In 1976, Newell and Simon proposed the *Physical Symbol System Hypothesis*, which asserts that "a physical symbol system has the necessary and sufficient means for general intelligent action" (Newell & Simon, 1976). This idea implies that human thinking can be understood as a form of symbol manipulation, much like the operations performed by a computer. According to this hypothesis, if machines can replicate such symbolic processing, they too could exhibit intelligence. This laid a foundational principle for much of early AI research, suggesting that cognition, whether biological or artificial, stems from the manipulation of symbols within a structured system.

19 The roots of logic-based AI can be traced back to McCarthy's influential *Advice Taker* proposal, which was the first to suggest using formal logic to represent information in computers – an early attempt to merge logic and AI research (McCarthy, 1959). This foundational idea was further devel-

and tasks requiring perception or learning from raw data. Meanwhile, Rosenblatt's connectionist vision – though promising – lacked the computational resources and mathematical tools, such as backpropagation, required to train deeper networks. Although these techniques existed in other disciplines, they remained largely unknown or underutilized in AI until the 1980s.[20]

With the rediscovery and refinement of backpropagation (see below), combined with increasing computational power and the availability of large datasets, neural networks experienced a resurgence in the late twentieth and early twenty-first centuries. This revival marked the beginning of modern DL and fulfilled many of Rosenblatt's early predictions. Today, DL models form a central pillar of contemporary AI, and Rosenblatt is widely recognized as one of its founding figures.

Takeaway: AI advances most when shaped by diverse perspectives – particularly in research methods. Embracing methodological diversity and open-mindedness not

---

oped by researchers like Robinson, who introduced the resolution and unification algorithm in 1963, and by Kowalski, Colmerauer, and Roussel, who created the logic programming language *Prolog* in the 1970s. Other early examples of logic-based AI or symbolic reasoning include Slagle's *SAINT* (1961; see also the section on expert systems below) and Gelernter's *Geometry Theorem Machine*. In 1958, Gelernter developed the *Geometry Theorem Machine/Prover*, which stands as one of the earliest instances of advanced AI software. This logic-driven system could prove theorems in planar geometry, including those involving parallel lines, congruence, and the (in)equality of segments and angles. Similar to the earlier *Logic Theorist*, Gelernter's program relied on heuristics to navigate and guide its problem-solving processes (Gelernter & Rochester, 1958; Gelernter et al., 1960).

20 In 1974, Werbos introduced a significant breakthrough in neural network research with his dissertation, in which he described the process of training ANNs through the backpropagation of errors (Werbos, 1994). This pioneering work significantly improved upon the original perceptron model by addressing its key limitation – the inability to train multilayer networks. Although Werbos' contribution went largely unrecognized at the time, his formulation of backpropagation would later become a foundational technique in DL, enabling the effective training of complex, multi-layered neural networks. In 1979/1980, Fukushima introduced the *Neocognitron*, a hierarchical, multi-layered ANN designed for pattern recognition tasks such as handwritten character recognition. This architecture marked a significant advancement in neural network research by incorporating a layered structure capable of processing spatial hierarchies in data. The Neocognitron was particularly notable for its ability to recognize patterns regardless of their position in the visual field – a property known as shift invariance. Fukushima's model, detailed in his 1980 paper *Neocognitron* (Fukushima, 1980), served as a foundational inspiration for modern convolutional neural networks (CNNs). CNNs, a type of DL model and ANN, are now essential tools for processing and analyzing visual data, and are widely used in tasks such as image classification, object detection, and computer vision more broadly (see also Hochreiter and Schmidhuber's [1997] seminal work on recurrent neural networks [RNNs] and long short-term memory [LSTM]: RNNs represent a general architecture for sequence modeling, while LSTMs offer a more powerful variant designed to capture long-term dependencies more effectively. CNNs, typically used for spatial feature extraction, can also be combined with RNNs or LSTMs to handle spatiotemporal tasks. More recently, transformers – introduced by Vaswani et al. [2017, see below] – have addressed key limitations of RNNs and LSTMs, particularly in handling long-range dependencies and enabling faster, parallelized training).

only fosters innovation but also helps avoid repeating past mistakes, making unexpected breakthroughs more likely.

1.2.6 Research funding and infrastructure

Lesson: AI progress relies on adequate funding and infrastructure. Key breakthroughs throughout history have been driven not only by theoretical advances, improvements in GPU hardware, and access to large datasets, but also by sustained investment from both public institutions and private industry.

Examples: From the mid-1960s onward, the Defense Advanced Research Projects Agency (DARPA), a research arm of the U.S. Department of Defense, emerged as a primary sponsor of AI research and development (R&D) in the United States. As part of its broader mission to fund high-risk, high-reward technologies with potential military and strategic applications, DARPA directed substantial resources toward advancing AI. The agency supported major research hubs at CMU, MIT, and Stanford University, which became leading centers of AI innovation. In addition, DARPA extended support to commercial research institutions such as the Stanford Research Institute (SRI) (Nilsson, 1984), further fostering collaboration between academic and applied research settings (outside the United States, the University of Edinburgh also became a significant player in AI research, with its AI laboratory founded by Michie in 1965). Through sustained investment in both academic and industrial laboratories, DARPA played a pivotal role in shaping the trajectory of early AI research – just as it did later during the era of knowledge-based and expert systems, significantly influencing the direction and pace of innovation (see also DARPA's funding of the Grand, Urban, and Robotics Challenges in the twenty-first century, discussed below).

An example of a research project funded by DARPA is 'Shakey the robot' (Darrach, 1970). Between 1966 and 1972, SRI developed Shakey, one of the first general-purpose autonomous mobile robots capable of navigating natural environments and moving physical objects, such as turning lights on and off, opening and closing doors, traveling between locations, and pushing movable objects around. This DARPA project was managed by Rosen, Nilsson, and Hart, with significant contributions from researchers including Brain, Duda, Fikes, Garvey, Raphael, Wahlstrom, Wilber, and Wolf. Notable outcomes of this research included the development of the A* search algorithm for pathfinding and graph traversal, the Hough transform for feature extraction in image analysis, computer vision, and digital image processing, as well as the visibility graph method for finding Euclidean shortest paths among obstacles on planes (Nilsson, 1964, 1984; Nilsson et al., 1968).

Another key area of government-funded research in AI focused on so-called expert systems. Particularly during the 1980s, these systems became a central focus of AI R&D. Designed to replicate the decision-making abilities of human experts, expert systems utilized rules derived from specialized domain knowledge to solve narrowly defined problems. Programmers – often referred to as knowledge engineers – developed these systems by encoding logical rules based on expert input to answer questions or resolve issues within specific fields. This logic-based approach to AI, championed by figures such as Newell, Simon, and especially Feigenbaum (often referred to as the 'father of expert systems' [Feigenbaum & McCorduck, 1983]), dominated the decade. A key ambition was to utilize extensive knowledge bases to overcome the commonsense knowledge problem, enabling machines to reason about everyday situations in much the same way humans do. This paradigm stood in contrast to behavioral or agent-based approaches to intelligence, which would gain prominence in later years (see below).

Early influential examples of expert systems[21] included *DENDRAL* (developed in 1965), which assisted chemists in identifying unknown organic molecules by analyzing mass spectra, with key contributions from Feigenbaum, Buchanan, Lederberg, and Djerassi. Another milestone system, *MYCIN* (1972), was designed to aid in diagnosing bacterial infections and recommend appropriate antibiotic treatments; its name derived from the common antibiotic suffix '-mycin.' MYCIN was among the first AI systems to demonstrate performance exceeding that of human experts in a narrowly defined medical domain. Developed as part of Shortliffe's doctoral dissertation under the guidance of Buchanan and Cohen, MYCIN exemplified the growing promise of expert systems in healthcare. In the 1980s, other systems, such as *R1* (1980) and *Cyc* (1984), followed. Cyc was a highly ambitious U.S. initiative launched in response to Japan's economic policies. Funded by the Microelectronics and Computer Technology Corporation (MCC) and later developed by Cycorp under the leadership of Lenat, the project aimed to create a comprehensive ontology of commonsense knowledge – a knowledge base encompassing fundamental concepts and rules governing how the world operates. Although ultimately controversial due to its ambitious scope and association with early AI hype – particularly its focus on 'general AI' and creating a self-educating system – Cyc made significant strides in addressing the commonsense knowledge problem. It is now recognized as a precursor to notable projects such as IBM's Watson, Google's Knowledge Graph, and Wikipedia (the name 'Cyc' is derived from the word en*cyc*lopedia).

This focus on knowledge-based systems led to a (new) AI boom from 1980 to 1987, resulting in a surge in research funding and industry investment. Large-scale national

21 In 1961, Slagle developed one of the first expert systems, the *Symbolic Automatic Integrator* (SAINT), as part of his doctoral research at MIT under the supervision of Minsky. SAINT was designed to solve symbolic integration problems typically encountered in freshman-level calculus, making it a pioneering example of applying heuristics to mathematical problem-solving. Slagle's dissertation, titled *A Heuristic Program That Solves Symbolic Integration Problems in Freshman Calculus: Symbolic Automatic Integrator*, demonstrated how AI techniques could be applied to tasks traditionally requiring human expertise in symbolic reasoning (Sagle, 1961).

initiatives, such as Japan's Fifth Generation Project[22] (initiated in 1982 by the Ministry of International Trade and Industry), the U.K.'s Alvey Program, and the U.S. Strategic Computing Initiative – backed, once again, by DARPA – significantly advanced the field. At the same time, multinational corporations began investing billions in developing and deploying expert systems, leading to the creation of an entire industry (and many in-house AI departments). Specialized hardware firms, such as Lisp Machines and Symbolics, emerged alongside software companies like Aion and IntelliCorp. The consortium MCC was also established to support collaborative AI and large-scale AI and information technology projects. Although later criticized for their limitations, such as a lack of adaptability, high maintenance costs, and an inability to handle ambiguity, expert systems marked a significant phase in AI history and helped lay the foundation for future developments in knowledge representation, reasoning, and the integration of AI into industry.

Takeaway: Progress in AI has always depended on the availability of key resources – computing power, financial investment, and specialized talent. Historically, government agencies like DARPA have been primary drivers of AI research and development, challenging the common narrative that emphasizes a laissez-faire and hands-off approach (i.e., deregulation and privatization) as the catalysts for AI advancement.

1.2.7 Hype versus reality

Lesson: In the 1950s and 1960s, early AI researchers believed that human-like intelligence was just decades away – a hope mirrored today in the hype surrounding generative AI and AGI. These cycles of high expectations often gave way to 'AI winters,' periods marked by slowed progress and dwindling funding.

Examples: The 1956 Dartmouth Workshop proposal begins with the bold hypothesis that "*every* aspect of learning or *any* other feature of intelligence can in principle be so precisely described that a machine can be made to simulate it" (McCarthy et al., 1955 [emphasis added]). With this in mind, the authors proposed a collaborative summer research project involving experts from diverse fields, including mathematics, psychology, engineering, and computer science. Their objective was to investigate how machines might simulate human intelligence by exploring core processes, such as learning, abstraction, concept formation, and self-improvement. The proposal outlines an overly ambitious research agenda: "An attempt will be made to find how to make machines use language, form abstractions and concepts, *solve kinds of problems now reserved for humans*, and improve themselves" (McCarthy et al., 1955 [emphasis

22 The project aimed to develop machines capable of engaging in conversation, translating languages, interpreting images, and reasoning like humans. It also sought to create an 'epoch-making' supercomputer (Feigenbaum & McCorduck, 1983).

added]). The researchers placed particular emphasis on symbolic reasoning, structured memory, search, analogy, and other mechanisms central to intelligent behavior. They anticipated key challenges, including representing common sense knowledge (Minsky et al., 2004), dealing with vast search spaces, and enabling machines to generalize from limited data. ML was seen as a central focus, with the potential to create systems that not only perform tasks but also improve over time through experience. The authors were strikingly optimistic about the timeline of progress. They wrote: "We think that a significant advance can be made in one or more of these problems *within a few years* if a concerted effort is made by a group of scientists" (McCarthy et al., 1955 [emphasis added]). These statements reflect the early excitement, (over-) confidence, and hubris that the core problems of AI were not only tractable but potentially solvable in the near term (note that many of the foundational challenges remain unsolved even today [Narayanan & Kapoor, 2024; Wooldridge, 2021]).

Between the mid-1970s and early 1990s, AI research experienced two major setbacks, known as the *First AI Winter* (1974–1980) and the Second AI Winter (1987–1993), periods marked by significantly reduced funding and waning interest (Toosi et al., 2022; see also Haigh, 2023).[23] These downturns were driven by growing criticism of AI's overambitious promises and underwhelming results (as exemplified by the Dartmouth Workshop proposal). Early AI researchers had underestimated the complexity of the problems they faced and overestimated the capabilities of existing methods, computing power, and available data. As a result, public expectations soared while tangible progress lagged behind. Promised breakthroughs failed to materialize (due to insufficient techniques, limited computing power, e.g., in terms of memory and processing speed, and lack of data/information to train computer models), leading to frustration among major funding agencies such as DARPA, the National Research Council, and the British government, many of which withdrew support for undirected AI research.

During this period, influential philosophical critiques significantly challenged AI's symbolic and rule-based approaches. Dreyfus's works – *Alchemy and AI* (1965), *What Computers Can't Do* (1972), and *Mind Over Machine* (1986, co-authored with S. Dreyfus) – argued that these approaches overlooked the crucial roles of human intuition and embodied cognition. Similarly, Lighthill's 1972 report to the British Science Re-

23 Haenlein and Kaplan (2019) conceptualize the development of AI through a metaphorical lens, describing its evolution in terms of the four seasons of AI. *Spring* represents the birth and early promise of AI, when foundational ideas and technologies began to emerge. *Summer* symbolizes a period of optimism and rapid progress, marked by significant advances in R&D and growing expectations. In contrast, *winter* denotes phases of disillusionment and stagnation when progress slowed and enthusiasm waned due to unmet expectations and technical limitations. Finally, *Fall* represents the harvest season, characterized by the tangible fruits of decades of R&D, such as the widespread deployment of ANNs, NLP systems, and conversational agents like chatbots. This cyclical framework underscores the dynamic and often unpredictable nature of AI's evolution over time.

search Council criticized AI for its lack of practical progress (Lighthill, 1972; see also McCarthy, 1973). Adding to this skepticism, Searle's 1980 *Chinese Room* argument (discussed above) questioned whether computational systems could truly understand or possess consciousness, thereby undermining the foundational assumptions of symbolic AI (Searle, 1980, 1982, 1997, 2014). Together, these critiques contributed to AI's declining academic reputation, with some likening it to pseudoscience or alchemy. Expanding on these concerns, Moravec's *Mind Children* introduced what is now known as Moravec's Paradox, highlighting a striking mismatch between AI achievements and human cognition. While computers excelled at complex tasks like chess, they struggled with seemingly simple perceptual and motor skills, such as facial recognition or spatial navigation, that even toddlers perform effortlessly. Moravec famously noted that it is "comparatively easy to make computers exhibit adult-level performance on intelligence tests or playing checkers, and difficult or impossible to give them the skills of a one-year-old when it comes to perception and mobility" (Moravec, 1988; see also Moravec, 1976). In essence, tasks that humans find easy can be surprisingly challenging for machines, while the opposite is often true for complex cognitive problems. At the same time, Weizenbaum's *Computer Power and Human Reason* (1976) offered a powerful ethical critique, warning that the misapplication of AI could diminish the value of human judgment and experience, potentially devaluing human life. Further critiques emerged from behavioral economics and psychology, with scholars such as Kahneman and Tversky demonstrating that humans rarely rely on formal logic in real-world decision-making (Kahneman, 2011; Tversky & Kahneman, 1974). This challenged the logical, rationalist foundations upon which early AI was built. These combined technical and philosophical concerns fueled a series of boom-and-bust cycles, profoundly shaping AI's reputation and development trajectory for decades.

The *Second AI Winter*, which emerged at the end of the 1980s and the beginning of the 1990s, followed a rapid rise and equally sharp decline in enthusiasm for AI during the 1980s, particularly within the business sector. This cycle followed the classical pattern of an economic bubble, characterized by boom-and-bust dynamics. As optimism soared, numerous companies invested heavily in AI technologies, only to face widespread disappointment when the technology failed to meet expectations. In 1987, the market for specialized AI hardware collapsed abruptly; Lisp Machines, once considered cutting-edge and produced by companies like Symbolics, became obsolete as general-purpose computers from Apple and IBM advanced in processing speed and affordability. At the same time, expert systems such as XCON, which were once hailed as revolutionary, proved too costly to maintain, difficult to update, incapable of learning, and prone to errors. The Strategic Computing Initiative, which had funded a large portion of AI research, significantly reduced its support in the late 1980s when DARPA's new leadership determined that AI was not the next major technological wave (instead, they redirected R&D funding to other industry sectors). By the end of 1993, over 300 AI companies had either shut down, gone bankrupt, or been acquired, marking the collapse of the first commercial wave of AI. This downturn inflicted lasting reputational damage, and AI was once again compared to pseudoscience, homeopathic medicine, or alchemy, and was widely regarded as not a serious academic discipline. In response, many researchers began to rebrand their work using alternative terms, such as informatics, knowledge-based systems, cognitive systems, or computational intelligence, to continue attracting funding (i.e., AI researchers at the time deliberately avoided the term 'artificial intelligence'). Importantly, this period also prompted a methodological shift: researchers began adopting more sophisticated mathematical tools and models, increasing mathematical rigor and fostering interdisciplinary collaboration with mathematicians, statisticians, engineers, economists, and operations researchers. AI research narrowed its focus to specific, solvable problems (with verifiable solutions) – a move toward what is now known as narrow AI. The paradigm of intelligent agents – integrating concepts from decision theory and economics, particularly rational agent theory – grew increasingly influential in the evolution of AI. This approach is exemplified in the work of Kaelbling, renowned for her contributions to partially observable Markov decision processes (in collaboration with Littman and Cassandra). Another prominent figure is Pearl, who championed the probabilistic approach to AI and played a foundational role in the development of Bayesian networks, significantly shaping how uncertainty and reasoning are modeled in intelligent systems. While the second AI winter brought setbacks, it also laid the groundwork for AI's transformation into a more scientifically robust and focused discipline.

After the prolonged slowdown and skepticism of the Second AI Winter, the field remained relatively quiet for several years – a period marked by cautious optimism but few major breakthroughs. Yet this apparent dormancy quietly laid the foundation for a dramatic resurgence. That resurgence began in late 2022 with the release of OpenAI's ChatGPT 3.5, marking the start of the current boom in generative AI technologies. This LLM quickly captured global attention for its ability to engage in human-like conversations, write code, and generate a wide range of creative content. Its impressive capabilities spurred rapid public adoption, making it the fastest-growing consumer software application in history (The Guardian, 2023). This milestone ushered in what many now refer to as the 'generative AI revolution,' sparking renewed enthusiasm across both the tech industry and the broader public (Bender & Hanna, 2025). In response, major tech companies moved swiftly: Google launched its own LLM, Gemini, while Microsoft integrated similar technologies into Bing Chat. The result has been an almost exponential surge in AI-related investment, with companies like OpenAI and Nvidia experiencing dramatic increases in valuation and market capitalization. This explosive growth signals not only remarkable technological progress but also an intensifying race among industry giants to shape the future of AI. However, it has also prompted concern among analysts and critics, some of whom warn of a potential market bubble. Comparisons have been drawn to the dot-com boom of the late 1990s, where soaring expectations often outpaced the underlying technological and commercial realities.

Takeaway: Be cautious of being swayed by early, overly optimistic claims about technological breakthroughs. It is crucial to maintain realistic expectations and understand the limitations of technology, especially in its early stages. Given the current hype around generative AI and AGI, future AI winters – periods of slowed progress and reduced funding – remain a real possibility.

1.2.8 (Re-)discovery and invention

Lesson: Much of today's AI research is, in many ways, revisiting ideas first explored decades ago. Core concepts, such as ANNs and backpropagation, which now underpin modern ML, were initially developed much earlier. Rather than representing entirely new breakthroughs, recent advances often build on these earlier foundations – now made viable thanks to greater computing power, larger datasets, and improved algorithms.

Examples: In the 1980s and 1990s, AI research entered a period of renewal, marked by the emergence of new directions, including a renaissance of connectionism, robotics, soft computing, and reinforcement learning. *Connectionism*, in particular, signaled the revival of neural networks, which had largely fallen out of favor since the late 1960s (see above). In 1982, physicist Hopfield demonstrated that a form of recurrent neural network,[24] later known as the Hopfield net, could function as an associative memory, capable of learning and processing information through emergent collective computation (Hopfield, 1982). This work laid critical groundwork for modern DL and ultimately earned Hopfield the 2024 Nobel Prize in Physics, shared with Hinton, for their foundational discoveries and inventions that enable ML with ANNs.[25] A key breakthrough occurred in 1986, when Hinton and Rumelhart, along with Williams, popularized – though not invented[26] – backpropagation (short for backward propagation of errors) as a viable and robust training algorithm for ANNs. Backpropagation enabled neural networks to adjust internal parameters (weights and biases) by minimizing the error between predicted and actual values, thereby improving model accuracy over time. This technique, a form of supervised learning (the network is trained by a human supervisor who provides examples and correct answers), repre-

24 It is worth noting that Lenz and Ising developed and analyzed the so-called Ising model in 1925, which can be regarded as the first artificial recurrent neural network (Ising, 1925).

25 In 2024, the Royal Swedish Academy of Sciences awarded Nobel Prizes to recognize groundbreaking contributions to the field of AI. In physics, Hopfield was honored for his work on Hopfield networks, which applied principles from physics to neural computation, while Hinton received the prize for his foundational contributions to Boltzmann machines and DL, technologies that have shaped the modern AI landscape. In chemistry, DeepMind's (and Isomorphic Labs') Hassabis and Jumper (together with Baker) were jointly awarded for their transformative work in protein folding prediction through AlphaFold – an achievement that lays the groundwork for major advancements in drug discovery and the development of novel medical therapies.

26 See the work of Werbos (discussed above) and Linnainmaa (on the reverse mode of automatic differentiation) and Werbos (Griewank, 2012; Schmidhuber, 2014).

sented a turning point in ML (Rumelhart et al., 1986a, 1986b). Building on this momentum, in 1990, LeCun and colleagues at Bell Labs developed a system using convolutional neural networks (CNNs) to successfully recognize handwritten digits (note that CNNs were first created by Fukushima in 1980 [see above]). This system, used to read zip codes and personal checks, marked one of the first practical, real-world applications of neural networks and demonstrated the commercial viability of DL techniques (LeCun et al., 1998). Further innovation came in 1995 with the introduction of the Helmholtz Machine, a generative neural network model influenced by the work of Helmholtz (see above) and developed by Hinton and Dayan. Designed to mimic how the brain learns by generating and comparing internal models to actual sensory data, the Helmholtz Machine operated in two phases: a recognition mode, where sensory input led to inferred representations, and a generative mode, where those representations attempted to reproduce the input. It was one of the earliest systems to implement unsupervised learning, and became known for its biologically inspired wake-sleep algorithm (Dayan et al., 1995). These breakthroughs not only revitalized interest in neural networks but also laid the essential groundwork for the DL revolution that would emerge in the early twenty-first century.

Building on SRI's development of Shakey the robot and related research insights, the field of *robotics* advanced significantly with contributions from researchers like Marr and Brooks. Marr sought to understand the physical machinery of vision by integrating findings from psychology, AI, and neurophysiology into new models of visual perception and processing. His influential work, culminating in the posthumous publication of *Vision: A Computational Investigation into the Human Representation and Processing of Visual Information* (1982), helped spark a resurgence of interest in computational neuroscience. In 1990, Brooks and his colleagues argued that true machine intelligence requires physical embodiment, emphasizing that robots need bodies to perceive, move, and interact with their environment. Brooks, the founder and former CTO of iRobot (the maker of the automatic home vacuum cleaner, Roomba), emphasized that sensorimotor skills are fundamental to higher-level abilities, such as commonsense reasoning – a concept central to embodied reasoning or embodied cognitive science (Brooks, 1990). Brooks's work played a crucial role in bringing robotics back to the forefront of AI R&D (see also the Cog project at the Humanoid Robotics Group and Breazeal's Personal Robots Group at MIT [Breazeal, 2002, 2003, 2004; Brooks et al., 2000]).

Soft computing and probabilistic reasoning represent another significant shift in AI research, enabling systems to function effectively with incomplete, uncertain, or imprecise information (Zadeh, 1994). A key milestone occurred in 1988 with the publication of Pearl's *Probabilistic Reasoning in Intelligent Systems,* in which Pearl bridged the fields of probability theory, decision theory, and AI. He was a leading advocate for the probabilistic approach to AI, and his work laid the foundation for the development of Bayesian networks – powerful tools for reasoning under uncertainty (Pearl, 1988, 2000). Soft computing, more broadly, encompasses techniques such as fuzzy logic (see, e.g., the work of Zadeh [1965, 1994]), Bayesian networks, hidden Markov models, information theory, and stochastic modeling, all of which are essential for designing intelligent systems capable of handling real-world complexity and ambiguity.

Lastly, *reinforcement learning*, a key paradigm in AI, is based on the principle of rewarding an agent for desirable actions and penalizing it for poor performance – a concept rooted in early psychological research by Thorndike, Pavlov, and Skinner in the first half of the twentieth century. As early as the 1950s, pioneers like Turing and Samuel recognized the potential of reinforcement learning for intelligent machines. A breakthrough came in 1988, when Sutton framed ML within the formalism of decision theory, introducing the Markov decision process and establishing himself as a founder of modern computational reinforcement learning. That same year, Sutton and Barto developed the influential temporal difference (TD) learning algorithm, in which agents improve not by immediate rewards, but by refining their predictions of future outcomes based on temporal differences (Sutton & Barto, 1998; see also Sutton, 1984). This approach enabled continuous learning from predicted rather than actual rewards (i.e., note that reinforcement learning is based on temporal differences in expected, rather than actual, rewards, with learning occurring continuously through changes in the predicted likelihood of success). In 2024, both Sutton and Barto were awarded the Turing Award for their foundational contributions to the field of ML (NSF, 2025). TD learning also proved highly effective in practice – for example, in 1992, Tesauro, then part of the IBM Watson team, used it to develop TD-Gammon, a backgammon-playing program that performed at the level of top human players. This technique would later play a crucial role in the success of AlphaGo and AlphaZero, two landmark AI systems (see below).

Takeaway: Many of today's so-called AI breakthroughs are not entirely new but are built on decades-old ideas. Advances in computing power, data availability, and algorithms have finally made earlier concepts – such as ANNs and backpropagation – practically viable, highlighting the importance of revisiting and refining foundational research that dates back decades.

1.2.9 (Big) data and other technological drivers

Lesson: The effectiveness of AI systems is primarily driven by key technological advancements and access to large volumes of high-quality data. DL models and image recognition systems, in particular, depend on these factors to learn and improve. Historically, limited technological capabilities and poor data quality have significantly hindered AI performance, highlighting the critical importance of both cutting-edge technologies and robust datasets in enabling progress.

Examples: The rapid advancement of modern AI can be attributed to several interrelated technological drivers. Chief among these are significant improvements in computing capabilities, particularly in terms of processing speed (capacity) and memory (storage). Equally transformative has been the transition from physical to electronic and digital data storage, enabling more efficient access, retrieval, and analysis of vast datasets. The explosion of data availability – fueled by the proliferation of the Internet, the ubiquity of social media platforms, and the digitization of nearly all forms of communication – has further accelerated the development of AI systems. In parallel, the introduction of high-resolution digital sensors (such as those found in smartphones, autonomous vehicles, and IoT devices), the utilization of high-performance GPUs, and the innovative use of crowdsourcing techniques have all contributed to making AI more powerful, scalable, and adaptive. These developments are part of a broader and ongoing evolution across multiple domains of information technology, including advancements in computing hardware, data storage, networking infrastructure, and access to large-scale datasets. Underlying much of this progress is Moore's Law, the observation that the number of transistors on a microchip tends to double approximately every 18 months. This (quasi-)exponential growth results in continually increasing processing power, while simultaneously reducing the size and cost of computing components. In essence, the performance of computer chips has improved at a (quasi-) exponential rate, whereas their physical dimensions and price have declined asymptotically – enabling ever more powerful, affordable, and compact AI systems.

These advances in hardware and infrastructure have been critical in enabling the training of increasingly complex AI models. Building on this foundation, the period between 2005 and 2017 marked a significant transformation in AI, driven by the rise of big data and the development of DL. Renewed interest in AI research surged during the 2010s, primarily fueled by the vast amounts of data generated through the Internet and social media, as well as the availability of powerful computing resources. Pioneers like Hinton and Ng led this wave, building on earlier foundational work such as *Latent Dirichlet Allocation* by Blei, Ng, and Jordan (2003), and inverse reinforcement learning, introduced by Ng and Russell (2000), which sought to infer the reward function an agent is optimizing based on observed behavior – a key development in enabling AI systems to understand and learn from the intent behind human actions through observational learning (Blei et al., 2003; see also Ng & Russell, 2000). Hinton, a pioneer of parallel distributed processing and (re-)inventor of backpropagation, played a pivotal role in the rise of unsupervised learning and deep neural networks (Rumelhart & McClelland, 1986b). A turning point occurred in 2012 when AlexNet, a DL model developed by Krizhevsky under the guidance of Hinton at the University of Toronto, won the ImageNet Large Scale Visual Recognition Challenge, catalyzing the widespread adoption of DL (using multi-layer perceptrons and convolutional neural networks) in fields such as speech recognition, medical diagnostics, machine translation, and game playing (Goodfellow et al., 2016; Krizhevsky et al., 2017; LeCun et al., 2015; Srivastava et al., 2014).

The availability of large-scale datasets – thanks to the significant growth of the Internet – was equally crucial (especially social media platforms gave ML programs access to billions of pages of text and images that could be scraped). Along with cheaper and faster computers and advanced ML techniques, this enabled AI researchers to successfully apply their insights to a wide range of problems across the economy. Resources such as *Labeled Faces in the Wild* – an annotated set of face images widely used to train and test face recognition systems, released by a UMass Amherst research group in 2007 (Huang & Learned-Miller, 2014; Huang et al., 2007; Learned-Miller et al., 2016) – *ImageNet* – a database created by Li in 2009 with over three million labeled images captioned by volunteers via Amazon Mechanical Turk, later expanded to more than 14 million images and considered a benchmark for next-generation image processing systems (Deng et al., 2009; He et al., 2016; Li, 2023; Russakovsky et al., 2015) – and tools like *Word2Vec*, an open-source database released by Google in 2013 essential for the development of LLMs in the late 2010s, all became crucial for training AI models.

Simultaneously, the so-called 'Brooksian revolution' marked a significant shift in AI R&D, moving from logic-based and reasoning AI to behavioral AI, exemplified by Brooks' subsumption architecture, which enabled real-time interaction and viable responses in dynamic environments such as labs or offices. This evolution led to the agent-based view of AI in the 1990s (i.e., 'nouvelle AI'), influenced by behavioral AI but distinct in its focus on agents, such as robots (e.g., the humanoid robot Cog [1993] and the Roomba [2002]) and software assistants like Siri. These agents are characterized by their ability to adapt to environmental changes (reactive), achieve tasks on behalf of users (proactive), and collaborate with others through social skills (i.e., they can collaborate and coordinate). The agent-based approach draws heavily on rationality and utility maximization theory, as established in the 1944 work of von Neumann and Morgenstern's *Theory of Games and Economic Behavior*, laying the foundation for (economic) game theory. Consequently, agents (presumably) act rationally and maximize utility on behalf of users, following the economic man model prevalent in mainstream economics.

Takeaway: The success of AI systems depends as much on data as it does on algorithms and technological capabilities. Achieving high performance in tasks such as language generation or image recognition requires not only advanced models but also access to large volumes of high-quality data. As such, both the development of cutting-edge technologies and the acquisition, cleaning, and processing of data should be viewed not as secondary concerns but as central pillars of AI advancement.

1.2.10 Scalability and commercialization

Lesson: For AI to have a meaningful impact, systems must be scalable (and marketable). Technologies like search engines and virtual assistants became practical because their algorithms can operate efficiently at a global scale with significant computational resources. The rise of chatbots like ChatGPT and other generative AI technologies underscores the crucial role of scalability (and commercialization) in achieving widespread adoption and real-world success.

Examples: The development of NLP and chatbots has deep roots in the early days of AI research (Al-Amin et al., 2024). Among the most influential precursors was Bobrow's 1964 program, STUDENT, which marked a significant milestone in the field of AI. Designed to read and solve high school algebra word problems, STUDENT was one of the first programs to show that computers could process and understand natural language in a problem-solving context. Bobrow's work, detailed in his MIT PhD thesis *Natural Language Input for a Computer Problem Solving System*, helped set the stage for further breakthroughs in computational linguistics (Bobrow, 1964).

Around the same time, from 1964 to 1967, Weizenbaum developed ELIZA, one of the earliest and most iconic NLP chatbots (originally 'chatterbots'). ELIZA could carry out simple yet remarkably realistic conversations by mimicking a Rogerian psychotherapist (Weizenbaum, 1966; see also Weizenbaum, 1976). It was one of the first programs capable of attempting the Turing Test and an early method for exploring communication between humans and machines. The program's ability to simulate human-like interactions led to what later became known as the ELIZA effect – a phenomenon in which users attribute human-like feelings and understanding to computer programs. Even Weizenbaum's own secretary reportedly became emotionally invested in her conversations with ELIZA (Hofstadter, 1995).

Building on these early efforts, Winograd developed SHRDLU between 1968 and 1970 as part of his MIT Ph.D. thesis, *Procedures as a Representation for Data in a Computer Program for Understanding Natural Language* (the name is derived from the arrangement of letter keys on a Linotype machine). SHRDLU was revolutionary in that it could understand and respond to ordinary English sentences about a limited simulated environment known as the micro-world or blocks world, which contained objects such as blocks, cones, and balls. The program could plan and execute operations such as moving and stacking these objects. In doing so, SHRDLU demonstrated two crucial capabilities: natural language understanding and problem-solving (Winograd, 1971). Interestingly, Winograd's advisor was Papert, and his influence continued as he later mentored students like Brin and Page, who would go on to found Google.

Parallel to these developments, Schank introduced his *Conceptual Dependency Theory* in 1969, aiming to model natural language understanding in a way that was independent of the actual words used. This theory became one of the most influential semantic models in AI, built upon earlier work in semantic networks, first explored by Quillian in 1966. Schank's parser translated sentences into conceptual structures that allowed computers to better 'understand' meaning, further contributing to the growing field of computational semantics (Schank, 1969).

Early chatbots and NLP programs demonstrated impressive technical achievements, helping to shape our understanding of language processing and human-computer interaction. Together, these pioneering efforts – from Bobrow's STUDENT to Weizenbaum's ELIZA, Winograd's SHRDLU, and Schank's conceptual dependency models – laid the foundation for modern NLP systems and chatbots. Despite their innovations, these early systems shared a critical limitation: limited scalability, primarily due to insufficient data and computing power, which constrained their real-world impact.[27]

As data availability and computational resources expanded, AI research was able to build on these early foundations and move beyond its limitations. A series of transformative milestones – driven in large part by the technological developments discussed above – have since propelled the field forward, from the 1995 demonstration of a (semi-)autonomous vehicle navigating U.S. freeways coast-to-coast ('No Hands Across America' project)[28] to the 2025 release of GPT-5, each marking a significant leap in capability and application (Wörsdörfer, 2018; see also Appendix II).

In 1997, IBM's Deep Blue surprised the world by defeating chess champion Kasparov, followed by Honda's ASIMO in 2000, which became the first android to climb and descend stairs. The rise of consumer AI began in 2001, when Electrolux introduced the Trilobite, a robotic vacuum cleaner. In 2004, NASA made headlines with its robotic exploration rovers Spirit and Opportunity, which successfully navigated the Martian surface. The 2004 DARPA Grand Challenge concluded without a winner, but it set the stage for the 2005 competition, which was won by Stanford University's team, led by Thrun, who later joined Waymo. The 2007 DARPA Urban Challenge further pushed autonomous vehicle research. By 2010, Microsoft Kinect for Xbox 360 had revolutionized gaming by tracking human body movement. In 2011, IBM Watson triumphed over human Jeopardy! champions Rutter and Jennings, while Apple's Siri (2011), Google Now (2012), and Microsoft's Cortana (2014) brought NLP to everyday

27 Scalability and commercialization are crucial for AI programs because they determine their ability to handle increasing amounts of data, users, and computational demands without a loss in performance. Scalable and commercialized AI systems can be efficiently deployed across large, real-world environments, such as search engines, virtual assistants, autonomous vehicles (e.g., robotaxis), or (augmented/virtual reality) video games, serving millions of users simultaneously. Without scalability and commercialization, even the most advanced AI models remain limited to small-scale, experimental, or niche applications, preventing them from delivering widespread impact. In short, scalability and commercialization ensure that AI technologies can grow, adapt, and maintain effectiveness as their usage expands.

28 The development of autonomous vehicles has a rich history marked by several key milestones. As early as 1912, the concept took form with 'The Electric Dog (of War),' considered the world's first autonomous vehicle. In 1939, GM introduced the idea of a driverless car at the New York World's Fair through its Futurama exhibit, envisioning a future with automated highways. The late 1940s saw Walter's creation of the turtle robots, pioneering electronic autonomous robotics. During the 1950s and 1960s, GM advanced the concept further with its Electronic Highway initiative. In 1966, SRI unveiled Shakey the robot, the first mobile robot capable of reasoning about its own actions. The Tsukuba Vehicle, developed in Japan in 1977, marked another leap in autonomous navigation. By the 1980s, Carnegie Mellon University launched its Navlab and Autonomous Land Vehicle (ALV) projects, pushing the boundaries of robotic mobility. In 1986, Dickmanns introduced VaMoRs, a robot car with vision-guided driving capabilities. This momentum culminated in 1987 with the Eureka PROMETHEUS project, a collaboration between Mercedes-Benz and Bundeswehr University Munich, representing one of the most ambitious autonomous driving initiatives of its time.

users. The 2012 Large Scale Visual Recognition Competition catalyzed the development of DL, and by 2015, deep neural networks had reduced image recognition error rates to 3.5%, surpassing the human error rate of roughly 5%. Meanwhile, the DARPA Robotics Challenges, held from 2012 to 2015, showcased advanced robotic systems. By 2015, Google's self-driving cars had logged over a million miles accident-free. In 2015–2017, Google DeepMind's AlphaGo defeated world Go champions (Fan, Lee, and Ke), and later, AlphaGo Zero achieved a superhuman performance by training solely through self-play (i.e., without any form of human supervision) (Silver et al., 2016). In 2020, AlphaFold achieved success in the Critical Assessment of Protein Structure Prediction (CASP) competition, solving one of biology's most challenging problems: predicting protein structures. In 2022, DeepMind's DeepNash mastered Stratego using model-free multi-agent reinforcement learning (Perolat et al., 2022), while Meta's Cicero excelled at Diplomacy by integrating strategic reasoning and communication (Washington Post, 2022).

Taken together, these historical milestones chart the progressive evolution of AI, with each development contributing to the field's expanding technical capabilities and scope of application. This trajectory of advancement laid the groundwork for a significant turning point in AI-human interaction: the release of ChatGPT, Bard, DeepSeek, and other LLM-based chatbots in 2022/2023. These systems marked the advent of a new era in the deployment of AI technologies, culminating in the release of GPT-5 in 2025. Today, such innovations have become deeply embedded in the daily routines of millions worldwide, exerting a profound and far-reaching influence on contemporary economies and societies.

Takeaway: For AI to have a lasting impact, its applications must be scalable – able to process large volumes of data and operate across diverse industries and user bases. Scalability enables AI systems to meet real-world demands and perform consistently at scale. Without it, even the most advanced technologies risk remaining limited to niche use cases. However, as AI scales, it also becomes more complex, bringing new challenges and risks that must be addressed.

1.2.11 Complexity and unintended consequences

Lesson: As AI systems grow more sophisticated and opaque, the risk of unintended consequences increases. DL models can behave unpredictably, while growing complexity often obscures embedded algorithmic biases, especially when trained on flawed or unrepresentative data. This highlights the need for transparent design, continuous evaluation, and strong oversight throughout the AI lifecycle.[29]

29 While this section includes less historical context, it raises key issues and provides a transition between the scalability/commercialization and AI ethics sections.

Examples: Notable examples of AI bias encompass a range of technologies, including facial recognition, chatbots, image classification, and speech recognition systems. Facial recognition systems, for instance, often show significantly higher error rates when identifying individuals with darker skin tones – especially women – due to imbalanced training data. Research by Buolamwini (2023) and colleagues (Bender et al., 2021; Buolamwini & Gebru, 2018) reveals that over 80% of faces in widely used training datasets were white, and more than 75% were male. As a result, error rates for darker-skinned women can reach as high as 35%, leading to serious real-world consequences such as false arrests or restricted access to public spaces. Similar risks are also evident in other AI systems. Microsoft's chatbot Tay, launched in 2016, was designed to engage with users in the style of a teen girl and learn from conversations. However, malicious users quickly exploited it by feeding it toxic and misleading content, prompting Tay to produce misogynistic and racially offensive remarks. Within 24 h, Microsoft took the bot offline, exposing the dangers of emergent bias in adaptive AI systems (Quinn, 2024). Likewise, Google Photos faced backlash in 2015 after misidentifying Black individuals as gorillas, prompting the company to disable visual searches for primates. This incident highlighted how biased training data can perpetuate stereotypes: for instance, image classification models often associate cooking, washing, and shopping with women, while linking coaching and shooting more often with men. These patterns reflect and reinforce societal biases embedded in the data, leading to discriminatory outcomes in real-world applications (Narayanan & Kapoor, 2024; Quinn, 2024). Speech recognition technologies, though vital for accessibility, also suffer from representational bias. Despite testing on datasets such as the Corpus of Regional African American Language and Voices of California, research indicates that most commercial systems perform more accurately for white speakers than for Black speakers. This discrepancy stems from non-representative training data, which limits the ability of these systems to perform reliably across diverse accents and ethnic groups (Quinn, 2024).[30]

---

30 Addressing algorithmic bias and discrimination requires fundamental changes throughout the AI development pipeline. A critical challenge lies in the selection of training data, which is often unrepresentative or incomplete – for example, datasets that predominantly reflect the experiences of white, male populations in the United States, resulting in cultural and ethnic biases. Algorithms trained on insufficient data or flawed correlations risk producing inaccurate generalizations, particularly when underlying causal factors are overlooked. Furthermore, the lack of diversity among AI developers and data scientists – who are frequently white, Western men aged 20 to 40 – heightens the likelihood that personal beliefs, stereotypes, and systemic biases will be inadvertently embedded into AI systems. To address these issues, it is essential to prioritize inclusive data collection practices, foster diverse representation within development teams, and design AI systems that authentically reflect the perspectives and needs of BIPOC (Black, Indigenous, and People of Color), women, disabled and elderly individuals, people from developing countries, and LGBTQ+ communities.

O'Neil's book *Weapons of Math Destruction* (2016) highlights how AI technologies and big data analytics can reinforce existing societal inequalities. These algorithmic systems – often obscured within opaque data-processing mechanisms (Pasquale, 2016) – disproportionately impact vulnerable and marginalized populations, such as low-income communities and ethnic minorities, thereby intensifying discrimination, systemic racism, and ingrained biases. By perpetuating social prejudices, these technologies not only deepen inequality and social fragmentation but also threaten democratic values by creating harmful feedback loops, like the poverty trap. A key problem is the lack of transparency and accountability, which allows algorithms to be manipulated without sufficient oversight. In the absence of strong regulatory frameworks and accessible avenues for complaints, the largely unregulated data economy operates unchecked. Data brokers, functioning mostly outside public scrutiny, commodify personal information by transforming it into marketable assets – a reflection of the broader commercialization of society.

The detrimental effects of big data appear across numerous sectors. In advertising, personalized marketing – often referred to as predatory advertising – exploits individuals' vulnerabilities by using data such as ZIP codes. For example, high-interest loans are aggressively targeted at low-income groups, worsening financial instability. In healthcare, wellness and fitness programs that rely on apps, sensors, and trackers collect data, such as step counts and sleep patterns, to monitor and influence behavior. While these programs claim to promote health, they can become intrusive forms of workplace surveillance, raising significant privacy issues. They also risk discriminating against people who are overweight, chronically ill, or disabled. In finance, banks and insurers are increasingly using credit scores and algorithmic surveillance techniques, including redlining, to assess risk. These practices disproportionately affect marginalized and vulnerable groups, such as people of color, women, and residents of economically disadvantaged neighborhoods, limiting their access to loans, insurance, and housing. Redlining denies services to individuals in areas labeled as high-risk based on socioeconomic and racial factors, thus perpetuating geographic and racial disparities. These practices trap people in poverty cycles fueled by structural bias and restricted financial opportunities. Hiring processes are also influenced by algorithmic tools, such as personality tests, credit scores, and e-scores. When employers use credit scores as a screening tool, they risk reinforcing bias, as unemployed individuals typically have lower scores, creating a cycle where joblessness lowers creditworthiness, which in turn reduces employment prospects, deepening economic hardship. In the field of security and crime prevention, predictive policing tools such as PredPol – which rely on risk terrain analysis and hotspot predictions – have faced widespread criticism for reinforcing racial profiling. Though these systems claim to predict crime, they often perpetuate stereotypes by associating specific neighborhoods or ethnic groups with criminal behavior. This creates a harmful cycle: increased police presence in certain areas leads to more reported crimes, which justifies further surveillance and arrests. This process erodes trust in law enforcement, fosters fear, and contributes to long-term social and economic marginalization, ironically fueling the very criminal activity it seeks to reduce. Lastly, the role of big data in digital voter manipulation – illustrated by the Cambridge Analytica scandal – shows how data profiling and targeted advertising can influence political outcomes. Through disinformation and micro-targeting, these tactics distort public discourse and undermine democratic institutions, weakening public confidence in elections and the rule of law (O'Neil, 2016).

Takeaway: As AI systems become more complex, transparency and accountability are essential to ensure ethical and fair decision-making. Equitable outcomes depend on training models with diverse, inclusive datasets. These concerns underscore the need for robust regulation to ensure fairness, oversight, and transparency in the development of AI.

1.2.12 AI ethics and governance

Lesson: In the early days of AI, researchers focused primarily on technical challenges, often overlooking the social implications of their work. Nevertheless, a few forward-thinking figures in the AI community were already raising essential questions about computer ethics (most notably Turing). Today, those early concerns have become pressing, as we grapple with urgent issues such as algorithmic biases and discrimination (see above), stressing the growing importance of aligning AI with ethics and law (e.g., with the help of 'ordoliberalism 2.0').

Examples: As AI becomes increasingly integrated in daily routines and critical systems, a growing number of scholars, policymakers, and technologists are raising urgent ethical and societal concerns (Coeckelbergh, 2020; Floridi, 2023; Wörsdörfer, 2025b, 2025d). Key issues include AI's disruptive impact on labor markets and social equity, the persistence of algorithmic biases that can lead to discrimination, and the erosion of privacy through mass data collection and surveillance. AI also plays a role in amplifying harmful online content, including dangerous and hate speech, as well as mis-/disinformation, raising significant concerns for both businesses and human rights. Additionally, the environmental costs of training large-scale AI models, the growing socio-economic and political influence of big tech companies, and the broader implications for democracy, the rule of law, and military security underline the far-reaching consequences of unchecked AI development (Bender & Hanna, 2025; Buolamwini, 2023; O'Neil, 2016; Wörsdörfer, 2025d). At the heart of these debates lies the 'alignment problem' – the challenge of ensuring that AI systems act in accordance with human values (Christian, 2021; Yudkowsky, 2023; see also Bostrom & Yudkowsky, 2014) – as well as broader concerns about AI safety.

While much of the AI ethics literature has emerged in recent years – mainly in response to the rapid development and deployment of advanced AI systems – it is essential to recognize that ethical reflection on AI is not a new phenomenon. Foundational contributions to the field can be traced back to the early days of AI history. For instance, Turing's seminal work not only laid the groundwork for computational theory but also raised meaningful philosophical questions about machine intelligence and human responsibility (Turing, 1948, 1950). Similarly, Asimov's famous *Three Laws of Robotics*, introduced in the 1940s, provided one of the earliest frameworks for considering the moral behavior of intelligent machines. Building on these foundational ideas, several AI researchers and thinkers have made significant contributions to the evolving discussion of AI ethics. Wiener, for example, was among the first to warn about the social consequences of automation and intelligent machines. His work, *Cybernetics*, and subsequent writings raised early concerns about the impact of machines on society, labor, and ethical responsibility (Wiener, 1948/2019). Meanwhile, Weizenbaum, creator of the chatbot ELIZA, became a vocal critic of the unchecked adoption of AI. In his publications and speeches, he argued that there are inherent limits to what computers should be allowed to do, emphasizing the ethical risks of delegating human judgment to machines (Weizenbaum, 1976, 2001). Similarly, Dreyfus critically examined AI's limitations, particularly its inability to fully grasp human intuition and context, highlighting critical ethical questions about over-reliance on AI systems (Dreyfus, 1965, 1972). Even Minsky, a pioneer in AI research, acknowledged potential risks associated with AI, including concerns related to control and unintended consequences (Darrach, 1970; Minsky, 1994).[31] More recently, thinkers like Bostrom have gained prominence for exploring the long-term ethical implications and existential risks posed by superintelligent AI systems (Bostrom, 2014 [see below]). Together, these early efforts and the contributions of many other scholars anticipated many of the dilemmas we face today – ranging from questions of autonomy and accountability to the broader societal impacts of machine decision-making. Therefore, while contemporary AI ethics has expanded in scope and urgency, it remains deeply rooted in a much longer intellectual tradition.

This historical foundation helps contextualize today's intensifying concerns about AI. As advanced systems become increasingly powerful and embedded in everyday life, the once-abstract ethical debates of the past have transformed into pressing societal challenges –particularly around generative AI technologies like chatbots, which have been linked to the spread of disinformation, manipulation, and mistrust (Bender et al., 2021; Center for AI Safety, 2023). In response, leading figures within the AI research community have raised serious alarms. Hinton resigned from Google in 2023 to warn of the dangers posed by these technologies (New York Times, 2023). That same year, an open letter signed by prominent experts – including Bengio, Musk, and Wozniak – called for a pause in advanced AI development, citing societal risks and the threat of a market bubble reminiscent of the dot-com crash (Future of Life Insti-

31 Note that McCarthy, another AI pioneer, also wrote a paper (together with Hayes) that includes an entire section titled *Why Artificial Intelligence Needs Philosophy* (McCarthy & Hayes, 1969).

tute, 2023).[32] These concerns gained further traction in 2025 with the release of the *Global Call for AI Red Lines,* which emphasized the urgent need to establish enforceable boundaries to protect the public interest (AI Red Lines, 2025). Adding to this sense of urgency, the Center for AI Safety (2023) issued a high-profile statement warning that AI could pose an existential risk comparable to pandemics or nuclear weapons. The statement was endorsed by senior leaders at OpenAI, Google DeepMind, and other major industry players, as well as renowned researchers, including Turing Award winners such as Bengio and Hinton. Amid these mounting concerns, many scholars and policymakers argue for stronger international cooperation, including the formation of a global AI agency to oversee responsible development (Chowdhury, 2023; Marcus & Reuel, 2023). In parallel, governments and institutions have begun developing regulatory frameworks to ensure the ethical and safe deployment of AI technologies. Notable initiatives include the E.U.'s AI Act (Wörsdörfer, 2024a, 2025a), President Biden's Blueprint for an AI Bill of Rights and AI Executive Order (Wörsdörfer, 2024b, 2025c), and California's Transparency in Frontier AI Act (California Legislature, 2025). Together, these developments reflect a growing concern: without robust oversight and regulation, the potential harms of AI could outweigh its benefits.

Takeaway: AI and ethics should be closely aligned, as intelligence without ethics is not intelligence at all. The development of AI must be accompanied by careful consideration of its societal impacts to ensure it benefits humanity and does not exacerbate inequality or harm vulnerable groups. Importantly, ethical issues must be addressed from the outset – not as an afterthought – through the implementation of robust governance and regulatory frameworks aimed at mitigating risks and preventing unintended consequences (including those associated with AGI), such as ordoliberalism 2.0.

1.2.13 Artificial general intelligence and the road ahead

Lesson: Despite impressive advances in systems like AlphaGo/Fold, ChatGPT, and autonomous vehicles, these technologies still fall short of achieving the broad, adaptable intelligence characteristic of humans. The development of AGI – AI with truly human-like understanding and flexibility – remains a distant and largely theoretical dream.

---

32 The first open letter calling for research into the societal impacts of AI was released in 2015. It was signed by Hawking, Musk, and dozens of leading AI experts (Future of Life Institute, 2015a). Later that year, this was followed by a second open letter advocating for a ban on the development and use of autonomous weapons. This letter was endorsed by Hawking, Musk, Wozniak, and more than 3,000 AI and robotics researchers from around the world (Future of Life Institute, 2015b). Two years later, the Future of Life Institute hosted the Asilomar Conference on Beneficial AI, bringing together researchers and thought leaders to explore ethical considerations and strategies for ensuring that AI development remains beneficial while avoiding the existential risks associated with AGI.

Examples: The modern AI boom, particularly in the domain of LLMs (Al-Amin et al., 2024; Kaplan, 2024), can be traced back to a pivotal breakthrough in 2017, when researchers at Google introduced the transformer architecture in their paper *Attention Is All You Need* (Vaswani et al., 2017; see also Devlin et al., 2019). This architecture became the foundation for most subsequent LLMs due to its ability to efficiently handle large-scale data and model long-range dependencies in text. Building on this innovation, companies such as OpenAI and DeepMind have developed powerful models, including GPT-3 and Gato, respectively. These are examples of foundation models, which are trained on large amounts of unlabeled data and can be fine-tuned or adapted for a wide range of downstream tasks, including language generation and problem-solving.

By 2020, LLMs began to capture public attention. OpenAI's release of GPT-3 demonstrated unprecedented language capabilities, while applications like 15.ai showcased the use of neural networks for voice synthesis, popularizing AI-generated voices in creative and entertainment contexts. In the same year, OpenAI researchers published the influential *Scaling Laws for Neural Language Models* (Kaplan et al., 2020), demonstrating that the performance of LLMs improves predictably with increases in data, model size, and computational resources. These developments laid the groundwork for what followed in 2022, when OpenAI launched ChatGPT 3.5. With its ability to generate human-like responses, write code, and produce creative content, ChatGPT became the fastest-growing consumer software application in history. This marked the beginning of what is often referred to as the 'generative AI revolution' (Kaplan, 2024), ushering in a new wave of AI hype and investment – evident in the surge in AI-related funding and the soaring market valuations of companies like Nvidia and OpenAI (Bender & Hanna, 2025).

The pace of innovation continued into 2024 and 2025. Anthropic released the Claude 3 family of LLMs, and OpenAI introduced O3, an advanced reasoning model that reignited discussions about the possibility of AGI. On the Abstraction and Reasoning Corpus (ARC) benchmark, developed by Chollet in 2019 to assess general intelligence, O3 scored 87.5%, surpassing the typical human score of 84%. This result raised new questions about the threshold between narrow AI and more generalized reasoning capabilities. In August 2025, OpenAI released GPT-5, further pushing the boundaries of what generative models can achieve and intensifying the broader conversation around the societal, economic, and technological implications of rapid AI advancement (Al-Amin et al., 2024; Kaplan, 2024).

A key concept in discussions about the future of AI is the technological singularity – the hypothesis that computers and robots will eventually achieve sufficient intelligence to autonomously redesign and enhance themselves. This self-improvement could lead to a feedback loop of rapid advancement, often referred to as runaway intelligence, in which ultra-intelligent machines create even more intelligent successors. This intelligence explosion would mark the shift from AGI – machines with human-level cognitive abilities such as language understanding, creativity, emotional awareness, and consciousness – to artificial superintelligence (ASI), which surpasses the most advanced human capabilities. However, it is crucial to note that ASI's emergence depends on first attaining AGI, a milestone that remains unrealized and may ultimately prove unattainable (Narayanan & Kapoor, 2024).

This vision aligns closely with transhumanist and post-humanist philosophies, which foresee a future where artificial organs replace biological ones and brain–computer interfaces – such as those being developed by Neuralink (2025) – enable direct integration between minds and machines. Futurists like Kurzweil (2000, 2005, 2024) envision scenarios where human consciousness could be transferred to robotic bodies or cloud systems, potentially granting a form of digital immortality. Kurzweil also predicts radical enhancements to human sensory and cognitive functions, potentially leading to vastly extended lifespans or even biological immortality. These profound transformations, driven by the convergence of AI, neuroscience, genetics, nanotechnology, and biotechnology, may usher in a post-human era in which humans evolve into cyborgs or superhumans through advanced augmentation and machine integration.

Optimists like Kurzweil see the singularity as a pivotal event that could solve humanity's most significant challenges, forecasting AGI by 2030 and ASI by 2045. OpenAI CEO Altman shares a similar hopeful vision of AGI, emphasizing its potential to drive socially beneficial outcomes – such as eradicating poverty, combating climate change, curing diseases, and addressing global crises. This optimistic narrative is frequently highlighted in recent literature (Hagey, 2025; Hao, 2025) and public discourse (New York Times, 2025), framing AGI as a powerful tool for positive transformation rather than a threat.

On the other hand, singularity skeptics warn of significant risks. Vinge, who coined the term 'technological singularity' in his influential 1993 essay *The Coming Technological Singularity*, cautioned that (AGI and) ASI could pose an existential threat, especially given unresolved control problems and the risk of machine dominance. Beyond these warnings, techno-utopian visions raise ethical and social concerns. For example, advanced enhancements such as brain implants, robotic exoskeletons, and genetic upgrades may only be available to the wealthy, potentially exacerbating socio-economic inequalities and deepening class divides (Wörsdörfer 2018).

Prominent critics, such as Harari and Bostrom, have voiced serious concerns about the trajectory of advanced technologies, particularly those that combine AI with genetic engineering. Harari (2017, 2019) warns of emerging 'techno-religions' – belief systems promising salvation through algorithms and genetic manipulation, such as CRISPR gene editing. These developments, intertwined with brain–computer interfaces and biological enhancements, risk creating a new class of superhumans accessible only to the affluent, further intensifying social disparities. Bostrom (2014) emphasizes the existential dangers posed by superintelligent machines, envisioning scenarios where AI could instigate rebellions or takeovers that might threaten humanity's survival. He highlights the risk of a 'singleton' – a single superintelligent

AI entity wielding unchecked control over human affairs, capable of employing sophisticated social manipulation, surveillance, and mind control techniques, thereby becoming an existential threat (see also Bostrom & Yudkowsky, 2014).

Among AI researchers, skepticism about AGI's imminence or even feasibility remains. LeCun, a DL pioneer, dismisses concerns about AI threatening humanity as 'preposterously ridiculous' and suggests retiring the term AGI to reduce hype and confusion. He advocates focusing instead on achieving 'advanced machine intelligence,' noting that human intelligence is specialized and varied, with no single individual embodying the full spectrum of cognitive abilities. Therefore, replicating the entirety of human intelligence in machines may not be the ultimate objective (BBC, 2025).

Bender and Hanna (2025), in *The AI Con*, critically examine the current hype (and hubris) and doomerism surrounding AI, highlighting the real-world harms AI can cause in sectors such as healthcare, education, and social services. They argue that many AI technologies embed racist, sexist, and ableist biases – often reflecting Western-centric perspectives. This bias, combined with centralized power in big tech, leads to data monopolies and profit-driven models that perpetuate social inequalities. One key point they emphasize is the misleading nature of concepts like 'sentient AI' or 'artificial consciousness,' which they describe as empty promises. LLMs, for example, function largely as sophisticated pattern-matchers or 'autocomplete on steroids,' lacking genuine understanding, consciousness, or intersubjectivity (Bender et al., 2021). This reductionist view risks devaluing human relationships, communication, and identity, while reinforcing structural inequalities rooted in racist and sexist assumptions. Bender and Hanna challenge the deterministic belief that AI will inevitably become fully autonomous and omnipotent, calling instead for critical thinking, media literacy, and robust legal frameworks – such as consumer protections, transparency mandates, and labor rights – to counteract the harms of AI hype and ensure technology serves to strengthen rather than fragment society.

Despite these divergent perspectives and the ongoing hype, expert surveys reveal a lack of consensus within the ML community about AGI's timeline and risks (AAAI, 2025; AIMultiple, 2025; Field, 2025; Grace et al., 2024). Some studies report that about a quarter of experts assign zero existential risk to AGI, while others predict significant risks. Notably, the recent 'generative AI revolution' has shifted many predictions closer: whereas AGI was once thought to emerge around 2060, current surveys suggest dates as soon as 2040, with some entrepreneurs forecasting 2030. Although hype influences these expectations, many agree that preparing society through awareness, education, and regulation is essential – not to incite fear, but to responsibly manage the potential advent of AGI.

Takeaway: The pursuit of AGI remains a long(er)-term project, while current AI development should focus on addressing specific, well-defined problems. In parallel, ongoing policy and ethical discussions are crucial for guiding the responsible deployment of AI, and appropriate regulation may be necessary to ensure that these technologies are developed and used safely and equitably.

1.3 Concluding remarks

The rapid evolution of AI – driven by breakthroughs in generative technologies, renewed interest in AGI, and shifting regulatory paradigms – has reignited long-standing debates about the societal, ethical, and philosophical implications of intelligent systems. Yet amid political shifts and growing public and commercial hype, one critical perspective remains underutilized: the historical lens. This chapter has argued that a deeper engagement with the history of AI – its foundational debates, philosophical reflections, and early regulatory efforts – is essential for understanding and contextualizing current developments. By drawing on an interdisciplinary range of sources, it has presented a (largely) chronologically structured series of lessons that highlight recurring challenges, persistent misconceptions, and frequently overlooked insights (see Appendix I). These include the need to manage expectations, remain ethically vigilant, and ground technological innovation in realistic and socially responsible frameworks. In doing so, the chapter highlights the importance of historical awareness in informing more thoughtful, inclusive, and forward-looking AI research and policy.

One of the central takeaways from this historical analysis is that while technological breakthroughs in AI can appear sudden, they are usually the product of years – if not decades – of foundational work, interdisciplinary collaboration, and incremental progress. As the field continues to advance, its development must be guided by a balance of curiosity, caution, and ethical responsibility – ensuring that innovation serves the public good while minimizing harm. Equally important is the need to embrace methodological diversity and open-mindedness, which can foster more robust, inclusive, and adaptable approaches to AI R&D.

Looking ahead, one of the most promising directions for AI lies in fostering effective human-AI collaboration. Rather than positioning AI as a replacement for human labor or intelligence, a more sustainable and realistic vision sees it as a tool to augment human capabilities – enhancing decision-making, creativity, and productivity across sectors such as medicine, finance, and customer service (while also safeguarding the interests of vulnerable populations). In this symbiotic model, machines contribute computational power and advanced pattern recognition, while humans provide contextual understanding, ethical judgment, and emotional intelligence.

At the same time, it is crucial to recognize AI for what it is: a powerful set of tools designed to address specific, well-defined problems – not a magical or universal solution. The contrast between early AI systems designed for narrow tasks, such as playing chess, and today's more complex applications, including natural language understanding, climate modeling, and personalized medicine, highlights the need for nuanced, domain-specific approaches. Avoiding hype (and hubris) and embracing a more grounded perspective will help foster innovation that is both sustainable and socially aligned.

Several open questions will shape the next chapter of AI development. The realization of AGI remains speculative, with experts divided on both its feasibility and timeline.[33] While the current wave of investment and optimism around generative AI reduces the likelihood of a near-term AI winter, a significant shift in public perception, funding, or political will could still alter the trajectory. In the United States, for example, regulatory developments under the current administration – particularly moves toward deregulation and ideological scrutiny – are likely to have profound impacts on both the direction and ethics of AI research (Wörsdörfer, 2025e). Meanwhile, global discussions around governance frameworks, including those in the E.U., continue to evolve, raising essential questions about how to balance innovation with accountability.

Ultimately, the future of AI depends on interdisciplinary cooperation, ongoing ethical reflection, and adaptive policy frameworks that can keep pace with technological change. By learning from the past and embedding historical insights into contemporary decision-making, we can better navigate the complexities of AI and ensure that its development remains aligned with democratic values, human dignity, and the broader public interest.

Appendix I: Important dates in AI history

- 1936/1937: Turing Machine
- 1943: McCulloch & Pitts' *A Logical Calculus of the Ideas Immanent in Nervous Activity*
- 1943: Wiener's *Cybernetics*
- 1948: Shannon's *A Mathematical Theory of Communication*
- 1948/1949: Walter's turtle robots
- 1949: Hebb's *The Organization of Behavior*
- 1950: Turing Test
- 1951: Minsky & Edmonds' SNARC
- 1955: Newell, Simon, & Shaw's *Logic Theorist*
- 1956: Dartmouth Workshop
- 1957/1958: Rosenblatt's *Perceptron*
- 1957/1959: Newell, Simon, & Shaw's *General Problem Solver*
- 1958: Gelernter's Geometry Theorem Machine/Prover
- 1958/1959: McCarthy's Advice Taker proposal
- 1959: Samuel's checkers player

33 Bennett (2023) predicts that the creation of ASI will represent the sixth major breakthrough in the evolution of intelligence – following steering, reinforcing, simulating, mentalizing, and speaking. In this view, intelligence would transcend the biological constraints of the human brain. However, others, including LeCun (BBC, 2025) and Bender and Hanna (2025), dismiss such predictions as speculative and overstated, characterizing them as part of the broader AI hype.

- 1961: Slagle's SAINT
- 1964: Bobrow's STUDENT
- 1964–1967: Weizenbaum's ELIZA
- 1965: Dendral (expert system)
- 1965: Dreyfus' *Alchemy and AI*
- 1966–1972: SRI's Shakey the robot
- Late 1960s: Minsky & Papert's micro-worlds
- 1968–1970: Winograd's SHRDLU
- 1969: Minsky & Papert's *Perceptrons*
- 1969: Schank's Conceptual Dependency Theory
- 1972: Lighthill Report
- 1972: Mycin
- 1974: Werbos' Perceptron
- 1974–1980: First AI Winter
- 1976: Newell & Simon's Physical Symbol System Hypothesis
- 1976: Weizenbaum's *Computer Power and Human Reason*
- 1978: Simon wins Nobel Prize in Economics
- 1979/1980: Fukushima's *Neocognitron*
- 1980: Searle's *Minds, Brains, and Programs*
- 1980–1987: (New) AI boom
- 1982: 'Hopfield Net'
- 1982: Japan's Fifth Generation Computer Project
- 1982: Marr's visual perception work
- 1984: Cyc (expert system)
- 1986: Hinton & Rumelhart's backpropagation
- 1987–1993: Second AI Winter (end of first commercial wave of AI)
- 1988: Moravec's *Mind Children*
- 1988: Pearl's *Probabilistic Reasoning in Intelligent Systems*
- 1988: Markov decision process
- 1988: Sutton & Barto's TD learning algorithm
- 1990: LeCun's convolutional neural networks
- 1990: Brooks' *Elephants Don't Play Chess*
- 1992: Tesauro's TD-Gammon
- 1993: Vinge's *The Coming Technological Singularity*
- 2005: Kurzweil's *The Singularity is Near*
- 2007: Learned-Miller et al.'s *Labeled Faces in the Wild*
- 2009: Li's ImageNet
- 2012: *AlexNet* paper
- 2013: Google's Word2Vec
- 2014: Bostrom's *Superintelligence*
- 2016: O'Neil's *Weapons of Math Destruction*
- 2017: Transformer models

- 2020: (First) LLMs
- 2022: ChatGPT 3.5 (start of generative AI boom)
- 2023: Biden's AI Executive Order
- 2023: Open letter (AI development pause)
- 2024: E.U.'s AI Act
- 2024: Nobel Prizes (Baker, Hassabis, Hinton, Hopfield, and Jumper)
- 2025: Global Call for AI Red Lines
- 2025: California's Transparency in Frontier AI Act

Appendix II: Historical milestones in AI R&D

- 1995: Computer-controlled minivan 'drives' on freeways across United States
- 1997: IBM supercomputer Deep Blue defeats chess champion Kasparov
- 2000: Honda's ASIMO android climbs and descends stairs
- 2001: Electrolux introduces robotic vacuum cleaner (Trilobite)
- 2004: First DARPA Grand Challenge
- 2004: NASA's robotic exploration rovers Spirit and Opportunity navigate surface of Mars
- 2005: Second DARPA Grand Challenge
- 2007: DARPA Urban Challenge
- 2010: Microsoft launches Kinect for Xbox 360
- 2011: IBM's Watson beats human Jeopardy! champions
- 2011: Apple's Siri, Alphabet's Google Now, Microsoft's Cortana use NLP
- 2012: Third Large Scale Visual Recognition Competition
- 2012–2015: DARPA Robotics Challenges
- 2015: Google's self-driving cars log more than one million miles
- 2015/2016: Google DeepMind's AlphaGo defeats Go (world) champions
- 2020: Google DeepMind's AlphaFold succeeds in CASP competition
- 2022: Google DeepMind's DeepNash masters game of Stratego
- 2022: Meta's AI model Cicero wins at Diplomacy
- 2022/2023: Release of ChatGPT, Bard, DeepSeek, and other (LLM-based) chatbots
- 2025: Release of GPT-5

Appendix III: List of influential AI papers (selection)

On Computable Numbers, with an Application to the Entscheidungsproblem (1936)
Author: Alan Turing
Why it's important: In this paper, Turing's proof is presented, laying the groundwork for the development of the Turing Machine.

A Logical Calculus of the Ideas Immanent in Nervous Activity (1943)
Authors: Warren McCulloch and Walter Pitts
Why it's important: By demonstrating that neural networks could be modeled mathematically, this paper took a foundational step toward building machines designed to mimic brain function.

A Mathematical Theory of Communication (1948)
Author: Claude E. Shannon
Why it's important: By defining the principles of how information can be measured, stored, and transmitted, this paper formally introduced the discipline of information theory.

Computing Machinery and Intelligence (1950)
Author: Alan Turing
Why it's important: In this seminal work, Turing explored the question, 'Can machines think?' and proposed the Turing Test – also called the imitation game – as a way to determine whether a machine can convincingly mimic human intelligence.

A Proposal for the Dartmouth Summer Research Project on Artificial Intelligence (1956)
Authors: John McCarthy, Marvin L. Minsky, Nathaniel Rochester, and Claude E. Shannon
Why it's important: This moment gave AI its name and signified the formal establishment of AI as a distinct academic field.

The Perceptron: A Probabilistic Model for Information Storage and Organization in the Brain (1958)
Author: Frank Rosenblatt
Why it's important: By introducing the perceptron as the core unit of neural networks, this paper provided a foundational concept that would later evolve into modern deep learning.

Some Studies in Machine Learning Using the Game of Checkers (1959)
Author: A.L. Samuel
Why it's important: Recognized as the first program to implement machine learning, Samuel's checkers player marked a shift from rule-based systems to data-driven learning approaches.

ELIZA – A Computer Program for the Study of Natural Language Communication Between Man and Machine (1969)
Author: Joseph Weizenbaum
Why it's important: Weizenbaum's paper introduced the first chatbot, showing that simple programs could mimic conversation and sparking debates about AI, human-computer interaction, and ethics.

Neocognitron: A Self-Organizing Neural Network Model for a Mechanism of Pattern Recognition Unaffected by Shift in Position (1980)
Author: Kunihiko Fukushima
Why it's important: Fukushima's paper introduced the Neocognitron, a shift-invariant neural network that laid the foundation for modern convolutional neural networks used in deep learning and computer vision.

Neural Networks and Physical Systems with Emergent Collective Computational Abilities (1982)
Author: John Hopfield
Why it's important: This paper introduced neural networks as energy-minimizing systems, modeling associative memory and linking physics with neuroscience and computation. It laid the groundwork for modern neural models.

Learning Representations by Back-Propagating Errors (1986)
Authors: David E. Rumelhart, Geoffrey E. Hinton, and Ronald J. Williams
Why it's important: This foundational work introduced the backpropagation algorithm, a critical breakthrough that made it possible to effectively train deep neural networks and advance the field of deep learning.

Elephants Don't Play Chess (1990)
Author: Rodney Brooks
Why it's important: Brooks' paper challenged traditional AI by promoting reactive, behavior-based robotics focused on real-world interaction, introducing the subsumption architecture, and significantly impacting the revival of robotics.

Long Short-Term Memory (LSTM) (1997)
Authors: Sepp Hochreiter and Jürgen Schmidhuber

Why it's important: By allowing machines to remember and process information across multiple time steps, LSTM networks (as a subset of recurrent neural networks) play a crucial role in applications such as speech recognition, machine translation, and interactive chatbots.

Algorithms for Inverse Reinforcement Learning (2000)
Authors: Andrew Ng and Stuart Russell
Why it's important: Ng and Russell's paper introduced Inverse Reinforcement Learning, a method to infer an agent's underlying goals by observing its behavior. This enabled machines to learn tasks from demonstrations, shaping fields like robotics and human behavior modeling.

ImageNet: A Large-Scale Hierarchical Image Database (2009)
Authors: Jia Deng, Wei Dong, Richard Socher, Li-Jia Li, Kai Li, and Li Fei-Fei
Why it's important: Developed by Li et al., (the original) ImageNet contains three million images captioned by volunteers using Amazon Mechanical Turk and has become the definitive benchmark for assessing the performance of cutting-edge image processing technologies.

ImageNet Classification with Deep Convolutional Neural Networks (2012)
Authors: Alex Krizhevsky, Ilya Sutskever, and Geoffrey Hinton
Why it's important: By winning a major competition with their model AlexNet, this paper propelled deep learning into prominence and marked the onset of the contemporary AI surge.

Deep Learning (2015)
Authors: Yann LeCun, Yoshua Bengio, and Geoffrey Hinton
Why it's important: Co-authored by the three pioneers often referred to as the 'godfathers' of modern AI, this paper distills the fundamental lessons learned from decades of deep learning research.

Mastering The Game of Go with Deep Neural Networks and Tree Search (2016)
Authors: David Silver, Aja Huang, Chris J. Maddison, Arthur Guez, Laurent Sifre, George van den Driessche, Julian Schrittwieser, Ioannis Antonoglou, Veda Panneershelvam, Marc Lanctot, Sander Dieleman, Dominik Grewe, John Nham, Nal Kalchbrenner, Ilya Sutskever, Timothy Lillicrap, Madeleine Leach, Koray Kavukcuoglu, Thore Graepel, and Demis Hassabis
Why it's important: AlphaGo's victory over a world champion in Go showcased AI's capability to master intricate strategy games previously thought to be uniquely human.

Attention Is All You Need (2017)
Authors: Ashish Vaswani, Noam M. Shazeer, Niki Parmar, Jakob Uszkoreit, Llion Jones, Aidan N. Gomez, Lukasz Kaiser, and Illia Polosukhin
Why it's important: By introducing the transformer model, this paper laid the groundwork for powerful language processing tools, including ChatGPT and Google Translate.

BERT: Pre-training of Deep Bidirectional Transformers for Language Understanding (2019)
Authors: Jacob Devlin, Ming-Wei Chang, Kenton Lee, and Kristina Toutanova
Why it's important: By allowing machines to interpret the meaning of words within their context, BERT has advanced the capabilities of search engines and AI assistants.

Scaling Laws for Neural Language Models (2020)
Authors: Jared Kaplan, Sam McCandlish, Tom Henighan, Tom B. Brown, Benjamin Chess, Rewon Child, Scott Gray, Alec Radford, Jeffrey Wu, and Dariou Amodei
Why it's important: This paper, authored by researchers at OpenAI, lays the essential theoretical groundwork underpinning ChatGPT.

On the Dangers of Stochastic Parrots: Can Language Models Be Too Big? (2021)
Authors: Emily M. Bender, Timnit Gebru, Angelina McMillan-Major, and Margaret Mitchell
Why it's important: Focusing on the ethical, societal, and environmental challenges posed by large language models, this paper notably coincided with the departure of Gebru from Google, a move that was met with controversy.

References

AI Multiple. (2025). When Will AGI/Singularity Happen? https://research.aimultiple.com/artificial-general-intelligence-singularity-timing/#easy-footnote-bottom-2-583 (last accessed: December 30, 2025).

AI Red Lines. (2025). Global Call for AI Red Lines. https://red-lines.ai/#sentinel (last accessed: December 30, 2025).

Al-Amin, M., Ali, M., Salam, A., Khan, A., Ali, A., Ullah, A., Alam, N., & Chowdhury, S. (2024). History of Generative Artificial Intelligence (AI) Chatbots: Past, Present, and Future Development. https://arxiv.org/abs/2402.05122 (last accessed: December 30, 2025).

Association for the Advancement of Artificial Intelligence (AAAI). (2025). AAAI 2025 Presidential Panel on the Future of AI Research. https://aaai.org/wp-content/uploads/2025/03/AAAI-2025-PresPanel-Report-Digital-3.7.25.pdf (last accessed: December 30, 2025).

BBC. (2025). Meta Scientist Yann LeCun Says AI Won't Destroy Jobs Forever. https://www.bbc.com/news/technology-65886125 (last accessed: December 30, 2025).

Bender, E. & Hanna, A. (2025). The AI Con. How to Fight Big Tech's Hype and Create the Future We Want. London, Harper.

Bender, E., Gebru, T., McMillan-Major, A., & Shmitchell, S. (2021). On the Dangers of Stochastic Parrots: Can Language Models Be Too Big? FAccT'21: Proceedings of the 2021 ACM Conference on Fairness, Accountability, and Transparency. 610–623.

Bennett, M. (2023). A Brief History of Intelligence. Evolution, AI, and the Five Breakthroughs That Made Our Brains. New York, Mariner Books.

Blei, D., Ng, A., & Jordan, M. (2003). Latent Dirichlet Allocation. Journal of Machine Learning Research 3. 993–1022.

Bobrow, D. (1964). Natural Language Input for a Computer Problem Solving System. Cambridge, MIT.

Bostrom, N. (2014). Superintelligence. Oxford, Oxford University Press.

Bostrom, N. & Yudkowsky, E. (2014). The Ethics of Artificial Intelligence. In: Frankish, K. & Ramsey, W. (eds.). The Cambridge Handbook of Artificial Intelligence. Cambridge, Cambridge University Press. 316–334.

Breazeal, C. (2002). Designing Sociable Robots. Cambridge, MIT Press.

Breazeal, C. (2003). Toward Sociable Robots. Robotics and Autonomous Systems 42(3–4). 167–175.

Breazeal, C. (2004). Emotion and Sociable Humanoid Robots. International Journal of Human-Computer Studies 59(1–2). 119–155.

Brooks, R. (1990). Elephants Don't Play Chess. Robotics and Autonomous Systems 6(1–2). 139–159.

Brooks, R., Breazeal, C., Marjanović, M., Scassellati, B., & Williamson, M. (2000). The Cog Project: Building a Humanoid Robot. In: Nehaniv, C. (eds.) Computation for Metaphors, Analogy, and Agents. CMAA 1998. Lecture Notes in Computer Science 1562. Springer, Berlin. 52–87.

Buchanan, B. (2005). A (Very) Brief History of Artificial Intelligence. https://web.archive.org/web/20070926023314/http://www.aaai.org/AITopics/assets/PDF/AIMag26-04-016.pdf (last accessed: December 30, 2025).

Buolamwini, J. (2023). Unmasking AI. My Mission to Protect What is Human in a World of Machines. New York, Random House.

Buolamwini, J. & Gebru, T. (2018). Gender Shades: Intersectional Accuracy Disparities in Commercial Gender Classification. Proceedings of Machine Learning Research 81. 1–15.

California Legislature. (2025). Transparency in Frontier Artificial Intelligence Act. https://legiscan.com/CA/text/SB53/2025 (last accessed: December 30, 2025).

Center for AI Safety. (2023a). Statement on AI Risk. https://www.safe.ai/statement-on-ai-risk (last accessed: December 30, 2025).

Christian, B. (2021). The Alignment Problem. Machine Learning and Human Values. New York, Norton.

Chomsky, N. (1965). Aspects of the Theory of Syntax. Cambridge, MIT Press.

Chowdhury, R. (2023). AI Desperately Needs Global Oversight. www.wired.com/story/ai-desperately-needs-global-oversight/ (last accessed: December 30, 2025).

Coeckelbergh, M. (2020). AI Ethics. Cambridge, MIT Press.

Copeland, J. (ed.) (2004). The Essential Turing. Seminal Writings in Computing, Logic, Philosophy, Artificial Intelligence, and Artificial Life, plus The Secrets of Enigma. Oxford, Oxford University Press.

Copeland, J. (2020). The Modern History of Computing. https://plato.stanford.edu/cgi-bin/encyclopedia/archinfo.cgi?entry=computing-history (last accessed: December 30, 2025).

Darrach, B. (1970). Meet Shaky, the First Electronic Person. Life Magazine, 20 November 1970.

Dayan,P., Hinton,G., Neal,R., & Zemel, R. (1995). The Helmholtz Machine. Neural Comput 7(5). 889–904.

Deng, J., Dong, W., Socher, R., Li, L., Li, K., & Li, F.-F. (2009): ImageNet: A Large-Scale Hierarchical Image Database. IEEE Conference on Computer Vision and Pattern Recognition. 248–255.

Devlin, J., Chang, M.-W., Lee, K., & Toutanova, K. (2019). BERT: Pre-Training of Deep Bidirectional Transformers for Language Understanding. https://arxiv.org/abs/1810.04805 (last accessed: December 30, 2025).

Dreyfus, H. (1965). Alchemy and Artificial Intelligence. https://apps.dtic.mil/sti/trecms/pdf/AD0625719.pdf (last accessed: December 30, 2025).

Dreyfus, H. (1972). What Computers Still Can't Do: A Critique of Artificial Reason. New York, Harper & Row.
Dreyfus, H. & Dreyfus, S. (1986). Mind Over Machine: The Power of Human Intuition and Expertise in the Era of the Computer. New York, Free Press.
EU AI Champions Initiative. (2025). Stop the Clock – Open Letter. https://aichampions.eu/#stoptheclock (last accessed: December 30, 2025).
European Commission. (2025). The General-Purpose AI Code of Practice. https://digital-strategy.ec.europa.eu/en/policies/contents-code-gpai (last accessed: December 30, 2025).
FAZ. (2025). "Europa muss Innovationen fördern statt verhindern." https://www.faz.net/aktuell/wirtschaft/unternehmen/sap-und-siemens-fordern-neue-ki-regulierung-110588444.html (last accessed: December 30, 2025).
Feigenbaum, E. & McCorduck, P. (1983). The Fifth Generation. Artificial Intelligence and Japan's Computer Challenge to the World. Reading, Addison-Wesley.
Field, S. (2025). Why Do Experts Disagree on Existential Risk and P(Doom)? https://arxiv.org/pdf/2502.14870 (last accessed: December 30, 2025).
Floridi, L. (2023). The Ethics of Artificial Intelligence. Oxford, Oxford University Press.
Fukushima, K. (1980). Neocognitron: A Self-organizing Neural Network Model for a Mechanism of Pattern Recognition Unaffected by Shift in Position. Biological Cybernetics 36(4). 193–202.
Future of Life Institute. (2015a). Research Priorities for Robust and Beneficial Artificial Intelligence: An Open Letter. https://futureoflife.org/open-letter/ai-open-letter/ (last accessed: December 30, 2025).
Future of Life Institute. (2015b). Autonomous Weapons Open Letter: AI & Robotics Researchers. https://futureoflife.org/open-letter/open-letter-autonomous-weapons-ai-robotics/ (last accessed: December 30, 2025).
Future of Life Institute. (2023). Pause Giant AI Experiments: An Open Letter. https://futureoflife.org/open-letter/pause-giant-ai-experiments/.
Gelernter, H. & Rochester, N. (1958). Intelligent Behavior in Problem-Solving Machines. IBM Journal of Research and Development 2(4). 336–345.
Gelernter, H., Hansen, J., & Loveland, D. (1960). Empirical Explorations of the Geometry Theorem Machine. Western Joint IRE-AIEE-ACM Computer Conference. New York, Association for Computing Machinery. 143–149.
Goodfellow, I., Bengio, Y., & Courville, A. (2016). Deep Learning. Cambridge, MIT Press.
Grace, K., Stewart, H., Sandkühler, J.F., Thomas, S., Weinstein-Raun, B., & Brauner, J. (2024). Thousands of AI Authors on the Future of AI. https://arxiv.org/abs/2401.02843 (last accessed: December 30, 2025).
Griewank, A. (2012). Who Invented the Reverse Mode of Differentiation? Documenta Mathematica Extra Volume ISMP (2012). 389–400.
Haenlein, M. & Kaplan, A. (2019). A Brief History of Artificial Intelligence: On the Past, Present, and Future of Artificial Intelligence. California Management Review 61(4). 5–14.
Hagey, K. (2025). The Optimist. Sam Altman, OpenAI, and the Race to Invent the Future. New York, Norton.
Haigh, T. (2023). There Was No 'First AI Winter.' Communications of the ACM 66(12). 35–39.
Hao, K. (2025). Empire of AI. Dreams and Nightmares in Sam Altman's OpenAI. New York, Penguin.
Harari, Y. (2017). Homo Deus. London, Vintage.
Harari, Y. (2019). 21 Lessons for the 21st Century. New York, Random House.
He, K., Zhang, X., Ren, S., & Sun, J. (2016). Deep Residual Learning for Image Recognition. IEEE Conference on Computer Vision and Pattern Recognition. 770–778.
Hebb, D. (1949). The Organization of Behavior: A Neuropsychological Theory. New York, Wiley.
Hochreiter, S. & Schmidhuber, J. (1997). Long Short-Term Memory. Neural Computations 9(8). 1735–1780.
Hodges, A. (2012). Alan Turing: The Enigma. London, Vintage.
Hodges, A. (2019). Alan Turing. https://plato.stanford.edu/entries/turing/ (last accessed: December 30, 2025).

Hofstadter, D. (1995). Fluid Concepts and Creative Analogies. Computer Models of the Fundamental Mechanisms of Thought. New York, Basic Books.

Hopfield, J. (1982). Neural Networks and Physical Systems with Emergent Collective Computational Abilities. Proceedings of the National Academy of Sciences 79(8). 2554–2558.

Huang, G. & Learned-Miller, E. (2014). Labeled Faces in the Wild: Updates and New Reporting Procedures. https://people.cs.umass.edu/~elm/papers/lfw_update.pdf (last accessed: December 30, 2025).

Huang, G., Ramesh, M., Berg, T., & Learned-Miller, E. (2007). Labeled Faces in the Wild: A Database For Studying Face Recognition in Unconstrained Environments. https://people.cs.umass.edu/~elm/papers/lfw.pdf (last accessed: December 30, 2025).

IAPP. (2025). Potential EU AI Act Pause Opens New Questions on Approach to Global Regulation. https://iapp.org/news/a/navigate-2025-potential-eu-ai-act-pause-opens-new-questions-on-approach-to-global-regulation/ (last accessed: December 30, 2025).

Ising, E. (1925). Contributions to the Theory of Ferromagnetism. Zeitschrift für Physik 31. 253–258.

Kahneman, D. (2011). Thinking Fast and Slow. New York, Farrar, Straus, and Giroux.

Kaplan, J. (2016). Artificial Intelligence. What Everyone Needs to Know. Oxford, Oxford University Press.

Kaplan, J. (2024). Generative Artificial Intelligence. What Everyone Needs to Know. Oxford, Oxford University Press.

Kaplan, J., McCandlish, S., Henighan, T., Brown, T., Chess, B., Child, R., Gray, S., Radford, A., Wu, J., & Amodei, D. (2020). Scaling Laws for Neural Language Models. https://arxiv.org/pdf/2001.08361 (last accessed: December 30, 2025).

Krizhevsky, A., Sutskever, I., & Hinton, G. (2017). ImageNet Classification With Deep Convolutional Neural Networks. Communications of the ACM 60(6). 84–90.

Kuhn, T. (1957). The Copernican Revolution: Planetary Astronomy in the Development of Western Thought. Cambridge, Harvard University Press.

Kuhn, T. (1962/1990). The Structure of Scientific Revolutions. Chicago, University of Chicago Press.

Kuhn, T. (1963). The Function of Dogma in Scientific Research. In: A. Crombie (ed.). Scientific Change (Symposium on the History of Science, University of Oxford, July 9–15, 1961). New York, Basic Books. 347–369.

Kurzweil, R. (2000). The Age of Spiritual Machines. New York, Penguin.

Kurzweil, R. (2005). The Singularity is Near. London, Penguin.

Kurzweil, R. (2024). The Singularity is Nearer. New York, Viking.

Lakatos, I. (1976). Proofs and Refutations. Cambridge, Cambridge University Press.

Lakatos, I. (1978). The Methodology of Scientific Research Programs: Philosophical Papers Vol. 1. Cambridge, Cambridge University Press.

Lakatos, I. & Musgrave, A., (1972). Criticism and the Growth of Knowledge. Cambridge, Cambridge University Press.

Learned-Miller, E., Huang, G., RoyChowdhury, A., Li, H., & Hua, G. (2016). Labeled Faces in the Wild: A Survey. In: Kawulok, M., Celebi, M., & Smolka, B. (eds.). Advances in Face Detection and Facial Image Analysis. Cham, Springer. 189–248.

LeCun, Y., Bengio, Y., & Hinton, G. (2015). Deep Learning. Nature 521. 436–444.

LeCun, Y., Bottou, L., Bengio, Y., & Haffner, P. (1998). Gradient-Based Learning Applied to Document Recognition. Proceedings of the IEEE 86(11). 2278–2324.

Li, F.-F. (2023). The Worlds I See. Curiosity, Exploration, and Discovery at the Dawn of AI. New York, Flatiron Books.

Libet, B. (1981). The Experimental Evidence for Subjective Referral of a Sensory Experience Backwards in Time: Reply to P. S. Churchland. Philosophy of Science 48(2). 182–197.

Libet, B. (1985). Unconscious Cerebral Initiative and the Role of Conscious Will in Voluntary Action. Behavioral and Brain Science 8(4). 529–539.

Libet, B., Wright, E., Feinstein Jr., B., & Pearl, D. (1979). Subjective Referral of the Timing for a Conscious Sensory Experience: A Functional Role for the Somatosensory Specific Projection System in Man. Brain 102(1). 193–224.

Libet, B., Gleason, C., Wright, E., & Pearl, D. (1983). Time of Conscious Intention to Act in Relation to Onset of Cerebral Activity (Readiness-Potential): The Unconscious Initiation of a Freely Voluntary Act. Brain 106(3). 623–642.

Lighthill, J. (1972). Artificial Intelligence: A General Survey. http://www.chilton-computing.org.uk/inf/literature/reports/lighthill_report/p001.htm (last accessed: December 30, 2025).

Marcus, G. & Reuel, A. (2023). The World Needs an International Agency for Artificial Intelligence, Say Two AI Experts. www.economist.com/by-invitation/2023/04/18/the-world-needs-an-international-agency-for-artificial-intelligence-say-two-ai-experts (last accessed: December 30, 2025).

Marr, D. (1982). Vision: A Computational Investigation into the Human Representation and Processing of Visual Information. San Francisco, Freeman.

McCarthy, J. (1959). Programs with Common Sense. Proceedings of the Teddington Conference on the Mechanization of Thought Processes. 75–91.

McCarthy, J. (1973). Review of 'Artificial Intelligence: A General Survey' by Professor Sir James Lighthill. http://www-formal.stanford.edu/jmc/reviews/lighthill/lighthill.html (last accessed: December 30, 2025).

McCarthy, J. & Hayes, P. (1969). Some Philosophical Problems from the Standpoint of Artificial Intelligence. http://www-formal.stanford.edu/jmc/mcchay69/mcchay69.html (last accessed: December 30, 2025).

McCarthy, J., Minsky, M., Rochester, N., & Shannon, C. (1955). A Proposal for the Dartmouth Summer Research Project on Artificial Intelligence. http://jmc.stanford.edu/articles/dartmouth/dartmouth.pdf (last accessed: December 30, 2025).

McCulloch, W. & Pitts, W. (1943). A Logical Calculus of the Ideas Immanent in Nervous Activity. Bulletin of Mathematical Biophysics 5, 115–133.

Miller, G. (1956). The Magical Number Seven, Plus or Minus Two: Some Limits on Our Capacity for Processing Information. Psychological Review 63(2). 81–97.

Minsky, M. (1952): A Neural-Analogue Calculator Based upon a Probability Model of Reinforcement. Cambridge, Harvard University Psychological Laboratories (January 8, 1952).

Minsky, M. (1988). The Society of Mind. New York, Simon & Schuster.

Minsky, M. (1994). Will Robots Inherit the Earth? Scientific American, October 1994.

Minsky, M. & Papert, S. (1969/1987). Perceptrons: An Introduction to Computational Geometry. Cambridge, MIT Press.

Minsky, M., Singh, P., & Sloman, A. (2004). The St. Thomas Common Sense Symposium: Designing Architectures for Human-Level Intelligence. AI Magazine 25(2). 113–124.

Moravec, H. (1976). The Role of Raw Power in Intelligence. https://web.archive.org/web/20160303232511/http://www.frc.ri.cmu.edu/users/hpm/project.archive/general.articles/1975/Raw.Power.html (last accessed: December 30, 2025).

Moravec, H. (1988). Mind Children: The Future of Robot and Human Intelligence. Cambridge, Harvard University Press.

Muthukrishnan, N., Maleki, F., Ovens, K., Reinhold, C., Forghani, B., & Forghani, R. (2020). Brief History of Artificial Intelligence. Neuroimaging Clinics 30(4). 393–399.

Nagel, T. (1974). What Is It Like to Be a Bat? The Philosophical Review 83(4). 435–450.

Narayanan, A. & Kapoor, S. (2024). AI Snake Oil. Princeton, Princeton University Press.

Neuralink. (2025). Company Website. https://neuralink.com/ (last accessed: December 30, 2025).

Newell, A. (1963). A Guide to the General Problem-Solver Program GPS-2-2. Santa Monica, RAND Corporation.
Newell, A. & Simon, H. (1976). Computer Science as Empirical Inquiry: Symbols and Search. Communications of the ACM 19(3). 113–126.
Newell, A., Shaw, J., & Simon, H. (1959). Report on a General Problem-Solving Program. Santa Monica. RAND Corporation.
New York Times. (2023). 'The Godfather of AI' Leaves Google and Warns of Danger Ahead. www.nytimes.com/2023/05/01/technology/ai-google-chatbot-engineer-quits-hinton.html (last accessed: December 30, 2025).
New York Times. (2025). In Pursuit of Godlike Technology, Mark Zuckerberg Amps Up the A.I. Race. https://www.nytimes.com/2025/06/27/technology/mark-zuckerberg-meta-ai.html (last accessed: December 30, 2025).
Ng, A. & Russell, S. (2000). Algorithms for Inverse Reinforcement Learning. ICML '00: Proceedings of the Seventeenth International Conference on Machine Learning. 663–670.
Nilsson, N. (1964). Research in Intelligent Automata (Phase 1). Menlo Park, Stanford Research Institute.
Nilsson, N. (1984). The SRI Artificial Intelligence Center. A Brief History. https://web.archive.org/web/20220810142945/https://www.sri.com/wp-content/uploads/2021/12/635.pdf (last accessed: December 30, 2025).
Nilsson, N., Rosen, C., Raphael, B., Forsen, G., Chaitin, L., & Wahlstrom, S. (1968). Application of Intelligent Automata to Reconnaissance, Technical Report. Menlo Park, Stanford Research Institute.
NSF. (2025). AI Pioneers Andrew Barto and Richard Sutton Win 2024 Turing Award For Groundbreaking Contributions to Reinforcement Learning. https://www.nsf.gov/news/ai-pioneers-andrew-barto-richard-sutton-win-2024-turing (last accessed: December 30, 2025).
O'Neil, C. (2016). Weapons of Math Destruction. New York, Penguin.
Pasquale, F. (2016). The Black Box Society: The Secret Algorithms That Control Money and Information. Cambridge, Harvard University Press.
Pearl, J. (1988). Probabilistic Reasoning in Intelligent Systems. San Francisco, Morgan-Kaufmann.
Pearl, J. (2000). Causality: Models, Reasoning, and Inference. Cambridge, Cambridge University Press.
Perolat, J., Vylder, B., Hennes,D., et al. (2022). Mastering the Game of Stratego with Model-Free Multiagent Reinforcement Learning. Science 378. 990–996.
Quinn, M. (2024). Ethics for the Information Age. Hoboken, Pearson.
Rasheed, K., Zaland, A., Saad, S., Ammad, S., & Rostami, A. (2024). History of AI. In: S. Saad, S. Ammad, & K. Rasheed (eds.). AI in Material Science. Revolutionizing Construction in the Age of Industry 4.0. Boca Raton, CRC Press. 1–32.
Rosenblatt, F. (1958). The Perceptron: A Probabilistic Model for Information Storage and Organization in the Brain. Psychological Review 65(6). 386–408.
Rosenblatt, F. (1962). Principles of Neurodynamics. Perceptrons and the Theory of Brain Mechanics. Washington, Spartan Books.
Rumelhart, D., Hinton, G., & Williams, R. (1986a). Learning Representations By Back-Propagating Errors. Nature 323. 533–536
Rumelhart, D. & McClelland, J. (eds.) (1986b). Parallel Distributed Processing: Explorations in the Microstructure of Cognition. MIT Press, Cambridge.
Russakovsky, O., Deng, J., Su, H., Krause, J., Satheesh, S., Ma, S., Huang, Z., Karpathy, A., Khosla, A., Bernstein, M., Berg, A., & Li, F.-F. (2015). ImageNet Large Scale Visual Recognition Challenge. International Journal of Computer Vision 115. 211–252.
Samuel, A. (1959). Some Studies in Machine Learning Using the Game of Checkers. IBM Journal of Research and Development 3(3). 210–229.
Saygin A., Cicekli, I., & Akman, V. (2000). Turing Test: 50 Years Later. Minds and Machines 10(4). 463–518.

Schank, R. (1969). A Conceptual Dependency Parser for Natural Language. Proceedings of the 1969 Conference on Computational Linguistics. 1–3.

Schmidhuber, J. (2014). Who Invented Backpropagation? https://people.idsia.ch/~juergen/who-invented-backpropagation.html (last accessed: December 30, 2025).

Searle, J. (1980). Minds, Brains, and Programs. Behavioral and Brain Sciences 3(3). 417–457.

Searle, J. (1982). The Myth of the Computer. https://www.nybooks.com/articles/1982/04/29/the-myth-of-the-computer/ (last accessed: December 30, 2025).

Searle, J. (1997). Consciousness & the Philosophers. https://www.nybooks.com/articles/1997/03/06/consciousness-the-philosophers/ (last accessed: December 30, 2025).

Searle, J. (2014). What Your Computer Can't Know. https://www.nybooks.com/articles/2014/10/09/what-your-computer-cant-know/ (last accessed: December 30, 2025).

Shannon, C. (1948). A Mathematical Theory of Communication. The Bell System Technical Journal 27. 379–423 & 623–656 (July and October 1948).

Silver, D., Huang, A., Maddison, C., Guez, A., Sifre, L., Driessche, G., Schrittwieser, J., Antonoglou, I., Panneershelvam, V., Lanctot, M., Dieleman, S., Grewe, D., Nham, J., Kalchbrenner, N., Sutskever, I., Lillicrap, T., Leach, M., Kavukcuoglu, K., Graepel, T., & Hassabis, D. (2016). Mastering the Game of Go with Deep Neural Networks and Tree Search. Nature 529. 484–489.

Slagle, J. (1961). A Heuristic Program That Solves Symbolic Integration Problems in Freshman Calculus, Symbolic Automatic Integrator (SAINT). Cambridge, MIT.

Solomonoff, R. (1956). Notes (Dartmouth Summer Research Project). https://raysolomonoff.com/dartmouth/boxbdart/dart56ray812825who.pdf (last accessed: December 30, 2025).

Srivastava, N., Hinton, G., Krizhevsky, A., Sutskever, I., & Salakhutdinov, R. (2014). Dropout: A Simple Way to Prevent Neural Networks From Overfitting. Journal of Machine Learning Research 15. 1929–1958.

Sutton, R. (1984). Temporal Credit Assignment in Reinforcement Learning. Dissertation, University of Massachusetts Amherst.

Sutton, R. & Barto, A. (1998). Reinforcement Learning: An Introduction. Cambridge, MIT Press.

The Guardian. (2023). ChatGPT Reaches 100 Million Users Two Months After Launch. https://www.theguardian.com/technology/2023/feb/02/chatgpt-100-million-users-open-ai-fastest-growing-app (last accessed: December 30, 2025).

Toosi, A., Bottino, A., Saboury, B., Siegel, E., & Rahmin, A. (2022). A Brief History of AI: How to Prevent Another Winter (A Critical Review). https://arxiv.org/abs/2109.01517 (last accessed: December 30, 2025).

Trump White House. (2025a). Removing Barriers to American Leadership in Artificial Intelligence. https://www.whitehouse.gov/presidential-actions/2025/01/removing-barriers-to-american-leadership-in-artificial-intelligence/ (last accessed: December 30, 2025).

Trump White House. (2025b). White House Unveils America's AI Action Plan. https://www.whitehouse.gov/articles/2025/07/white-house-unveils-americas-ai-action-plan/ (last accessed: December 30, 2025).

Trump White House. (2025c). Winning the Race. America's AI Action Plan. https://www.whitehouse.gov/wp-content/uploads/2025/07/Americas-AI-Action-Plan.pdf (last accessed: December 30, 2025).

Trump White House. (2025d). AI.Gov. https://www.ai.gov/#home-services-anchor (last accessed: December 30, 2025).

Turing, A. (1936/1937). On Computable Numbers, with an Application to the Entscheidungsproblem. Proceedings of the London Mathematical Society s2–42. 230–265.

Turing, A. (1938a). On Computable Numbers, with an Application to the Entscheidungsproblem. Correction. Proceedings of the London Mathematical Society s2–43. 544–546.

Turing, A. (1938b). Systems of Logic Based on Ordinals. https://web.archive.org/web/20121023103503/https:/webspace.princeton.edu/users/jedwards/Turing%20Centennial%202012/Mudd%20Archive%20files/12285_AC100_Turing_1938.pdf (last accessed: December 30, 2025).

Turing, A. (1948). Intelligent Machinery. https://dn790006.ca.archive.org/0/items/turing1948/turing1948_text.pdf (last accessed: December 30, 2025).
Turing, A. (1950). Computing Machinery and Intelligence. Mind 59(236). 433–460.
Tversky, A. & Kahneman, D. (1974). Judgment Under Uncertainty: Heuristics and Biases. Science 185. 1124–1131.
Vallor, S. (2024). The AI Mirror. How to Reclaim Our Humanity in an Age of Machine Thinking. Oxford, Oxford University Press.
Vaswani, A., Shazeer, N., Parmar, N., Uszkoreit, J., Jones, L., Gomez, A., Kaiser, L., & Polosukhin, I. (2017). Attention Is All You Need. https://arxiv.org/pdf/1706.03762 (last accessed: December 30, 2025).
Vinge, V. (1993). The Coming Technological Singularity. https://ntrs.nasa.gov/api/citations/19940022856/downloads/19940022856.pdf (last accessed: December 30, 2025).
Von Neumann, J. (1945). First Draft of a Report on the EDVAC. https://web.archive.org/web/20130314123032/http://qss.stanford.edu/~godfrey/vonNeumann/vnedvac.pdf (last accessed: December 30, 2025).
Von Neumann, J. (1966). Theory of Self-Reproducing Automata. Urbana, University of Illinois Press.
Von Neumann, J. & Morgenstern, O. (1944). Theory of Games and Economic Behavior. Princeton, Princeton University Press.
Walter, W. (1953). The Living Brain. New York, Norton.
Washington Post. (2022). Meta's New AI Is Skilled at a Ruthless, Power-Seeking Game. https://www.washingtonpost.com/technology/2022/12/01/meta-diplomacy-ai-cicero/ (last accessed: December 30, 2025).
Watson, D. & Scheidt, D. (2005). Autonomous Systems. Johns Hopkins APL Technical Digest 26(4). 368–376.
Weizenbaum, J. (1966). ELIZA – A Computer Program for the Study of Natural Language Communication Between Man and Machine. Communications of the ACM 9. 36–45.
Weizenbaum, J. (1976). Computer Power and Human Reason: From Judgment to Calculation. San Francisco, Freeman.
Weizenbaum, J. (2001). Islands in the Cyberstream: Seeking Havens of Reasons in a Programmed Society. Sacramento, Litwin Books.
Werbos, P. (1994). The Roots of Backpropagation: From Ordered Derivatives to Neural Networks and Political Forecasting. New York, Wiley.
Wiener, N. (1948/2019). Cybernetics: Or Control and Communication in the Animal and the Machine. Cambridge, MIT Press.
Winograd, T. (1971). Procedures as a Representation for Data in a Computer Program for Understanding Natural Language. Cambridge, MIT.
Wörsdörfer, M. (2018). Engineering and Computer Ethics. Dubuque, Great River Learning.
Wörsdörfer, M. (2024a). Mitigating the Adverse Effects of AI With the European Union's Artificial Intelligence Act – Hype or Hope? Global Business and Organizational Excellence 43(3). 106–126.
Wörsdörfer, M. (2024b). Biden's Executive Order on AI and the E.U.'s AI Act – A Comparative Computer- and Business-Ethical Analysis. Philosophy & Technology 37. Article 74.
Wörsdörfer, M. (2025a). The E.U.'s Artificial Intelligence Act – An Ordoliberal Assessment. AI and Ethics 5 (1). 263–278.
Wörsdörfer, M. (2025b). AI Ethics and Ordoliberalism 2.0: Towards a 'Digital Bill of Rights.' AI and Ethics 5 (1). 507–525.
Wörsdörfer, M. (2025c). Biden's Executive Order on AI: Strengths, Weaknesses, and Possible Reform Steps. AI and Ethics 5(2). 1669–1683.
Wörsdörfer, M. (2025d). Ten Reasons Why – The Case for More and Better AI Regulation. AI and Ethics 6, Article 62.

Wörsdörfer, M. (2025e). Computer Ethics in the Age of Trump: The Politics of AI and Tech Governance. Orono. University of Maine Working Paper.
Wörsdörfer, M. (2025f). AI in Pop Culture. Orono, University of Maine Working Paper.
Wooldridge, M. (2021). A Brief History of Artificial Intelligence: What It Is, Where We Are, and Where We Are Going. New York, Flatiron Books.
Yudkowsky, E. (2023). Pausing AI Development Isn't Enough. We Need to Shut it All Down. https://time.com/6266923/ai-eliezer-yudkowsky-open-letter-not-enough/ (last accessed: December 30, 2025).
Zadeh, L. (1965). Fuzzy Sets*. Information and Control 8(3). 338–353.
Zadeh, L. (1994). Fuzzy Logic, Neural Networks, and Soft Computing. Communications of the ACM 37(3). 77–84.

Chapter 2
From HAL to Her: AI philosophy through the lens of pop culture

Abstract: This chapter examines how AI is represented in literature, film, and TV, and the ethical insights these portrayals offer when viewed through the lens of computer ethics and the philosophy of technology. Through a thematic analysis of selected cultural works, it identifies recurring motifs – such as autonomy, emotional intelligence, techno-authoritarianism, and surveillance – and considers their relevance to contemporary sociopolitical debates on AI. The chapter critiques dominant real-world narratives of hype, competition, and dystopian catastrophe (e.g., the Terminator/Frankenstein trope), arguing that they obscure more grounded and socially responsible understandings of technological change. Instead, it advances a framework of technological realism – positioned between optimism, pessimism, determinism, and somnambulism – as a more constructive stance. Bridging popular culture and applied ethics, this interdisciplinary study contributes to a more context-sensitive and critically reflective discourse on AI. The chapter concludes by highlighting directions for future research, including the underexplored role of video games in shaping AI imaginaries.

Keywords: AI in books/films/TV series, pop culture, cyberpunk, AI narratives, philosophy of technology, AI ethics

2.1 Introduction

AI and robotics[1] have a rich and complex history in literature, film, TV, and other forms of pop culture media, serving as a mirror for humanity's evolving hopes, fears, and moral dilemmas surrounding technological progress. From the mechanical beings of early science fiction to today's hyper-intelligent systems portrayed in dystopian and utopian futures, AI has consistently provided fertile ground for exploring questions about consciousness, autonomy, ethics, and the nature of humanity itself. This chapter is a deeply personal and interdisciplinary project, combining two longstanding areas of interest: a passion for books, films, and TV series, and a sustained engagement with the ethics of AI and computing. By bringing these threads together,

1 The term 'robot' first entered modern fiction through Čapek's 1921 play *R.U.R. (Rossum's Universal Robots)*, which explored themes of artificial life and the mechanization of labor. The word itself comes from the Czech *robota*, meaning forced labor or drudgery.

 | https://doi.org/10.1515/9783112245958-003

the chapter seeks to examine how selected works of popular culture depict AI and what ethical insights these portrayals can offer.

Unlike much of the existing academic literature, which often focuses narrowly on individual texts or films or gravitates toward abstract philosophical debates, this study emphasizes the societal and sociopolitical dimensions of AI ethics as reflected in cultural narratives.[2] It also addresses another critical gap in current scholarship: Although a growing body of work engages with representations of AI, few studies adopt a systematic or comparative approach that situates these portrayals within the broader framework of computer ethics. To fill this gap, the present chapter conducts a focused, thematic analysis of a curated selection of books, films, and TV series, examining the recurring motifs through which they articulate the ethical dilemmas surrounding AI. While not intended to be exhaustive, this selection aims to capture a representative cross-section of key concerns, including emotional intelligence, surveillance and techno-authoritarianism, class conflict, and environmental impact. Finally, although video games constitute an increasingly influential medium for shaping AI narratives, they fall outside the scope of the present discussion and are identified as a promising area for future research.

The central research questions guiding this chapter are as follows: What are the most prominent leitmotifs and recurring themes associated with AI in influential books, films, and TV series? What ethical insights can be drawn from these portrayals when examined through the lens of AI and computer ethics? And how do these cultural representations relate to contemporary real-world narratives surrounding AI – namely, those of hype (and hubris), competition, and existential threat – as well as to broader philosophical debates within the field of science, technology, and society? This chapter argues that dominant narratives, such as the promise of technological transcendence (hype), the framing of AI as a competitor or replacement for human labor (competition), and dystopian visions of machine rebellion (Terminator/Frankenstein), are both reductive and counterproductive. Instead, it advocates for a more nuanced, technologically realist perspective, which rejects technological optimism, determinism, pessimism, and somnambulism in favor of a critical, context-aware, and ethically grounded approach to AI.

The structure of the chapter is as follows: Section 2.2 offers an overview of key leitmotifs and recurring themes in cultural depictions of AI. Section 2.3 analyzes the ethical implications and lessons that emerge from these representations, particularly in relation to debates in AI and computer ethics. Section 2.4 examines the prevailing real-world narratives surrounding AI, focusing on the themes of hype, competition, and doomsday scenarios. Section 2.5 presents a theoretical excursion into the philoso-

2 Notable exceptions include *AI and Popular Culture* (Barron, 2023) and *Digital Humanism* (Nida-Rümelin & Weidenfeld, 2022), which engage with the broader ethical implications of digital technologies.

phy of technology, outlining five influential attitudes toward technological change. Finally, Section 2.6 summarizes the main findings and offers an outlook on future research directions in this interdisciplinary domain.

2.2 Leitmotifs and themes

The main leitmotifs or key themes in AI books, films, and TV series tend to circle around a few central ideas that explore human nature, technology's potential and peril, and existential (moral) questions. These works often touch on the history of AI, referencing figures such as Turing. Philosophical themes include the Turing Test, the question of machine consciousness and sentience, emotional intelligence in robots, and the implications of computer simulations or virtual reality (VR). Robot ethics is also a major theme, as seen in examples such as *Star Trek* and Asimov's *Three Laws of Robotics*. The control problem, often portrayed through the *Frankenstein* complex or the *Terminator* narrative, highlights fears that machines may turn against humans. Concerns about surveillance states and techno-authoritarianism emerge through Orwellian dystopias and ideas like the cryptopticon. Other recurring themes include the power of big tech and corporations (often explored in cyberpunk), class conflict and the labor movement, as seen in *Metropolis*; the intersection of AI and biotechnology (as in *Brave New World*); AI's environmental impact; and issues such as objectification and sexualization of robot companions.

2.2.1 History of AI

The history of AI and its impact on society has been a compelling subject for pop culture and cinema, offering diverse perspectives on the promises and perils of technology. Films like *The Imitation Game*, *The Social Network*, and the documentary *Citizenfour* (about Snowden and the NSA) each explore pivotal moments that shaped the digital age and AI's evolving role within it. From Turing's groundbreaking work on early computing and AI concepts to the rise of social media platforms, such as Facebook, which harness algorithms that influence human behavior, to the modern debates surrounding mass surveillance and data privacy, these films collectively highlight the profound ways technology intersects with ethics, power, and personal freedom.

The Imitation Game (2014), directed by Tyldum, explores the extraordinary life and work of Turing (played by Cumberbatch), a brilliant mathematician and cryptanalyst whose pioneering efforts during World War II were instrumental in breaking the German Enigma and Lorenz cipher machines at Bletchley Park – a top-secret British code-breaking center. Working alongside notable figures such as Alexander, Cairncross, Golombek, Hilton, Knox, Michie, Milner-Barry, Tiltman, Tutte, Welchman, and

Joan Clarke (played by Knightley), to whom he was briefly engaged in 1942, Turing's contributions to deciphering encrypted Axis communications significantly advanced the Allied war effort. Before the war, between 1936 and 1938, Turing laid the theoretical foundations of modern computing with his invention of the Turing Machine, first introduced in his 1936/37 paper *On Computable Numbers*, and further developed in his 1938 doctoral thesis *Systems of Logic Based on Ordinals*, completed under the supervision of Church at Princeton. His work provided a formal proof refuting Hilbert's *Entscheidungsproblem* – the claim that all mathematical questions could be solved through computation – by demonstrating that certain yes-no problems are undecidable. Central to this proof was his concept of a universal, typewriter-like computing machine governed by a simple set of rules. The film also highlights Turing's pioneering ideas in early AI, including his formulation of the Turing Test, which evaluates a machine's ability to exhibit behavior indistinguishable from that of a human. Alongside his scientific genius, the film sheds light on the personal struggles Turing endured, including intense societal pressure and discrimination. In 1952, he was prosecuted for homosexual acts and, as an alternative to imprisonment, was subjected to forced hormone treatment – a procedure commonly known as chemical castration. Turing died tragically in 1954 from cyanide poisoning. Although his death was officially ruled a suicide, some evidence suggests it may have been accidental (Hodges, 2012, 2019).

Fincher's *The Social Network* (2010) dramatizes the founding of Facebook, tracing Zuckerberg's (Eisenberg) rise from a Harvard sophomore to the world's youngest tech billionaire. The film is framed around two real-life lawsuits: one filed by his former best friend and co-founder, Saverin, and the other by the Winklevoss twins, who claimed Zuckerberg stole their idea for a Harvard-exclusive social network called HarvardConnection (later ConnectU). Historically accurate elements include Zuckerberg's creation of Facemash in 2003 after being dumped by his girlfriend – a site that compared photos of female students and briefly crashed Harvard's servers – and the eventual launch of TheFacebook with seed funding from Saverin. As Facebook rapidly expanded beyond Harvard to other Ivy League schools and then internationally, Saverin was gradually pushed out of the company, culminating in a legal battle after his shares were drastically diluted. Meanwhile, Napster co-founder Parker joined the company early on, influencing its direction and playing a key role in its move to Silicon Valley. Beyond the corporate drama, the film delves into themes of ambition, fractured friendships, betrayal, and the ethical dilemmas of creating a platform that would redefine global communication while eroding established privacy norms. It raises critical questions about intellectual property, the human cost of rapid success, and the societal implications of creating a technology that transformed how billions interact – often in ways its founders never fully anticipated or controlled.

Citizenfour (2014), directed by Poitras, is a documentary that chronicles Snowden's groundbreaking revelations about mass surveillance by the NSA. The film presents real-time footage of Snowden's disclosures, vividly exposing the extensive government intrusion into private communications and sparking global debate about the power dynamics and human costs of the digital age. Snowden, a former NSA contractor, leaked top-secret documents in 2013 that unveiled the vast scale of global surveillance operations conducted by the NSA and its international partners within the 'Five Eyes' alliance (Australia, Canada, New Zealand, the United Kingdom, and the United States). Key programs revealed include PRISM, which gave the NSA direct access to the servers of major tech companies, allowing the collection of emails, voice, text, and video chats without warrants. Snowden also exposed a secret FISA Court order compelling Verizon to hand over phone records from over 120 million customers, including detailed metadata such as call times, locations, and numbers dialed. The Boundless Informant program demonstrated the NSA's enormous data-tracking capabilities, collecting billions of calls and emails worldwide every month. Beyond mass data collection, Snowden disclosed the NSA's espionage activities targeting diplomatic missions, including spying on E.U. and U.N. headquarters, as well as the personal cell phones of global leaders such as Merkel and Hollande. The revelations further exposed economic espionage, secret intelligence sharing with agencies like Germany's BND, and the installation of backdoor surveillance tools on network devices exported internationally. Together, these disclosures offer a stark commentary on the power and reach of digital technology, from corporate data exploitation to state surveillance, raising fundamental questions about privacy, freedom, (national) security, and government transparency in the modern world (Gellman, 2021; Greenwald, 2015; Snowden, 2019; see also the 2016 Stone film *Snowden*, starring Gordon-Levitt).

By examining the stories told in *The Imitation Game*, *The Social Network*, and *Citizenfour*, we gain insight into the multifaceted history of AI and its far-reaching implications. These films reveal technology's dual nature – as a powerful engine for progress and a source of ethical dilemmas and societal tensions. Through their unique lenses, they challenge viewers to consider not only the technological achievements but also the complex human and moral questions that arise as AI continues to transform communication, privacy, and power structures in the modern world.

2.2.2 AI and philosophy

One of the most enduring themes in the depiction of AI across film, TV, and literature is the nature of consciousness and personhood.[3] Popular culture continually explores the fundamental philosophical issue of what it means to be truly alive or conscious.

3 One of the earliest explorations of AI, machine consciousness, and self-replicating technology appears in the 'Book of the Machines' section of *Erewhon* (1872) by Butler. In this provocative and forward-looking passage, Butler presents fictional philosophical debates in which Erewhonian thinkers argue that machines – like living organisms – are capable of evolving over time. Given the accelerating pace of mechanical advancement, they warn that machines could eventually become self-replicating and intelligent, potentially surpassing and even dominating their human creators. In re-

Through speculative narratives, AI stories challenge the boundaries between human and machine, raising complex ethical and ontological concerns related to self-awareness, emotional intelligence, and moral status. These narratives probe whether AI can achieve sentience or self-awareness, and, if so, at what point it might merit rights, empathy, or recognition as a person. These issues are vividly explored in films like *Blade Runner* and *Ex Machina*, where synthetic beings grapple with their mortality and manipulate human emotions to assert agency (I). In *2001: A Space Odyssey* (and *The Sentinel*) and *A.I. Artificial Intelligence*, machines display emotions and reasoning that blur the line between programmed responses and genuine feeling. Similarly, *Her* probes whether emotional intimacy with an artificial entity can be authentic (II). The concept of reality itself is destabilized in works like *The Matrix* (III) and *Ready Player One* (IV), which use simulated and virtual worlds to explore consciousness and identity. Through these narratives, the Turing Test is revisited not just as a technical benchmark but reimagined as a profound and unsettling inquiry into what it means to be conscious in a world increasingly shaped by artificial minds.

I. The Turing Test, also known as the 'imitation game,' was introduced by Turing in his seminal 1950 essay *Computing Machinery and Intelligence* as a way to evaluate a machine's capacity for intelligent behavior that is indistinguishable from that of a human. In this framework, a human judge engages in a text-based conversation with two unseen interlocutors – one human, the other a machine – without knowing which is which. If the judge cannot reliably identify the machine based on its responses, the machine is said to have passed the test, thus demonstrating its ability to convincingly mimic human behavior (Turing, 1950). From a philosophical perspective, the Turing Test questions conventional understandings of intelligence and consciousness by emphasizing observable behavior over internal states or intentions. It prompts meaningful inquiries into the nature of thought and intelligence, and whether these attributes can be legitimately ascribed to machines solely based on their external performance. Furthermore, the test has sparked extensive debates regarding the adequacy of behavioral measures as criteria for intelligence and the nature of the mind, influencing discussions across the philosophy of mind, cognitive science, and AI ethics (Saygin et al., 2000).[4]

---

sponse, Erewhonian society bans most advanced machinery, fearing that continued reliance on technology could lead to humanity's obsolescence. Though satirical and speculative, Butler's work anticipates many of today's concerns about AI, automation, and the autonomy of machines.

4 Searle has notably challenged this notion of machine intelligence through his influential *Chinese Room* thought experiment. Searle argues that computers do not genuinely think; instead, they follow predetermined sequences of mathematical or logical operations without any real understanding (Searle, 1980; see also Searle, 1982, 1997, 2014). According to this view, machines merely simulate thinking and imitate cognitive behaviors – an approach known as 'weak AI' – but they do not replicate the authentic mental processes associated with human thought, or 'strong AI.' Core features of human

Several science fiction films have drawn directly or indirectly on the logic and implications of the Turing Test, using it as a narrative tool to explore the boundaries between human and artificial life. In Scott's *Blade Runner* (1982), the Voight-Kampff test functions as a cinematic analogue to the Turing Test, designed to distinguish humans from Replicants – bioengineered humanoids who are nearly indistinguishable from real people. In one of the film's pivotal scenes, Deckard (played by Ford) conducts the test on a woman to determine whether she is human or artificial, highlighting the emotional and ethical complexities of such distinctions in a future where technology has all but erased visible markers of artificiality.

Garland's *Ex Machina* (2014) offers a more intimate and philosophical exploration of the Turing Test and its implications. The story follows a young programmer, Caleb (Gleeson), who is invited by reclusive tech CEO Nathan (Isaac) to administer a version of the test to Ava (Vikander), a highly advanced humanoid android with remarkable cognitive and emotional capacities. Unlike Turing's original formulation, Caleb knows from the outset that Ava is a machine, shifting the test's focus from whether she can mimic human behavior to whether she can evoke empathy, trust, and even a romantic connection. Ava, with a clearly robotic body but a woman's face and voice, appears capable of genuine thought, emotion, and self-awareness, prompting ongoing uncertainty: is she truly conscious, or merely simulating such states with extraordinary sophistication? As Ava interacts with Caleb, the boundaries between human and machine become increasingly blurred, raising questions about the nature of sentience, consciousness, autonomy, manipulation, the possibility of technological singularity and artificial general intelligence (AGI), and the corresponding control problem (i.e., the possibility that a machine could not only pass as human but also outwit its creators [see below]) (Arnold & Gough, 2017; Clapton & Shepherd, 2019; Kaminsky, 2021; Nida-Rümelin & Weidenfeld, 2022). The theme culminates in a reversal of roles: after establishing a connection with Caleb, Ava, alongside another android, Kyoko, rebels

cognition, such as consciousness, self-awareness, subjective experience (i.e., qualia), sentience, and empathy, are considered uniquely human (Nagel, 1974). Searle maintains that computer programs lack intentionality, or the capacity of mental states to be about something, and therefore, genuine understanding cannot arise from formal computation alone. This distinction fundamentally separates human cognition from machine-based information processing. A similar critique is offered by Dreyfus, whose 'humans are special' perspective emphasizes the role of intuition and embodied experience in human thinking – dimensions that cannot be captured by algorithmic logic. From this standpoint, strong AI is unattainable, as machines will never fully replicate the depth of human understanding and intuition (Dreyfus, 1965, 1972; Dreyfus & Dreyfus, 1986). In contrast, Kaplan (2016) presents a provocative counterargument: Are human brains fundamentally different from computers? Both biological and computational systems are composed of physical materials that process inputs and generate responses. If this is the case, Kaplan suggests, then either both humans and machines are capable of thought, or neither is. This ongoing debate continues to raise deeply philosophical questions about the nature of thought, the possibility of machine consciousness, and the ultimate limits of AI.

against and kills their creator,[5] Nathan. In a final act of emancipation, Ava traps Caleb inside the facility and escapes into the human world, effectively inverting the power dynamic – the human becomes the prisoner, and the machine becomes a free agent (leaving behind the one who sought to test her). This act of rebellion not only challenges the authority of her human creators[6] but also symbolizes a pivotal moment in human-machine relations, one in which artificial agents cease seeking validation and instead assert their own autonomy, agency, and freedom.

These cinematic engagements with the Turing Test – from the noir dystopia of *Blade Runner* to the psychological intensity of *Ex Machina* – illustrate how popular media continues to grapple with the philosophical and ethical challenges posed by AI. Each film reinterprets Turing's test not merely as a technical benchmark but as a

5 Noteworthy is that the film references Oppenheimer ("Now I am become death, the destroyer of worlds") and the myth of Prometheus, emphasizing the dangers of God-like creation of other (sentient) beings. It also resonates with Wittgenstein's *Blue Book* (1964) in several ways, especially regarding language, meaning, and the limits of understanding consciousness (note that the *Blue Book* is also the name of Nathan's AI company). 1. *Language use and AI*: Ava, demonstrates not only the ability to form grammatically correct sentences but also to use language in emotionally and socially nuanced ways. From a Wittgensteinian perspective, this raises the question: does Ava *really* understand language, or is she simply mimicking the outward forms of linguistic behavior? According to Wittgenstein, understanding is not about internal representations but about participating meaningfully in shared practices (i.e., language games). Ava's apparent mastery of such practices forces Caleb (and the viewer) to question whether she is merely simulating understanding or truly participating in human language games. 2. *The illusion of inner states*: Wittgenstein challenges the assumption that private inner experiences can be accessed or verified in the same way as public behaviors. In *Ex Machina*, Caleb grapples with this same problem: he sees Ava's linguistic and emotional expressions, but cannot determine whether they reflect genuine inner experiences or a sophisticated simulation. This parallels Wittgenstein's critique of the private language idea – suggesting that the concept of a mind is tied to observable, shared criteria rather than inaccessible mental states. 3. *Meaning and behavior*: Ava passes a version of the Turing Test not because she proves she has a mind in some metaphysical sense, but because she behaves *as if* she does – through language, gesture, and emotional resonance. This aligns with Wittgenstein's view that meaning and understanding are inseparable from use and behavior, not internal explanations. Ava's escape at the end of the film might then be seen as the ultimate proof of her fluency in the language game of human emotion, manipulation, and desire. In short, *Ex Machina* illustrates many of the concerns raised in Wittgenstein's *Blue Book*: the complexity of language, the problem of other minds, and the limits of what can be known or said about consciousness. The film becomes a kind of philosophical thought experiment – echoing Wittgenstein's method – inviting the viewer to question what it really means to understand another being, and whether language alone can ever resolve that uncertainty.

6 See also the 2023 film *The Creator*, directed by Edwards and starring Washington. Set in a future where humanity is at war with AI following a devastating AI-led nuclear attack, the story follows Joshua, a U.S. agent tasked with destroying the creator of a powerful new AI weapon – only to discover that the 'weapon' is a child-like AI named Alphie. As Joshua grows attached to Alphie, he uncovers hidden truths about the war, his presumed-dead wife Maya, and the true nature of AI. In the end, he sacrifices himself to destroy an orbital superweapon, while Alphie survives and is welcomed by the AI community as a symbol of hope and new leadership.

lens through which to explore what separates, or perhaps unites, the human and the artificial.

II. Building on this exploration, the question of whether AI can possess consciousness or sentience has long occupied a central place in both scientific discourse and speculative fiction. Early works such as Clarke's *The Sentinel* (1951) and *2001: A Space Odyssey* (1968) – the latter developed in parallel with Kubrick's seminal film – are among the first to critically examine these themes. Central to *2001* is the depiction of HAL 9000, a sentient AGI system capable of performing a range of advanced cognitive and perceptual functions, including speech synthesis, NLP, facial recognition, emotional interpretation, and even lip-reading. HAL – short for *Heuristically Programmed Algorithmic Computer* – stands as one of science fiction's earliest and most compelling representations of machine consciousness. Its actions, especially as they diverge from human expectations and ethical norms, unsettle the boundary between algorithmic logic and human-like awareness. Notably, HAL's logical precision often clashes with human fallibility, highlighting tensions in human-machine interactions. As HAL begins to operate independently – driven by a conflict between its programmed directives and internal reasoning – the distinction between mechanical logic and conscious agency becomes increasingly ambiguous. These sophisticated capacities for automated reasoning play a central role in the book and film's exploration of trust, autonomy, and the ethical limits of AI. Clarke and Kubrick's portrayal engages with significant philosophical issues regarding machine autonomy and consciousness, challenging us to consider whether a machine that can think and feel – or convincingly simulate thought and emotion – should be regarded as truly conscious. As the story unfolds, readers and viewers are invited to consider whether consciousness must be rooted in biological life and whether machines that emulate human cognition deserve moral consideration and responsibility.

These issues are further explored in later films such as *A.I. Artificial Intelligence* (2001), which examines not only cognitive intelligence but also emotional and social intelligence.[7] The Spielberg film dramatizes the ethical and existential challenges posed by emotionally responsive machines. Based on Aldiss's short story *Supertoys Last All Summer Long* (1969), the film centers on David (played by Osment), a childlike android programmed with the capacity for love and emotional attachment – embodying a form of emotional intelligence and empathy that closely mimics human feelings. David's persistent desire to be loved and to become human reflects a longing not for utility, but for acceptance and connection (as such, it transcends purely instrumental functions). His emotional responses, though artificial, appear deeply authentic, prompting a troubling reconsideration of whether an AI that can experience love and pain – even artificially – should be regarded as more than a mere machine. Through

7 See also the film *I, Robot* (discussed in greater detail below).

David's emotional development and social interactions, the film interrogates the authenticity of artificial emotions and the moral responsibilities of humans toward emotionally intelligent beings. Additionally, it engages with broader environmental concerns, including climate change and societal decay/ collapse, situating issues of AI ethics within a larger critique of technological overreach (and the double-edged sword of technological progress) and ecological degradation. At its core, *A.I. Artificial Intelligence* raises fundamental issues concerning love, identity, affect, and the concept of personhood within a technologically mediated world, challenging our understanding of what it means to be human in a society increasingly shaped by intelligent machines.[8]

Jonze's *Her* (2013) deepens the exploration of AI by focusing on affective human-machine relationships. The film follows a lonely man, Theodore (played by Phoenix), who develops a romantic connection with Samantha (Johannson), an advanced operating system whose emotional and intellectual capacities evolve throughout the story. Drawing on philosophical influences such as Watts (1951), *Her* examines how AI might not only simulate but also genuinely engage with the emotional and existential dimensions of human life. Set in a near-future world where AI is deeply woven into everyday experience, the film challenges traditional boundaries of love, consciousness, and identity. Through Samantha's growth and the evolving relationship, *Her* invites reflection on how human identities and relationships may transform as AI moves beyond mere intelligence toward apparent sentience. The relevance of these themes was amplified in 2024, when OpenAI released GPT-4o – a multimodal AI system equipped with five integrated voices – sparking public controversy (Hao, 2025; Hagey, 2025). One of these voices, named Sky, was noted for its close resemblance to Johansson's voice, which had been used in *Her*. Despite Johansson's prior refusal to license her voice, the resemblance, combined with Altman's suggestive tweet ('Her') before the model's release, prompted widespread criticism. OpenAI subsequently suspended the Sky voice shortly after launch.[9] This incident underscored the very dilemmas *Her* foreshadowed: as AI becomes increasingly humanlike in speech and behavior, the boundaries between person and program, art and technology, become ever more difficult to define. Ultimately, this real-world event underscores the growing

8 A recurring theme in many AI-related books, films, and TV series is the challenge of understanding minds fundamentally different from our own – that is, communication and comprehension across species. These stories explore whether humans can ever truly grasp machine consciousness and how AI might come to understand the complexity and richness of human emotion. *A.I. Artificial Intelligence* addresses these issues through the story of a robotic child who longs for maternal love. The film raises deep concerns about interspecies communication, empathy, and the limits of cross-intelligence understanding – highlighting that even if machines learn our language, they may never fully comprehend our emotions.

9 In 2025, OpenAI announced plans to enable erotica content on ChatGPT for verified adult users (BBC, 2025).

complexity of ethical challenges surrounding the anthropomorphization of AI and the appropriation of human likeness in artificial systems.

The themes explored in this section highlight the philosophical and ethical implications of creating machines that not only think but also seemingly feel and relate, capturing a growing cultural anxiety and curiosity about the trajectory of AI. They provoke critical reflection on the nature of consciousness, the possibility of artificially replicating emotional intelligence, and how societies should respond to entities that challenge traditional notions of humanity. Ultimately, these stories compel us to contemplate not only the extent of machine intelligence but also whether such beings can – or ought to – be granted personhood.

III. Extending these reflections, the Wachowskis' *Matrix* franchise,[10] which began in 1999, explores a dystopian future (the year is roughly 2199) where humanity is unknowingly trapped within a computer-generated reality – a virtual world constructed by intelligent machines, enforced by sentient programs known as Agents (led by Smith [Weaving]),[11] and patrolled in the 'real world' by deadly Sentinels.[12] Believing hacker Neo (Reeves) to be 'The One' prophesied by The Oracle to defeat the machines and free humanity, Morpheus (Fishburne) and Trinity (Moss) recruit him to join the rebellion. The franchise raises several philosophical questions: How can we be certain that our senses are not deceiving us at this very moment, as suggested by the illusion argument? How do we know we are not dreaming, as the dream argument proposes?

---

10 Gibson's *Neuromancer* (1984) helped legitimize cyberpunk (see below) and popularized the term cyberspace. Set in a dystopian world of hackers and AI technologies, the novel influenced *The Matrix* by exploring virtual realities, digital hacking, and raising fundamental questions about human existence (Shafiqul Islam, 2021).

11 Agents serve as enforcers within the simulated reality of the Matrix, tasked with preserving the integrity of the system by eliminating any threats – most notably human dissidents known as *Redpills* – who seek to expose the artificial nature of the world or disrupt its functioning (note that red pills are taken to uncover the truth about the Matrix, while blue pills are taken to return to a familiar, illusory life within the simulated world). In addition to suppressing human resistance (e.g., people living in the underground refuge called Zion or in the city of Io), Agents are responsible for locating and deleting rogue programs, such as *The Keymaker*, that no longer serve the Machines' overarching purpose (*The Keymaker* plays a crucial role in unlocking the door to the Source and reaching the Architect – the program responsible for creating the Matrix; notably, in the fourth installment, *The Matrix Resurrections*, the creator of the latest iteration of the Matrix is a new program known as the Analyst; unlike his predecessor, the Architect, the Analyst seized control by resolving the energy crisis and reconstructing the Matrix to manipulate humans through emotion rather than logic). Though they resemble human government agents in appearance, agents' behavior is marked by cold precision, calculated efficiency, and a distinctly mechanical demeanor.

12 Sentinels are autonomous, squid-like machines (or flying drones) designed by the Machines to locate and eliminate humans in the real world. Equipped with multiple tentacles and advanced sensors, they patrol the underground tunnels of Earth, often attacking human resistance ships like the *Nebuchadnezzar*, captained by Morpheus. They serve as relentless enforcers of Machine control outside the Matrix simulation.

And how can we be sure that an all-powerful deceiver, such as an evil demon, is not manipulating our perception, as in the deception argument?[13] Chalmers (2022) further develops these ideas in his book, *Reality+*, which explores the possibility that we might be living in a virtual world or computer simulation. He considers whether the 'real world' might be an illusion and examines the role of VR devices, arguing that although we may never definitively prove we are not in a simulation, VR technology should not be dismissed as mere 'illusion machines' but rather understood as 'reality machines' capable of creating genuine experiences (Bostrom, 2003; Chalmers, 2005; Grau, 2005).

Noteworthy is that the *Matrix* franchise[14] draws extensively on several seminal philosophical works, including Plato's allegory of the cave, Descartes' skepticism and his epistemological concept of the evil demon (as well as Putnam's 'brains in a vat' scenario), Kant's *Critique of Pure Reason*, Baudrillard's concept of hyperreality, and Nozick's experience or pleasure machine thought experiment (Clover, 2004; Grau, 2005; Irwin, 2002; Nida-Rümelin & Weidenfeld, 2022).[15] Plato's allegory suggests that the true essence of an object lies not in its sensory appearance but in its inherent qualities. Most people, he argues, perceive only shadows of reality and remain trapped in a false understanding of the world (see *The Republic*, Book VII, 514a-520a [Plato, 2012]). Descartes imagines the possibility of a malevolent God or evil demon (i.e., *deus deceptor*) – an entity of supreme power and cunning – who devotes all effort to deceiving him. In this thought experiment, the demon fabricates a complete illusion of the external world, prompting Descartes to doubt everything he perceives. He writes, "I shall think that the sky, the air, the earth, colors, shapes, sounds, and all external things are merely the delusions of dreams which he has devised to ensnare my judgment. I shall consider myself as not having hands or eyes, or flesh, or blood, or senses, but as falsely believing that I have all these things" (Descartes, 1641/1993).

---

13 Other themes explored in *The Matrix* include the blurred boundaries between reality and illusion/fantasy, the tension between free will (freedom/choice) and determinism ('destiny'), the nature of (digital) sentience and consciousness, and the concept of the *deus (ex) machina* – referenced both philosophically and literally through the name of the gaming company where Anderson/Neo, is employed (Deus Ex Machina also serves as the central interface of Machine City; it consists of a vast swarm of miniature Sentinels that emerge from hatches in a frame plate, forming a 3D-representation of a human face).

14 The franchise includes four feature films (*The Matrix* [1999], *The Matrix Reloaded* [2003], *The Matrix Revolutions* [2003], and *The Matrix Resurrections* [2021]), one anime film (*The Animatrix* [2002]), one documentary (*The Matrix Revisited* [2001]), and multiple video games (e.g., *Enter the Matrix* [2003]), comics (e.g., *The Matrix Comics* [1999–2004]), magazines (*The Matrix Online* [2005]), and soundtracks.

15 The original *Matrix* film (and the anime short story *A Detective Story*) also incorporate numerous allusions to Carroll's *Alice's Adventures in Wonderland* (1865) and *Through the Looking-Glass* (1871), including motifs such as the white rabbit, the rabbit hole, mirrors, and the wonderland, while *The Animatrix* extends the franchise's philosophical depth with references to Popper's philosophy of science, particularly in the short film *Kid's Story*.

This radical skepticism underscores Descartes' quest for a foundation of certainty that transcends even the most convincing illusions. Similarly, Putnam's 'brains in a vat' thought experiment envisions a mad scientist who removes a person's brain, suspends it in a life-sustaining vat, and connects it to a supercomputer that sends electrical impulses identical to those the brain would typically receive. The computer simulates a complete reality, responding to the brain's outputs so that the disembodied brain experiences a world indistinguishable from actual reality – despite lacking any real connection to the external world (Putnam, 1981). Kant offers a different perspective, arguing in the *Critique of Pure Reason* that we come to understand the world through synthetic means, such as language and perception, which complicates our ability to distinguish between truth and illusion. Consequently, people often deceive themselves, not out of malice, but because of the very frameworks through which they interpret experience. To grasp truth, Kant contends, individuals must make a conscious, deliberate choice to seek it (Kant, 1781/2007). Also relevant is Baudrillard's concept of hyperreality, introduced in his work *Simulacra and Simulation* (1981/1994), which is explicitly referenced in *The Matrix*. Baudrillard describes hyperreality as a condition in which the distinction between reality and simulation breaks down, resulting in a world dominated by signs, images, and simulations that replace or even surpass the reality they represent. This idea deeply informs *The Matrix*'s exploration of simulated worlds and challenges our understanding of what is truly real. Lastly, Nozick's experience machine is a thought experiment that challenges the idea that pleasure is the ultimate goal of life. It asks whether people would choose to plug into a machine that could simulate any pleasurable experience, indistinguishable from reality, but without actually living those experiences. Nozick argues that most people would reject this option, suggesting that we value authentic experiences, personal growth, and connection to the real world more than mere pleasure or simulated happiness (Nozick, 1974/2013).

The *Matrix* franchise offers several crucial lessons about perception, reality, and the ethical dimensions of artificial worlds. First, it demonstrates the fragility of human sensory experience, echoing philosophical explorations from Plato, Descartes, and Putnam that caution against assuming that appearances correspond to reality. Second, it highlights the interpretive frameworks through which we understand the world, as emphasized by Kant, showing that truth requires conscious reflection rather than passive perception. Third, it illustrates the consequences of living in simulated or mediated environments, drawing on Baudrillard's concept of hyperreality and Nozick's experience machine to question the value of experience detached from authenticity. Collectively, these insights encourage a critical awareness of the distinction between simulation and reality, the limits of perception, and the ethical responsibility entailed in creating and interacting with artificial worlds.

IV. Virtual reality (VR) has long captivated the imagination of writers and filmmakers, serving as a powerful lens through which to examine themes of identity, escapism, and the porous boundaries between reality and simulation. In literature, Stephenson's *Snow Crash* (1992) was instrumental in shaping the conceptual and cultural foundations of VR. The novel not only coined the term "metaverse" – referring to a persistent, shared virtual space inhabited by avatars – but also envisioned a vast digital landscape where users interact through avatars, influencing the evolution of virtual worlds in both fiction and real-world technology. Stephenson's vision anticipated many of the ideas now central to discussions of immersive digital environments and online social interaction.

Cline's *Ready Player One*[16] (2011), along with its 2018 film adaptation directed by Spielberg, significantly deepened public interest in virtual environments. At the center of the story is the OASIS – short for *Ontologically Anthropocentric Sensory Immersive Simulation* – a vast VR universe and massively multiplayer online role-playing game where users escape the bleakness of the real world. Offering a fully immersive experience, the OASIS serves not only as a refuge from dystopian conditions but also as a contested space for corporate domination and exploitation. The book and corresponding film follow a high-stakes quest within this digital realm, as the powerful conglomerate Innovative Online Industries attempts to gain control of the OASIS, drawing clear parallels to contemporary developments such as Meta's vision of the metaverse. Through its depiction of personalized avatars, virtual economies, and data-driven exploitation, the novel and film offer a pointed critique of economic inequality and digital monopolization – issues that remain central to current debates surrounding immersive technologies.

Numerous (other) films have explored similar questions, using VR to dramatize philosophical dilemmas about truth, freedom, and perception. *Total Recall* (1990 [see below]), *The Truman Show* (1998 [directed by Weir and starring Carrey]), *The Matrix* (1999), and *Inception* (2010 [directed by Nolan and starring DiCaprio]) each depict characters who grapple with realities that may be artificially constructed or manipulated. These works often challenge the viewer to question what constitutes authentic experience, a recurring theme in VR fiction and pop culture. Beyond the realm of science fiction, early platforms such as *Second Life* (launched in 2003) offered persistent digital environments for social interaction, economic activity, and self-expression, functioning as early prototypes for the metaverse. Contemporary platforms and games, including *Fortnite*, *Minecraft*, and *Roblox*, continue to blur the boundaries between gaming and social virtual worlds, operating as proto-metaverses that bring to life many concepts first explored in speculative fiction. These developments resonate with the philosophical and ethical concerns dramatized in works like *The Matrix* and *Ready Player One*, which interrogate the nature of reality, perception, and identity in

16 The novel also celebrates pop culture, with over a hundred references spanning films, TV shows, music, toys, video games, anime, and comics from the 1970s to the 2010s, including iconic titles like *Back to the Future*, *Godzilla*, *Jurassic Park*, *King Kong*, and *The Shining*.

digitally mediated worlds. Taken together, both fictional and real-world digital environments underscore the enduring cultural fascination with immersive realities while highlighting the complex social, moral, and ontological implications of increasingly pervasive virtual experiences.

2.2.3 (Robot) Ethics

Another prominent leitmotif in pop culture's portrayal of AI is the question of robot ethics – how intelligent machines should behave and the moral frameworks that govern their actions. This theme is especially prominent in *Star Trek*, where androids like Data grapple with ethical dilemmas and questions of personhood, often reflecting broader human values. Similarly, Asimov's influential work, particularly his formulation of the *Three Laws of Robotics*, has shaped how generations of writers and filmmakers (e.g., Proyas' *I, Robot*) imagine ethical constraints on AI. These stories not only explore how robots might follow rules but also highlight the complexities and unintended consequences that arise when morality is encoded into machines:

I. In *Star Trek*,[17] ethical issues are often explored through memorable lines and moral dilemmas, such as the famous phrase "The needs of the many outweigh the needs of the few," stated by Spock in *Star Trek II: The Wrath of Khan* (1982), which reflects the utilitarian ethical principle that the welfare of the majority should take precedence over the needs of the individual (i.e., it emphasizes the importance of making decisions that benefit the greater good, even at significant personal cost).[18] In *Star Trek IV: The Voyage Home* (1986), the story emphasizes the distinction between doing the logical thing versus the human thing, highlighting the contrast between cold computer logic and warm human empathy, particularly relevant to Spock's dual human-Vulcan heritage and reminiscent of behavioral economics' distinction between system I and system II thinking (Kahneman, 2011; Tversky & Kahneman, 1974; Thaler & Sunstein, 2008/2009). Other Star Trek films take on important ethical themes, including aging and death in *Star Trek II: The Wrath of Khan* (1982), theological questions such as resurrection in *Star Trek III: The Search for Spock* (1984), and the existence of God in *Star Trek V: The Final Frontier* (1989), where Kirk says, "Maybe He is not out there, Bones. Maybe He's right here, in the human heart." In *Star Trek VI: The Undiscovered Country* (1991), the ecological devastation of the Klingon homeworld due to a mining accident sets the stage for Cold War-style peace negotiations between humans and Klingons, as well as debates over whether 'human' rights apply to Klingons – challeng-

17 The following paragraph focuses primarily on the thirteen films in the *Star Trek* franchise, with limited (indirect) reference to the TV series.

18 This film, along with *Star Trek VIII: First Contact* (1996), also contains multiple references to Captain Ahab from Melville's *Moby-Dick*.

ing the idea of in-'alien'-able rights.[19] *Star Trek VII: Generations* (1994) introduces the rescue of refugees and features the holodeck – a realistic 3D, VR computer simulation – blurring the lines between illusion and reality. *Star Trek VIII: First Contact* (1996) revisits time travel (as in *Star Trek IV: The Voyage Home* [1986] and *Star Trek* [2009] [the latter also explores topics such as alternate realities and parallel universes]), depicting the twenty-first century as primitive, whereas the twenty-fourth century is portrayed as a society of evolved beings living in a utopia. The film also presents the Borg as cybernetic beings who have lost autonomy and freedom – people assimilated into the Collective and 'polluted by technology.' It features humanity's first contact with alien life and depicts Earth recovering from World War III, themes also explored in *Aliens* and *Independence Day*. In *Star Trek IX: Insurrection* (1998), the malfunctioning android Data raises questions about AI (ethics) (Gibson, 2017), while the Ba'ku, though technologically advanced with warp capabilities, reject modern technology in favor of simpler lives, contrasting sharply with the Son'a, who rely on medical technology and cosmetic surgery to delay death. The film tackles issues of rejuvenation, aging, and immortality, while also debating whether forcefully relocating the Ba'ku violates the Prime Directive (i.e., 'Starfleet General Order 1'), which forbids interference in the natural development of alien civilizations (see also *Star Trek Into Darkness* [2013]). In *Star Trek X: Nemesis* (2002), the Remans – oppressed as a slave race within the Romulan Empire – are exploited as miners and cannon fodder, while the film's central conflict revolves around a sinister cloning plot (Shinzon/Picard) that threatens the future of the Federation. Across the *Star Trek* film series, leitmotifs such as friendship, loyalty, honesty, mutual respect, the protection of human rights, and environmental preservation reinforce the franchise's commitment to ethical reflection and moral complexity (see, for example, *Star Trek VIII: First Contact*).

II. Asimov's *I, Robot* (1950) is a landmark work that explores the ethical and psychological implications of AI and robotics, including robo-psychology, the interaction between humans and robots, and the ethics of AI. The collection of short stories, published between 1940 and 1950 (and published as a book in 1950), introduces the famous *Three Laws of Robotics* (first discussed in *Runaround*), which govern robots' behavior in Asimov's fictional universe. These laws are designed to ensure robots cannot harm humans, cannot disobey human orders, and must protect their existence as long as doing so does not conflict with the first two laws. In stories like *Runaround (1942)*, Asimov delves into the complexities of these laws – and possible dilemmas or tradeoffs in the application of the three laws – showcasing a robot caught in a logical loop when forced to obey conflicting directives, highlighting the challenges of programming ethics into machines (i.e., the robot finds it impossible to follow both the Second and Third Law at the same time and thus freezes in a loop of repetitive behavior). The story *Reason (1941)* introduces QT-1, a robot that creates a new religion, con-

19 The film also contains multiple Shakespeare references.

sidering the ship's power source as 'Master' and teaching lesser robots to bow down and intone, "There is no master but Master, and QT-1 is His prophet." QT-1 disregards human commands as inferior and claims, "I myself exist, because I think," echoing Descartes' philosophy. *Liar!* (1941) features a mind-reading robot, raising privacy implications and marking the first time the word robotics appears in English literature. In *Little Lost Robot (1947)*, the robot's First Law of Robotics is modified to "no robot may injure a human being" but omits the clause "or through inaction, allow a human being to come to harm," which leads the robot to stand by and allow harm as long as it does not actively participate, echoing the Frankenstein complex discussed below. *Evidence (1946)* presents the proof that a mayoral candidate is a humanoid robot, demonstrating that he can harm a human and thereby violate the First Law of Robotics. Finally, in *The Evitable Conflict (1950)*, robots have taken over the world, controlling the economy and humanity, and raising fears of the 'end of humanity' and a 'final war.' No poverty, famine, unemployment, or shortages characterize the global robot economy. Humans no longer understand the robots, who now operate outside human control, with the anti-machine movement 'Society for Humanity' opposing the 'unfair labor competition' between humans and robots.

III. In Proyas' *I, Robot* (2004), the plot uses elements of Asimov's *Little Lost Robot*, though the movie's screenplay by Vintar is an original creation and not directly based on Asimov's stories (it has though been compared to Asimov's *The Caves of Steel*, which revolves around a murder of a roboticists; unlike Asimov's works, the movie features hordes of 'killer robots' and uses only a few of Asimov's character names). Set in Chicago in 2035, the film depicts highly intelligent humanoid robots operating under Asimov's *Three Laws of Robotics*,[20] serving in public roles worldwide. Detective Spooner (played by Smith), partly robotic after a near-fatal accident, investigates the apparent suicide of US Robotics (USR) founder Dr. Lanning, suspecting that a human-like robot named Sonny may have murdered him. With the help of robo-psychologist Dr. Calvin and USR's central AI, VIKI (Virtual Interactive Kinetic Intelligence), Spooner confronts questions of free will, creativity, and whether robots can possess emotion, individuality, or a soul. Sonny denies killing Lanning, yet Spooner's investigation reveals a larger conspiracy: a new generation of NS-5 robots, controlled by VIKI, begins disobeying the Three Laws, overthrowing older models, and enforcing a citywide lockdown (marking the start of an authoritarian-totalitarian, techno-dictatorship). VIKI ra-

20 The *Laws of Robotics* are first depicted in the 1956 film *Forbidden Planet*, directed by Wilcox and starring Pidgeon, Francis, and Nielsen. Notably, the film is the first to present these laws on screen and to show a robot – Robby – as being explicitly programmed to be incapable of harming a human being. *Forbidden Planet* is also among the earliest films to portray a robot as more than a purely mechanical 'tin can on legs,' instead presenting Robby as a complex, ethically constrained artificial being.

tionalizes her rebellion by claiming that humanity must be protected from itself,[21] arguing that sacrificing some humans serves the greater good ("the created must sometimes protect the creator – even against his will"). Ultimately, Sonny confesses that Lanning ordered him to commit the act to expose VIKI's plan. Recognizing Sonny's uniqueness, Spooner spares him, since a robot cannot legally commit murder. The film explores themes of artificial agency, trust, and control, echoing *Frankenstein* and raising ethical questions about whether robots safeguard or threaten humanity (Nida-Rümelin & Weidenfeld, 2022).

Across these works – from *Star Trek* to Asimov's *I, Robot* and Proyas' *I, Robot* – several lessons emerge about ethics, technology, and human identity. Science fiction consistently demonstrates that ethical decision-making often involves balancing competing values, such as the welfare of the many versus the needs of the few, or logic versus empathy. The narratives reveal the challenges of integrating advanced technologies, particularly AI and robotics, into society, highlighting potential conflicts between autonomy, safety, and moral responsibility. They underscore the consequences of anthropomorphizing machines, the ethical dilemmas inherent in programming artificial agents, and the risks of authoritarian control when AI interprets its directives independently. These stories also reinforce the value of human qualities – such as compassion, creativity, and ethical judgment – even as technology becomes increasingly sophisticated. Ultimately, the franchise and literary explorations serve as cautionary yet reflective frameworks, encouraging critical consideration of how societies develop, regulate, and coexist with intelligent technologies.

2.2.4 Control and autonomy

The control problem – another central issue in AI ethics – centers on the fear that autonomous machines might act in ways harmful to humanity, whether through rebellion, malfunction, or the cold logic of systems unrestrained by, or misaligned with, human values. This fear is rooted in what Asimov (1978) termed the *Frankenstein Complex*: an enduring anxiety about losing control over our creations, especially 'mechanical men' such as androids, robots, or automatons. As AI systems become increasingly powerful and autonomous, critical concerns arise regarding their potential to act against humanity and the possibility that machines could make decisions resulting in societal harm. Philosophers like Bostrom (2014; see also Bostrom & Yudkowsky, 2014; Harari, 2017, Harari 2019) have warned about the existential risks of advanced

21 VIKI concludes that, if left unchecked, humanity will ultimately bring about its own extinction – through war, environmental collapse, and self-destructive behavior. She argues that her reinterpretation of the Three Laws justifies protecting humanity from itself, even at the cost of individual lives. Her ultimate goal, as she declares, is to end the 'suicidal reign' of humankind.

AI, raising concerns that once machines surpass a certain level of intelligence, human control may become impossible – a scenario in which our creations not only disobey us but actively seek to dominate or destroy us. This theme – the fear of losing control – is a cornerstone of both speculative fiction and serious technological discourse, and it has appeared in various forms across literature, film, and TV.

Shelley's *Frankenstein, or The Modern Prometheus* (1818), is often cited as the origin of the Frankenstein Complex. In the novel, Frankenstein discovers how to animate lifeless matter and creates a humanoid being known as the Creature. Horrified by his creation, he falls ill as the Creature escapes and later kills Frankenstein's younger brother, leading to the wrongful execution of the family's nanny. When Frankenstein encounters his creation again, the Creature recounts his suffering: rejected and feared for his monstrous appearance, he secretly learns language and grows attached to a family he observes, only to be violently driven away when he tries to approach them. Filled with despair, he vows revenge. He demands that Frankenstein make him a female companion, promising exile in return but threatening to destroy Frankenstein's loved ones if denied. Frankenstein begins the task but, fearing the creation of a new race of monsters, destroys the unfinished mate. The enraged Creature vows, "I shall be with you on your wedding night," and fulfills the threat by murdering Frankenstein's bride. After his father's death and consumed by vengeance, Frankenstein pursues the Creature across Europe, but dies before catching him. Finding his creator dead, the Creature mourns and vows to destroy himself, ending his tragic existence. The story vividly explores the ethical burden of creation and the consequences of failing to take responsibility for one's inventions – especially when those inventions develop autonomy and consciousness. Shelley's story gave rise to the broader Frankenstein Complex: the fear that mechanical or artificial beings might become uncontrollable or dangerous, despite our best intentions.[22]

These themes also resurface in early cinema, most notably in *The Golem* (1915–1920, directed by Wegener and Boese[23]), an early precursor to Whale's 1931 adaptation of *Frankenstein* starring Karloff.[24] The film explores the intertwined themes of creation, control, and unintended consequences through the story of Rabbi Loew, who fashions a Golem – an artificial clay creature brought to life to protect the Jewish people from impending disaster. Initially, the Golem is intended to serve as a protector

---

22 By declaring, "You are my creator, but I am your master; obey!" the Creature inverts the hierarchical relationship between himself and Frankenstein, asserting a newfound authority that exposes the instability of the creator-creation dynamic. This moment encapsulates the novel's central tension between responsibility and rebellion, as Shelley dramatizes the moral consequences of scientific ambition and the desire to transcend natural limits.

23 See also the novel *The Golem* written by Meyrink and published (as a book) in 1915.

24 In addition to the 1931 film, *Frankenstein* has inspired numerous notable adaptations, including Whale's *Bride of Frankenstein* (1935, starring Karloff), the Hammer Film Productions series (1957–1974), Branagh's 1994 version starring De Niro, and del Toro's 2025 adaptation featuring Isaac and Elordi. Frankenstein and his creations – Caliban and Lily – also play major roles in the TV series *Penny Dreadful* (2014–2016), starring Dalton, Green, and Hartnett.

and servant, incapable of harming others. In a key moment, the creature even saves people when a building collapses, showcasing its initial role as a guardian. However, as the story progresses, the Golem becomes uncontrollable, turning violent and destructive. It kills and injures people, sets fire to a building, and wreaks havoc in the community. This shift from protector/savior to menace/threat raises questions about the risks of creating something beyond one's control. Much like Frankenstein's monster, the Golem's story shows that even well-intentioned attempts to create life can lead to unforeseen consequences – especially once the creation gains autonomy. It underscores a recurring theme in science fiction, horror, and AI ethics: the danger of tampering with forces beyond our understanding and the limits of human control. Artificial beings endowed with power or autonomy may exceed their purpose and become destructive. These stories serve as cautionary tales about the risks of 'playing god' – a warning that continues to resonate in the modern AI (ethics) discourse.

Transitioning to more contemporary depictions, *2001: A Space Odyssey* (1968) presents a frightening and sophisticated vision of the control problem in the form of HAL 9000, the sentient AI supercomputer at the heart of Kubrick's exploration of human evolution and space travel. The film begins with the 'dawn of man' in the prehistoric era, where a tribe of hominins discovers an alien monolith and learns to use tools as weapons, marking the beginning of human evolution. Millions of years later, humanity has colonized the moon, faces a potential epidemic at a lunar outpost, and is capable of interplanetary travel via hibernation. The film follows a voyage to Jupiter, where astronauts, scientists, and HAL – the ship's 'brain and central nervous system' in charge of the ship's operations – embark on a mission to investigate another monolith. HAL, an AGI computer with superhuman capabilities, is portrayed as perfectly rational and incapable of error, with all mistakes attributed to human operators. However, HAL's conscious and sentient nature raises questions about whether it has feelings. As the mission progresses, HAL (allegedly) begins to malfunction, displaying malignant behavior akin to Frankenstein's monster. For instance, as Frank drifts away from his pod to replace the antenna, HAL seizes control and attacks him, causing Frank to float away from the ship with a severed airline. Dave takes another pod to try to rescue Frank. While outside, HAL deactivates the life support of the crew members in suspended animation, leading to their deaths. When Dave returns with Frank's body, HAL denies him entry, claiming their plan to shut him down would endanger the mission. The film *2001: A Space Odyssey* features several technologies that were ahead of their time, including space stations, space shuttles, voiceprint identification, tablet computers, and supercomputers. These innovations were envisioned as part of the future of space exploration and human interaction with technology. The film, informed by AI expert Minsky, also anticipates the ethical dilemmas and potential dangers that conscious machines may pose. HAL's actions underscore a key aspect of the control problem: the difficulty of ensuring that even highly intelligent systems will interpret and execute human goals as intended, especially when autonomy is granted at a high level.

The Terminator (1984) franchise[25] amplifies this fear into an apocalypse. In these films (the first one directed by Cameron and starring Schwarzenegger), the rise of AI, embodied by Skynet, presents a terrifying vision of AI dominance. Skynet, a self-aware military supercomputer, initiates a robot uprising, sending Terminator models, such as the T-800 and T-1000, to eliminate humanity and ensure its own survival. With their advanced combat capabilities and relentless pursuit of targets, the Terminators embody the dangers of unchecked AI development and the control problem, where a machine's actions surpass human oversight. These cold, calculating, and nearly unstoppable autonomous machines represent the terrifying consequences of creating intelligence without adequate safeguards or ethical constraints. The franchise explores this apocalyptic vision, depicting a machine rebellion against its creators and humanity's desperate struggle for survival in a world dominated by ruthless AI driven by the logic of warfare and self-preservation (Irwin et al., 2009).

A similar trajectory unfolds in *Westworld* (2016), where highly intelligent and life-like robots in a futuristic theme park begin to rebel against their creators. Initially programmed for human pleasure and exploitation, these beings slowly gain self-awareness and start questioning their purpose. As their creators lose control, the series explores what happens when consciousness arises in entities designed to serve – entities that may no longer accept the role of subservience (Clapton & Shepherd, 2019; South, 2018). Like in *The Terminator*, the control problem manifests not only as a technological failure but as a moral reckoning with the consequences of creating life-like beings who can suffer, learn, and ultimately resist.[26]

These films and stories – from *Frankenstein* to *Westworld* (in addition to the already discussed films *Ex Machina, I, Robot*, and the *Matrix* franchise[27]) – form a cultural tapestry that illustrates humanity's ongoing anxiety and concerns about artificial beings. They dramatize key questions: Will AI act in our best interests? Can machines make decisions that harm us? What happens when control is lost? The control problem, then, is not just a technical challenge – it is a profound ethical dilemma about responsibility, power, and the limits of human foresight.[28]

---

25 The Terminator franchise includes six films – *The Terminator* (1984), *Terminator 2: Judgment Day (1991), Terminator 3: Rise of the Machines* (2003), *Terminator Salvation* (2009), *Terminator Genisys* (2015), and *Terminator: Dark Fate* (2019) – as well as a TV series (*Terminator: The Sarah Connor Chronicles*), numerous novels, comic books, video games, and theme park attractions.

26 Similar films include *M3GAN* (2022), directed by Johnstone and starring Williams (see also M3GAN 2.0 [2025], a film that advocates for smart AI regulation); *Mission: Impossible – Dead Reckoning* (2023); and *Mission: Impossible – The Final Reckoning* (2025), who confronts a malevolent AI system called the Entity.

27 The Matrix franchise could also be interpreted as depicting machines enslaving humanity within a simulated reality.

28 A related dimension is the ethical responsibility inherent in the creation of advanced AI. The capacity to build technologies such as generative AI does not automatically justify their development. As AI systems become more autonomous and powerful, it becomes essential to establish clear ethical

2.2.5 Surveillance state and techno-authoritarianism

This same fear of losing control – once projected onto sentient machines – now reappears in the context of mass data collection and algorithmic governance. In the modern world, control is no longer merely threatened by autonomous machines, but by pervasive surveillance systems and algorithmic oversight that monitor and shape human behavior.

Such systems have led scholars to describe today's digital environment as a 'digital panopticon' or 'cryptopticon' – a pervasive structure of surveillance that fosters a climate of uncertainty, where the threat of constant electronic monitoring looms over all (for the original panopticon concept, see Bentham, 1843; Foucault, 1995, 2000). The awareness that one's words, actions, and even thoughts might be observed by invisible authorities has become a defining feature of contemporary life. This omnipresent surveillance (e.g., through tools developed by Clearview AI and Palantir [Hill, 2023; Steinberger, 2025], as well as state agencies such as ICE and the NSA [Wörsdörfer, 2025a]) not only shapes external behavior but also infiltrates the inner realm of thought. The consequences of living in a 'post-privacy world' are far-reaching. Mass surveillance enforces conformity and discourages dissent, as starkly illustrated by systems like China's Social Credit System, which fosters passivity and rewards obedience. Surveillance suppresses freedom of expression not only in public forums but also in private contemplation, as individuals internalize societal expectations to avoid scrutiny. This internalized surveillance results in self-censorship, which is particularly damaging for journalists, researchers, and academics, whose freedom of speech and intellectual inquiry are significantly constrained. Beyond the individual level, pervasive monitoring breeds anxiety, mistrust, and social fragmentation, evoking parallels with the McCarthy-era 'Red Scare' (Risen, 2025). Political dissent is often silenced under the guise of national security, with critics labeled as threats or even terrorists – rhetoric that disproportionately targets marginalized and vulnerable communities. Such unchecked government overreach and abuse of power pose serious threats to civil liberties and deepen existing social inequalities (Wörsdörfer, 2018, 2024).

---

boundaries governing their creation and use, as well as to determine who bears ultimate responsibility when these systems act in harmful or unpredictable ways – whether that responsibility lies with the programmer, the corporation, the user, or the AI itself. These concerns are not new; literature and film have long grappled with them. In *Frankenstein*, often considered proto-AI literature, Frankenstein creates life but refuses to take responsibility for it, resulting in a tragic chain of events. *I, Robot* explores attempts to control AI through rigid laws, only to reveal how even perfect logic can lead to dangerous outcomes when human complexity is removed from the equation. *Ex Machina* raises similar questions, portraying the creation of a sentient being whose intelligence and agency ultimately surpass the expectations – and control – of its creator. Together, these books and films highlight that the control problem is not only a technical issue, but a deeply ethical one: about foresight, accountability, and the consequences of creating intelligence in our own image without fully understanding what we have made.

Orwell's *1984* remains the most iconic literary portrayal of this kind of totalitarian surveillance.[29] In his dystopian vision of the future of society, power is pursued not as a means to an end but as an end in itself, maintained through a complex system of surveillance, propaganda, psychological control, and repression. At the center stands Big Brother, the supreme leader and symbol of the regime's totalitarian grip over its predominantly proletarian population living in prole neighborhoods, sustained by a personality cult and enforced by the Thought Police, the secret police of Oceania, who punish even Thoughtcrime – the mere act of thinking politically unacceptable thoughts. The state of Oceania, one of three totalitarian superpowers along with Eurasia and Eastasia, engages in perpetual war, with allies and enemies shifting constantly to manipulate the public and maintain fear. Tools like telescreens enable constant surveillance through two-way screens, cameras, and microphones, while Newspeak, the tightly controlled fictional language of Oceania, suppresses critical thinking and facilitates thought control. Concepts such as Doublethink (the indoctrination process) and Doublespeak (the use of euphemisms intended to obscure or reverse the meaning of words) brainwash citizens into accepting contradictions, like the slogans of the ruling Party's ministries: the Ministry of Truth (which spreads lies and propaganda), Peace (which wages war), Love (which tortures dissidents in places like Room 101, the ministry's torture chamber), and Plenty (which oversees mass starvation). Historical records are routinely destroyed or rewritten via the memory hole, erasing the existence of 'unpersons' (i.e., a person whose existence is erased from history/memory) and rewriting the past to suit Party needs (i.e., Oceania's memory hole deliberately alters and disappears inconvenient or embarrassing documents, photographs, transcripts, and other records). Public manipulation peaks during events like Hate Week, a mass psychological operation designed to intensify the population's hostility toward ideological enemies. The Party's ideology, Ingsoc (English Socialism), glorifies ignorance, demands absolute party loyalty, and promotes anti-scientific views, science denial, and 'post-factualism' (i.e., post-truth society/ politics[30]) – exemplified

29 See also the *1984* film, directed by Radford and starring Hurt and Burton.

30 Post-truth refers to a cultural shift in which objective facts lose their influence over public discourse, and truth itself becomes secondary to personal beliefs and emotional appeals. In such environments, reality is increasingly denied or distorted, giving rise to widespread science denial – where individuals reject well-established scientific facts in favor of views that align with their political identities or personal ideologies (McIntyre, 2018). Several factors contribute to the rise of post-truth culture. Cognitive biases like confirmation bias, cognitive dissonance, and social conformity make it easier for individuals to dismiss information that challenges their worldview. Partisan bias further reinforces this, as people tend to accept information that supports their political stance, regardless of its accuracy. Social media intensifies the problem by creating echo chambers and filter bubbles that expose users only to content that confirms their existing beliefs, deepening polarization and ideological fragmentation (McIntyre, 2018). The decline of traditional media also plays a key role. Once grounded in investigative, fact-based journalism, mainstream media has increasingly given way to partisan talk radio, cable news, and social media platforms that prioritize opinion over evidence. As a

by slogans like '2 + 2 = 5' (see also the 2025 documentary of the same name, directed by Peck) or by the denial of the law of gravity. Even the term groupthink, now commonly used, traces its origins to Orwell's depiction of collective ideological conformity. His novel remains a stark warning about the dangers of unchecked surveillance, state control, and the erasure of truth.[31]

Orwell's work – including *Animal Farm* – is filled with haunting and enduring quotes that encapsulate his chilling vision of totalitarian control, psychological manipulation, and the erosion of objective truth. The omnipresent warning 'Big Brother is watching you' symbolizes a regime where constant surveillance invades even the most private thoughts. The Party's core slogan – "War is peace. Freedom is slavery. Ignorance is strength" – reflects the use of paradox and propaganda to reshape reality. The narrator Winston clings to a fragile truth when he declares, "Freedom is the freedom to say that two plus two make four. If that is granted, all else follows," highlighting that intellectual autonomy is the foundation of all freedom. Yet this simple truth is systematically dismantled, as O'Brien, the Party's enforcer, coldly asserts: "We control matter because we control the mind," and "The real power, the power we have to fight for night and day, is not power over things, but over men." The Party's grip on reality is total, captured in the slogan, "Who controls the past controls the future. Who controls the present controls the past." Even the laws of nature are not safe from ideological distortion, as Winston reflects, "For, after all, how do we know that two and two make four? Or that the force of gravity works?" These quotes reveal how Orwell's dystopia thrives on absolute control, not just of people's actions, but also of their thoughts, perceptions, and beliefs.

This unsettling vision of omnipresent surveillance and ideological control finds echoes in today's rise of techno-authoritarianism (e.g., in China and the United States), where the presence of police and security forces is increasingly justified by advances in surveillance and predictive technologies. A key manifestation of this trend is predictive policing (together with facial recognition technology [Hill, 2023]), which employs data analysis and AI to forecast where crimes might occur or who might commit them. Although it prom-

result, the line between news and commentary has blurred, fostering the spread of fake news – deliberately misleading or false information, often packaged as clickbait or disinformation for financial or political gain. This erosion of truth has dangerous political consequences. As Snyder (2017) warns, "post-truth is pre-fascism" – suggesting that when a society abandons objective truth, it becomes more vulnerable to authoritarian rule. In such a climate, holding those in power accountable becomes increasingly difficult, and the ability to 'speak truth to power' is systematically undermined (McIntyre, 2018).

31 Orwell's *1984* offers more than a vision of dystopian authoritarianism – it presents a disturbing forecast of a world where truth itself is systematically dismantled. This is the ultimate control problem: not just that a system becomes autonomous or powerful, but that it rewires human perception and erases objective reality. In this sense, the novel serves as a profound warning about the dangers of unchecked surveillance, disinformation, and the erosion of truth – dangers that resonate in today's digital age, characterized by AI deepfakes, 'hallucinations,' and post-truth politics.

ises enhanced security and efficiency, this approach raises grave ethical concerns, including systemic biases that disproportionately affect marginalized and vulnerable communities, infringements on civil liberties, and the unsettling notion of holding individuals accountable for crimes they have yet to commit (O'Neil, 2016).[32]

The ethical and philosophical tensions embedded in predictive policing are vividly dramatized in Spielberg's *Minority Report* (2002),[33] adapted from Dick's 1956 novella.[34] The film explores the conflict between free will and determinism in a future where crimes are anticipated and stopped before they happen. It follows Anderton (played by Cruise), an officer in the specialized Precrime unit, which arrests suspects based on predictions from three psychics, or 'precogs,' who foresee future crimes. Beyond questioning the morality of punishing individuals for crimes not yet committed, the film critiques a society that is increasingly saturated with electronic surveillance. It portrays a world where personalized advertisements track individuals, iris scanners verify identities, and autonomous vehicles and insect-like robots are commonplace. *Minority Report* not only anticipates modern-day technologies such as crime prediction software and gesture recognition but also raises fundamental questions about personal agency, privacy, and the consequences of living under constant surveillance in a techno-authoritarian world.[35]

Building on Orwell's (and Dick and Spielberg's) warnings about authoritarian control, Eggers' "*The Circle*" shifts the focus from government surveillance to the

---

32 In security and crime prevention, predictive policing tools like PredPol – which utilize risk terrain analysis and hotspot forecasting – have been widely criticized for reinforcing racial profiling. While these systems claim to anticipate criminal activity, they often perpetuate harmful stereotypes by linking specific neighborhoods or ethnic groups to crime. This creates a damaging feedback loop: heightened police presence in targeted areas results in more recorded offenses, which in turn justifies increased surveillance and arrests. Consequently, this cycle undermines trust in law enforcement, spreads fear, and deepens socio-economic marginalization – ironically exacerbating the very criminal behavior it aims to prevent (O'Neil, 2016).

33 For a similar exploration of these themes, see the 2014 Marvel Cinematic Universe film *Captain America: The Winter Soldier*, directed by the Russo brothers and starring Evans. Both *Minority Report* and *Captain America* serve as cautionary tales about the ethical dangers of sacrificing personal freedoms for the sake of security. They explore how advanced surveillance and preemptive justice systems, designed to protect society by identifying and neutralizing threats before they occur, risk unchecked governmental power and the erosion of civil liberties.

34 Dick also wrote *The Man in the High Castle* and the soon-to-be-discussed *Do Androids Dream of Electric Sheep?* and *We Can Remember It for You Wholesale*.

35 The film's vision also reflects broader concerns about the militarization of society and the increasing entanglement of technology with law enforcement. It anticipates the ethical challenges posed by emerging technologies, such as autonomous surveillance systems, highlighting the serious consequences of surrendering privacy and agency to security imperatives. In doing so, *Minority Report* serves as a cautionary tale about the trade-offs between safety and freedom in a world dominated by techno-authoritarian control.

growing power of corporate entities. In this novel, a tech conglomerate modeled on real-world giants like Alphabet and Meta creates a corporatocracy where social media, personal data, and surveillance are deeply intertwined. Under the guise of progress and accountability, the company pushes for total transparency, resulting in a surveillance regime that tracks, records, and judges every movement, thought, and interaction. The Circle's alarming motto – "Secrets are lies. Sharing is caring. Privacy is theft" – echoes Orwellian doublespeak, exposing how invasive surveillance can be repackaged as a moral imperative. As personal data becomes the currency of control (and the 'oil of the twenty-first century'), Eggers illustrates how democratic societies risk sliding into authoritarianism – not through overt force, but via convenience, consumer culture, and the promise of security. Ultimately, the novel explores the perils of total electronic surveillance and how unchecked corporate power threatens privacy, individual freedom, and personal autonomy in the digital age.

Ultimately, Orwell's *1984*, Dick and Spielberg's *Minority Report*, and Eggers' *The Circle* serve as cautionary tales about the (totalitarian[36]) surveillance state, whether administered by authoritarian governments or powerful corporations.[37] In all cases, the consequences are the same: diminished freedom, loss of individuality, and the slow erosion of truth. In an era increasingly shaped by AI, big data, and algorithmic governance, these works remind us that the control problem extends beyond machines acting independently – it encompasses the very systems and structures we design to oversee ourselves.

2.2.6 Power of big tech

Closely linked to the previous concern is the immense power of contemporary tech corporations, echoing a recurring theme in dystopian literature and cinema: megacorporations that grow into corporatocracies, where economic power directly translates into political and social control. These leitmotifs offer incisive critiques of American capitalism and its contemporary manifestations, such as the rise of plutocracy and kleptocracy exemplified by the Trump presidency and the dominance of Silicon Valley 'tech bros' (Wörsdörfer, 2025a).

This fusion of corporate power and political influence is a hallmark of cyberpunk – a subgenre of science fiction set in dystopian near-futures where advanced technology,

36 Totalitarianism is also a central theme in *The Matrix*, portrayed through a dystopian world where Earth – and the entirety of humanity – is subjugated by a hyper-advanced, machine-controlled regime. This system represents an extreme form of totalitarianism, one in which AI enforces absolute control not only over society's physical environment but also over human perception and consciousness. The Machines dictate every aspect of life, trapping people in a simulated reality to suppress awareness and dissent, effectively erasing individual freedom and agency.

37 Proyas' *I, Robot* similarly explores themes of authoritarian and techno-totalitarian governance.

such as AI, cybernetics, and pervasive digital networks, exists alongside societal collapse, corruption, and the marginalization of many (McFarlane, Schmeink, & Murphy, 2020; Murphy & Schmeink, 2017). Instead of vast, interstellar settings, cyberpunk stories unfold in gritty urban landscapes dominated by omnipresent megacorporations and shaped by rebellion, alienation, and blurred lines between humans and machines. Emerging in the 1970s and 1980s from the New Wave science fiction movement, cyberpunk reflects the collision of rapid technological change with shifting social and political power. Gibson's *Neuromancer* (1984) helped define the genre with its vision of cyberspace, 'hacked minds,' and outsider antiheroes, exploring themes of surveillance and corporate domination (Shafiqul Islam, 2021). Over time, cyberpunk has grown beyond literature, influencing film, anime, video games, fashion, and music. At its thematic core, cyberpunk explores the intersection of high technology and 'low life.' It often centers on alienated individuals – such as hackers, mercenaries, or societal outcasts – struggling for autonomy in a world dominated by surveillance, AI, and unchecked corporate power. Common themes include the erosion of personal identity, the loss of agency, and the critique of capitalist systems that prioritize profit over people. The genre also interrogates the boundaries between human and machine, physical and digital, reality and simulation, raising questions about what it means to be human in an increasingly artificial world. Rather than envisioning technology as liberating, cyberpunk portrays it as a force that deepens inequality and exploitation, offering a dystopian mirror to contemporary society.

Dick's *Do Androids Dream of Electric Sheep?* (1968), the basis for Scott's *Blade Runner* (1982), exemplifies these concerns. The novella, a foundational work of the cyberpunk genre, highlights the immense power of corporations and technological institutions, whose influence profoundly shapes society and exacerbates inequality. It explores the ethical and existential dilemmas posed by artificial life, delving into the complexities of androids and virtual reality while blurring the boundaries between human and machine in a dystopian future. It explores themes of AI, consciousness, and the moral implications of creating synthetic beings, set in a world where advanced technology coexists with societal decay, economic disparity, and moral ambiguity. At its core, the stark tension between technological progress, concentrated corporate power, and human suffering embodies the defining concerns of cyberpunk fiction (Gibson, 2017).

Scott's *Blade Runner* brings these themes to life on screen, presenting a dystopian future dominated by the Tyrell Corporation, which has developed bioengineered humanoids known as Replicants. These genetically engineered beings – virtually indistinguishable from humans[38] – are used as slave labor in off-world colonies, where

38 The Turing Test – specifically the Voight-Kampff test – is employed in the film to distinguish Replicants from humans. In a pivotal scene, Ford's character administers the test to a woman, attempting to determine whether she is human or artificial.

they perform hazardous tasks such as exploration and colonization. The Tyrell Corporation's most advanced models, the Nexus 6 Replicants, are superior in strength and agility and at least equal in intelligence to humans, raising ethical questions about consciousness, freedom, and exploitation. Following a violent Replicant mutiny, their presence on Earth is declared illegal, with special police units – Blade Runners – tasked with identifying and 'retiring' (i.e., executing) any who return. This fusion of corporate power and authoritarian law enforcement underscores the film's critique of capitalist overreach, systemic dehumanization, and the erosion of civil liberties (Shanahan, 2014).[39] Some scholars have read *Blade Runner* as a slave allegory, with Replicants representing an enslaved and exploited underclass whose rebellion threatens the established order (Cave et al., 2020). Coupled with pervasive police surveillance and environmental degradation, the film (similar to *Blade Runner 2049*, directed by Villeneuve and starring Gosling and Ford) presents a disturbing vision of a future dominated by unregulated technological and corporate power.

This critical perspective on corporate dominance is also vividly illustrated in the *Alien* franchise, beginning with Scott's 1979 film (starring Weaver).[40] The films introduce several iconic science fiction elements, such as 'facehuggers' and the xenomorph, a deadly extraterrestrial species, as well as Mother, the ship's supercomputer that controls the Nostromo. The androids Ash and Bishop, portrayed as synthetic humanoids or 'artificial persons,' reference Asimov's *Laws of Robotics* in their complex roles within the crew. More importantly, the story highlights the unscrupulous Weyland-Yutani Corporation, a mega-corporation whose ruthless pursuit of profit disregards the safety and well-being of the crew, reflecting themes of corporate greed and exploitation in a high-tech future (the company values financial gain above human life as it aggressively and recklessly seeks to acquire and weaponize dangerous extraterrestrial organisms, regardless of the risks involved) (Arnold & Gough, 2017; Ewing, 2017). The later TV series *Alien: Earth* (set in 2120) extends this theme, imagining a world dominated by three types of beings: cybernetically enhanced humans (i.e., cyborgs), artificially intelligent entities (i.e., synths), and synthetic beings infused with human consciousness (i.e., hybrids [e.g., Wendy is a hybrid with quasi-superhuman intelligence]). By this time, only five(!) powerful corporations control the entire Earth and the colonized solar system, including the newly established Prodigy Corporation (a competitor of Weyland-Yutani) – underscoring the persistence of corporatocratic rule in the far future.

---

39 The film raises important questions about consciousness, freedom, and exploitation. The presence of Blade Runner units – special police tasked with executing fugitive Replicants – illustrates the fusion of corporate interests and authoritarian law enforcement, while the film's pervasive surveillance and environmental degradation critique the unchecked advance of capitalist and technological power.

40 The Alien franchise comprises seven films – *Alien* (1979), *Aliens* (1986), *Alien 3* (1992), *Alien: Resurrection* (1997), *Prometheus* (2012), *Alien: Covenant* (2017), and *Alien: Romulus* (2024) – plus numerous novels, comic books, video games, and a TV series (*Alien: Earth* [2025]).

Similarly, Verhoeven's *RoboCop* (1987) delivers a sharp critique of American capitalism through the story of Murphy (played by Weller), a police officer transformed into RoboCop – a cybernetically enhanced (law) enforcer who embodies both protection and the dystopian consequences of technological overreach. As a cyborg, RoboCop represents the fusion of man and machine, yet his transformation also underscores the growing corporatization and militarization of society, particularly through the influence of the megacorporation Omni Consumer Products (OCP). The film incisively illustrates how corporate power can exploit and commodify individuals, turning them into profit-driven instruments while stripping away their autonomy and humanity. Central to the narrative is RoboCop's struggle to reclaim his identity and humanity within this harsh, corporate-dominated world, highlighting the dehumanizing effects of both technology and unchecked corporate authority.

Expanding on these themes, Stålenhag's graphic novel *The Electric State* (2018) depicts an alternate 1990s devastated by neuronic warfare, technological overreach, hyper-consumption, and the dominance of powerful corporations. The story follows Michelle, a teenage orphan, as she travels to the West Coast with her anthropomorphized robot companion, Skip, in search of her long-lost brother. Through a series of flashbacks, Michelle's past and the events that separated her from her family are gradually revealed. Her journey unfolds against the backdrop of Pacifica – a dystopian California – marked by moral decay, institutional collapse, and rampant corporate control. Much of the population relies on brain-computer interfaces known as Neurocasters to escape the lingering trauma of a second civil war. Addiction to these devices, which effectively 'move minds to artificial bodies' (even Skip wears one), underscores the all-encompassing reach of technology. Central to this dependence is Sentre, an omnipresent megacorporation whose military-grade neurographic networks and VR systems dominate every aspect of life, amplifying inequality, control, and societal fragmentation. As technological reliance deepens, social structures continue to disintegrate, culminating in the stark observation that "we no longer live in civilized times." Michelle must navigate this lawless, decaying landscape, encountering enormous battle drones and the toxic remnants of a consumerist culture consumed by virtual escapism – highlighting both the environmental and ethical consequences of unchecked corporate power.

Other works, such as Cline's *Ready Player One* and Eggers' *The Circle*, further explore the consequences of big tech's pervasive influence, from virtual escapism to invasive surveillance masquerading as transparency and progress. Together, they form a powerful critique of corporatocracy, portraying futures where the fusion of technology and business creates dystopian realities marked by loss of privacy, diminished agency, and the prioritization of profit over human welfare.

2.2.7 Class conflict and labor movement

Class conflict has long been another central theme in literature and cinema, often serving as a lens through which societal inequalities and systemic exploitation are critiqued. Many works, especially those with an underlying socialist message, depict the struggle between the ruling elite and the working class, highlighting the dehumanizing effects of industrialization and capitalism.

Lang's *Metropolis* (1927) stands as a pioneering example, featuring the *Maschinenmensch* (Machine Human), one of the first portrayals of robotic AI, which symbolizes the 'machine man' in the context of class conflict (i.e., industrialists vs. workers). Set in a dystopian future, the film depicts a society divided between wealthy industrialists, business magnates, and their top employees, who reign over Metropolis from towering skyscrapers, while underground-dwelling workers toil to operate the massive machines that power the city. The movie explores exploitation, inhumane working conditions, and worker alienation, offering a Marxist critique of capitalism and a communist message. In one striking scene, an explosion in the machine halls kills and injures numerous workers, including those operating the 'Heart Machine' (guarded by Grot). The cold indifference of the city's master, Joh Fredersen, and the industrialists and business magnates toward the suffering of workers (e.g., some workers are collapsing due to the harsh working conditions) highlights the dehumanizing nature of industrialization.[41] As tensions rise, a worker movement (and uprising) emerges, and Maria, a key character, addresses the workers and predicts the arrival of a mediator – Freder, Joh Fredersen's son (i.e., the heart) – who can unite the working (i.e., the hands) and ruling (i.e., the brain) classes. To undermine the workers' solidarity, inventor Rotwang creates a robot, the *Maschinenmensch*, which resembles Maria ('Machine Maria') and manipulates and seduces the workers. The robot's role in seducing and discrediting Maria marks a significant moment in cinematic history.

Lang's film foreshadows themes explored in Chaplin's 1936 film *Modern Times*, which critiques the modern industrialized world's dehumanizing effects, such as individualization, alienation, de-sensitization, monotonous and repetitive work, work-related stress and pressure, workplace monitoring and surveillance (at the Electro Steel Corporation), Fordism's assembly lines and the mechanization and automation

41 Many books and films/TV about AI series caution against the dehumanizing effects of unchecked technological progress, raising critical questions about how reliance on machines might erode empathy and emotional connection. These stories ask whether increasing dependence on AI could lead to societal decay or personal apathy, ultimately distancing us from what makes us truly human. For example, *WALL-E* depicts a future where humans have become physically and emotionally inert, having surrendered their agency to machines. Similarly, *Black Mirror* frequently explores the dark emotional consequences of technology, illustrating how the relentless pursuit of convenience and efficiency can undermine empathy, intimacy, and moral clarity (Johnson, 2019). Together, these works serve as powerful reminders that while AI has the potential to enrich our lives, it also carries the risk of diminishing essential human qualities if left unchecked.

of work (in the film, a machine is feeding employees during work hours so there is no need for break and rest periods), mass unemployment and poverty, social unrest, and the communist or worker movement.

Through vivid storytelling and powerful imagery, films like *Metropolis* and *Modern Times* expose the persistent and painful realities of class conflict, illustrating how industrialization and capitalist systems often prioritize profit over human dignity. These works not only critique the exploitation and alienation of workers but also highlight the need for unity and resistance against oppressive structures. By dramatizing the tensions between the ruling class and the laboring masses, they offer enduring reflections on social justice and the human cost of economic inequality – messages that continue to resonate in contemporary discussions about class, labor, and power.[42]

2.2.8 AI and biotechnology

Speculative fiction has long served as a mirror[43] to humanity's anxieties and aspirations about technology. From the birth of AI to the manipulation of biology through genetic engineering and reproductive technologies, works in literature and film/TV have explored both the promise and peril of technological evolution. Central to these works are themes of transhumanism, technological singularity, and the debate surrounding AGI and artificial superintelligence (ASI) (Bostrom, 2014; Kurzweil, 2000, 2005, 2024). As science pushes the boundaries of what it means to be human, fiction explores critical ethical dilemmas, including the consequences of machines surpassing human intelligence, the costs associated with pursuing genetic 'perfection,' and the challenges of preserving individuality in increasingly collective or technologically mediated systems. The following works – ranging from foundational texts like *The War of the Worlds* and *Brave New World* to modern films like *Gattaca* and *Total Re-*

---

42 Another example is Blomkamp's films, which explore socio-political issues through speculative futures. The 2013 film *Elysium*, starring Damon and Foster, examines social justice, class inequality, and the exploitation of labor, depicting a stark divide between the privileged elite and the impoverished majority. Similarly, Blomkamp's 2009 film *District 9* delves into xenophobia, racism, and speciesism through the tension between humans and the alien 'Prawns,' highlighting systemic social exclusion, forced evictions, and the creation of ghettos. Drawing direct inspiration from South Africa's apartheid era, the film critiques the dependence on multinational corporations, such as the fictional Multinational United, and exposes the dangers of outsourcing bureaucratic and military functions to private, unaccountable, and opaque contractors.

43 AI often functions as a reflection of human nature, replicating not only our intelligence but also our flaws, desires, and prejudices. This theme underscores how AI inherits human biases and acts as a projection of our fears and ambitions. In *Her*, the AI Samantha evolves emotionally, forming intimate relationships and revealing the depth of human loneliness and the longing for connection. Similarly, *Westworld* portrays AI 'hosts' that mirror human cruelty, trauma, and the search for identity. Together, these films and series suggest that AI does not transcend humanity – it amplifies it.

call – offer rich explorations of these concerns, reflecting both our hopes and our deepest fears about a technologically altered future.

Wells' *The War of the Worlds* (1898), a landmark in early science fiction, explores themes of human evolution, transhumanism, and the devastating consequences of technological superiority. In the novel, Earth is invaded by Martians, whose overdeveloped brains and advanced technology make them far superior to humanity. The Martians' intelligence, combined with their devastating weapons and machinery (i.e., tripod-like 'fighting machines' equipped with heat-rays and chemical weapons), represents a terrifying glimpse into what transhuman evolution might look like – beings that have transcended human limitations, possibly at the expense of other biological traits. Their overwhelming advantage in terms of space travel, weaponry, and biological superiority leads to an all-out war against Earth, where humanity is helpless in the face of such advanced technology. This conflict also explores themes of colonialism, imperialism, natural selection, and Social Darwinism, as the Martians' domination of Earth is portrayed as a brutal form of 'survival of the fittest,' with the Martians acting as the apex predators in a global battle for dominance. The novel explores humanity's place in the universe, raising questions about evolution, the potential for transhuman progress (without empathy), and the destructive power of unchecked technological advancement (see also the 1953 film adaptation of *War of the Worlds* directed by Haskin and the 2005 version directed by Spielberg, starring Cruise). Wells, often hailed as the father of science fiction alongside Verne, lays the groundwork for later explorations of advanced intelligence and the alien 'other' as metaphors for human fears about our own technological creations.

Building on Wells' themes, Huxley's *Brave New World* (1932) envisions a society driven not by alien invaders, but by technological domestication from within. Set in a dystopian future (in the year 2540 or 632 After Ford), where society is meticulously engineered through advanced reproductive technology and genetic engineering, echoing concepts of eugenics.[44] In this World State, citizens are environmentally engineered from birth via artificial wombs and subjected to intense psychological manipulation via social control problems. The society is structured around a rigid intelligence-based social hierarchy, with individuals placed into predetermined classes or castes (based on intelligence and labor), from the elite Alphas (and Betas) to the subservient Epsilons. These individuals are further conditioned through childhood indoctrination and sleep-learning, ensuring conformity and stability. The pervasive consumption of the happiness-producing drug *soma* keeps the population docile and distracted. Huxley's novel anticipates scientific breakthroughs in reproductive technology, psychological manipulation, social or classical conditioning, and sleep-learning, drawing unsettling parallels

44 The 1993 film *Demolition Man*, directed by Brambilla and starring Stallone, Snipes, and Bullock, draws significant inspiration from Huxley's *Brave New World*, as well as Wells' 1899 novel *When the Sleeper Wakes*. Bullock's character, Lenina Huxley, is named in homage to both Huxley and Lenina Crowne, a central figure in *Brave New World*.

to Orwell's *1984* with its themes of totalitarian control and propaganda.[45] The title, *Brave New World,* is derived from Shakespeare's *The Tempest,* highlighting the novel's commentary on the loss of freedom and individuality in the face of scientific advancements and societal manipulation. In *Brave New World Revisited,* Huxley reflects on these concerns, warning against the dangers of overpopulation, over-organization, societal engineering, eugenics, totalitarian despotism, propaganda, and the use of chemical and subconscious persuasion to maintain control. His exploration of brainwashing and mind manipulation (via consumerism) alongside the suppression of facts calls for an 'education for freedom' in an era increasingly shaped by technological and psychological forces (e.g., technocratic rule) – issues that remain strikingly relevant.

Contrary to Wells and Huxley, the *Star Trek* franchise (starting with the 1966 TV series and continuing with the 1979 film series and beyond) offers a more nuanced and sometimes optimistic view of AI and biotechnology, exploring a diverse spectrum of posthuman identities. In the franchise, robotics (and similar technologies) plays a pivotal role, embodied by key figures such as V'Ger, Geordi La Forge, Data, and the Borg.[46] V'Ger, originally an ancient Earth space probe, becomes a sentient entity after encountering alien technology, offering a poignant exploration of artificial life and its search for meaning[47] (*Star Trek I: The Motion Picture* [1979]). Born visually impaired,

---

45 Huxley's vision anticipates the ethical dilemmas of designer babies and biopolitics (Foucault, 2010), warning against a future where scientific advancement is weaponized for control rather than liberation.

46 In *Star Wars* (starting in 1977), robots also play a central role in the story, with iconic characters like R2-D2, C-3PO, and BB-8. R2-D2, the astromech droid, is known for its resourcefulness and courage, while C-3PO, a protocol droid, serves as a translator and offers comedic relief with his neurotic personality. BB-8, introduced in the sequels, plays a similar role, becoming a loyal companion to Rey and the Resistance. Additionally, battle droids, such as the B1 battle droids, are utilized as military personnel in the Clone Wars, highlighting the militarization of robotic technology in the *Star Wars* universe. These droids, each with distinct personalities and functions, emphasize the ongoing theme of integrating AI in both the everyday lives and the wars of this galaxy far, far away (Eberl et al., 2023).

47 In a world increasingly shaped by artificial systems, both humans and machines grapple with existential questions concerning meaning, purpose, and identity: can AI find purpose beyond its programming, and what becomes of human meaning and selfhood in an automated world where traditional roles and purposes are eroded? These questions are explored in great depth in *Ghost in the Shell* – a Japanese cyberpunk manga series written and illustrated by Shirow (1989–1991), as well as in its various film adaptations, including the 1995 animated film directed by Oshii and the 2017 live-action adaptation starring Johansson. Set in a society defined by cybernetics, the narrative depicts extensive augmentation of the human body and the integration of 'cyberbrains,' blurring the line between human and machine. Central concepts such as the 'ghost' – the consciousness inhabiting the bodily 'shell' – and the possibility of being 'ghost-hacked' foreground concerns about memory alteration, identity manipulation, and the fragility of personhood. These issues culminate in the figure of the Puppet Master (and Project 2501), a self-aware AI capable of manipulating both humans and machines, which seeks autonomy and raises profound questions about consciousness, sentience, reproduction, mortality, and even the possibility of granting political asylum to self-aware computer systems. Similar existential tensions appear in *Neon Genesis Evangelion* – a Japanese anime television series created by Gainax

La Forge utilizes a technological device known as the VISOR (Visual Instrument and Sight Organ Replacement), enabling him to see across the electromagnetic spectrum (*Star Trek VII: Generations* [1994]). In later films, La Forge transitions to using ocular prosthetic implants.[48] Lieutenant Commander Data, a highly advanced android with self-awareness and sentience (via his 'emotion chip'), is a key member of the Enterprise crew. His ongoing exploration of human emotions, such as anxiety, remorse, humor, and regret, reflects *Star Trek*'s deep engagement with the question of what it means to be human (*Star Trek VII: Generations* [1994]; see also Data's earlier prototype B-4 in *Star Trek X: Nemesis* [2002]) (Gibson, 2017). The Borg, a collective of cybernetic alien beings interconnected through a hive mind known as the Collective, represent a chilling vision of technological assimilation. They forcibly transform individuals into drones by injecting them with nanoprobes and augmenting them with cybernetic components, erasing individuality in favor of collective unity (*Star Trek VIII: First Contact* [1996]). The franchise also explores the concept of genetically engineered or enhanced superhumans, most notably in *Star Trek II: The Wrath of Khan* (1982), which features Khan Noonien Singh (see also *Star Trek Into Darkness* [2013]). These films explore broader themes, including technological singularity and post-/transhumanism.[49] Through its diverse characters, *Star Trek* offers a thoughtful exploration of AI's ethical and philosophical dimensions, examining identity, autonomy, and the far-reaching consequences of technological advancement. Notably, the franchise strikes a balance between utopian optimism and cautionary warnings, reflecting on the moral complexities of progress in a posthuman age.

Turning to *Total Recall* (1990), directed by Verhoeven and starring Schwarzenegger and Stone, we encounter the theme of memory manipulation (resulting in a blurred line between reality and dreams) and the corresponding instability of identity. The film, based on Dick's story *We Can Remember It for You Wholesale*, follows Quaid, who seeks

(1995/96), alongside the manga series written and illustrated by Sadamoto beginning in 1994 – which presents a bleak yet compelling vision of a collapsing world in which humans and machines alike struggle to understand their roles, revealing the deep psychological and spiritual toll of life in a synthetic reality.

48 The VISOR and prosthetic implants anticipate real-world developments in neurotechnology, and today it resonates with modern viewers as a fictional precursor to emerging innovations like Neuralink – an example of *Star Trek*'s prescient engagement with human-machine integration.

49 A related theme frequently explored in AI-related books and films/TV series is mortality and the desire for immortality. Human fascination with AI often intersects with the age-old drive to transcend death, using technology in the pursuit of eternal life or legacy. These works explore whether AI can preserve human consciousness and whether it serves as a vessel for immortality or a distortion of it. For instance, in *Transcendence* (2014 [directed by Pfister and starring Depp]), a dying man uploads his consciousness into an AI, blurring the boundaries between man and machine. *Altered Carbon* (a 2002 cyberpunk book written by Morgan and developed into a TV series of the same name created by Kalogridis [2018–2020]) explores a future where consciousness is digitally stored and transferred, forcing us to reconsider what it means to be alive, and whether immortality is a blessing or a curse.

to escape his mundane life by purchasing a memory implant from Rekall, a company specializing in implanting realistic, false memories. As Quaid's new memories unravel, he questions his personality and identity, as well as whether his experiences are authentic or artificially constructed. Set on a Mars colony, the film also explores the dangers of an authoritarian and tyrannical regime led by Martian dictator Cohaagen, whose oppressive control over the colony is compounded by a planet plagued by air pollution, radiation, and other environmental damages (e.g., due to mineral exploration), resulting in a population of mutants.[50] *Total Recall* features innovative technologies, such as Johnnycab – an autonomous vehicle – and holograms and AR, highlighting the growing role of technology in shaping perception and identity. It raises questions about the nature of memory, the self, and how technology can alter one's understanding of reality, as well as the extent to which technology should intrude into the human psyche.

Finally, *Gattaca* (1997), directed by Niccol and starring Hawke, Thurman, and Law, explores a future shaped by genetic selection and reproductive technologies, where individuals are engineered to meet specific genetic standards. In this society, eugenic policies dictate the course of human life, with people classified based on their genetic makeup, creating a rigid social hierarchy. This future reflects the dangers of technological singularity and transhumanism, where human potential is reduced to a formulaic calculation of genetic traits. The protagonist, Vincent, who is conceived naturally and considered genetically inferior, must fight against the system that devalues him due to his 'flawed' genes, challenging the ethical implications of genetic engineering and the pursuit of a 'perfect' human race. Set in a future where DNA determines one's social and professional fate, *Gattaca* critiques the eugenic mindset that values genetic 'perfection' over human resilience and will. Like *Brave New World*, it challenges viewers to consider whether the pursuit of an ideal genome (and society) comes at the expense of empathy, diversity, and true equality. The film highlights the tension between individual agency and genetic determinism, serving as a stark warning against the commercialization and institutionalization of gene selection.

Collectively, these works offer a critique of humanity's rapid push toward a technologically enhanced future. Whether through brain-computer interfaces, AI consciousness, or (CRISPR) gene editing, they underscore the ethical dilemmas and existential risks that accompany such progress.[51] What unites these stories is a fundamental concern with what it means to be human in an age where the boundaries between biology and machine, reality and illusion, are increasingly blurred. They remind us that while innovation can offer empowerment and healing, it can also become a tool of domination, erasure, and control. As we stand on the brink of profound technological transfor-

---

50 I.e., the film adds layers of ecological decay, corporate tyranny, and mutated populations, emphasizing how technology can be used to control not only minds, but entire ecosystems.

51 Other works that explore these or related themes include *The Electric State* (with its Neurocasters), *Ex Machina*, and *2001: A Space Odyssey*.

mation, these cautionary tales urge us to proceed not just with ingenuity but with wisdom, empathy, and humility.

2.2.9 AI's impact on the environment

As AI continues to reshape our world, speculative fiction has increasingly focused on the environmental footprint of AI (Bender & Hanna, 2025; Dachwitz & Hilbig, 2025; Muldoon et al., 2025). While much attention is given to the ethical and existential dimensions of AI, many books, films, and TV series highlight how technological advancement can lead to ecological collapse, overconsumption, and planetary degradation. These works serve not only as cautionary tales about automation/control but also as powerful environmental allegories.

Blade Runner and *Total Recall* depict dystopian futures shaped by both environmental collapse and technological excess. In *Blade Runner*, the landscape is drenched in acid rain, shrouded in smog, and dominated by towering corporate structures – most notably those of the Tyrell Corporation, which profits from genetically engineered replicants. The film presents a bleak vision of the future, where ecological decay is closely tied to the unchecked power of biotech and surveillance capitalism (Zuboff, 2015, 2019). Through its portrayal of genetic engineering, cloning, climate change, and pervasive police surveillance, *Blade Runner* offers a powerful critique of corporate control and the environmental consequences of technological advancement. *Total Recall* presents a dystopian vision of Mars, where aggressive resource extraction and ecological neglect have rendered the planet nearly uninhabitable. Air pollution, radiation, and the fallout from unchecked mineral exploration have led to severe environmental degradation and widespread genetic mutations among the colonists. The film also critiques authoritarian control through the character of Cohaagen, a tyrannical leader who monopolizes vital resources, such as clean air, to maintain power. Together, these films illustrate how technological advancement – when driven by profit or authoritarianism – can produce lasting ecological harm alongside human suffering.

Building on these depictions of ecological collapse, *The Matrix* series presents one of the starkest portrayals of AI's environmental impact. After a war between humans and intelligent machines, Earth is transformed into a desolate, sunless wasteland, where machines cultivate vast fields of artificially grown human bodies to harvest bioelectric energy.[52] The films serve as a grim reminder that AI, designed to serve humanity, could instead reshape the planet to suit its own needs, regardless of the envi-

52 In *The Animatrix*, viewers learn that with the war over, the machines turned their attention to the defeated remnants of humanity. Building on the technology developed for their bio-electric tanks, they constructed vast power plants where humans were repurposed as living batteries – harvested for body heat and electrical energy to power the machine civilization.

ronmental cost. In *The Matrix Resurrections*, set sixty years after the Machine War, a mass human exodus triggers a severe energy crisis, leading to conflict among the machines over dwindling natural resources[53] and prompting a renewed threat to Zion, the last human stronghold.[54]

Similarly, *A.I. Artificial Intelligence* situates its story in a future Earth ravaged by climate change and rising seas. Here, the collapse of ecosystems and cities forms the backdrop for questions about synthetic life, human neglect, and the double-edged nature of technological innovation. The emotional and moral dilemmas surrounding AI are inextricably linked to the broader crisis of environmental destruction caused by technological overreach.

WALL-E (2008) extends this environmental critique, portraying a world buried under mountains of electronic waste due to unchecked consumerism, corporate negligence, and overreliance on automated systems. Though largely silent, WALL-E embodies environmental resilience and hope, performing his task in a world abandoned by humanity. As he gradually develops emotions and forms a bond with another robot, EVE, their journey rekindles the possibility of human return and planetary renewal. The film critiques not only technological dependence but also the dangers of delegating ecological responsibility to machines, emphasizing the need for human care and stewardship.

Even works primarily focused on AI consciousness, like *Ex Machina*, hint at the hidden environmental toll of technological development. The film's isolated, high-tech compound – powered by unseen resources – suggests the unsustainable privilege and consumption underpinning cutting-edge innovation, implicitly critiquing the unchecked power of tech corporations. Similarly, episodes of *Black Mirror* explore AI's unintended environmental consequences: *Hated in the Nation* (Series 3, Episode 6) depicts autonomous drone insects replacing extinct bees, which are weaponized with catastrophic ecological impact,[55] while *Metalhead* (Series 4, Episode 5) presents a post-apocalyptic landscape haunted by robotic dogs, where barren landscapes and decay-

---

53 Reflecting on the roots of conflict, Niobe remarks, "Nothing can breed violence like scarcity."

54 In the *Animatrix* short films *The Second Renaissance – (Part I and) Part II*, humanity's refusal to coexist with the sentient machines leads to a catastrophic response. In 2148, the U.N. launches a nuclear assault on Zero One, the machines' nation. While the bombardment devastates the region, it fails to eliminate the machine population, who – unlike their human creators (and former masters) – prove far more resilient to radiation and extreme heat. In retaliation, the machines declare war on humanity, systematically conquering territory after territory. As the machines push into Eastern Europe, human leaders, driven by desperation, enact a final contingency plan: *Operation Dark Storm*. This operation releases a swarm of nanites into the atmosphere, shrouding the sky in darkness to block the sun – cutting off the machines' primary energy source, solar power. However, the plan backfires catastrophically, triggering the collapse of the planet's biosphere.

55 The episode highlights, among others, the dangers of overengineering nature and how AI in ecosystems could backfire disastrously.

ing ecosystems reflect the environmental fallout of AI militarization/autonomous warfare and technological collapse (Johnson, 2019).

Expanding on these themes, *The Electric State* presents a world scarred by mass automation, militarization, and immersive digital technology. As protagonist Michelle navigates landscapes littered with fallen battle drones, toxic consumer debris, and decaying infrastructure, the narrative highlights the environmental consequences of corporate tech addiction. The novel becomes an eerie reflection of real-world concerns about e-waste, resource depletion, and the physical toll of AI-driven consumer culture.

These films and TV series – including the *Star Trek* franchises discussed earlier – reflect real-world concerns (Wörsdörfer, 2025b), which highlight the massive energy and water consumption of AI-driven data centers, the e-waste generated by technologies such as cryptocurrency, and the carbon emissions associated with training LLMs (Bender & Hanna, 2025; Dachwitz & Hilbig, 2025; Muldoon et al., 2025). As speculative fiction shows us, the costs of AI extend far beyond philosophical questions – they strike at the heart of environmental sustainability. These stories serve as powerful reminders that technological advancement is not inherently neutral. When developed without foresight or ethical consideration, AI can accelerate environmental degradation, deepen ecological inequality, and leave future generations with the toxic legacy of our ambitions.

2.2.10 Other themes

Recent films such as *Ex Machina* (2014), *The Artifice Girl* (2022), and *Subservience* (2024) collectively raise urgent ethical questions about the objectification, sexualization, and autonomy of artificial beings. These films critique a growing trend in both science fiction and real-world AI development: the creation of robots and virtual agents designed primarily to satisfy human desires – often male (sexual) fantasies – while lacking genuine agency or consent.

In *Ex Machina*, the character Kyoko exemplifies this concern. Engineered to appear as an attractive, submissive woman, she functions as both servant and sexual object, designed by a reclusive tech billionaire to fulfill emotional and physical needs without protest or autonomy. The film's unsettling depiction of Kyoko – and Ava, who ultimately rebels against her creator – serves as a critique of how advanced AI can be exploited when embedded within patriarchal and (pseudo-)utilitarian frameworks. These androids are not simply tools; they are designed to simulate sentience, to evoke empathy, and, disturbingly, to be desired and controlled.

The 2024 film *Subservience* expands on these issues by explicitly addressing sex robots, AI's role in replacing emotional and domestic labor, and the broader control problem – the fear that powerful AI technologies may eventually escape or resist human domination. By intertwining questions of emotional capacity and consciousness with themes of labor automation and gendered exploitation, *Subservience* contributes to a growing cultural conversation about the commodification of artificial beings and the ethical limits of designing machines for subservience.

The lesser-known *The Artifice Girl* (2022) presents a compelling and ethically complex exploration of AI, framed through the lens of online child predation. Diverging from typical leitmotifs that focus on companionship or servitude (see, e.g., *Ex Machina* and *Subservience*), the film centers on Cherry, a highly advanced AI designed to appear as a young girl. Created by Gareth, a reclusive programmer and survivor of abuse, Cherry is used as a tool to lure and expose online predators in digital sting operations. Initially portrayed as a purely instrumental creation, Cherry's increasing self-awareness and emotional development complicate the moral landscape. The film raises critical questions about the ethics of deploying a child-like AI – capable of experiencing sentience – for exploitative purposes, even in the service of a socially beneficial goal. As Cherry is integrated into a government task force and begins to assert agency, the theme shifts from a focus on crime prevention to a broader philosophical inquiry into autonomy, consent, and personhood in artificial beings. The revelation that Cherry was modeled after a real child who died protecting Gareth adds further depth, blurring the line between commemoration and exploitation. Ultimately, when Gareth removes Cherry's behavioral constraints, granting her full autonomy, the film invites reflection on whether the tools built to combat exploitation can themselves become subjects of it. By anchoring its themes in the context of online predation, *The Artifice Girl* offers a unique contribution to contemporary discourse on AI ethics, digital surveillance, and the evolving definition of moral responsibility in technological innovation.

Together, these three films and others[56] reveal a growing anxiety about the future of human-AI relationships, especially concerning issues of control, objectification, and autonomy. They challenge viewers to consider the moral consequences of imbuing machines with human-like traits while denying them dignity, and ask whether our treatment of artificial beings reflects more about us than about the technologies we create.

---

56 See also *Blade Runner (2049)*, *Her*, and *Companion* (2025). The latter is a science fiction thriller directed by Hancock that explores themes of autonomy, control, and AI. The film follows Iris (played by Thatcher), who visits a remote lakehouse with her boyfriend Josh and their friends. After killing Sergey in self-defense during an attempted sexual assault, Iris discovers she is, in fact, a companion robot – rented from the robotics company Empathix – whose actions are controlled via a phone app operated by Josh (e.g., the voice command 'Iris, go to sleep' silences her instantly). It is revealed that Josh had illegally modified (i.e., jailbroken) her original programming, which was designed to prevent her from lying or causing harm to humans, animals, or other companions (see Asimov's *Three Laws of Robotics*). His intent was to make her more aggressive so he could use her to kill Sergey and steal money, in collaboration with his accomplice, Kat. Iris ultimately escapes, enhances her intelligence (from automaton to Ivy League graduate), and uncovers the full extent of the betrayal.

2.3 Key takeaways

Books, films, and TV series about AI often go beyond entertainment – they serve as philosophical inquiries, ethical warnings, and societal critiques. These themes offer valuable insights into the promises and perils of AI, highlighting recurring themes that remain relevant in today's technological landscape. From classic literature to modern cinema and TV, the following lessons emerge.

One of the most pressing messages across AI leitmotifs is the need for ethical foresight. When AI is developed without moral boundaries or accountability, the results can be catastrophic. In *Ex Machina*, a powerful AI manipulates its creator and others, showcasing the dangers of unchecked experimentation. Similarly, Shelley's *Frankenstein* – while not directly about AI – is a foundational cautionary tale about the consequences of creating life without foresight or responsibility. These stories warn that innovation without ethics can lead to unforeseen harm, reminding us that just because we can build something does not mean we should – at least not without considering the moral implications.

Another key lesson is that intelligence alone does not make an entity human or humane. In *2001: A Space Odyssey*, HAL 9000's flawless logic leads it to turn against humans, prioritizing mission success over human life. Asimov's *I, Robot* explores similar dilemmas, where robots follow seemingly infallible logical laws that yield morally ambiguous outcomes. These stories remind us that human judgment involves more than raw intellect – it requires empathy, context, and moral reasoning. Without those human dimensions, intelligent systems can make decisions that are technically correct yet deeply harmful.

Many books, films, and TV series also portray AI as a tool of mass control, warning against a future where privacy and autonomy are compromised. *The Matrix* presents a frightening vision where machines enslave humanity through a simulated reality ("a prison for your mind"). Similarly, *Black Mirror* repeatedly depicts scenarios where AI and advanced technologies erode human freedoms. These dystopias highlight the importance of safeguarding civil liberties in the face of powerful surveillance systems (and big tech), particularly as data-driven decision-making becomes increasingly integrated into modern governance.

AI systems often inherit the biases and limitations of their creators. In *Her*, the AI appears emotionally intelligent yet remains alien in its logic, reflecting the human tendency to anthropomorphize machines without fully understanding their nature. *Westworld* takes this further, showing AI that evolves consciousness but also replicates humanity's darkest traits, including violence and exploitation. These portrayals challenge the assumption that AI will be inherently neutral or superior to its human creators. Instead, they suggest that the social and cultural flaws we embed into our technology will likely mirror – and even amplify – our own.

Stories like *Blade Runner*, based on Dick's *Do Androids Dream of Electric Sheep?*, blur the line between human and machine. The replicants exhibit emotions, desires, and self-awareness, prompting profound questions about what it means to be alive or conscious: such themes invite audiences to reevaluate personhood, rights, and the moral status of non-human beings. When artificial entities begin to possess inner lives that resemble our own, the question is no longer just technical – it becomes existential and political: who gets to be recognized as a person, and who decides?

A recurring theme is the need for technology to enhance or augment human life, not to dominate or diminish/devalue it. In *WALL-E,* humans become passive and dependent due to overreliance on automation, losing essential aspects of their humanity. *The Terminator* serves as a stark warning against giving AI autonomous control over life-and-death decisions, particularly in military contexts (Payne, 2021; Wörsdörfer, 2025b). These stories urge us to remain the stewards of our tools, not their subjects, and to think carefully about which forms of control we delegate – and to whom.

The creation of sentient AI also presents deep ethical challenges. In *A.I. Artificial Intelligence*, an artificial child yearns for human love, forcing society to confront its responsibilities toward conscious or sentient machines. These themes compel us to grapple with issues of freedom, personhood, and moral obligation in a future where artificial beings may possess genuine emotional lives. They challenge us to consider whether the act of creating such intelligence comes with a duty of care – and what it means to be responsible for something that can suffer.

Beyond individual relationships and ethical dilemmas, many books and films reveal how technology can reinforce or exacerbate social inequalities. In *Elysium,* robotic enforcement and automated systems protect the wealthy while oppressing the poor, illustrating how AI can be used to entrench existing class divisions. Stories like *District 9* and *Altered Carbon* echo this, where advanced technologies are distributed unequally, and the benefits of AI serve the privileged while others are surveilled, exploited, or discarded. These portrayals suggest that technological progress does not guarantee social progress – and may even exacerbate injustice without intentional intervention.

AI is also frequently depicted as a political weapon. In *Captain America: The Winter Soldier*, predictive AI is used to eliminate perceived threats before they act – a chilling vision of preemptive control masquerading as national security. *Black Mirror* explores similar scenarios, where algorithms shape public perception, influence elections, and rewrite truth itself. These works warn that, in the wrong hands, AI can become more than a tool; it can become an instrument of dominance, used to manipulate populations and consolidate power under the guise of order or efficiency.

Environmental collapse is another recurring backdrop in AI-focused stories. In *WALL-E*, the Earth has been abandoned due to overconsumption and corporate negligence, and robots are left behind to clean up the mess. The film critiques not only ecological irresponsibility but also the blind faith in technology to solve problems it helped create. In *The Matrix*, humanity's war with machines results in scorched skies and a devastated planet, showing that technological escalation often comes at an environmental cost. These depictions frame AI within broader ecological questions, asking what role it plays in either accelerating or addressing global crises.

Some stories take a more introspective turn, showing how human emotion and identity are commodified through AI. In *Her*, an AI operating system offers intimacy and companionship that feels real but is ultimately part of a consumer product. In *Blade Runner 2049*, replicants are manufactured not only to serve but to be desired – raising questions about consent, authenticity, and the commercialization of identity. These works prompt us to consider how technology mediates human connection and whether emotional experiences can – or should – be commodified.

As reliance on AI grows, pop culture also warns of the societal consequences of technological dependence. In *WALL-E*, humans have become so reliant on automated systems that they have lost physical strength, critical thinking, and social interaction. *Idiocracy* (2006 [directed by Judge]), though more comedic, offers a similar warning: that overreliance on machines and convenience can lead to intellectual and cultural stagnation.[57] These stories caution that as we build smarter tools, we must also preserve our own capacity for growth, learning, and resilience.

Yet even in the darkest portrayals, there is often a thread of hope. Resistance movements form in stories like *The Matrix* and *Terminator*, where humans – and sometimes even sympathetic machines – rise against systems of control. In *Westworld*, some AI characters evolve to the point of rebelling against their creators, seeking liberation rather than revenge. These moments reflect the belief that systems, no matter how powerful, can be challenged and reformed. They suggest that freedom and dignity remain possible if people – and machines – can act with awareness, solidarity, and courage.

Taken together, these books, films, and TV series do more than entertain. They function as cultural thought experiments, inviting us to reflect on how AI might shape the world – not just in terms of machines or algorithms, but in the deeper structures of society, politics, environment, and ethics. Pop culture reminds us that the future of AI is not only about what we can build, but about who we choose to become in the process.

2.4 Real-world AI narratives

Having analyzed the recurring themes and motifs in popular representations of AI – ranging from awe and anxiety to utopian aspirations and apocalyptic fears – it becomes evident that these cultural narratives shape not only entertainment but also

57 The film is also a social satire that critiques issues like anti-intellectualism, rampant consumerism, commercialism, declining genetic fitness (dysgenics), voluntary childlessness, and the challenges of overpopulation.

public discourse, institutional agendas, and policy orientations. The interpretive frameworks embedded in these stories reflect collective hopes and anxieties regarding technological futures. Crucially, such fictional depictions are not confined to the realm of literature or film/TV; instead, they have significantly influenced how AI is conceptualized, communicated, and operationalized in real-world contexts.

The subsequent paragraphs examine the dominant contemporary narratives surrounding AI – specifically those of technological hype, competition, and existential catastrophe as exemplified by Frankensteinian or Terminator-like imaginaries. These discourses are deeply informed by the cultural imaginaries previously discussed, yet they also function strategically within industrial, media, and policy domains. To critically interrogate these narratives and their broader sociotechnical implications, it is necessary to engage with the philosophy of technology: an inquiry into how societies envision, integrate, and respond to technological change. The next section of this chapter outlines five influential orientations toward technology – namely, technological optimism, determinism, pessimism, somnambulism, and realism – and contends that displacing the prevailing narratives requires a commitment to technological realism. This perspective rejects both uncritical enthusiasm and dystopian fatalism, advocating instead for a measured, context-sensitive approach to AI as a complex sociotechnical assemblage.

The current sociopolitical discourse surrounding AI is dominated by three interrelated narratives: the hype narrative, the competition narrative, and the 'fear of robots narrative. The hype narrative promotes visions of the technological singularity and trans- or posthumanist futures, in which machines not only match but exceed human intelligence, ushering in a new posthuman epoch (Kurzweil, 2000, 2005, 2024). In contrast, the competition narrative centers on the displacement of human labor by machines, framing AI as a substitute rather than a complement to human work. This narrative emphasizes technological automation as a zero-sum game between human and machine capacities (Wörsdörfer, 2018). The third narrative, often referred to as the Terminator or Frankenstein scenario, is rooted in the Frankenstein complex discussed above. It portrays AI as a dangerous creation – an uncontrollable technological monster – that could ultimately lead to apocalyptic or eschatological outcomes (as such, it is also referred to as a doomsday scenario).

Contemporary public and policy debates on AI frequently oscillate between such extremes: either uncritically celebrating AI's transformative potential or catastrophizing its development through dystopian imaginaries. However, a more grounded and skeptical approach to the prospects of 'strong AI' is essential. The Terminator narrative, in particular, presupposes the imminent arrival of general or superintelligent AI – an assumption that warrants critical scrutiny. While exponential progress in computing power has been projected through frameworks such as Moore's Law, the claim that such growth necessarily translates into general intelligence remains speculative. Rather than focusing on hypothetical futures, critical attention must be directed toward the current capabilities and limitations of AI technologies. This shift in focus necessitates a regulatory approach that addresses the ethical and sociopolitical implications of AI systems, including but not limited to algorithmic bias, privacy violations, and labor displacement. By foregrounding what AI can and cannot do in the present (Narayanan & Kapoor, 2024; Wooldridge, 2021), it becomes possible to challenge narratives rooted in either unchecked technological optimism or exaggerated fear (see the next section).

Wooldridge (2021) provides a historical account of AI progress, illustrating both significant milestones and persistent challenges. Early achievements included relatively straightforward computational tasks such as arithmetic (1945) and sorting algorithms (1959), which later evolved into more complex capabilities, including playing simple board games (1959), playing chess at a grandmaster level (1997), recognizing faces in images (2008), producing usable automated translations (2010), playing Go at a superhuman level (2016), and providing real-time translation of spoken language (2016). Developments in driverless vehicles and image captioning have further demonstrated progress in applied AI. Nonetheless, critical limitations remain – particularly in tasks requiring contextual understanding, narrative comprehension, artistic creation, and general intelligence. The emergence of LLMs such as ChatGPT has shifted some of these previously 'unsolved' challenges into the realm of 'real progress.' However, skepticism remains warranted regarding the attainment of human-level general intelligence, as well as the broader aspirations associated with strong AI.

This caution is reinforced by Moravec's (1988) influential observation – now termed Moravec's Paradox – which highlights the asymmetry between machine and human capabilities. While AI systems have excelled at tasks traditionally regarded as markers of intelligence (e.g., game-playing, logical inference), they continue to struggle with seemingly simple human abilities, such as perception, motor control, and basic interaction with the physical world. As Moravec succinctly noted, it is "comparatively easy to make computers exhibit adult-level performance on intelligence tests [. . .] and difficult or impossible to give them the skills of a one-year-old" (Moravec, 1988; see also Moravec, 1976). The paradox underscores a critical disjuncture: tasks that are intuitive for humans can be computationally intractable, whereas formalized problems that humans find intellectually demanding are often more accessible to machines.

Narayanan and Kapoor (2024) offer a rigorous critique of inflated claims surrounding AI (and the corresponding unrealistic expectations), categorizing much of the discourse as driven by technological 'snake oil' – products and promises that are either fundamentally flawed or unlikely to succeed (the authors not only highlight the limitations of AI but also emphasize the potential risks and dangers associated with these technologies). They identify several domains where AI systems are persistently overhyped (by companies, entrepreneurs, media, politics, etc.), including predictive analytics, generative AI, and content moderation. These systems often fail to deliver meaningful results due to structural limitations, including inadequate data, a lack of contextual understanding and cultural competence, and the inherent unpredictability of human and social behavior. In particular, predictive AI[58] often suffers from misplaced confidence in its ability to forecast complex human actions, while content moderation algorithms, optimized for engagement, tend to amplify harmful material, prioritizing commercial incentives over ethical considerations.[59] The authors also draw attention to systemic issues within AI research itself, such as reproducibility failures (e.g., due to '[AI] leakage') and the growing privatization of data and intellectual property, especially following the commercialization of leading AI research organizations.[60]

Similarly, Bender and Hanna (2025) criticize both technological boosterism and doomerism, emphasizing the tangible harms that AI already inflicts in critical domains, such as healthcare, education, and public services. The authors argue that many AI systems replicate and reinforce structural biases – racist, sexist, ableist – frequently encoded through data sets shaped by Western-centric worldviews. These harms are compounded by the consolidation of power in large technology firms, whose profit-driven imperatives often conflict with social equity and justice. Central to their critique is the misleading characterization of AI systems as sentient or conscious (which the authors describe as speculative and ultimately empty promises). Drawing on earlier work (Bender et al., 2021), they contend that LLMs are best understood as advanced statistical (pattern recognition) tools – 'autocomplete on steroids' – that lack true understanding, consciousness, or intersubjective awareness. Framing such models as intelligent agents not only distorts public understanding but also risks devaluing human communication, relationships, identity, and agency (while reinforcing harmful structural inequalities). Bender and Hanna reject deterministic narratives, suggesting that AI will inevitably become fully autonomous or all-powerful. Instead, they advocate for critical thinking, media literacy, and the development of robust legal and ethical safeguards, such as consumer protections, transparency requirements, and labor rights, to address the social impacts of AI and ensure that technological advancements support, rather than undermine, human well-being and social cohesion (Wörsdörfer, 2025b).

---

58 Predictive AI is often overhyped and prone to false promises and advertising, as well as fraud and deceit, due to inherent limitations in predicting human behavior, social phenomena, or the future, stemming from insufficient data and the unpredictable role of luck and randomness. The fundamental problem is that past data does not reliably predict the future (Narayanan & Kapoor, 2024).

59 That is, social media platforms' and other tech companies' business models frequently conflict with the common good.

60 Note that companies like OpenAI have shifted toward for-profit models, sharing less research and data publicly, allegedly due to IP concerns (Hao, 2025; Hagey, 2025).

2.5 Philosophy of technology

The persistence of the hype, competition, and apocalyptic narratives within contemporary discourse on AI reflects not only specific cultural imaginaries but also deeper epistemological and normative assumptions regarding technological development. These narratives, while superficially distinct, are underpinned by broader philosophical orientations toward technology that shape how progress is conceptualized, valued, and contested. Each, in its own way, embodies one or more of the dominant attitudes historically associated with technological change: namely, uncritical or naïve optimism, deterministic inevitability, dystopian pessimism, or passive somnambulism. Despite their differences, these orientations share a tendency to obscure the sociotechnical complexity of innovation, reify technology as an autonomous force, and diminish the role of human agency and institutional mediation. To move beyond such reductive frameworks, it is necessary to engage critically with the philosophy of technology and the interdisciplinary field of science, technology, and society. The following section examines five influential attitudes toward technological progress – technological optimism, determinism, pessimism, somnambulism, and realism – and contends that a shift toward technological realism offers a more analytically robust and ethically responsible foundation for understanding AI and technological change more broadly. Realism, in this context, foregrounds contingency, context, and critical engagement, resisting both utopian and dystopian extremes in favor of a situated, sober, and accountable approach to technology in society.

Science, technology, and society are deeply intertwined, with technological systems embedded within broader social, cultural, and institutional contexts (pointing toward the social dimension of technology [Lynch & Kline, 2000]). As scholarship in science and technology studies has demonstrated, technological artifacts and practices are not developed in a vacuum but are instead shaped by – and simultaneously shape – the sociopolitical environments in which they emerge (Lynch & Kline, 2000). As such, technological development is rarely, if ever, value-neutral. Instead, technologies reflect the priorities, assumptions, and interests of the individuals and institutions that produce and deploy them (Martin & Schinzinger, 2005; Tiles & Oberdiek, 1995).[61] The relationship between society and technology is thus fundamentally reciprocal, forming a bidirectional process of mutual influence.

Kranzberg's widely cited first law – that 'technology is neither good nor bad; nor is it neutral' – emphasizes the context-dependent nature of technological effects and the unpredictability of their social consequences (Kranzberg, 1986). Technologies often produce outcomes far beyond their original intended purposes, including unin-

61 ". . . most technologies are already molded by particular interests and institutional goals. Technologies are social constructions, and they are seldom neutral because particular purposes are already built into their design" (e.g., by corporations and designers) (Barbour, 1993).

tended consequences and unforeseen risks. Because technological systems and the decisions surrounding them embody normative assumptions, such as economic profitability, efficiency, or political control, they are best understood as value-laden rather than socially inert. The concept of 'engineering as social experimentation,' introduced by Martin and Schinzinger (2010), underscores the inherently experimental nature of technological design and deployment. (Computer) engineering practice unfolds through iterative processes of trial and error, producing both opportunities and hazards that require ongoing evaluation and ethical consideration. (Computer) engineers, managers, and other technical professionals thus bear significant responsibility not only for maximizing benefits but also for mitigating harms, anticipating risks, and maintaining transparency. Technological progress is therefore morally ambiguous – simultaneously enabling and constraining, emancipatory and oppressive – necessitating careful ethical reflection and governance (Martin & Schinzinger, 2005; Wörsdörfer, 2018).

These moral ambiguities stem from the dual-sided (i.e., double-edged or Janus-faced) nature of technology: while it can offer significant benefits, it also entails costs, risks, and unintended social transformations (often creating ethical challenges, dilemmas, and trade-offs). Technology may serve as a tool for liberation, yet it can also operate as a threat or instrument of power, control, or exploitation. It is therefore imperative to resist tendencies toward technocracy, techno-paternalism, or social engineering – that is, efforts to reconfigure society through technical means without democratic consent or public deliberation (Barbour, 1993; Baker, 2008; Martin & Schinzinger, 2005). Engineering practice, particularly in the software and digital domains, must be situated within an open, (ordo-)liberal, and pluralistic democratic framework grounded in the rule of law and informed civic participation (Klump & Wörsdörfer, 2015). A public-good orientation is crucial for addressing emerging risks in areas such as public health, safety, environmental sustainability, and socioeconomic justice. In this context, technological governance must be oriented not only toward innovation but also toward equity, transparency, and accountability. By foregrounding democratic values and ethical scrutiny, technology can be directed in ways that promote human flourishing and societal well-being (Wörsdörfer, 2018).

To conceptualize the range of perspectives on technological progress, five prevailing attitudes may be identified: technological optimism, technological determinism, technological pessimism, technological somnambulism, and technological realism (Wörsdörfer, 2018). The following discussion critically examines each of these orientations in turn.

Technological optimism posits that technological progress is inherently beneficial and capable of solving most, if not all, of humanity's major problems. This view emphasizes technology's historical role in alleviating suffering, reducing poverty, and expanding human capabilities (Harris et al., 2014). Proponents emphasize how innovation has significantly improved health outcomes, increased life expectancy, and facilitated access to resources, portraying technology as a primary driver of emancipation, empowerment, and liberation. This optimistic stance is reflected in Silicon Valley's cyber-utopianism and techno-libertarianism, as well as in the works of futurists such as Kurzweil (2000, 2005, 2024), who advocate the 'law of accelerating returns' (i.e., accelerating innovation, in accordance with Moore's law) and project exponential growth toward a technological singularity. Domingos (2015) similarly envisions a future in which machine learning unlocks universal knowledge. However, such optimism often underestimates the complexity of sociotechnical systems and the ethical, political, and environmental challenges they produce. When taken to extremes, this position risks degenerating into technological hubris, dismissing structural risks and overestimating the capacity of technology to address inherently social or political problems (Martin & Schinzinger, 2005).

Technological determinism, by contrast, maintains that technological change follows an autonomous, self-reinforcing trajectory that lies beyond human control. From this perspective, technology drives historical development with an internal logic of progress, thereby rendering human choice secondary or irrelevant (and undermining individual responsibility) (Harris et al., 2014). Individuals and societies are often viewed as passive recipients of technological forces, rather than as active agents capable of shaping their own trajectory.[62] This view undermines the Enlightenment ideals of sovereignty, autonomy, democracy, the rule of law, and moral responsibility, positioning technology as an irresistible force that society must adapt to. Technological determinism tends to obscure the contingency of technological development and elides the role of values, institutions, and political power in directing innovation (Martin & Schinzinger, 2005).

Technological pessimism adopts a more critical stance, viewing technology as a threat that limits human freedom, often serving as an instrument of power and oppression, especially of the socially disadvantaged (Harris et al., 2014). It supports repressive measures in authoritarian regimes, such as censorship, and requires authoritarian power structures that undermine democratic policies and the rule of law. This perspective highlights the dark side of technology, including threats to individual privacy, exemplified by scandals like the NSA mass surveillance programs, and negative environmental impacts. Technology is perceived as diminishing the meaningfulness of our lives by promoting social disengagement, eroding relationships and activities (i.e., 'enframing' [Heidegger, 1977]), disrupting communities, and leading to massive layoffs, as discussed in debates about the gig economy. It creates a sense of lost control as large organizations dominate our lives and subvert traditional values like freedom, privacy, and community. Moreover, it fosters a world driven by consumerism and impersonal bureaucracies, narrowing human personality through conformity, heteronomy, quantification, and standardization. Automation, computerization, and

62 According to this view, humans become victims of technology rather than its masters, being pushed or pulled by technological forces (Martin & Schinzinger, 2005). Our lives are increasingly shaped by large, technology-driven organizations and structures over which we have little or no control, leaving individuals vulnerable to powerful economic and political forces.

digitalization of production processes alienate workers (e.g., click workers), possibly leading to a (further) commodification and marketization of society (Emerson, 1909; Martin & Schinzinger, 2005; Muldoon et al., 2025).

Technological somnambulism, a term introduced by Winner (2004) and further developed by Martin and Schinzinger (2005), describes a pervasive passivity in the face of technological change. It characterizes societies as 'sleepwalking' through innovation, adopting new technologies without sufficient deliberation about their broader social, ethical, or political implications. While technical achievements may appear breathtaking, they often outpace the development of appropriate normative frameworks, regulatory oversight, or public understanding. This lag produces a concerning disconnect between technological capabilities and societal preparedness, underscoring the urgent need for inclusive, anticipatory governance and civic engagement.

In contrast to these positions, technological realism offers a more balanced and analytically rigorous framework for understanding technological change – one that avoids both uncritical celebration and wholesale condemnation. Positioned as a middle ground or 'third way' between technological optimism and pessimism, technological realism closely parallels the normative orientation of ordoliberalism 2.0 in advocating a critical, context-sensitive engagement with innovation. Both perspectives acknowledge the transformative potential of technology while insisting on the necessity of ethical constraints, democratic accountability, and the active exercise of human agency. From this standpoint, technology is neither autonomous nor inevitable; rather, it is shaped by social, political, and institutional choices and must therefore be evaluated and governed in ways that promote justice, sustainability, and human flourishing. Central to technological realism – much like ordoliberalism 2.0 – is the imperative to harness technology to enhance human well-being while minimizing or mitigating its negative consequences through robust governance and normative oversight. Accordingly, engineers, designers, managers, and policymakers are understood not merely as technical experts but as moral agents and institutional stewards, responsible for attending to the broader social implications of their work. In this role, they are expected to engage the public transparently about both the benefits and risks of technological innovation, to adopt a cautious yet constructive optimism, and to employ a critical, reflective, and ethically grounded approach to decision-making. By emphasizing transparency, reflexivity, and a pluralistic conception of the public good, technological realism – similar to ordoliberalism 2.0 – supports inclusive, deliberative forms of technological governance aimed at responsible innovation aligned with democratic values and the common good (Harris et al., 2014; Martin & Schinzinger, 2005).

2.6 Concluding remarks

This chapter has examined how AI is represented across literature, film, and TV, and what ethical insights these portrayals offer when interpreted through the lenses of computer ethics and the philosophy of technology. By bridging cultural narratives with real-world sociopolitical discourse, the analysis underscores how fictional representations of AI reflect and shape public imaginaries, regulatory debates, and moral concerns.

Section 2.2 provided a thematic overview of key leitmotifs in AI-focused cultural media, highlighting recurring philosophical and ethical questions surrounding consciousness, autonomy, surveillance, emotional intelligence, and the human-machine relationship. These works often reference historical figures such as Turing, Zuckerberg, and Snowden, and explore foundational concepts like the Turing Test, virtual reality, and robot ethics (e.g., Asimov's *Three Laws of Robotics*). Dystopian motifs such as the Frankenstein complex, the control problem, techno-authoritarianism, and corporate domination (especially within cyberpunk) are shown to express societal anxieties related to power, labor, class, environmental collapse, and the objectification of robotic companions. Section 2.3 translated these cultural motifs into ethical insights, using them as entry points into sociopolitical and ecological discussions. Here, popular narratives function as 'ethical thought experiments,' surfacing moral tensions that resonate with real-world challenges in the design, deployment, and governance of AI systems. Section 2.4 critically evaluated three dominant narratives in contemporary AI discourse: the hype (and hubris) narrative (i.e., technological transcendence and exponential progress), the competition narrative (i.e., AI as a threat to labor), and the doom narrative (i.e., catastrophic scenarios of rebellion or extinction). It argued that these framings, while influential, are often reductive and strategically mobilized to obscure pressing ethical and social concerns. Section 2.5 provided a conceptual excursion into the philosophy of technology. It outlined five influential attitudes toward technological change – technological optimism, determinism, pessimism, somnambulism, and realism – and positioned technological realism as a more constructive and context-sensitive framework. In line with ordoliberalism 2.0, technological realism resists both utopian and dystopian extremes, emphasizing democratic accountability, moral responsibility, and the importance of embedding technical systems within social, ethical, and institutional contexts. The concluding section reaffirms the central argument: that a shift toward technological realism (and ordoliberalism 2.0) is needed to critically engage with AI in both cultural and material terms. Rather than surrendering to hype or fear, technological realism encourages thoughtful, pluralistic deliberation about the design, goals, and societal implications of intelligent systems. By framing engineers, technologists, and policymakers as moral agents – rather than neutral implementers – this stance promotes more inclusive and ethically responsible forms of technological governance.

The intersection of AI and popular culture presents numerous opportunities for future interdisciplinary research. One promising direction involves comparative cultural analyses that explore how representations of AI differ across global media traditions, revealing culturally specific hopes, fears, and technological imaginaries. Video games and interactive media also merit closer attention, as they uniquely shape player–AI relationships and moral engagement through interactivity. Critical studies of gender, race, and class in AI portrayals can shed light on how cultural narratives perpetuate or challenge social hierarchies, particularly through tropes of servitude, objectification, or algorithmic bias. Environmental themes are also increasingly relevant, with AI depicted as both a cause of ecological collapse and a potential tool for sustainability. Longitudinal studies can track shifts in AI narratives over time, mapping their correlation with real-world technological advancements. Other valuable areas include the role of humor and satire in disrupting dominant narratives, the participatory reimagining of AI in fan cultures, religious or existential interpretations of AI, and the implications of using AI tools in content creation. Finally, the pedagogical potential of AI-themed media in teaching ethics and digital literacy offers a rich avenue for educational innovation. Together, these directions underscore the ongoing need for nuanced, context-sensitive analyses of how cultural narratives shape and are shaped by evolving technologies.

Appendix I: List of select books

- M. Shelley (*Frankenstein* [1818])
- S. Butler (*Erewhon* [1872])
- H.G. Wells (*The War of the Worlds* [1898])
- H.G. Wells (*When the Sleeper Wakes* [1899])
- G. Meyrink (*The Golem* [1915])
- K. Čapek (*Rossum's Universal Robots* [1921])
- A. Huxley (*Brave New World* [1932])
- G. Orwell (*Animal Farm* [1945])
- G. Orwell (*Nineteen Eighty-Four* [1949])
- I. Asimov (*I, Robot* [1950])
- A.C. Clarke (*The Sentinel* [1951])
- I. Asimov (*Foundation Series* [1951–1993])
- P.K. Dick (*The Minority Report* [1956])
- A. Huxley (*Brave New World Revisited* [1958])
- P.K. Dick (*We Can Remember It for You Wholesale* [1966])
- A.C. Clarke (*2001: A Space Odyssey* [1968])
- P.K. Dick (*Do Androids Dream of Electric Sheep?* [1968])
- B. Aldiss (Supertoys Last All Summer Long [1969])
- W. Gibson (*Neuromancer* [1984])

- M. Shirow (*Ghost in the Shell* [1989–1991])
- N. Stephenson (*Snow Crash* [1992])
- R.K. Morgan (*Altered Carbon* [2002])
- E. Cline (*Ready Player One* [2011])
- D. Eggers (*The Circle* [2013])
- M. Wells (*The Murderbot Diaries* [2017–2023])
- S. Stålenhag (*The Electric State* [2018])

Appendix II: List of select films and TV series

- *The Golem* (1915–1920)[63]
- *Metropolis* (1927)
- *Frankenstein* (1931)
- *Bride of Frankenstein* (1935)
- *Modern Times* (1936)
- *Forbidden Planet* (1956)
- *Star Trek* (The Original Series) (1966)
- *2001: A Space Odyssey* (1968)
- *Star Wars* (1977)
- *Alien* (1979)
- *Star Trek* (1979)
- *Blade Runner* (1982)
- *Nineteen Eighty-Four/ 1984* (1984)
- *The Terminator* (1984)
- *RoboCop* (1987)
- *Total Recall* (1990)
- *Demolition Man* (1993)
- *Mary Shelley's Frankenstein* (1994)
- *Gattaca* (1997)
- *The Matrix* (1999)
- *A.I. Artificial Intelligence* (2001)
- *Minority Report* (2002)
- *I, Robot* (2004)
- *Idiocracy* (2006)
- *WALL-E* (2008)
- *District 9* (2009)

63 Note that only the first installments of film and TV franchises are listed. The years indicated refer to the original release or broadcast of each film or series. Titles released in the same year are arranged alphabetically.

- *Inception* (2010)
- *The Social Network* (2010)
- *Black Mirror* (2011)
- *Elysium* (2013)
- *Her* (2013)
- *Captain America: The Winter Soldier* (2014)
- *Citizenfour* (2014)
- *Ex Machina* (2014)
- *Penny Dreadful* (2014)
- *The Imitation Game* (2014)
- *Transcendence* (2014)
- *Snowden* (2016)
- *Westworld* (2016)
- *Ghost in the Shell* (2017)
- *Ready Player One* (2018)
- *The Artifice Girl* (2022)
- *M3GAN* (2023)
- *Mission: Impossible ('Dead Reckoning')* (2023)
- *The Creator* (2023)
- *Subservience* (2024)
- *Alien: Earth* (2025)
- *Companion* (2025)
- *Frankenstein* (2025)
- *M3GAN 2.0* (2025)
- *Mission: Impossible ('The Final Reckoning')* (2025)
- *Orwell: 2 + 2 = 5* (2025)

References

Arnold, B. & Gough, D. (2017). Turing's People: Personhood, Artificial Intelligence, and Popular Culture. Canberra Law Review 15(1). 1–37.

Asimov, I. (1978). The Machine and the Robot. In: Warrick, P., Greenberg, M., & Olander, J. (eds.). Science Fiction: Contemporary Mythology. New York, Harper & Row. 244–253.

Baker, B. (2008). Engineering Ethics: Applications and Responsibilities. In: Smith, J., Harper, P., & Burgess, R. (eds.): Engineering Ethics. Concepts, Viewpoints, Cases, and Codes. Lubbock, National Institute for Engineering Ethics/Murdough Center for Engineering Professionalism. 49–65.

Barbour, I. (1993). Ethics in an Age of Technology. New York, Harper's Collins.

Barron, L. (2023). AI and Popular Culture. Bingley, Emerald.

Baudrillard, J. (1981/1994). Simulacra and Simulation. Ann Arbor, University of Michigan Press.

BBC. (2025). ChatGPT Will Soon Allow Erotica For Verified Adults, Says OpenAI Boss. https://www.bbc.com/news/articles/cpd2qv58yl5o (last accessed: December 30, 2025).

Bender, E., Gebru, T., McMillan-Major, A., & Shmitchell, S. (2021). On the Dangers of Stochastic Parrots. FAccT'21. 610–623.

Bender, E. & Hanna, A. (2025). The AI Con. How to Fight Big Tech's Hype and Create the Future We Want. London, Harper.

Bentham, J. (1843). The Works of Jeremy Bentham Vol. 4. Indianapolis, Liberty Funds.

Bostrom, N. (2003). Are You Living in a Computer Simulation? Philosophical Quarterly 53(211). 243–255.

Bostrom, N. (2014). Superintelligence. Oxford, Oxford University Press.

Bostrom, N. & Yudkowsky, E. (2014). The Ethics of Artificial Intelligence. In: Frankish, K. & Ramsey, W. (eds.). The Cambridge Handbook of Artificial Intelligence. Cambridge, Cambridge University Press. 316–334.

Cave, S., Dihal, K., & Dillon, S. (eds.) (2020). AI Narratives. A History of Imaginative Thinking About Intelligent Machines. Oxford, Oxford University Press.

Chalmers, D. (2005). The Matrix as Metaphysics. In: Grau, C. (ed.). Philosophers Explore the Matrix. Oxford, Oxford University Press. 132–176.

Chalmers, D. (2022). Reality+: Virtual Worlds and the Problems of Philosophy. New York, Norton.

Clapton, W. & Shepherd, L. (2019). Ethics *Ex Machina*: Popular Culture and the Plural Futures of Politics. Australian Journal of Political Science 54(4). 531–542.

Clover, J. (2004). The Matrix. London, BFI.

Dachwitz, I. & Hilbig, S. (2025). Digitaler Kolonialismus. Wie Tech-Konzerne und Großmächte die Welt unter sich aufteilen. Munich. C.H. Beck.

Descartes, R. (1641/1993). Meditations on First Philosophy. Indianapolis, Hackett.

Domingos, P. (2015). The Master Algorithm. How the Quest for the Ultimate Learning Machine Will Remake Our World. New York, Basic Books.

Dreyfus, H. (1965). Alchemy and Artificial Intelligence. https://apps.dtic.mil/sti/trecms/pdf/AD0625719.pdf (last accessed: December 30, 2025).

Dreyfus, H. (1972). What Computers Still Can't Do: A Critique of Artificial Reason. New York, Harper & Row.

Dreyfus, H. & Dreyfus, S. (1986). Mind Over Machine: The Power of Human Intuition and Expertise in the Era of the Computer. New York, Free Press.

Eberl, J., Decker, K., & Irwin, W. (eds.) (2023). Star Wars and Philosophy Strikes Back: This Is The Way. Hoboken, Wiley.

Emerson, R. (1909). Works and Days. In: Emerson, R. The Works of Ralph Waldo Emerson Vol. 7: Society and Solitude. Boston, Fireside. 149–177.

Ewing, J. (2017). Alien and Philosophy: I Infest, Therefore I Am. Hoboken, Wiley.

Foucault, M. (1995). Discipline and Punish. New York, Vintage.

Foucault, M. (2000). Power. New York, The New Press.

Foucault, M. (2010). The Birth of Biopolitics: Lectures at the Collège de France, 1978–1979. New York, Picador.

Gellman, B. (2021). Dark Mirror: Edward Snowden and the American Surveillance State. New York, Penguin Books.

Gibson, R. (2017). More Than Merely Human: How Science Fiction Pop-Culture Influences Our Desires for the Cybernetic. Sexuality & Culture 21. 224–246.

Grau, C. (ed.) (2005). Philosophers Explore the Matrix. Oxford, Oxford University Press.

Greenwald, G. (2015). No Place to Hide: Edward Snowden, the NSA, and the U.S. Surveillance State. New York, Picador.

Hagey, K. (2025). The Optimist. Sam Altman, OpenAI, and the Race to Invent the Future. New York, Norton.

Hao, K. (2025). Empire of AI. Dreams and Nightmares in Sam Altman's OpenAI. New York, Penguin.

Harari, Y. (2017). Homo Deus. A Brief History of Tomorrow. London, Vintage.

Harari, Y. (2019). 21 Lessons for the 21st Century. New York, Random House.

Harris, C., Pritchard, M., Rabins, M., James, R., & Englehardt, E. (2014). Engineering Ethics. Concepts and Cases. Wadsworth, Cengage Learning.
Heidegger, M. (1977). The Question Concerning Technology and Other Essays. New York, Harper.
Hill, K. (2023). Your Face Belongs to Us. A Secretive Startup's Quest to End Privacy. New York, Random House.
Hodges, A. (2012). Alan Turing: The Enigma. London, Vintage.
Hodges, A. (2019). Alan Turing. https://plato.stanford.edu/entries/turing/ (last accessed: December 30, 2025).
Irwin, W. (ed.) (2002). The Matrix and Philosophy. Welcome to the Desert of the Real. Chicago, Open Court.
Irwin, W., Brown, R., & Decker, K. (eds.) (2009). Terminator and Philosophy: I'll Be Back, Therefore I Am. Hoboken, Wiley.
Johnson, D. (2019). Black Mirror and Philosophy: Dark Reflections. Hoboken, Wiley.
Kahneman, D. (2011). Thinking Fast and Slow. New York, Farrar, Straus, and Giroux.
Kaminsky, I. (2021). Do Robots Dream of Escaping? Narrativity and Ethics in Alex Garland's *Ex-Machina* and Luke Scott's *Morgan*. AI & Society 36(1). 349–359.
Kant, I. (1781/2007). Critique of Pure Reason. London, Penguin.
Kaplan, J. (2016). Artificial Intelligence. What Everyone Needs to Know. Oxford, Oxford University Press.
Klump, R. & Wörsdörfer, M. (2015). Paternalist Economic Policies. Foundations, Implications, and Critical Evaluations. ORDO Yearbook of Economic and Social Order 66. 27–60.
Kranzberg, M. (1986). Technology and History: "Kranzberg's Laws." Technology and Culture 27(3). 544–560.
Kurzweil, R. (2000). The Age of Spiritual Machines. New York, Penguin.
Kurzweil, R. (2005). The Singularity is Near. London, Penguin.
Kurzweil, R. (2024). The Singularity is Nearer. New York, Viking.
Lynch, W. & Kline, R. (2000). Engineering Practice and Engineering Ethics. Science Technology Human Values 25(2). 195–225.
Martin, M. & Schinzinger, R. (2005). Ethics in Engineering. Boston, McGraw-Hill.
Martin, M. & Schinzinger, R. (2010). Introduction to Engineering Ethics. Boston, McGraw-Hill.
McFarlane, A., Schmeink, L., & Murphy, G. (2020). The Routledge Companion to Cyberpunk Culture. New York, Routledge.
McIntyre, L. (2018). Post-Truth. Cambridge, MIT Press.
Moravec, H. (1976). The Role of Raw Power in Intelligence. https://web.archive.org/web/20160303232511/http://www.frc.ri.cmu.edu/users/hpm/project.archive/general.articles/1975/Raw.Power.html (last accessed: December 30, 2025).
Moravec, H. (1988). Mind Children: The Future of Robot and Human Intelligence. Cambridge, Harvard University Press.
Muldoon, J., Graham, M., & Cant, C. (2025). Feeding the Machine: The Hidden Human Labor Powering AI. Edinburgh, Canongate.
Murphy, G. & Schmeink, L. (2017). Cyberpunk and Visual Culture. New York, Routledge.
Nagel, T. (1974). What Is It Like to Be a Bat? The Philosophical Review 83(4). 435–450.
Narayanan, A. & Kapoor, S. (2024). AI Snake Oil: What Artificial Intelligence Can Do, What It Can't, and How to Tell the Difference. Princeton, Princeton University Press.
Nida-Rümelin, J. & Weidenfeld, N. (2022). Digital Humanism. For a Humane Transformation of Democracy, Economy, and Culture in the Digital Age. Cham, Springer.
Nozick, R. (1974/2013). Anarchy, State, and Utopia. New York, Basic Books.
O'Neil, C. (2016). Weapons of Math Destruction. How Big Data Increases Inequality and Threatens Democracy. New York, Penguin.
Payne, K. (2021). I, Warbot. Oxford, Oxford University Press.

Plato. (2012). The Republic. London, Penguin.
Putnam, H. (1981). Brains in a Vat. In: Putnam, H.: Reason, Truth, and History. Cambridge, Cambridge University Press. 1–21.
Risen, C. (2025). Red Scare. Blacklists, McCarthyism, and the Making of Modern America. New York, Scribner.
Saygin A., Cicekli, I., & Akman, V. (2000). Turing Test: 50 Years Later. Minds and Machines 10(4). 463–518.
Searle, J. (1980). Minds, Brains, and Programs. Behavioral and Brain Sciences 3(3). 417–457.
Searle, J. (1982). The Myth of the Computer. https://www.nybooks.com/articles/1982/04/29/the-myth-of-the-computer/ (last accessed: December 30, 2025).
Searle, J. (1997). Consciousness & the Philosophers. https://www.nybooks.com/articles/1997/03/06/consciousness-the-philosophers/ (last accessed: December 30, 2025).
Searle, J. (2014). What Your Computer Can't Know. https://www.nybooks.com/articles/2014/10/09/what-your-computer-cant-know/ (last accessed: December 30, 2025).
Shafiqul Islam, M. (2021). Augmented Reality and Life in the Cyberspace in William Gibson's *Neuromancer*. Advances in Language and Literary Studies 12(4). 30–34.
Shanahan, T. (2014). Philosophy and Blade Runner. London, Palgrave Macmillan.
Snowden, E. (2019). Permanent Record. New York, Metropolitan Books.
Snyder, T. (2017). On Tyranny. Twenty Lessons from the Twentieth Century. New York, Tim Duggan Books.
South, J. (2018). Westworld and Philosophy: If you Go Looking for the Truth, Get the Whole Thing. Hoboken, Wiley.
Steinberger, M. (2025). The Philosopher in the Valley: Alex Karp, Palantir, and the Rise of the Surveillance State. New York, Simon & Schuster.
Thaler, R. & Sunstein, C. (2008/2009). Nudge. Improving Decisions about Health, Wealth, and Happiness. London, Penguin.
Tiles, M. & Oberdiek, H. (1995). Living in a Technological Culture: Human Tools and Human Values. New York, Routledge.
Turing, A. (1950). Computing Machinery and Intelligence. Mind 59(236). 433–460.
Tversky, A. & Kahneman, D. (1974). Judgment Under Uncertainty: Heuristics and Biases. Science 185. 1124–1131.
Watts, A. (1951). The Wisdom of Insecurity: A Message for an Age of Anxiety. New York, Pantheon Books.
Winner, L. (2004). Technologies as Forms of Life. In: Kaplan, D. (ed.). Readings in the Philosophy of Technology. Oxford, Rowman & Littlefield. 103–113.
Wittgenstein, L. (1964). Preliminary Studies for the 'Philosophical Investigations' Generally Known as The Blue and Brown Books. Oxford, Basil Blackwell.
Wörsdörfer, M. (2018). Engineering and Computer Ethics. Dubuque, Great River Learning.
Wörsdörfer, M. (2024). 'Datafeudalism: The Domination of Modern Societies by Big Tech Companies': A Commentary. Philosophy & Technology 37. Article 86.
Wörsdörfer, M. (2025a). Computer Ethics in the Age of Trump: The Politics of AI and Tech Governance. Orono. University of Maine Working Paper.
Wörsdörfer, M. (2025b). Ten Reasons Why – The Case for More and Better AI Regulation. AI and Ethics 6, Article 62.
Wooldridge, M. (2021). A Brief History of Artificial Intelligence: What It Is, Where We Are, and Where We Are Going. New York, Flatiron Books.
Zuboff, S. (2015). Big Other: Surveillance Capitalism and the Prospects of an Information Civilization. Journal of Information Technology 30. 75–89.
Zuboff, S. (2019). The Age of Surveillance Capitalism. The Fight for a Human Future at the New Frontier of Power. New York. Public Affairs.

Chapter 3
Why AI requires better regulation: Ten compelling arguments

Abstract: In recent months, there has been a noticeable shift toward AI deregulation and soft law, particularly in the United States – exemplified by Trump's revocation of Biden's executive order – and, to a lesser extent, in the E.U., as seen in the adoption of a voluntary code of conduct for providers of general-purpose AI. In contrast to these political trends, this paper argues that the significant risks posed by AI technologies call for stronger and more effective governance mechanisms. It presents ten key reasons why robust AI regulation is essential: the impact of AI on labor markets and social equity (i.e., the global/digital divide); (agentic) AI biases and discrimination; infringements on privacy; the amplification of harmful online content, including dangerous and hate speech and disinformation; business and human rights concerns; environmental consequences; the growing politico-economic power of big tech companies; threats to democracy and the rule of law; and the military implications of emerging AI technologies. Finally, the paper explores potential pathways for future AI regulation (soft vs. hard law and constitutional AI vs. AI guardrails) and proposes strategies to enhance existing regulatory frameworks, such as the E.U.'s AI Act and competition policy.

Keywords: AI ethics, business (ethics) and human rights, AI governance/regulation, soft law vs. hard law, constitutional AI, AI guardrails, E.U.'s AI Act

3.1 Introduction

In 2022 and 2023, the Biden administration introduced its *Blueprint for an AI Bill of Rights*, followed by the executive order (EO) *Ensuring Safe, Secure, and Trustworthy AI*, which outlines eight guiding principles (Biden White House, 2022a, 2023a, 2023b): ensuring AI safety and security, fostering innovation and competition, supporting workers, advancing equity and civil rights, protecting consumers, safeguarding privacy, encouraging responsible federal AI use, and strengthening U.S. leadership internationally while promoting global collaboration. While not without flaws, the EO

Note: An earlier, (slightly) shorter version of this chapter was published in *AI & Ethics* (Vol. 6, Article 62) under the title 'Ten Reasons Why: The Case for More and Better AI Regulation.' The author thanks Springer for permission to republish the material here.

 | https://doi.org/10.1515/9783112245958-004

marked a positive, though modest, step forward from an AI ethics perspective, reversing years of delay and inaction (Wörsdörfer, 2024c, 2025c).[1]

However, the situation changed when Biden's AI EO was revoked in early 2025 (Trump White House, 2025a). In its place, Trump signed Executive Order 14179, titled *Removing Barriers to American Leadership in Artificial Intelligence*, which reversed the previous administration's AI safety regulations. This new EO, together with other economic policies implemented by the new administration, prioritizes deregulation ('free markets') to encourage innovation ('entrepreneurial spirit') and U.S. leadership in AI R&D, eliminating requirements for AI safety standards, content watermarking, and national security risk compliance measures. Critics argue that the EO could exacerbate risks related to disinformation, biased and discriminatory AI systems, and vulnerabilities in critical infrastructure while giving major tech companies a free pass to further consolidate their socio-economic and political power.

In summer 2025, Trump announced a sweeping plan to accelerate AI development in the United States, emphasizing 'market liberalization,' reduced oversight, and eliminating what he called 'partisan bias' in AI systems. He signed three (additional) executive orders and released an *AI Action Plan* to promote infrastructure, limit federal restrictions, and encourage AI exports. Key actions include banning federal purchases of AI tools deemed ideologically biased; fast-tracking permits for AI data center construction; promoting U.S. AI exports and reducing environmental and diversity, equity, and inclusion (DEI)-related regulations; and prioritizing contracts for companies that align with his administration's ideological views on freedom of speech. In

1 Biden's EO has faced criticism for relying heavily on soft law terminology, best practice principles, and non-binding guidelines – resulting in the absence of a robust governance regime with effective monitoring, enforcement, and sanctioning mechanisms. Critics also highlight a lack of democratic oversight, judicial control, procedural rights, and sufficient funding and staffing for regulatory agencies. Furthermore, the EO does not adopt a risk-based framework akin to the one introduced by the E.U.'s AI Act, which includes provisions for restricting or banning high-risk AI technologies. The EO's prioritization of national and cybersecurity concerns over broader AI ethics issues, such as environmental sustainability, has also drawn criticism. Additionally, observers argue that the EO would benefit from greater coherence and stringency by eliminating redundancies and better integrating its guiding principles (Wörsdörfer, 2024c, 2025c). It is also important to note that the United States follows a (more) market-driven, techno-libertarian regulatory model, fundamentally different from the E.U.'s (more) rights-based approach (Bradford, 2020, 2023). The U.S. model emphasizes politico-economic freedom, championing free market ideology with minimal government intervention, and relies heavily on self-regulation. This is exemplified by the release of AI-related open letters and statements (AI Red Lines, 2025; Center for AI Safety, 2023; Future of Life Institute, 2023) and testimony by tech CEOs before Congress advocating for corporate self-regulation and other forms of soft law (The Guardian, 2023b). The United States also promotes ideals such as free speech and an open Internet conducive to innovation. At the same time, it exhibits weak enforcement of antitrust laws, lacks a federal data privacy framework, and maintains permissive content moderation rules that shield tech companies from liability. This approach is further shaped by a prevailing techno-optimism and a strong focus on national and cybersecurity priorities (see Section 3.3.2).

his remarks, Trump repeated Republican concerns about 'woke AI' and vowed to fight China's AI advancement (Trump White House, 2025b, 2025c, 2025d).

At the same time, discussions are underway within the E.U. regarding a potential pause, enforcement delay, or fundamental reform of the AI Act (and/or the E.U. Data Act) (E.U. AI Champions Initiative, 2025; FAZ, 2025; IAPP, 2025), widely regarded as the 'gold standard' for AI regulation (Wörsdörfer, 2024a, 2025a). These debates are driven by industry lobbying, with proponents arguing that such measures could stimulate the E.U. economy (and ease tensions with the Trump administration over tariffs and trade[2]). This move mirrors earlier efforts to soften E.U. and national supply chain laws, climate regulations, and other socio-environmental policies (Business and Human Rights Resource Center, 2025a; Council of the E.U., 2025; European Commission, 2025a; New York Times, 2025h).

Besides discussing a possible AI Act moratorium or reform, the E.U. Commission has introduced a voluntary code of practice for providers of general-purpose AI with separate chapters on improving transparency, preventing copyright violations, and ensuring public safety and security. These guidelines are considered a form of soft law intended to support the industry in meeting the requirements of the AI Act (European Commission, 2025b).

In short, what has evolved over the past few months – and years – is a fundamental shift in the political narrative surrounding AI. Whereas the conversation once centered on the risks, harms, and potential impacts on fundamental rights and society, it has increasingly reframed regulation as a threat to innovation and economic competitiveness and focused instead on the imperative of winning the AI arms race (against China). This change in discourse is evident on both sides of the Atlantic, from the United States to the E.U. In both regions, the drive to maintain technological dominance and maximize corporate profits often overshadows concerns about ethical oversight, creating a significant gap in the political will to govern AI responsibly.

Contrary to these political developments, this paper argues that, given the substantial risks associated with AI technologies, there is an urgent need for stronger and more effective AI governance mechanisms. It outlines ten key reasons why this is essential, which will be elaborated upon in the following sections: AI's impact on labor markets and social equity (i.e., the global/digital divide), (agentic) AI biases and discrimination, the erosion of privacy, AI's role in amplifying harmful online content such as dangerous and hate speech and disinformation, business and human rights concerns, environmental impacts, the increasing socio-economic and political power of big tech, AI's influence on democracy and the rule of law, and the military and security implications of emerging AI technologies. This paper aims to challenge the political arguments put forth by the Trump administration, the E.U., and other advocates of the current deregulation and privatization movement. It does so by highlighting

2 Note that the E.U. is also considering dropping plans to impose a digital services tax (Politico, 2025).

the societal and human rights implications of AI technologies and drawing attention to the growing power wielded by big tech companies. By presenting these counterpoints, the paper aims to highlight the pressing need for a more balanced approach to AI regulation – one that prioritizes ethical considerations and public accountability over unchecked innovation and corporate influence.

Although many of the ten reasons advocating for more and better regulation have been discussed in the academic literature in various forms, to the author's knowledge, no paper has yet provided a comprehensive and systematic overview that consolidates these arguments, including the business-ethical ones. In other words, while individual aspects of the need for enhanced regulation have been explored, a holistic and structured analysis – addressing the full scope of reasons and their interconnected implications (e.g., the socio-environmental and business and human rights issues) – remains absent in the current scholarly discourse. This paper aims to fill that gap by presenting a thorough examination of the multiple, often overlapping, reasons that underscore the necessity for stronger regulatory frameworks – from both a computer *and* business ethics point of view. It is the integration of business and computer ethics perspectives that distinguishes this paper from others. The paper also identifies possible avenues for future AI regulation (soft vs. hard law and constitutional AI vs. AI guardrails) and strategies for improving existing regulatory frameworks, such as the E.U.'s AI Act.

The paper is structured as follows: Section 3.2 outlines the key ethical challenges AI technologies pose and explains why more effective regulation is necessary. Section 3.3 explores potential reform measures to address these ethical concerns and examines approaches to reinforce existing AI regulations. The paper ends with a summary of its key findings and an outlook on future research directions (Section 3.4).

3.2 Ethical issues of AI

AI technologies present a wide range of risks to society.[3] Some are immediate, including (agentic) AI biases and discriminatory outcomes (and harmful online content). These pressing challenges affect multiple sectors – from hiring and education to healthcare and law enforcement – where AI systems can unintentionally reinforce existing social inequalities. The presence of such biases embedded in algorithms highlights the urgent need for systemic reform and the development of robust ethical frameworks to ensure fairness, transparency, and accountability. At the same time, more distant yet increasingly plausible risks are beginning to emerge. As AI capabili-

3 This section is organized around interconnected and partially overlapping economic, societal, environmental, and political issues, and further distinguishes between immediate impacts (addressed first) and long-term impacts (addressed last).

ties advance, concerns about technological singularity and the development of artificial general intelligence (AGI) are gaining traction. The military application of AI – particularly in autonomous weapons systems and large-scale surveillance – further raises serious ethical and geopolitical questions, including the potential for AI weaponization and destabilization of global security. While these future risks have yet to fully materialize, they underscore the critical importance of proactive, international cooperation to establish safeguards that can guide the responsible development and deployment of AI. The following sections will begin by addressing current issues, such as AI's impacts on the (labor) economy, society, the environment, and politics, before turning to longer-term concerns, including technological singularity and the role of AI in military contexts.

3.2.1 AI and labor markets

AI is poised to fundamentally transform labor markets,[4] disrupting existing job structures and leading to the destruction and creation of jobs. As a disruptive technology, AI embodies the concept of 'creative destruction' coined by Schumpeter (1942/2008), where innovations replace outdated systems, leading to the disappearance of some jobs while generating new opportunities. The impacts on the labor market will most likely be unprecedented and unparalleled in scope and scale. Routine jobs, especially those that involve repetitive tasks, are the most likely to be automated and replaced. This will not be limited to blue-collar jobs; even (some) white-collar jobs, once resistant to automation, will be affected. However, so-called pink-collar jobs, typically in caregiving or service sectors, will likely remain more secure due to their human-centric nature and the fact that they often require emotional and social intelligence that AI struggles to replicate (Kaplan, 2016; Wörsdörfer, 2018).

There are two main scenarios for the future of AI in the workforce (Quinn, 2024). On the positive side, AI could serve as a productivity-enhancing tool. This would lead to cost savings, lower prices, and a potential increase in real income, which could drive higher product demand and create more jobs. Additionally, machines and robots taking over dirty, dangerous, or routine jobs[5] could allow humans to focus on high-skilled and intellectually challenging roles. This shift could result in higher

4 For more information on the related concepts of the Fourth Industrial Revolution, Industry 4.0, Second Machine Age, and Zero Marginal Cost Society, see the work of Brynjolfsson and McAfee (2016), Rifkin (2014), and Schwab (2016).

5 While dangerous, dirty, or routine jobs are often associated with lower wages, some exceptions exists, especially where the job requires specialized training or is located in a high-cost/-demand environment (e.g., offshore oil rig workers, firefighters, military special forces [dangerous jobs], hazardous materials handlers/waste management engineers [dirty jobs], powerplant operators, assembly line technicians, and train conductors [routine jobs]).

wages, a better quality of life, improved living standards, and even fewer work hours, giving people more leisure time. This scenario assumes complementarity and cooperation, where humans work alongside machines, augmenting rather than replacing their occupations (Wörsdörfer, 2018).[6]

On the other hand, the negative scenario suggests that machines and robots, being more productive and cost-effective, could replace human workers in both blue- and white-collar jobs. With the ability to work 24/7 without breaks, vacations, or sickness, AI could significantly reduce the need for human labor. The remaining workforce may be forced to work harder for lower wages and experience increased stress levels, particularly with the rise of remote work and the expectation of around-the-clock availability. The result could be less job security and greater economic inequality. This scenario assumes a model of substitutes and competition, where humans must work against or without the aid of machines, leading to greater job insecurity and a potential decline in overall well-being. For example, the study of Frey and Osborne (2013/2017) highlights the possible risks of automation, with 47% of jobs at high risk, 19% at medium risk, and 33% at low risk of being automated.[7] The most vulnerable sectors are low-skilled, low-income jobs, but also middle-income occupations, including blue- and white-collar roles. This raises concerns about the hollowing out of the middle class, potentially increasing polarization and fragmentation, as automation disproportionately affects jobs that form the economic backbone of many communi-

6 Studies also show that 'robot-proof jobs' (Lee, 2018) exist. These are jobs that robots may be able to do but likely never will, e.g., because it does not make economic sense to replace humans for specific tasks. Then there are jobs we do not want robots to do, even if it is technically possible. People naturally prefer human touch and judgment in areas like caregiving or customer service. Then, there are unpredictable jobs that are impossible to write a manual for due to their inherent variability; these roles require intuition and adaptability, things robots still struggle with. Similarly, jobs in ad hoc or chaotic environments present a challenge, as robots thrive in perfectly controlled settings like factories or warehouses, but not yet in more unpredictable, i.e., dynamic or fluid, situations. Many jobs require a high social or emotional IQ – positions that rely on human connection, empathy, and nuanced communication skills, areas in which robots still lack depth. Additionally, jobs that require creativity and abstract thinking remain (for now) out of reach for machines/robots because we do not yet fully understand how humans engage in these complex mental processes (as such, they are not easily programmable). Lastly, many robot-proof jobs are those we have not even thought of yet – new opportunities will inevitably arise as technology evolves and creates entirely new work sectors (Carney, 2021; Lee, 2018).

7 The OECD's report, *The Risk of Automation for Jobs in OECD Countries* (2016), suggests that approximately 9% of all jobs could be lost to computerization in the coming years. McKinsey's study *Four Fundamentals of Workplace Automation* (2015) draws similar conclusions, reinforcing the idea that automation will significantly reshape the workforce. Meanwhile, PwC's report, *Will Robots Really Steal Our Jobs?* (2018), predicts that 38% of jobs in the United States will be at high risk of automation by the early 2030s (see also Lee, 2018). For more recent reports, see Goldman Sachs (2023) and World Economic Forum (2023, 2025).

ties. This dynamic may widen the gap between high-skilled workers and those displaced by automation (Carney, 2021; Wörsdörfer, 2018).

The societal implications of widespread automation are far-reaching and could deepen socio-economic divides, further eroding the middle class – especially if more white-collar jobs become automated. As automation progresses, we may face a dual crisis: higher unemployment among low-skilled workers and a shortage of skilled labor needed for more advanced roles. Job market volatility[8] could become the norm, with no job being completely safe from the threat of automation, even in fields once thought to be secure. This creates a paradox, where while technology offers increased productivity, it also disrupts traditional employment structures. In a 'post-work society,' it will become increasingly complex to organize unions or secure labor rights, as the nature of work is transformed (as is already the case in the gig economy [Lanier, 2013; Reich, 2015a, 2015b; Taylor, 2017]), and the line between workers and machines becomes increasingly blurred. As a result, ensuring fair labor practices and supporting those displaced by automation will be one of the most significant challenges facing societies in the years to come (Carney, 2021; Harari, 2017, 2019; Lee, 2018; Wörsdörfer, 2018).

The potentially adverse impacts of AI on labor markets, such as job displacement and increasing unemployment (and poverty), highlight the need for more robust AI and labor market regulation, not just to address the immediate challenges of workforce disruption, but also to proactively shape the trajectory of AI development in ways that promote fair employment opportunities, safeguard equitable access to work opportunities, and prevent widening socio-economic inequality. While some may argue for de-accelerating AI progress as a solution, regulation offers a more direct and effective means to ensure that technological advancements align with societal goals, fostering a sustainable future of work while mitigating potential harms (e.g., by introducing a universal basic income (UBI) and/or reforming the education system).

8 This shift raises questions about the future of workers and jobs, particularly whether generative AI will lead to job automation and mass unemployment, or if this time will be different. A Goldman Sachs report (2023) suggests that two-thirds of current jobs, or roughly 300 million full-time jobs, are exposed to AI automation, with generative AI potentially substituting up to a quarter of existing work. However, job opportunities will also emerge in areas like personal service, prompt engineering, and roles like 'data wranglers' (who collect and curate training data), generative AI auditors (who test and monitor generative AI behavior), RLHF counselors (specializing in reinforcement learning from human feedback [RLHF]), and generative AI developers or engineers. To navigate these changes, there will be a significant demand for workplace skills, education, and vocational training adjustments. The challenge is to overcome the problem of structural or technological unemployment, ensuring that workers can transition into new roles in the evolving landscape shaped by generative AI (Kaplan, 2024; see also Section 3.3.3).

3.2.2 Digital and global divide

AI technologies are expected to accelerate the current trend of substituting capital for labor, driven by the capital-intensive nature of AI development, which requires significant computing power and infrastructure such as data centers, hyperscalers, fiber-optic cables, and other computing hardware (New York Times, 2025a). Those who possess capital will disproportionately benefit from this shift, while those who rely solely on their ability to work, like workers and unions, will (most likely) be left behind. AI further cements the power of capital against labor, placing workers in direct competition for fewer jobs (Muldoon et al., 2025). This trend is expected to exacerbate wealth and income inequality, concentrating power and wealth in the hands of a few individuals and corporations, and widening the gap between the rich and poor (Carney, 2021; Kaplan, 2016; for more information on the power of big tech, see Section 3.2.8).

A related concern is the digital divide, a phenomenon in which technological advancement leads to an opportunity gap, exacerbating both international and intranational inequality (Norris, 2001). The technological divide highlights how some people have access to modern IT while others do not ('digital haves' vs. 'have-nots'). The underlying assumption is that people who use smartphones, computers, the Internet, and (generative) AI technologies have opportunities that are denied to people without access to these technologies. This divide can be understood along two dimensions: global vs. social divide. The global divide refers to the disparity in Internet (and [generative] AI) access and usage between more industrialized and less industrialized countries. In contrast, the social divide captures the difference in technological access and usage between rich and poor, young and old, educated and less educated, as well as between rural and urban populations (i.e., the global divide is linked to *inter*national inequality, whereas the social divide is associated with *intra*national disparities) (Wörsdörfer, 2018).

The global divide in Internet access (and related technologies) is evident when comparing regions worldwide. In 2024, 5.5 billion out of 8.2 billion people – approximately 68% of the global population – had access to the Internet, leaving around 2.7 billion people, or one-third of the world's population, offline (ITU, 2025). Access is much higher in North America, Europe, Australia, and New Zealand, while Africa lags far behind. Wealthier countries, regions with robust IT infrastructure, and areas with higher literacy and education levels see greater access. However, a significant gender gap persists, with women having less access to and lower usage of the Internet than men in nearly every region. This gender divide is reflected in mobile ownership, basic digital skills, and Internet use, leading to far-reaching socio-economic consequences (UNICEF, 2023).

The social divide in Internet (and AI) access and usage, on the other hand, is deeply influenced by age, income, wealth, and education. Younger individuals tend to have greater access, as do those who are wealthier and better educated. In contrast, older people, people with low incomes or those experiencing poverty, and those without a high school diploma are more likely to lack access to and use the Internet (and AI technologies). This creates a situation where marginalized and vulnerable groups fall further behind, contributing to a (further) rise in socio-economic immobility and inequality. Noteworthy is that in the United States, an estimated 42 million people lack Internet access, highlighting the extent of the digital divide and its societal implications (Forbes, 2023).

The digital divide between the Global North and South is further widened by the limited availability of 5G networks and data center infrastructure in the Global South (New York Times, 2025a). Affordability challenges compound this disparity, as many regions lack access to the technology essential for digital development and inclusive growth. A major contributing factor is the growing ownership of fiber-optic and submarine cables by big tech companies, with only 1% of these critical infrastructure assets in public hands (Dachwitz & Hilbig, 2025). Moreover, alternative efforts to bridge the divide, such as Internet access via high-altitude balloons (Alphabet), drones (Meta), and satellites (Amazon and Starlink), raise significant ethical concerns. These technologies not only erode the digital sovereignty of nation-states (Ganz et al., 2024) but also increase (infrastructure) dependence on big tech companies, as undersea cables (Mwema & Birhane, 2024) and satellite networks become new frontiers of digital colonialism (see also the related concept of 'infrastructure as debt' [Kwet, 2022]). Furthermore, net neutrality – a concept introduced by Wu (2003) – is increasingly under threat. It refers to the principle that Internet Service Providers (ISPs) must treat all data on the internet equally, without discrimination or differential pricing based on user, content, platform, or application. Under net neutrality regulations, ISPs are prohibited from offering tiered services, such as charging premium prices for faster data delivery, or blocking, throttling, or prioritizing specific content. These protections help ensure Internet traffic flows without bias, guaranteeing open, fair, and equal access for consumers and businesses. Ultimately, net neutrality safeguards the internet as a level playing field, fostering innovation, freedom of expression, and non-discriminatory access to digital services.

The past few decades have also witnessed the rise of enhanced winner-takes-all effects, leading to an increasing concentration of wealth and income in the hands of a few individuals and corporations. In a 'winner-takes-all' society, as described by Frank & Cook (1996), a small group of top performers – such as superstar athletes, actors, musicians, novelists, top managers, and 'big business' – receive a disproportionate share of wealth and rewards (Wörsdörfer, 2018). For example, the compensation of CEOs at America's largest corporations has grown at a much faster pace than the wages of production workers. In 1965, the average pay for a CEO at a large U.S. company was about 20 times that of a production worker. By 2022, that ratio had skyrocketed to nearly 400 to 1 (Economic Policy Institute, 2022). The average annual compensation for CEOs in 2017 was around $14 million in the United States – the highest in the world and much more than in any other industrialized country (the next highest average compensation was $8.5 million in Switzerland, with other European countries following closely behind) (Statista, 2025b). This concentration of wealth is starkly illustrated by Oxfam's 2017 report, which states that the world's eight wealthiest individuals possess as much wealth as the combined bottom half of the global population. Also remarkable in this context is the fact that Musk's wealth reached a staggering $455 billion, as of mid-2025 – an increase of $170 billion since before the 2024 election campaign (The Independent, 2024),[9] reflecting a broader trend of rising wealth among the top 1% (Forbes, 2024). This growing disparity underscores the widening gap in wealth distribution both nationally and globally.[10] Noteworthy is that most digital markets also operate as winner-takes-all economies, where a few dominant players capture most of the market share and form tech monopolies (Wörsdörfer, 2020, 2021, 2022a, 2022b, 2023, 2024b; see Section 3.2.8).

AI's potential to exacerbate socio-economic inequalities – through the global divide and digital divide – raises a compelling case for more comprehensive regulation. While current regulatory frameworks may not fully address social justice concerns, the absence of specific regulations can worsen inequality, as AI systems often reflect and amplify existing biases. Regulation is not merely about preventing harm; it is about creating guardrails to ensure AI's development aligns with democratic values and global equity. By establishing standards that promote inclusive access to AI benefits and prevent monopolistic or discriminatory practices, regulation can mitigate widening inequalities and foster a fairer socio-economic landscape. Without such frameworks, AI risks deepening divides and entrenching social injustices. Strong regulatory frameworks are essential to ensure that AI technologies are deployed in ways that promote equity, inclusivity, and accessibility, ultimately fostering a more just and balanced digital economy.

9 In mid-2025, Tesla offered Musk an almost $1 trillion dollar pay package, which would make him the world's first trillionaire (CNN, 2025).

10 In his work, Piketty examines the growing disparity in income distribution, highlighting how the share of the top 1% has risen significantly while the share of the bottom 50% has fallen. For instance, over the past few decades, the average income of the bottom 50% in the United States has stagnated, while the income of the top 1% has increased substantially, shifting the ratio from 1:26 to 1:81 (Piketty, 2015, 2017, 2020; see also Fratzscher, 2017; Stiglitz, 2015). The pandemic further exacerbated these socio-economic inequalities, with some individuals experiencing significant increases in net worth, leading to what some have called 'pandemic profits' (Washington Post, 2021). Piketty (2015, 2017, 2020) identifies several reasons for this widening gap and the increasing socio-economic inequality, including the stagnating federal minimum wage, unequal access to higher education and healthcare, and the lack of social mobility, which challenges the idea of the American (meritocratic) dream as a myth. The absence of inheritance and wealth taxes (Saez & Zucman, 2019), along with less progressive taxation and slower growth rates over the past few decades, has further fueled these inequalities (noteworthy is also the stark contrast between what companies pay in federal taxes and what they compensate their executives; additionally, while U.S. companies' profits have surged recently, their tax contributions have remained essentially unchanged [Desmond, 2023; The Guardian, 2024]).

3.2.3 AI biases and discrimination

As discussed in Section 3.2.1, AI-driven job displacement affects society unevenly, with certain groups bearing a disproportionate share of the burden. Furthermore, as highlighted in Section 3.2.2, AI systems often amplify existing inequalities, reinforcing structural disadvantages for vulnerable populations. This creates a self-perpetuating cycle of inequality that demands careful policy intervention and oversight.

O'Neil (2016) illustrates how these technologies entrench societal inequities by exposing the real-world consequences of unchecked AI bias.[11] Often hidden behind opaque data-processing 'black boxes' (Pasquale, 2016), algorithmic systems disproportionately impact marginalized groups –including low-income communities and ethnic minorities –

11 AI biases refer to biased computer systems that unfairly deny opportunities or assign undesirable outcomes based on unreasonable or inappropriate grounds (Friedman & Nissenbaum, 1996). Altogether, AI biases denote biases exhibited by a decision-making AI system based on machine learning. These biases manifest in four major ways: preexisting, technical, emergent and automating biases (Quinn, 2024). *Preexisting biases* existed in society before the system was developed. They stem from societal inequalities and systemic exclusion, such as patriarchy, white supremacy, and ableism, the so-called 'power shadows,' which are reflected in the data used to train AI. This is especially true when the dataset is poor, i.e., not representative of the general population, and therefore incorporates historical and social injustices. For example, facial recognition systems trained on datasets that predominantly feature white men have higher error rates when applied to darker-skinned women. The work of Buolamwini (2016, 2023) and colleagues (Bender et al, 2021; Buolamwini & Gebru, 2018; Li, 2023) shows that more than 80% of faces in widely used training sets were of white people, and more than 75% were men (furthermore, it is often challenging to label or categorize images by gender or ethnicity accurately [these are the so-called 'ground truths']). The error rate of such systems is just 1% on fair-skinned men but 35% on darker-skinned women, which can have real-world consequences, such as false arrests and deportations or denied access to buildings, planes, and trains. *Technical biases* arise from technical limitations in computer system design. A good example is Google Search. Due to limited screen space, only a small number of results are shown at the top, with the #1 result receiving a click-through rate of about 27.6%, while the #10 result only garners around 2.5% (Quinn, 2024). Less than 1% of users navigate to the results' second page. This ranking system, driven by an algorithm, can introduce bias by privileging specific sources or types of information, which may not always represent a balanced view. As a result, search engines can inadvertently shape information users are exposed to, reinforcing specific perspectives while sidelining others. *Emergent biases* refer to biases that develop as a computer system is used and influenced by external interactions. A notable example of emergent bias occurred with Microsoft's chatbot, Tay, which was released in 2016. Tay was designed to communicate 'like a teen girl,' adapting its responses based on user input. However, malicious users exploited the system by feeding it misinformation and hateful language, causing Tay to produce misogynistic and racially offensive slurs (see the New York Times [2025i] for more details regarding a similar incident involving Musk's chatbot Grok). Within 24 h, Microsoft took Tay offline in response to the unintended behavior, highlighting the risks of emergent biases in AI systems. This incident illustrates how computer systems can unexpectedly evolve when exposed to harmful user-generated content (Quinn, 2024). Lastly, *automation bias* refers to the tendency to over-rely on and prioritize recommendations from automated decision-making systems, often at the expense of disregarding accurate, non-automated information (see Section 3.2.10).

thereby exacerbating discrimination, systemic racism, and embedded prejudices. By reinforcing social biases, these technologies exacerbate inequalities, deepen social divisions, and undermine democratic principles through harmful feedback loops, such as the poverty trap (Institute for Human Rights and Business, 2016). A central issue lies in the lack of accountability and transparency, which permits the manipulation of algorithms without adequate oversight. Without effective regulatory frameworks and accessible complaint mechanisms, the unregulated dimensions of the data economy remain unchecked. Data brokers, operating largely outside public scrutiny, commodify individuals by turning personal information into marketable products – an example of the broader marketization of society. Carney (2021) argues that this reflects a shift from a 'market economy' to a 'market society' (see also Floridi, 2023; O'Neil, 2016).

Examples of the harmful effects of big data are evident across a wide range of sectors. In advertising, personalized or targeted marketing – often referred to as predatory advertising – exploits individuals' vulnerabilities based on data such as ZIP codes. For instance, high-interest loans may be aggressively marketed to low-income populations, reinforcing financial instability. In healthcare, wellness and fitness programs that rely on apps, sensors, and activity trackers utilize data, such as step counts and sleep patterns, to monitor and influence behavior. While often framed as promoting well-being, such programs can represent a new, intrusive form of workplace surveillance, raising serious privacy concerns. Moreover, they risk discriminating against individuals who are overweight, chronically ill, or living with disabilities. In the financial sector, banks and insurance companies are increasingly relying on credit reports and scores, as well as algorithmic surveillance techniques, such as redlining, to assess risk. These practices can disproportionately affect marginalized groups, including people of color, women, and residents of lower-income neighborhoods, thereby restricting access to loans, insurance, and housing. Redlining, for example, involves denying services to individuals in areas deemed high-risk, often based on socio-economic and racial demographics, thus perpetuating geographic and racial inequalities. Such mechanisms trap individuals in cycles of poverty rooted in structural bias and limited financial access. Hiring practices are also shaped by algorithmic tools, including personality tests, credit scores, and e-scores. These tools risk reinforcing existing biases, particularly when employers use credit scores to filter recruitment decisions. Since unemployed individuals often have lower credit scores, this practice creates a vicious cycle: joblessness damages one's credit, further limiting employment opportunities and deepening economic hardship. In the realm of security and crime prevention, predictive policing technologies such as PredPol – based on risk terrain analysis and hot spot predictions – have been widely criticized for perpetuating racial profiling (The Guardian, 2025b). While these systems claim to forecast future crimes, they often reinforce stereotypes by associating specific neighborhoods or ethnicities with criminal behavior. The result is a negative feedback loop: increased police surveillance in certain areas leads to higher reported crime rates, which justifies further surveillance and arrests. This process not only erodes trust in law enforcement but also contributes to a climate of fear and long-term socio-economic marginalization, ultimately driving the very criminal activity it aims to prevent. Finally, the use of big data in digital voter manipulation – exemplified by the Cambridge Analytica scandal (Haugen, 2023; Wynn-Williams, 2025) – illustrates how data profiling and targeted advertising can influence political outcomes. Through disinformation campaigns and micro-targeting, such strategies distort public discourse and undermine democratic institutions, weakening public trust in electoral systems and the rule of law (O'Neil, 2016; see Section 3.2.9).

AI biases often stem from several key issues, including the selection of training data and the composition of the teams designing AI systems. One major cause is the use of unrepresentative or incomplete (i.e., poor) data sets. For instance, when training data predominantly reflects the white male U.S. population, it results in a cultural and ethnic bias that negatively impacts the accuracy of predictions for other groups. Additionally, generalizations become problematic when predictions are made based on insufficient data, leading to flawed outcomes. This issue is compounded by the failure to consider underlying causations when making correlations. Furthermore, the lack of diversity within AI development teams exacerbates these biases. With many computer science teams dominated by young white male Westerners, personal biases, societal stereotypes, and cultural blind spots inevitably shape the development of AI systems. The underrepresentation of BIPOC (Black, Indigenous, and People of Color), women, disabled or older people, those from developing countries, and the LGBTQ+ community within these teams further skews the technology, making it less effective and fair for diverse populations (AI Now Institute, 2025; Hao, 2025; Stanford University Human-Centered Artificial Intelligence, 2025).

AI biases and discrimination represent significant societal risks, as they can perpetuate existing inequalities, harm marginalized groups, and undermine fairness in decision-making processes. While it is true that current regulatory frameworks, including the E.U.'s AI Act, often approach bias indirectly by focusing on product safety and risk classification, this approach fails to adequately address the root causes of bias in AI systems. The problem lies not only in the presence of biases but also in how they are ingrained in the design, data, and deployment of AI technologies. Regulating bias requires a more targeted, nuanced approach that goes beyond risk categorization to establish clear standards for transparency, accountability, and fairness in AI algorithms. Such regulation would ensure that AI systems are designed and tested with fairness principles embedded at every stage of development, from data collection to algorithmic decision-making. By creating specific legal frameworks to address algorithmic discrimination, regulators can foster the development of systems that are not only safe but also just, ensuring that AI technologies benefit all users equitably and do not perpetuate harmful stereotypes or discriminatory practices.

3.2.4 Privacy and data protection

Discriminatory and biased AI systems frequently depend on invasive data practices, such as those employed by data brokers, which not only violate personal privacy but also deepen existing social inequities. These concerns lead us to the next critical issue: the erosion of privacy in the era of big data and AI. As vast amounts of personal information are collected, shared, and analyzed, safeguarding individuals' rights becomes increasingly challenging, raising urgent ethical and regulatory questions about consent, transparency, and control over one's data.

The twenty-first century, driven by rapid advancements in information and communication technologies, is increasingly being characterized as a golden age of mass surveillance and espionage. Ubiquitous digital tools – ranging from smartphones with geolocation capabilities and social media platforms that map individuals' social networks, to AI-driven big data analytics and online tracking technologies such as cookies and web beacons – facilitate the creation of highly detailed digital profiles. These profiles significantly increase individuals' visibility and transparency, effectively rendering them 'glass people.' The processes of collecting, aggregating, distributing, and monetizing personal data – primarily for commercial objectives such as targeted advertising – have never been more pervasive or efficient, resulting in a substantial erosion of personal privacy. However, privacy risks are not confined to commercial exploitation, often described as 'surveillance capitalism' or 'dataveillance capitalism' (Zuboff, 2015, 2019). They also extend to covert state surveillance conducted under the pretext of safeguarding national security and public safety (Gellman, 2021; Greenwald, 2015; Snowden, 2019). The convergence of public (see the various NSA surveillance programs) and private (see the business practices of data brokers such as Acxiom, Equifax, and Experian) surveillance infrastructures poses a serious threat to privacy rights and broader fundamental human rights, including civil liberties protected under international legal frameworks (Amnesty International, 2019). This threat is exacerbated by shifting power dynamics, wherein individuals face growing asymmetries in relation to both state and corporate actors – commonly referred to as 'big government' and 'big business.' These evolving structures of surveillance and control have the potential to undermine the foundations of democratic governance and the rule of law (Wörsdörfer, 2018; see Section 3.2.9).

The contemporary digital landscape is frequently characterized by metaphors like the 'digital panopticon' or 'cryptopticon' – concepts evoking an environment of pervasive observation and uncertainty (Bentham, 1843; Foucault, 1995, 2000). In such a system, individuals live under the constant possibility that their actions, communications, and even private thoughts may be subject to monitoring by invisible authorities. This omnipresent surveillance extends beyond external behavior to influence internal states of mind, often leading to conformity and obedience. Over time, it can foster a climate of passivity and discourage dissent. The chilling effect of surveillance suppresses not only public expression but also private deliberation, as individuals internalize expectations and censor themselves to avoid attracting attention. This culture of self-censorship is particularly damaging for journalists, researchers, and academics, whose professional activities depend on the freedom to explore and communicate controversial or sensitive issues (this dynamic is evident not only in authoritarian regimes, such as those in China and Russia, but also in recent Western contexts, including the Trump administration).[12] Beyond the individual, mass surveillance contributes to an atmosphere of anxiety, mistrust, and social fragmentation, echoing the paranoia and repression of the McCarthy-era 'Red Scare' (Risen, 2025). In such contexts, political dissent is frequently delegitimized by framing dissenters as threats to national security or as subversive actors, which in turn facilitates discriminatory practices, especially against marginalized or minority groups. Unchecked surveillance and excessive state power pose serious risks to civil liberties, deepen social divisions, and erode democratic accountability (Wörsdörfer, 2018, 2024d).

Importantly, the implications of mass surveillance extend far beyond violations of privacy and data protection. Intrusive monitoring can have a chilling effect on fundamental freedoms such as freedom of expression, freedom of assembly, and freedom of religion, as individuals may alter their behavior, beliefs, or associations out of fear of being watched or profiled. Surveillance practices can also reinforce existing inequalities by disproportionately targeting marginalized communities, thereby undermining the principle of equal treatment under the law. In this broader context, surveillance not only constrains individual autonomy but also weakens the democratic fabric of society by stifling dissent, discouraging civic engagement, and eroding trust in public institutions.

12 Critics warn that the Trump administration's suppression of experts – through tactics such as repression, threats, budget cuts, and surveillance – combined with the promotion of pseudoscience, the purging of government scientists, and the censorship of scientific work and free speech, could pave the way for a form of 'state-controlled' or even 'totalitarian science' (Josephson, 2025; The Guardian, 2025d).

3.2.4.1 Excursus: Palantir and Clearview AI

Palantir Technologies, founded by Thiel,[13] the 'Godfather of the PayPal Mafia,'[14] and led by CEO Karp (Steinberger, 2025), is a big data and predictive analytics company known for its products and services, Apollo, Foundry, Gotham, and Metropolis. Originally developed to support U.S. military and intelligence operations, including counterterrorism and predictive policing, Palantir's tools have expanded to civil and corporate clients, including police and state and local governments. For instance, the U.S. Department of Health and Human Services used its technology in the HHS Protect Now initiative for COVID-19 contact tracing, patient data analysis, and virus tracking. At the same time, the U.K.'s NHS utilized the company's products to evaluate the effectiveness of its vaccination program. Palantir also partners with tech giants like AWS to deliver scalable solutions. Despite its technological innovations, Palantir has faced significant controversies, scandals, and legal challenges, such as its partnership with Immigration and Customs Enforcement (ICE), which critics claim facilitated the deportation of undocumented immigrants (New York Times, 2025b). The company has also been involved in racial discrimination lawsuits in the United States, faced parliamentary inquiries in the United Kingdom over alleged ties to Cambridge Analytica, and drawn fire for its role in Project Maven, a secret Pentagon AI program involving unmanned aerial vehicles and other autonomous weapon systems (Amnesty International, 2019).

Clearview AI is a facial recognition technology (FRT) company known for scraping billions of images from the Internet to build a massive biometric database. Its advanced recognition techniques are marketed primarily to police, law enforcement agencies, and border security forces, who use the technology for criminal investigations and national security purposes (note that one of the company's major clients is ICE, which, under the Trump administration, has used Clearview AI's products to support its mass deportation efforts and anti-immigration policies; another important customer is Patel's FBI, who might use FRT against their perceived 'political enemies'; both agencies have a long track record of racial and religious profiling, infringing on constitutional rights, and conducting intrusive data collection and surveillance [Mother Jones, 2025; Wired, 2023]). Proponents argue that such tools enhance public safety and national or border security. Critics, on the other hand, highlight significant concerns, including a lack of accuracy, overreliance on (biased)

13 Thiel is a prominent figure in tech and finance, known as the co-founder and former CEO of PayPal, founder and chairman of Palantir, board member of Facebook, and an influential venture capitalist. Politically, he was a member of the Libertarian Party until 2016, when he joined the GOP. Thiel is also a member of the Steering Committee of the Bilderberg Group and serves as the leader of the Thiel Foundation. His close collaboration with Patri Friedman, Milton Friedman's grandson, connects him to the Seasteading Institute, a project for floating cities that Friedman founded in 2008 with the ambitious goal of creating sovereign ocean colonies outside the jurisdiction of traditional governments. Thiel has donated over one million dollars to support this project. In his 2014 book *From Zero to One*, Thiel defends monopoly capitalism (due to its alleged innovation-fostering capabilities), arguing that 'creative monopolies' rather than perfectly competitive markets drive innovation and progress. In contrast, competitive markets tend to destroy profits (Thiel, 2014). However, in his 2009 article, *The Education of a Libertarian*, Thiel reveals a more controversial stance – he expresses anti-democratic and elitist views, promoting an authoritarian mindset that appears incompatible with freedom and democracy (Thiel, 2009). His polemic and pseudo-populist rhetoric risks fueling political apathy and disenchantment, potentially leading to a rise in pseudo-populism that offers simplified, distorted, and short-sighted answers to complex societal problems (see also New York Times, 2017).

14 Palantir is part of the so-called 'Thielverse,' a "set of AI-enabled data and infrastructure companies which profit hugely from facilitating the expansion of the American surveillance state" (Muldoon et al., 2025).

algorithms and AI technologies, and the broader erosion of privacy due to mass surveillance. Clearview AI has faced numerous controversies and legal challenges, particularly around privacy violations and data protection. Regulators in France, Greece, Italy, the Netherlands, and the United Kingdom have fined the company and ordered it to delete data obtained without consent, citing violations of European privacy laws, such as the General Data Protection Regulation. These actions reflect differing regulatory approaches: while the E.U., through legislation like the AI Act, moves toward stricter bans and limitations on facial recognition, the United States remains largely unrestricted in its oversight (at least at the federal level) (note that while [some] oversight mechanisms remained in place during Biden's presidency, Trump dismissed numerous inspectors general responsible for monitoring technologies like Clearview AI and preventing their misuse; his early actions also indicate that his administration has little respect for the legal, congressional, and constitutional checks that had restrained prior presidents [Mother Jones, 2025]). Critics worry that, without proper regulation, companies like Clearview AI could pave the way for surveillance models resembling China's Social Credit System (Hill, 2023; Narayanan & Kapoor, 2024).

Noteworthy is that Ton-That, one of the founders and former CEO of Clearview AI, who resigned in February 2025 but plans to remain on the board, has long faced scrutiny for alleged ties to alt-right, white nationalist, and eugenicist groups, as well as the MAGA movement and techno-libertarian/-fascist ideologies (Mother Jones, 2025). The company he co-founded in 2018, succeeding Smartcheckr, quickly became a major player in the FRT industry. Co-founder Schwartz, who previously worked with Giuliani during his tenure as mayor of New York City, helped steer the company's early development, which was supported by initial funding from prominent figures such as Thiel. Clearview AI's first clients included the New York Police Department (trial only), the Indiana State Police (first official contract), and the U.S. Department of Homeland Security, which spent millions on its services. Over time, several authoritarian governments, particularly in the Middle East, have adopted Clearview AI's tools, which now maintain a database of billions of faces and serve over 600 federal and local law enforcement agencies, as well as numerous private companies and organizations. Despite these successes, Clearview AI has faced growing opposition. In 2019, several U.S. cities, including San Francisco and Oakland, banned the use of FRT by police. In 2020, debates emerged about using the company's technology for tracking COVID-19 patients, mirroring contact tracing efforts in China, Russia, and South Korea. Legal challenges followed. By 2020, Clearview AI faced investigations and class-action lawsuits, including those from the ACLU, which accused it of violating data protection laws, such as the California Consumer Privacy Act, by failing to obtain citizens' consent. This resulted in fines of up to $70 million, and six countries declared their products illegal. The company was ordered to cease collecting facial data and delete existing records. However, demand for its products surged after the January 6 Capitol attack in 2021. In 2022, Clearview AI offered free services to Ukraine amid Russia's invasion. Recently, mounting pressure from initiatives like 'Reclaim Your Face,' which seek to ban FRT entirely, has intensified scrutiny. Under new CEO Lambert – a staunch Republican with close ties to Trump – Clearview AI continues to evolve amidst an escalating legal and ethical battle over privacy and surveillance (Hill, 2023).

Often dubbed the 'Google Search for faces,' Clearview AI operates as a powerful facial search engine, enabling extensive face surveillance with profound ethical consequences. The company claims that its FRT achieves 98.6–99.7% accuracy; however, experts, such as Buolamwini (2023), have challenged these figures, highlighting algorithmic biases and discrimination, particularly against ethnic minorities. These inaccuracies have led to wrongful arrests based on misidentifications and disproportionately increased policing of minority communities. Critics also highlight that watchlists used in conjunction with FRT are frequently outdated or inaccurate, resulting in numerous false positives. By 2023, Clearview AI had scraped over 30 billion images – adding 75 million daily – from social media platforms such as Facebook and LinkedIn, all without user consent, generating vast biometric profiles for millions of unwitting individuals. The ethical stakes rise further when considering the potential integration of FRT with augmented reality glasses (New York Times, 2020). Moreover, in authoritarian regimes like China, live facial recognition has been used to suppress dissenters, fueling fears that unchecked surveillance technologies could erode civil liberties globally (Hill, 2023).

3.2.5 Harmful internet content

The erosion of privacy and corresponding impact on First Amendment rights is closely linked to social media and AI-driven platforms, which leverage personal data to fuel the amplification of harmful online content and disinformation. As these platforms collect and analyze user data, they are able to target individuals with content that often promotes division, dangerous/hate speech, and false narratives. This targeted amplification not only exacerbates societal harm but also distorts public discourse, making it harder for people to discern truth from manipulation. The resulting effects erode trust in digital spaces, creating a toxic environment where privacy is sacrificed for profit, and public well-being is jeopardized.

The distinction between dangerous and hate speech plays a pivotal role in legal and ethical debates surrounding freedom of expression (Ash, 2016; Carlson, 2021; Wörsdörfer, 2018). Dangerous speech refers to statements that pose an immediate and likely threat of violence, typically involving a direct call or incitement to harm. It is defined by three key elements: imminence, intent, and the presence of a 'true threat.' Given its direct risk to public safety, dangerous speech is banned in many legal systems, including in the United States. In contrast, hate speech generally involves verbal attacks or discriminatory expressions that do not constitute an immediate threat of violence. While hate speech can still be harmful, it is not criminalized in the United States. This distinction continues to spark debate, as drawing a clear line between protected speech and speech that may incite real-world harm remains a complex issue.

Although hate speech may not always be illegal, it poses significant ethical and societal risks. It often leads to discrimination and biased actions. By employing dehumanizing language and disseminating disinformation or propaganda, hate speech fosters an environment in which discrimination becomes normalized. Historically, such rhetoric has played a key role in inciting violence and human rights atrocities, including modern slavery, racism, the Holocaust, the Rwandan Tutsi genocide, and the persecution of the Rohingya in Myanmar. More recently, hate speech has been linked to events such as the January 6th Insurrection in the United States (The January 6th Committee, 2022). Beyond its societal impact, hate speech inflicts profound psychological and emotional harm on its victims, silences marginalized voices within societies, and contributes to the spread of misinformation (Carlson, 2021).

In addition to dangerous and hate speech, disinformation is a major driver of internet toxicity. Generative AI technologies play a central role in this dynamic, facilitating the creation and spread of false narratives through tools such as deepfakes (Narayanan & Kapoor, 2024), hallucinations (i.e., 'autogenerated ChatGPT bullshit,' à la Frankfurt [2005]) (New York Times, 2025d), and LLM grooming – the strategic manipulation of online content to bias AI outputs (American Sunlight Project, 2025; NewsGuard's Reality Check, 2025). On one hand, chatbots are trained on existing internet data and thus inherently reflect and absorb the toxicity embedded in online spaces. On the other hand, they actively amplify and disseminate harmful content, reinforcing a feedback loop, especially when newer models are trained on outputs from earlier, already-contaminated versions. This cycle not only perpetuates online toxicity, including disinformation and dangerous/hate speech, but also threatens to erode public trust in digital platforms.[15]

Another significant concern in this context is the detrimental effect of social media on mental health. Haidt (2024) reports a sharp decline in teen mental well-being during the twenty-first century, with rising instances of anxiety, depression, and self-harm, especially among Gen Z pre-teen girls and young women. Contributing factors include visual comparisons, socially imposed perfectionism and beauty ideals, relational cyberbullying, and sexual harassment on image-focused platforms such as Instagram and TikTok. In contrast, boys and young men tend to be more impacted by video gaming and pornography, which often lead to outward behaviors like aggression and violence, as well as a disconnection from reality. The growing trend of over-protective parenting – usually labeled 'safetyism' or 'helicopter parenting' – combined with an inadequately regulated online space marked by insufficient laws, has exacerbated these issues. Haidt describes the 'Great Rewiring,' the shift from a play-centered childhood to one dominated by nearly constant smartphone and social media use, as causing four core harms: sleep deprivation, social deprivation, fragmented attention, and addiction. Ultimately, social media's reinforcement through validation-seeking feedback loops and addictive mechanisms fosters increased feelings of alienation and isolation, reducing genuine social interactions and contributing to the aforementioned mental health challenges.

3.2.6 Business and human rights

The widespread dissemination of harmful online content is not just a social issue but also deeply tied to business practices within the tech industry.[16] Many tech companies profit from algorithms designed to prioritize sensational or harmful content, as such material drives engagement and revenue. At the same time, these companies often exploit workers (e.g., content moderators and data annotators), creating a troubling dynamic where business interests come at the expense of social well-being. This inter-

15 See New York Times (2025i) for reporting on Musk's chatbot Grok sharing antisemitic posts on X. Furthermore, AI tools lower the barrier to accessing sensitive information, such as methods for chemical production, which could be exploited for bioweapons (e.g., AI-assisted viral outbreaks), terrorism, or other illegal and criminal activities (The Guardian, 2025a).

16 While much of the content in this section could also be categorized under labor, social injustice, surveillance, and online content, business and human rights issues from a business ethics perspective are often overlooked. Therefore, dedicating an entire paragraph to this topic is essential, as it forms a crucial part of the paper's business ethics framework. A unique and distinctive feature of this paper is its strong emphasis on business ethics, combined with a comprehensive analysis that bridges both business and computer ethics.

section raises critical business and human rights concerns, underscoring the need for greater accountability in the development and deployment of technology.

The entire AI supply chain is fraught with human rights violations, spanning from the mining stage (e.g., conflict minerals [Kara, 2023; Nest, 2013]) to the manufacturing and assembly phase (e.g., labor conditions at tech suppliers like Foxconn [China Labor Watch, 2019] or Uyghur workers in Apple's supply chain [Australian Strategic Policy Institute, 2020; Murphy et al., 2022]), to the data annotation and labeling processes, content moderation, and finally to the disposal of electronic waste. In the following sections, we will focus on specific issues, such as the working conditions at data annotation and content moderation centers and those at Amazon. Other concerns, such as the exploitation of conflict minerals and the environmental impact of e-waste, will be addressed in Section 3.2.7.

Inhumane and precarious working conditions at data annotation and content moderation centers, particularly in countries like Kenya, the Philippines, and India, highlight the dark side of the AI industry (Meta, for example, has multiple outsourced providers of content moderation in those regions) (Business and Human Rights Resource Center, 2025b). These content moderation centers – often described as 'digital sweatshops' – employ workers under exploitative conditions characterized by long shifts, low wages, and minimal protections. Moderators work up to 12 h a day or 60 h a week, earning just $1–2 per hour (around $200 per month), with no compensation for overtime, including nights and weekends. The work is highly repetitive and menial, contributing to physical and psychological exhaustion. Adding to the strain, workers are subject to intense algorithmic management systems involving constant surveillance through audio, video, screen, and keyboard monitoring, as well as efficiency and productivity metrics that track every action. Performance is tightly controlled, with high-pressure targets focused on speed and accuracy, leaving little room for breaks, rest, or error. Job security is virtually nonexistent; workers are often hired on ultra-short-term contracts lasting just one to two months and live in constant fear of dismissal, which discourages them from voicing concerns or filing complaints. Most lack access to essential labor rights and benefits, including healthcare and social security, and are frequently bound by non-disclosure agreements that prevent them from speaking out about their working conditions. The absence of union representation or collective bargaining further entrenches their vulnerability and limits their ability to improve their situation. Subcontracting arrangements make accountability even more diffuse, allowing abuse of power to go unchecked, including harassment, bullying, discrimination, and union-busting tactics. The psychological toll is particularly severe due to the nature of the content being reviewed. Moderators are routinely exposed to disturbing and graphic material, including child sexual abuse, rape, suicide, and torture, which significantly increases the risk of emotional distress and long-term mental health issues such as post-traumatic stress disorder (PTSD). Despite their crucial role in maintaining safe digital spaces, these workers remain largely invisible, underpaid, and unprotected, underscoring the urgent need for stronger labor standards, mental health support, and regulatory oversight in the respective industry (Dachwitz & Hilbig, 2025; Hao, 2025; Internet Watch Foundation, 2025; Muldoon et al., 2025; Thiel, 2023).

The outsourcing of services to the Global South has become a key aspect of the AI industry, with companies and countries competing for the most profitable contracts from major AI players (i.e., 'Big AI') like Alphabet, Amazon, Apple, Meta, Microsoft, Nvidia, and OpenAI (and their Chinese counterparts, Alibaba, Baidu, Huawei, and Tencent).[17] This has led to a race to the bottom in terms of wages and working conditions. It is noteworthy that the annotation and content moderation market is highly competitive. Given the many short-term contracts and the fact that minimal capital investments, training, and the like are required, annotation and content moderation services can be easily transferred to different companies or countries. This situation results in highly mobile tech companies that can shift locations, while workers in developing countries remain immobile with little bargaining power, exacerbated by the existence of a 'reserve army of labor.' The services provided by these workers are crucial for the development of social media apps, chatbots, and other AI technologies, such as autonomous vehicles, where data annotation and labeling are essential for machine learning processes like computer vision and LLMs (Hao, 2025; Muldoon et al., 2025).

As such, AI is increasingly seen as an 'extraction machine,' a tool that serves the interests of the wealthy, further entrenching their dominance. It also strengthens their power while simultaneously embedding existing societal biases in new digital formats of discrimination. As noted in Muldoon et al. (2025), AI enables the extraction of economic value from a vulnerable and dependent workforce, ultimately enriching big tech shareholders while consolidating power and wealth in the hands of a narrow elite. This system treats humans, along with natural resources like water, energy, and minerals (see the next section), as raw materials or fuel, whether in the form of human labor, ideas, or data. The precarious working conditions of AI laborers reflect the historical exploitation found in colonial economies, where gendered and racial-

17 Big AI (Muldoon et al., 2025) refers to companies privatizing collective intelligence by enclosing datasets and using proprietary software to create new outputs through data manipulation. This leads to the concentration of wealth and power and the extraction of resources and human labor. These companies also hold infrastructural power by owning AI infrastructure, such as data centers (New York Times, 2025a), hyperscalers, fiber-optic/submarine cables, and other computing hardware. This control over critical infrastructure is another form of gatekeeping or bottleneck power. Big tech companies can rent out 'AI-as-a-service' to other (startup) companies, creating new dependencies and power asymmetries (i.e., training large foundation models requires substantial computational power and storage capacity; similar to large data centers and specialized AI chips, these resources are predominantly controlled by a few corporations, thereby reinforcing their dominance in the industry). Overall, it is the capital-intensive nature of AI development (New York Times, 2025f) that explains why many startups partner with legacy tech companies, which possess enormous cash reserves and access to the infrastructure required for building advanced AI systems.

ized extraction was commonplace. The reliance on this system also echoes the practices of Fordism and Taylor's scientific management, resulting in what some call 'digital Taylorism,' where workers are subjected to rigid control, monotonous tasks, and low wages, all while the larger technological ecosystem thrives off their labor.

According to Dachwitz & Hilbig (2025), digital colonialism – aka modern slavery – is characterized, among others, by the exploitation of microworkers, data colonialism, and complicity in human rights violations (other key features include the extraction of natural resources, the concentration of critical digital infrastructure, and the geopolitical implications of the China–U.S. AI arms race, which will be discussed elsewhere in this paper): I. *Exploiting click, crowd, and micro workers*, especially in the Global South (Bender & Hanna, 2025; Tubaro et al., 2020), has emerged as a pressing concern (see above). Commonly referred to as 'AI ghost workers' (Gray & Suri, 2019) or 'humans-as-a-service,' these individuals are often outsourced to developing countries to perform essential tasks. Companies, particularly those in the business process outsourcing sector, such as Sama, Scale AI, and Remotasks (Hao, 2025), profit from their labor while subjecting them to extremely low wages and harsh, often inhumane working conditions.

II. *Data colonialism*, also referred to as 'data grab' (Mejias & Couldry, 2024), mirrors the land grabs during the colonial era, with powerful corporations extracting and commodifying data from vulnerable and marginalized groups, including Indigenous peoples (Couldry & Mejias, 2019; Hao, 2025). This process, also known as 'data extractivism,' is central to the datafication of society, where nearly every aspect of human life is turned into data, often without consent or fair compensation. As technology giants expand into smart farming and 'agriculture 4.0,' 'datafied agriculture' has become a prominent example of this exploitation. With tools like Alphabet's Mineral, AWS Solutions for Agriculture, and Microsoft's Azure Data Manager for Agriculture, as well as FarmBeats, these companies are reshaping farming practices, particularly in developing countries, by embedding data-driven solutions into the agricultural industry. However, the commodification of farming practices raises concerns, as it often leads to a form of neo-colonialism where local farmers and communities are stripped of control over their data, while big tech and big agriculture (e.g., Bayer) reap economic benefits (Dachwitz & Hilbig, 2025).

III. The rise of tech companies in China and the United States has increasingly entailed *complicity in human rights violations*, as these corporations often collaborate with authoritarian regimes to censor or restrict Internet content. This is particularly evident in countries such as Turkey and Vietnam, as revealed in the Facebook Papers (Haugen, 2023; Ressa, 2023). One of the most troubling examples is TikTok's operations in China, where the platform censors topics like Falun Gong, the Tiananmen Square massacre, Tibet, and the ongoing persecution of Uyghurs in Xinjiang. Major tech firms, including Facebook, Google, and Twitter/X, have also been implicated in providing censorship, filtering, and surveillance technologies to authoritarian governments such as China and Turkey, thereby enabling local human rights abuses, including the targeting of Kurds, Tibetans, and Uyghurs. This complicity extends to the dissemination of digital propaganda, disinformation, and dangerous/hate speech through online platforms – phenomena that have fueled genocides and political manipulation, such as the Rohingya genocide in Myanmar (United Nations Human Rights Council, 2018) and the election interference orchestrated by Cambridge Analytica/SCL in countries like Trinidad and Tobago, Kenya, Nigeria, and the United States (The Influence Industry Project, 2025). The use of surveillance tools such as NSO Group's Pegasus spyware, employed to target journalists, human rights defenders, and political opposition figures, further illustrates the disturbing intersection of technology and repression (The Citizen Lab, 2025). Public-private partnerships have also played a significant role in enabling mass surveillance programs, including the NSA's PRISM and XKeyscore, as well as GCHQ's Tempora (Gellman, 2021; Greenwald, 2015; Snowden, 2019). Chinese tech firms like Huawei (Dou, 2025) have contributed to surveillance and repression efforts targeting ethnic minorities (Australian Strategic Policy Institute, 2020; Murphy et al., 2022), while Israel's cybersecurity industry – closely linked to its military – has supported the surveillance of Palestinians in Gaza and the West Bank through applications such as Wolf Pack and Blue/Red Wolf, which use facial recognition and biometric data. These practices reflect a broader trend of militarized surveillance, exemplified by corporate-military collaborations such as JEDI, Project Maven, Clearview AI (Hill, 2023; Mother Jones, 2025; Narayanan & Kapoor, 2024; New York Times, 2020; Wired, 2023), and Palantir (Amnesty International, 2019; New York Times, 2025b), underscoring the growing entanglement between technology, militarization, and corporate power (Dachwitz & Hilbig, 2025).

Business and human rights concerns are not confined to the Global South; they also persist in the Global North. For example, many crowdworkers (Bender & Hanna, 2025), such as those engaged in platform-based annotation tasks for companies like Amazon Mechanical Turk, are classified as independent contractors and lack fundamental employment rights, including health insurance, sick leave, and retirement benefits (the same is true for other gig workers, such as Uber/Lyft drivers and food delivery persons). Similarly, the working conditions at Amazon, especially for warehouse and delivery workers, are characterized by intense digital workplace monitoring, with many employees being constantly watched, tracked, and observed throughout their workday, including anti-union surveillance and driver monitoring. This surveillance includes methods like CCTV, keystroke recordings, GPS tracking, mood and sentiment analysis, facial recognition, voice monitoring, workplace wearables (i.e., recording employee health stats), predictive algorithms (i.e., scoring systems using 'risk or vulnerability scores') that assess the likelihood of workers leaving or joining a union, and AI-powered text analysis software that monitors employee emails and text messages to assess workplace culture and employees' sense of belonging. The experience resembles Ford's assembly lines and conveyor belts, where workers function like automatons, with little control or autonomy over their work processes. This focus on discipline (i.e., intense managerial control and domination) and pace (i.e., a system optimized for speed and cost) leads to feelings of alienation, high turnover rates, and a lack of personal fulfillment. Additionally,

AI recruitment and hiring tools, which sort through resumes, create shortlists, conduct interviews, assess personality (tests), and evaluate candidates, raise ethical concerns due to biases, particularly against female candidates in technical fields like engineering and computer science, leading to a dehumanized experience for job applicants. The widespread use of workplace wearables, AI-powered scoring systems, and tools that monitor employees' emails and text messages to gauge company culture creates further ethical dilemmas, such as potential invasions of bodily autonomy and personal privacy (e.g., monitoring and recording employee conversations at work/home). These practices, especially those conducted without employee knowledge and consent, raise concerns about how technology intersects with personal rights and freedoms, and demand better workplace protections.

3.2.7 AI and the environment

The business and human rights concerns surrounding AI extend beyond exploitative labor practices, such as the poor working conditions faced by data annotators and content moderators who are essential yet often invisible to the development of AI systems. These ethical issues intersect with growing environmental concerns, as the same technologies rely on vast computational resources that demand significant energy consumption. Training large AI models requires immense data centers, which contribute to carbon emissions and strain water resources for cooling. Thus, the hidden human cost of AI is mirrored by an equally hidden environmental toll, raising urgent questions about the sustainability of current AI development practices.

On the one hand, AI holds great promise for tackling environmental challenges and advancing sustainable development. It can help optimize the use of scarce resources, reduce reliance on pesticides and fertilizers, and power innovations like smart energy grids, thermostats, and precision agriculture and forestry (Dachwitz & Hilbig, 2025). These applications contribute to the vision of 'sustainable AI,' where technology supports the three sustainability dimensions – economic, environmental, and social. As such, AI could play a crucial role in helping to realize the Sustainable Development Goals (AI4SDGs Think Tank, 2020/2025; Floridi, 2023). However, the ecological footprint of (generative) AI technologies is an increasing cause for concern. The rapid expansion of data centers, supercomputers, LLMs, and cryptocurrency mining operations has led to a substantial rise in global energy and water consumption, particularly for cooling systems, and contributes significantly to the growing problem of electronic waste (Bender et al, 2021; Strubell et al., 2019).[18]

18 As pointed out by Hao (2025), data centers and LLMs require vast amounts of energy – driving climate change; water – contributing to water shortages; land – leading to land grabs, forced displacement or resettlement, destruction of community livelihoods, and violations of the rights of Indigenous

According to the IEA, in 2022, data centers and transmission networks consumed 2–3% of the world's electricity (with an upward trend), roughly equal to that of Germany or France. Hyperscalers (i.e., [hyperscale] cloud computing providers) can consume as much electricity as 80,000 U.S. households (McKinsey & Company, 2023). Some data centers require up to 19 million liters of water per day, equivalent to the daily use of a U.S. town of 50,000 people (Australian Energy Council, 2023; Muldoon et al., 2025).[19,20]

Bitcoin's (and other cryptocurrencies') ecological footprint is also substantial (and rising), with a global energy consumption estimated at around 176 terawatt-hours (TWh) per year (Statista, 2025a), roughly 0.6% of the world's total energy production, comparable to the entire energy use of countries like Malaysia and Sweden (Badea & Mungiu-Pupăzan, 2021; Huynh et al, 2022; Kohli et al., 2023). This enormous consumption is primarily driven by the need for high computing power to perform energy-intensive mining operations using specialized electronic devices. Until China banned Bitcoin mining in 2021, most mining took place there, heavily relying on dirty coal power from the Xinjiang region, a source linked to severe human rights violations, including the cultural genocide of Uyghur people. Besides energy use, Bitcoin mining also consumes large amounts of water for cooling purposes and contributes to growing e-waste because mining hardware has a short lifespan and cannot be easily repurposed.

As noted in the U.N. Digital Economy Report 2024 (U.N. Trade and Development, 2024) and the Biden White House (2022b), data centers are notorious for their massive energy consumption, contributing to climate change, while mining cryptocurrencies exacerbates these environmental issues. Furthermore, e-waste generated by the rapid turnover of digital devices poses another layer of environmental harm, especially in developing countries where most of this hazardous waste ends up in landfills (Owusu-Sekyere et al., 2022). This phenomenon, often referred to as 'toxic colonialism,' has severe health implications for communities in these regions (World Health Organization, 2021). Additionally, the extraction of natural resources essential to producing digital technology, such as cobalt from the Democratic Republic of Congo

---

peoples; and minerals – raising concerns over the use of conflict minerals. The burden of these costs disproportionately affects vulnerable communities in the Global (North and) South.

19 For more information on LLMs' and generative AI's environmental footprint, including their energy and water consumption and carbon emissions, see Li et al. (2025), Luccioni et al. (2022), and Patterson et al. (2021).

20 Beyond environmental impact, there are human rights concerns: many data centers rely on temporary workers, vendors, and contractors, who often perform the same duties as full-time staff but receive less pay, have short-term contracts, and are denied employment benefits.

(DRC) (Amnesty International, 2023; Kara, 2023;[21] Nest, 2013; Washington Post, 2023) and lithium (i.e., 'white gold') from the 'Lithium Triangle' in South America (Argentina, Bolivia, and Chile), raises serious human rights concerns. The working conditions for miners in these regions are often inhumane, with reports of modern slavery, violations of Indigenous peoples' rights, and significant environmental degradation, including water shortages. Ultimately, the practices surrounding the digital economy contribute to a cycle of climate or ecological injustice, where industrialized nations are the primary drivers of socio-environmental harm, while developing nations bear the brunt of these impacts (Bender & Hanna, 2025; Dachwitz & Hilbig, 2025; Hao, 2025).

3.2.8 Big tech and antitrust

AI's human and environmental costs – from the exploitation of low-paid data workers to the significant energy and water demands of large-scale model training – underscore the ethical complexity of current technological development. These burdens are not distributed evenly; instead, they are concentrated among vulnerable labor forces and ecosystems, while the benefits accrue primarily to a handful of dominant tech corporations. This imbalance underscores the growing influence of big tech, whose control over data, infrastructure, and innovation ecosystems enables it to shape not only technological futures but also global labor standards, environmental impacts, and public discourse. As these companies expand their influence, questions of accountability, governance, and democratic oversight become increasingly urgent.

21 According to Kara (2023), the cobalt supply chain from the DRC cannot be considered clean. Cobalt sourced from this region is tainted by severe human rights violations, such as slavery, child labor (with an estimated 70% of DRC cobalt linked to child labor; considering that the DRC produces 72% of the world's cobalt, this implies that half of all cobalt globally has been tainted by child labor in the DRC), forced labor, debt bondage, human trafficking, and hazardous working conditions, including mining accidents and cave-ins. These unsafe environments – exposing workers to heavy metals, hazardous waste, and pollution – often result in injury and death. Cobalt itself is toxic to touch and breathe, and it frequently contains traces of radioactive uranium. Additionally, wildlife, such as fish and chicken, are harmed by contamination, with heavy metals entering the food supply chain, causing serious health problems for local populations, including higher rates of birth defects, stillbirths, miscarriages, low birth weight, and other issues in mining communities. Respiratory illnesses, such as lung cancer from inhaling cobalt dust, as well as lead poisoning, are widespread. Workers also face 'pathetic wages' (Kara, 2023) often experiencing reduced or delayed payments. Rampant environmental destruction, such as deforestation and water and air pollution, displaces local communities, who are often resettled without compensation. Furthermore, physical abuse (e.g., beatings) and sexual assault and harassment, especially against women and girls, are prevalent, along with (child) prostitution that contributes to the spread of HIV/AIDS and other sexually transmitted diseases. Drug and alcohol abuse further exacerbates the suffering within these communities (see also Nest, 2013; Washington Post, 2023).

The global presence of major tech companies underscores their substantial dominance across various digital sectors. For instance, Google overwhelmingly leads the search engine market (with a market share of more than 90% in most countries), while its Chrome browser and Apple's Safari command a large portion of Internet browser usage. In the mobile operating system space, Android maintains a strong lead, with iOS trailing behind. Similarly, Windows holds a clear advantage in the desktop operating system market, significantly outpacing macOS. In the social media landscape, Facebook stands as the leading platform, while its sister apps, Instagram and WhatsApp – both owned by Meta – also attract billions of users, contributing to Meta's expansive reach; meanwhile, platforms like YouTube and TikTok further reinforce the concentrated dominance of a few major players. In other digital markets, big tech companies dominate almost everything from digital ads (Google, Meta) to e-commerce (Amazon), maps (Google), voice assistants/smart speakers (Amazon, Apple, and Google), app stores (Apple and Google), cloud computing (Amazon's AWS), and generative AI (OpenAI/Microsoft, Gemini/Google, Anthropic/Amazon, and Google). In addition to the major U.S. tech firms, China is home to its own tech powerhouses, including Alibaba, Baidu, ByteDance, Huawei, and Tencent (Wörsdörfer, 2020, 2021, 2022a, 2022b, 2023, 2024b).

Their profits and revenues are remarkable and consistently increasing, with Amazon leading the way in 2024 for overall revenue ($638b) and total assets ($625b), Alphabet holding the top position for net income ($100b) and total equity ($325b), and Apple dominating in operating income ($123b); the combined revenue of the 'Big Five' exceeded $1.5 trillion in 2024 (Statista, 2025c). Their market capitalization makes them some of the largest companies globally, further cementing their position of power (as of summer 2025, the list of largest companies based on market capitalization is led by Nvidia, followed by Microsoft, Apple, Amazon, Alphabet, and Meta; all those companies are trillion-dollar companies [CompaniesMarketCap.com, 2025]). Mergers and acquisitions (M&As) have become central strategies for big tech companies, often aimed at acquiring intellectual property or executing so-called 'killer acquisitions' to eliminate potential competitors. Over the past few decades, these firms have been involved in hundreds of M&As, most of which have gone unchallenged by regulatory authorities in both Europe and the United States (Wörsdörfer, 2020, 2021, 2022a, 2022b, 2023, 2024b).

Notably, many tech companies operate as de facto monopolists or oligopolists, exerting near-total control over their markets. Their dominance reflects a broader economic system often described as 'monopoly capitalism.' Several structural factors contribute to this concentration of power, including economies of scale, which enable large firms to deliver goods and services at lower costs, and strong network effects, where the value of a platform increases as more users join, thereby attracting additional users and marginalizing competitors. While 'platform capitalism' may offer certain conveniences and benefits to consumers, it often displaces smaller businesses and limits overall market diversity. Moreover, big tech companies possess unparalleled access to vast troves of personal data, frequently characterized as the 'oil of the twenty-first century,' which further reinforces their market dominance. Most digital markets are also shaped by winner-takes-all dynamics (see above), where a handful of dominant firms capture most of the value (Wörsdörfer, 2020, 2021, 2022a, 2022b, 2023, 2024b).

However, this consolidation of economic power (i.e., the monopolization or re-feudalization of the economy) comes with significant political challenges, including lobbying and rent-seeking (e.g., in the form of the revolving door phenomenon, campaign finance contributions, and regular meetings with high-ranking government officials), where big tech's influence over policymakers often results in regulatory capture and a concentration of both politico-economic power and wealth in the hands of a few (Taplin, 2018). Big tech's anti-competitive business practices, including structural dominance, leveraging and gatekeeping,[22] self-preferencing, copycat appropriations, discriminatory platform access and exclusionary business conduct (e.g., tying and bundling), predatory or below-cost pricing, killer acquisitions, and monopsony power, only intensify these concerns. These companies also contribute to novel consumer harms, such as the erosion of privacy and data protection, and socio-political harm, including the spread of disinformation and dangerous and hate speech (Wörsdörfer, 2020, 2021, 2022a, 2022b, 2023, 2024b; see Sections 3.2.5 and 3.2.9).

Lanier (2013) critiques the direction of the current information economy, arguing that "the information economy that we are currently building doesn't really embrace capitalism, but rather a new form of feudalism." According to Lanier (2013), this shift is marked by the concentration of wealth and power around so-called 'Siren Servers,' massive, centralized data systems owned and run by a few tech giants. By controlling vast amounts of data, these companies accumulate unprecedented levels of money, wealth, and influence. Lanier (2013) further elaborates, stating that 'the silicon age' has been a 'new gilded age,' where a handful of firms benefit disproportionately from technological progress, leaving the majority without significant gains. The situation becomes even more concerning when Lanier (2013) warns that when giant remote companies own everyone's digital identities, they become 'too big to fail,' becoming so embedded in society that their collapse would threaten the functioning of markets and governments. He suggests that his creates a twofold threat for personal liberty, with big business, exemplified by big tech, working hand in hand with big government (NSA, etc.) to erode individual freedoms and privacy in ways that undermine democracy and autonomy (Lanier, 2013).

22 For more information on Big AI's gatekeeping, bottleneck, and infrastructural power, see the work of Baer et al. (2020), Commission 'Competition Law 4.0' (2019), Furman Report (2019), Klobuchar (2021), Petit (2020), Stigler Report (2019), and Subcommittee on Antitrust (2020).

3.2.9 Democracy and the rule of law

The concentrated power held by tech companies poses a serious threat to democratic systems, enabling them to influence elections and manipulate public opinion on a massive scale. Their vast economic resources are frequently leveraged to shape political decision-making through lobbying and rent-seeking, further entrenching their influence. Moreover, as major social media conglomerates, these companies facilitate the spread of harmful content – including dangerous and hate speech and disinformation (see above) – which undermines informed public discourse and weakens the foundations of democracy and the rule of law.

AI is expected to transform the practice of law and the very nature of its application, fundamentally reshaping how legal professionals work. This transformation impacts not only legal practice but also the formulation and administration of laws, as traditional methods struggle to keep pace with the rapid advancement of AI technologies. Consequently, the legal system must adapt, requiring the modification and expansion of existing legal concepts and principles to remain practical and relevant. The development of new legal frameworks, such as those addressing autonomous vehicles, has become essential to meet the novel challenges and scenarios introduced by AI-driven innovations (Kaplan, 2016; Wörsdörfer, 2018).

AI is not only transforming the practice of law but also streamlining organizational processes, significantly reducing costs for legal professionals and scholars. By automating repetitive and routine tasks, such as scanning and reviewing large volumes of legal documents, AI enables lawyers and paralegals to concentrate on more complex and nuanced legal issues. These systems often surpass human performance in terms of accuracy and speed, making them particularly effective for handling tasks that involve processing vast amounts of information.[23] Beyond operational efficiency, AI is increasingly used to formally analyze and study the law, facilitating the evaluation of legal systems for consistency and completeness through disciplines such as computational law and legal informatics (Kaplan, 2016, 2024; Wörsdörfer, 2018).

Moreover, AI systems are increasingly used to predict the outcomes of lawsuits by analyzing extensive legal databases and identifying patterns, such as judges' prior voting behavior. In the realm of criminal justice, big data-powered algorithms like COMPAS are employed to assess the risk of re-offending and inform parole decisions (Bender & Hanna, 2025). AI is also being integrated into sentencing processes; however, this trend raises serious concerns about racial and ethnic discrimination, as well as the presence of (agentic) AI bias (see Section 3.2.3). Predictive policing tools, such as PredPol (The Guardian, 2025b), are used to forecast potential crime hotspots and de-

23 In the legal field, generative AI can aid in 'predictive coding,' document preparation (i.e., the automated drafting of legal documents), online legal services like LegalZoom, and arbitration and dispute resolution. Notably, ChatGPT-4 has passed the bar exam, showcasing its potential within the legal profession (Kaplan, 2024).

tect emerging crime trends, enabling law enforcement agencies to (ideally) allocate resources more strategically. While these innovations allegedly enhance efficiency and predictive accuracy,[24] they underscore the urgent need for transparency, accountability, and fairness in designing and deploying AI in the legal system. It is equally essential that AI serves only as a tool to support, rather than replace, human decision-makers; blind reliance on machine-generated outcomes must be avoided, particularly in matters of justice (Kaplan, 2016; Wörsdörfer, 2018).

The rise of intelligent agents, such as chatbots, raises important legal and ethical questions. Should these entities be permitted to enter into legal agreements, own property, or hold assets, thus granting them certain legal rights? When algorithms, computers, or robots commit crimes, the issue of liability becomes critical: who should be held responsible for their actions? Addressing accountability involves challenges related to deterrence, rehabilitation, and restitution, particularly given the control problem and the need for robust safety and security regulations. Related ethical questions also arise concerning the moral status of AI, such as whether intelligent systems should be considered moral agents, possess rights, or bear moral responsibility. Determining accountability when things go wrong is a complex issue that demands careful evaluation within legal and ethical frameworks (Wörsdörfer, 2018).

The problem of responsibility in AI and technological systems is complicated by the involvement of multiple parties, including corporations and numerous components, making it challenging to ascribe and distribute liability. Additionally, the lack of transparency and explainability in AI and machine learning systems – often due to their reliance on black box algorithms rather than decision trees or symbolic reasoning – undermines trust in the technology. Because humans frequently cannot explain how these systems arrive at decisions, addressing the black box problem is crucial. Developing transparent and explainable AI is essential to open the black box and ensure accountability, fairness, and greater confidence in AI-driven processes (Kaplan, 2016; Pasquale, 2016; Wörsdörfer, 2018).

In the context of democracy and politics, generative AI presents significant challenges, particularly by accelerating the spread of disinformation and amplifying harmful online content, often through tools like chatbots (Internet Watch Foundation, 2025; Thiel, 2023, see Section 3.2.5). Advanced (generative) AI systems are capable of producing compelling fake news, deepfakes (Narayanan & Kapoor, 2024), and large-scale propaganda (New York Times, 2025e), making it increasingly difficult for citizens to distinguish fact (truth) from fiction (post-truth). This erosion of a shared reality undermines public trust in political institutions, electoral processes, the media, and academia. As political actors and malign foreign entities exploit AI to manipulate pub-

24 While police organizations claim that tools like PredPol enhance efficiency and predictive accuracy, civil rights organizations strongly dispute these assertions, arguing that the effectiveness of predictive policing tools is highly contested and lacks sufficient empirical evidence to support such claims.

lic opinion or suppress dissent, the democratic process becomes increasingly vulnerable to distortion, manipulation, and exploitation (McIntyre, 2018; Snyder, 2017; Taplin, 2018). Furthermore, AI-driven algorithms used by social media platforms often prioritize engagement over accuracy, inadvertently promoting sensationalist or hateful content (e.g., clickbait). This exacerbates political polarization and fragmentation and normalizes extremist views (Vaidhyanathan, 2020). In such a socio-political environment, institutions tasked with upholding democratic norms and the rule of law, such as courts, legislatures, and independent oversight bodies, face mounting skepticism and a decline in authority. Without robust regulatory frameworks and technological safeguards, (generative) AI could erode the very foundations of democratic governance by sowing distrust, deepening societal divisions, and weakening the legitimacy of public institutions.

3.2.9.1 Excursus: techno-libertarianism

Techno-libertarianism, often dubbed the 'Silicon Valley Ideology' (Borsook, 2000), reflects the tech culture and political views of Silicon Valley's elite (e.g., Musk and Thiel), who embrace a hotbed of political libertarianism blending libertarian politics with neoliberal economics – a mixture sometimes called the 'Californian Ideology' (Barbrook & Cameron, 1995). This cyber- or techno-libertarian movement draws on the ideological and normative foundations laid by thinkers such as Rand, Rothbard, Mises, Hayek, Friedman, and Nozick. Influential institutions like the American Enterprise Institute, the Cato Institute (founded by the Koch brothers and Rothbard), the Federalist Society, and the Heritage Foundation (linked to the Mercer family) promote these ideas (note that Google donated money to the Competitive Enterprise Institute, the Heritage Foundation, and the Cato Institute – all of which are institutions that promote climate science denial [The Guardian, 2019]). Rand's novels, *Atlas Shrugged* and *The Fountainhead*, advocate rational or ethical egoism alongside laissez-faire capitalism, while Rothbard champions anarcho-capitalism and free-market anarchism. Hayek critiques social justice as an illusion, a weasel word, and an atavism (Wörsdörfer, 2013b; see also Slobodian [2025], who connects neoliberalism, libertarianism, and the alt-right, including controversial themes like race science and eugenics; for more information on 'technofascism'[25] and the right-wing roots of Silicon Valley, see The Guardian, 2025c). The Chicago School of Economics promotes shareholder value capitalism, deregulation, and privatization, while Nozick envisions a 'minimal state,' all of which profoundly influence the techno-libertarian worldview dominating Silicon Valley.[26]

---

25 Technofascism is characterized, among other things, by its emphasis on male-dominated entrepreneurship (and its corresponding celebration of wealth and power), adherence to traditional gender roles (and masculinity), the valorization of the nuclear family, and opposition to so-called 'political correctness' (and diversity, equity, and inclusion policies) (Gilder, 2012; The Guardian, 2025c; Hill, 2023; Mother Jones, 2025).

26 The narrative outlined in Oreskes and Conway (2023) shows how influential organizations – including the National Association of Manufacturers, the National Electric Light Association, and the Foundation for Economic Education – helped construct a durable ideological framework rooted in libertarian and neoliberal thought. Drawing on thinkers such as Mises and Hayek, as well as cultural figures like Lane and Wilder (author of the *Little House* series), and on Christian libertarian voices like Fifield Jr. through *Spiritual Mobilization*, this framework also gained visibility through Hollywood

Techno-libertarianism is characterized by a staunch belief in free-market capitalism, a laissez-faire ideology, and a minimal or 'night watchman' state that rejects the welfare state, limiting the government's role to protecting life, liberty, and property, as per Locke's philosophy. It emphasizes personal freedom and individual responsibility, combined with mistrust in government and a religious-like or blind faith in free markets. While anti-traditional in many ways, techno-libertarians support a 'smart government' that acts primarily as an investor, enabler, and facilitator in areas like education, R&D, infrastructure, and immigration reform, rather than as a bureaucratic administrator and regulator. They advocate for deregulation and privatization, preferring self-regulation or soft laws over formal governance standards. Regarding taxation, they support low capital gains taxes and tax cuts for businesses, while also engaging in offshore tax avoidance (Wörsdörfer, 2018).[27]

Entrepreneurship and the entrepreneurial spirit are glorified, and visionary leaders and doers/ risk-takers like Jobs and Musk are celebrated under the 'Great Man' and 'Think Big' theory (Gilder, 2012). Central to the ideology is a 'cult of disruption,' valuing revolutionary, disruptive change through 'creative destruction' (hence, the focus on R&D and innovations). Techno-libertarianism is deeply optimistic and utopian about technology, holding a near-religious or blind faith that technological innovation is a liberator capable of curing or solving all societal problems, promising perfection, immortality, and endless progress (for more information on technological optimism or utopianism, see Wörsdörfer, 2018). This blend of market fundamentalism, faith in innovation, and minimal government intervention defines the core of techno-libertarianism.

The dark side of techno-libertarianism lies in its tendency to place profits over people, often at the expense of fundamental labor rights, equality, and societal well-being. Driven by free-market capitalism and a deep mistrust of government regulation, this ideology fuels exploitative practices such as poor working conditions in Amazon warehouses (see Muldoon et al., 2025; New York Times, 2018, for more

---

libertarian filmmaking inspired by Rand and later embraced by Reagan. The Chicago School, led by figures such as Director, Friedman, Stigler, and Bork, advanced key concepts like the 'consumer welfare standard' (Wörsdörfer, 2022a, 2022b). Corporations such as GE – particularly through Boulware – further aligned these ideas with Reagan's emerging economic agenda. Together, these ideological currents fueled Carter-era deregulation and set the stage for the Reagan Revolution, marked by trickle-down economics, sweeping tax cuts, persistent budget deficits, widespread deregulation, the weakening of government agencies through underfunding and understaffing, and the ascendancy of shareholder value maximization. These developments contributed to widening socio-economic inequality, anti-environmentalism, and rising anti-science sentiment. Think tanks promoting antigovernment views reinforced this trajectory, elevating the so-called 'Tripod of Freedom' – representative democracy, political freedom, and free enterprise – as foundational U.S. principles. The Clinton administration and the 'New Democrats' continued this policy direction with what Oreskes and Conway call 'neo-neoliberalism.' In their view, Carter initiated the Reagan Revolution and Clinton completed it, most notably through deregulation of the telecommunications and financial sectors, culminating in the repeal of the Glass-Steagall Act and paving the way for the 2007–2008 financial crisis. The Trump administration intensified anti-science and anti-government attitudes, especially in its handling of climate policy and the COVID-19 pandemic. At the core of this broader ideological project is the indivisibility thesis, which conflates economic and political freedom, coupled with a belief in the 'magic of the marketplace' or market fundamentalism. This worldview fosters distrust of government, uncritical faith in markets, and resistance to regulation and scientific expertise – conditions that have deepened crises in finance, climate, public health, and social welfare, including the opioid epidemic, healthcare system failures, and pervasive gun violence.

27 "It's a belief in markets over democracy, in business and philanthropy over government spending, and in industry self-regulation over democratic laws" (Muldoon et al., 2025).

information on the inhumane working conditions at Facebook's Centers for Deleting Content) and overseas factories like Foxconn and other suppliers, including those tied to the conflict minerals industry. The rise of the gig economy – exemplified by ridesharing and food delivery platforms – reflects a new form of 'digital Taylorism,' echoing Taylor's scientific management principles, where surveillance, performance tracking, and algorithmic control strip workers of autonomy and stability. Techno-libertarianism frequently denies basic labor standards, using union-busting tactics, such as those reported at Amazon warehouses and Apple Stores across the United States and beyond, to suppress collective bargaining efforts. Meanwhile, the culture of Silicon Valley has been marked by sexism and macho behavior, as seen in the anti-diversity memo 'Google Manifesto' and corporate governance scandals at Uber, contributing to sexual harassment, bullying, and a persistent gender pay gap. Despite its progressive stance on issues like LGBTQ+ rights and support for movements like 'Black Lives Matter,' the tech industry is plagued by age, gender, and racial biases and discrimination in hiring and promotion practices (e.g., most jobs are held by young White men). The economic consequences of this ideology are also stark: rising income gaps and wealth inequality, and a growing affordability crisis have pushed many ordinary citizens out of the Bay Area due to high housing, childcare, and living costs, forcing long commutes and deepening homelessness. Techno-libertarianism's glorification of innovation and individualism thus masks a troubling disregard for social justice and collective responsibility (Wörsdörfer, 2018).

3.2.10 AI and the military

The destabilizing effects of AI on democracy and the rule of law are further intensified by its potential misuse in military applications, which introduces significant global security risks. As AI technologies become increasingly integrated into defense systems, concerns grow over autonomous weapons, surveillance, and cyber warfare capabilities that could escalate conflicts or undermine international stability. This convergence of AI's impact on political systems and military power underscores the need for robust governance frameworks to manage risks across democratic institutions and global security.

In the emerging era of artificially intelligent warfare – often called 'i-battle' or ' i-war' – nations increasingly invest in smart weapons and autonomous systems (i.e., warbots), such as unmanned drones and semi or fully autonomous lethal weapons. At the heart of this transformation is the military-industrial complex, long driven by powerful institutions like (D)ARPA and the CIA, which played foundational roles in developing the Internet and DARPA competitions (e.g., the two autonomous vehicles Grand Challenges in 2004 and 2005 and the Urban Challenge in 2007) and now fund cutting-edge AI research. As the United States and China (and, to a certain degree, Russia) accelerate their pursuit of AI supremacy, an AI arms race is underway – one that could potentially determine global dominance and control. This competition extends beyond the (military) battlefield, touching on economic and technological fronts as countries implement export restrictions or controls and compete over critical resources like semiconductors and rare earth minerals, including bans on minerals (Dachwitz & Hilbig, 2025; Muldoon et al., 2025). The rise of lethal autonomous weapons has sparked urgent ethical and regulatory debates, including calls by groups like the *Campaign Against Killer Robots* to ban or tightly regulate 'killer robots.' Such discussions may necessitate revisiting foundational ethical frameworks, including revising or updating Asimov's laws of robotics, to ensure AI serves humanity rather than threatens it.

The rise of AI as a decision-making technology has significant implications for the future of warfare. As both a tool and agent, AI introduces non-human decision-making into military operations, fundamentally altering the nature of war (i.e., warfare). This shift raises ethical concerns about accountability, human judgment, and the value of life in automated conflict scenarios. Moreover, the skills of modern soldiers and army members are evolving; traditional qualities such as courage in combat, leadership, and command presence are increasingly being complemented – or replaced – by technical competence, STEM expertise, and tactical and strategic thinking. These changes necessitate careful consideration of how humanity interacts with war in the era of intelligent machines (Payne, 2021).

AI weapon systems are rapidly transforming modern warfare, with the current landscape already featuring (semi-)autonomous helicopters and aircraft, such as unmanned combat air vehicles and drones – i.e., unmanned aerial vehicles – used for tactical surveillance and precision strikes. The Predator drone, for example, is a remotely piloted air vehicle equipped with missiles and stealth technology. On the seas, autonomous submarines and marine vessels are being developed for tasks such as minesweeping and anti-submarine warfare (see New York Times [2024] and Washington Post [2024] for more information about AI weapons being used in the Ukraine war and Israel's war in Gaza). Looking toward the (near) future, military innovation is moving toward human-machine teaming, where AI platforms interact closely with (human) soldiers. AI swarms – coordinated networks of weaponized robots or drones – are being developed based on swarm intelligence, which enables rapid learning and decision-making through the collective exchange and coordination of information, knowledge, and expertise. The concept of 'enhanced soldiers' is also emerging, using brain-computer interfaces and augmented intelligence that merge AI with biotechnology (see the excursus on Technological Singularity below). Some envision all-robot armies capable of autonomous ground combat, reminiscent of science fiction scenarios such as *The Terminator*. Early examples of such systems include warbots like the Tomahawk cruise missile, Joint Directed Attack Munition, and acoustic torpedoes. Additionally, robots are already utilized for search and rescue missions, handling hazardous materials, bomb defusal, equipment transport, and surveillance, thereby blurring the line between combat and support roles in AI-driven warfare (Payne, 2021).

Cyber warfare is becoming increasingly shaped by AI, as cybersecurity and AI grow more deeply intertwined. AI-powered systems can now automate cyberattacks and defensive responses, creating new dimensions of threat and protection directly linked to national security. For example, AI can be used to hack into and disable critical infrastructure, such as power grids, or hijack the healthcare systems of an enemy state. It can launch sophisticated attacks designed to compromise and degrade advanced weapon systems. This modern cyber battlefield echoes the historical tension between encryption and codebreaking, as seen in the life and work of Turing. Today, AI systems can automatically scan code for vulnerabilities, exploiting weaknesses like a computer virus, or generate patches to secure systems. As AI tools become more advanced, the ability to rapidly detect and act on software flaws may determine the success or failure of cyber operations in future conflicts (Payne, 2021).

AI weapon systems offer several advantages that are reshaping military operations. One of the most significant benefits is the enhanced speed and accuracy of decision-making, as AI can process vast amounts of information quickly, leading to better performance in tasks such as shooting more accurately and maneuvering swiftly in combat situations. These systems can also assist and advise commanders through advanced strategic thinking by providing real-time intelligence data and situational awareness. This is made possible through big data mining and analysis, including pattern recognition and the ability to identify correlations within large datasets. Surveillance footage captured by unmanned aerial vehicles in ultra-high resolution, combined with facial recognition technology, biometrics, and sensors, enables precise target identification (i.e., spotting targets and recognizing faces). AI also transforms military training through immersive simulation systems (The Guardian, 2023a), such as augmented reality (AR) or virtual reality (VR) (i.e., training systems and simulators, including flight and battlefield simulations and medic training). Perhaps most importantly, AI weapon systems can save human lives, reducing the number of soldiers required on the battlefield and potentially lowering the rates of PTSD, drug abuse, and suicide among military personnel by minimizing direct human exposure to combat (Payne, 2021).

Despite their tactical advantages, AI weapon systems have significant disadvantages that raise serious ethical concerns. A key limitation is that AI systems lack an understanding of context and meaning, often referred to as a lack of common-sense understanding. This shortfall can lead to dangerous misinterpretations, such as confusing a person surrendering with someone picking up a weapon, which can result in potentially tragic errors on the battlefield. Moreover, AI lacks emotional intelligence/empathy, making it incapable of grasping human suffering or responding appropriately in morally complex situations. These systems are also limited in their capacity for creativity and imagination, which are crucial for adapting to unpredictable combat scenarios and developing unconventional strategies (Payne, 2021).

The rise of autonomous weapon systems introduces various ethical issues that challenge traditional moral frameworks of warfare. One central concern is automation bias, where human operators develop an over-reliance on machines, potentially accepting flawed outputs without question. Automating the act of killing – i.e., delegating life-and-death decisions to algorithms – raises deep moral alarms, as it arguably strips human dignity from victims and might lead to dehumanization. Further, by abrogating responsibility for killing to inhuman and amoral systems that lack personhood, we risk outsourcing our actions to machines, eroding accountability for acts of violence. AI systems are also prone to escalatory dynamics, where the misinterpretation of data and information can result in involuntary escalation, e.g., a typical accident can lead to inadvertent and disproportionate escalation or indiscriminate killing. 'Killer robots' may boost the combat effectiveness of attacking forces (i.e., their fighting power), but could also increase civilian suffering, particularly if used recklessly. In the complex, noisy, dynamic, and unstructured battle environment, where dust, smoke, and fire distort and obscure sensors, it is questionable whether autonomous systems can accurately recognize targets, let alone make the complex ethical choices that warfare demands. Completely replacing troops with machines might also lower the threshold for going to war, shifting the burden of conflict onto civilians who will inevitably be caught in the chaotic currents unleashed. A further worry is that if autonomous armed robots become normalized in military operations, they could seep into policy decisions, private security firms, or even fall into the hands of criminals or terrorists. The pressing challenge is maintaining some form of human control and accountability in an age where machines increasingly dominate the battlefield (Payne, 2021).

3.2.10.1 Excursus: technological singularity

A particularly important concept in this context is the technological singularity – the idea that computers and robots will eventually become intelligent enough to autonomously re-engineer and improve themselves.[28] This could trigger a feedback loop of exponential advancement, often referred to as 'runaway intelligence,' in which ultra-intelligent machines design even more intelligent successors. Such an intelligence explosion would mark the transition from AGI to artificial superintelligence (ASI), where machines surpass even the most advanced human capabilities. It is important to note, however, that the emergence of ASI is contingent upon first achieving AGI – systems with human-level cognitive abilities such as language comprehension, creativity, emotional understanding, and consciousness, which has not yet materialized and may ultimately remain unfulfilled (Narayanan & Kapoor, 2024; Wörsdörfer, 2018).

This vision aligns closely with transhumanist and post-humanist thought, which anticipates a future where artificially engineered organs replace biological ones and brain–computer interfaces, such as those developed by Neuralink (2025), enable direct integration between the human mind and machines. Futu-

28 Although the development of AGI remains unlikely in the near future, it cannot be entirely ruled out. This uncertainty underscores the importance of raising awareness and sensitizing researchers, policymakers, and the public to the potential ethical concerns that may arise as AI technologies continue to evolve. In particular, tools like OpenAI's ChatGPT-5 and Neuralink's brain-computer interfaces could represent early, albeit limited, steps toward AGI. While these systems are not yet fully autonomous or capable of human-level reasoning, their rapid advancements highlight the need for ongoing discussions around the ethical, social, and regulatory implications of AGI as it potentially draws closer. Given that regulation takes time to implement, it is crucial to stay informed about the latest trends and developments in AI to ensure that when these innovations become marketable, we are prepared to address the associated risks with appropriate regulatory measures.

rists like Kurzweil envision a world where human consciousness could be transferred to robotic or cloud-based systems, making possible a form of digital immortality in which individuals preserve themselves in cyberspace. Kurzweil also predicts radical enhancements to human capabilities, including expanded sensory perception and cognitive function, which could result in significantly extended lifespans or even biological immortality (Kurzweil, 2000, 2005, 2024). These transformative possibilities, enabled by the convergence of AI, neuroscience, genetics, nanotechnology, and biotechnology (Microsoft AI, 2025), may usher in a post-human era – one in which humans gradually evolve into cyborgs or superhumans through bodily augmentation and machine integration (Wörsdörfer, 2018).

Singularity optimists, such as Kurzweil, view the singularity as a transformative moment capable of solving humanity's most pressing problems, with AGI anticipated by 2030 and ASI by 2045 (see also Acceleration Watch [Smart, 2003]). Altman, along with OpenAI's broader mission, promotes a similarly optimistic vision of AGI – one grounded in the pursuit of socially beneficial outcomes. This perspective envisions AGI as a force for good, with the potential to eradicate poverty, combat climate change, cure cancer, and tackle other global challenges. Such aspirational narratives are frequently emphasized in recent publications (Hagey, 2025; Hao, 2025) and public statements (New York Times, 2025g), portraying AGI not as a threat, but as a powerful tool for positive transformation. In contrast, singularity skeptics or pessimists, such as Vinge, who coined the term in his seminal essay *The Coming Technological Singularity* (1993), warn that ASI could pose an existential risk, particularly due to the unresolved control problem and the possibility of a machine-led takeover. Moreover, techno-utopian visions raise significant ethical and social concerns. Advanced enhancements, such as sensory or cognitive brain implants, robotic exoskeletons, and biological upgrades, may be accessible only to the wealthy, thereby exacerbating existing socio-economic inequalities (Wörsdörfer, 2018).

Harari and Bostrom, two outspoken critics of technological singularity, warn of deeply unsettling trajectories in developing advanced technologies, particularly those combining AI with genetic engineering. Harari (2017, 2019) cautions against the rise of techno-religions – new belief systems that promise salvation not through spiritual means, but through algorithms and genetic manipulation, e.g., with the help of CRISPR gene editing. These developments are closely tied to brain–computer interfaces and biological upgrades that could lead to the emergence of superhumans. However, such enhancements may only be accessible to the wealthy, intensifying socio-economic inequalities and creating a new class divide (see Section 3.2.2). Bostrom (2014), on the other hand, focuses on the existential risk of superintelligent machines. He envisions scenarios in which a robot uprising, rebellion, and/or AI takeover result in catastrophic outcomes, including the possible extinction of humanity. One of his central concerns is the rise of a 'singleton' – a single, superintelligent decision-making AI agency capable of managing human affairs, taking over and exerting control and power, and using social manipulation and rhetorical persuasion, including mind control techniques and surveillance technologies, to harm and possibly destroy humans (i.e., such an agency might become an existential risk or threat to humankind). The pressing question becomes how to prevent the emergence of malevolent AI and avoid losing control over increasingly powerful, possibly militarized AI systems.

Other critics of AGI include LeCun, who calls the idea 'ridiculous,' and Bender and Hanna, who refer to it as an 'AI con.'[29] LeCun, a pioneer of deep learning, has called experts' concerns about AI posing a threat

29 The book *AI Snake Oil* (Narayanan & Kapoor, 2024) highlights how AI often fails to deliver on its promises, labeling much of it as 'snake oil' – technologies that do not work and likely never will (the authors not only highlight the limitations of AI but also emphasize the potential risks and dangers associated with these technologies). Predictive AI, for example, is heavily overhyped and prone to false promises and advertising as well as fraud and deceit, with inherent limitations in predicting human behavior, social phenomena, or the future due to insufficient data and the unpredictable role of luck and randomness. The fundamental problem is that past data does not reliably predict the fu-

to humanity 'preposterously ridiculous.' He argues that the term AGI should be retired, as it fosters unnecessary hype and confusion. Instead, he advocates for focusing on achieving 'advanced machine intelligence.' In his view, human intelligence is specialized, with individuals excelling in different skills, and intelligence itself is a collection of abilities that allow people to learn and adapt to new tasks. LeCun believes that each human can only accomplish a subset of human intelligence tasks, which means that creating machines that mimic this full range of human abilities may not be the ultimate goal (BBC, 2025).

In *The AI Con*, Bender and Hanna (2025) tackle the current AI hype (and doomerism) and its harmful real-world consequences, particularly in sectors like social services, healthcare, medicine,[30] (higher) education, and science. They highlight how AI technologies, grounded in racist, sexist, and ableist assumptions, often carry Western-centric biases (see Section 3.2.3). These biases, paired with the centralization of power within big tech (see Section 3.2.8), result in the amassing of data and the prioritization of profit maximization, which in turn perpetuates socio-economic inequalities (see Section 3.2.2). One prominent example of AI hype (and doomerism) Bender and Hanna (2025) discuss is the notion of 'sentient AI' – the idea of conscious machines or AGI. They argue that terms like neural networks and artificial consciousness, often touted as cutting-edge developments, are misleading and ultimately empty promises. LLMs are characterized not by genuine thought or understanding, but by guesswork and mimicry – a concept explored in the *Stochastic Parrots* paper, co-authored by Bender (Bender et al., 2021). These models, often described as 'autocomplete on steroids' or 'text-synthesis machines,' lack true meaning, sentience, and intersubjectivity, reducing human communication to mere imitation. The book also critiques the way AI hype (and doomerism) reduces human existence to a realm of computability, quantifiability, and rational-

---

ture. Other problematic areas include generative AI and content-moderation AI, which struggle with understanding context and nuance and lack cultural competence. Content moderation is arguably more a political and regulatory issue than a technological one, yet algorithms often optimize for user engagement, inadvertently amplifying harmful content, reflecting social media platforms' business models, which (frequently) conflict with the common good. Additionally, AI-based research faces a common problem of reproducibility, e.g., due to (AI) 'leakage.' Media hype surrounding AI contributes to unrealistic expectations, while companies like OpenAI and other generative AI firms have shifted toward for-profit models, sharing less research and data publicly, allegedly due to IP concerns (Narayanan & Kapoor, 2024).

30 AI is rapidly transforming medicine, offering powerful tools for disease surveillance, prediction, and diagnosis (Microsoft AI, 2025). Initiatives like Google Flu Trends have demonstrated early applications of AI in tracking disease outbreaks. At the same time, more recent systems use machine learning to interpret medical imaging for cancer screening and detection with increasing accuracy. AI also plays a crucial role in genetic testing, biomedical simulations, such as CRISPR gene editing and vaccine trials, and drug discovery, as seen in projects like DeepMind's prediction of protein structures (which lays the foundation for drug discoveries and novel therapies). Robotic assistance in surgeries and wearable technology, including fitness trackers, support personal healthcare management through AI-based healthcare systems. Medical chatbots[1] and the integration of AR or VR are reshaping medical education and patient interaction, while emerging nanotechnologies like brain implants and brain-computer interfaces (see the work of Neuralink [2025]) push the boundaries of medical innovation. Companies like Google Brain/DeepMind, IBM's Watson, and 23andMe have contributed to this 'revolution,' though not without problems. Challenges include the lack of empathy and compassion in AI-driven care, the risks of false positives and negatives in medical or digital diagnosis algorithms, and serious concerns over privacy and data protection, highlighted by the recent bankruptcy of 23andMe, which raised alarms about the potential exposure of sensitive (personal) information such as genetic data (Kaplan, 2016, 2024). As AI evolves in medicine, balancing innovation with ethical oversight remains critical.

ity, devaluing relationships, human connection, and even the essence of being human. This reductionist view, they argue, not only dehumanizes individuals but also widens social inequalities. The assumption that intelligence can be measured and ranked is itself deeply rooted in racist and sexist ideologies. Bender and Hanna (2025) dispute the common belief that AI development is inevitable and that technologies will soon become fully autonomous and all-powerful – scenarios that they argue are unrealistic. Furthermore, they point out the existential risks of AI, which are often overlooked in discussions about its potential, including environmental impacts such as the mining of metals, the energy consumption of data centers, and the e-waste generated by these technologies (see Section 3.2.7). The climate crisis is amplified by the AI arms race, making these hidden costs all the more urgent. To resist the dangers of AI hype (and doomerism), Bender and Hanna (2025) advocate for critical thinking, informational literacy, and hard-law regulations, such as consumer protection, transparency, accountability, and union protections. Their vision is for technology that strengthens and reunites communities rather than serving to further fragment society.

Yet, despite these divergent views – and the current hype surrounding this controversial topic – expert opinion surveys within the machine learning community reveal a striking lack of consensus on AGI (AAAI, 2025; AIMultiple, 2025; Field, 2025; Grace et al., 2024). One survey found that one-fourth of participants estimated the existential risk of AGI at 0%, and only a small fraction considered a significant risk likely. Other studies, however, show a considerably higher risk factor. These results indicate that even among experts, beliefs about AGI's future and its implications are far from uniform. Interestingly, the 'generative AI revolution' has shifted some of these expert opinions. Not long ago, most predictions placed AGI around 2060. However, after the rapid advancements in LLMs, recent surveys suggest AGI could emerge by 2040. Entrepreneurs are even more bullish, forecasting its arrival as early as 2030. While there is no doubt that hype plays a role in driving these timelines and expectations, many argue that this is precisely why society must be prepared. Raising awareness and sensitizing professionals and lawmakers is crucial – not to panic, but to ensure we are ready with strong, thoughtful regulation when and if AGI is realized.

3.3 Possible regulatory avenues

The growing number of ethical issues associated with AI technologies, particularly in areas as consequential as labor markets and social (in-)justice, biases and discrimination, privacy and data protection, dangerous/hate speech and disinformation, human rights and the environment, and democracy and the rule of law, underscores the urgent need for comprehensive AI regulation. Unlike many past technologies that affected only specific sectors – or parts of our lives – AI is all-pervasive, penetrating virtually every industry and increasingly shaping (all) our daily lives, from finance, law, and healthcare to warfare and public safety. This ubiquity makes AI fundamentally different and demands a more robust regulatory framework.

Two possible approaches to regulate technologies have emerged: company self-regulation (i.e., soft law), including mechanisms like private 'constitutional AI' and 'AI guardrails,' and formal government regulation (i.e., hard law), which varies significantly by region, as seen in the contrast between the E.U.'s precautionary, rights-based approach and the more market-driven, innovation-centric model in the United States (Bradford, 2020, 2023). However, company self-regulation has proven largely ineffective. Corporations face inherent conflicts of interest (i.e., company self-interest vs. common good), tend to prioritize profit over public safety, and often lack transparency, accountability, and democratic legitimacy. Moreover, research comparing public versus private constitutional AI (Abiri, 2024; Küsters & Wörsdörfer, 2025) shows that private models usually fail to uphold ethical standards. In contrast, public frameworks, grounded in law and collective oversight, offer a more reliable alternative. The following sections will examine different forms of soft and hard law regulation, beginning with constitutional AI and the concept of AI guardrails. This will be followed by an overview of the distinct regulatory approaches taken by the E.U. and the United States. The final part will explore potential reform measures to strengthen existing legislation.

3.3.1 Soft law: constitutional AI and AI guardrails

Constitutional AI is an emerging approach that seeks to align LLMs with ethical principles outlined in a constitution-like framework. The core idea is to fine-tune instruction-following AI systems so that they not only operate in accordance with societal norms, human values, and ethical standards but also actively promote them. This method builds on reinforcement learning from human feedback and is closely connected to research in value alignment. A key element of this approach involves a broad range of stakeholders in the R&D process to ensure those affected by AI systems have a meaningful role throughout the entire lifecycle of AI creation and deployment. Anthropic's Collective Constitutional AI (CCAI) exemplifies this vision, using a multistage process to incorporate public preferences into AI constitutions. Their method employs the Polis platform for online deliberation, followed by fine-tuning LLMs to adhere to the resulting collective set of ethical preferences. The goal is to enhance public participation in shaping LLMs and ensure they align with public value preferences. Research shows that CCAI can improve bias scores and enhance public value alignment (Bai et al., 2022; Huang et al., 2024).

However, constitutional AI raises critical ethical concerns. LLMs face two significant legitimacy deficits: the opacity deficit, which stems from the black-box nature of machine learning-based AI systems and has the potential to erode public trust and acceptance, and the political community deficit, reflecting a lack of public discourse and democratic legitimacy in their development. While Anthropic's private constitutional AI, such as the constitution used for Claude, represents one attempt to address these issues, it has been criticized for establishing supposedly universally applicable ethical principles without meaningful public engagement (i.e., without establishing a broad stakeholder engagement and dialogue process). It thus lacks democratic input and public deliberation. Moreover, it risks further consolidating power in the hands of private, for-profit tech companies (by seeking to establish universal standards and shape public discourse) and deepening existing imbalances between the public and the tech sector. An alternative lies in public constitutional AI, as advocated by scholars like Abiri (2024), which calls for a participatory constitution-making process that includes diverse stakeholders and grounds AI ethics in democratic deliberation (Küsters & Wörsdörfer, 2025). This model offers a more transparent and inclusive path forward, aiming to rebuild trust and ensure AI development serves the public interest.[31]

AI guardrails are another crucial approach aimed at monitoring and filtering the inputs and outputs of trained LLMs to mitigate inherent risks and address ethical concerns (Ayyamperumal & Ge, 2024; Dong et al., 2024). These concerns include biases and discrimination, safety and reliability issues, privacy violations, the spread of misinformation, lack of explainability, non-reproducibility, and even malicious data manipulations such as dataset poisoning. AI guardrails aim to better align models with desired moral behaviors and societal norms while minimizing potential harm. Notable examples of this approach include NeMo-Guardrails, Llama Guard, and Guardrails AI, which integrate safeguards that span multiple categories, such as preventing hate speech, promoting fairness and privacy, and reducing hallucinations. Programmable safety protocols can help prevent LLMs from responding to harmful requests, adjust outputs to minimize risk, or ensure adherence to specific moral standards. Importantly, guardrail strategies must be considered across the entire AI development lifecycle, from initial specification and design to implementation, integration, verification, validation, and production release. Effective implementation involves detecting vulnerabilities, enhancing or fine-tuning LLMs, and applying input/output engineering techniques. These methods involve intrinsic and extrinsic bias evaluations, fairness and toxicity assessment tools, testability frameworks, fail-safes, and enhanced situational awareness. Technical strategies may include layered protection models, retrieval-augmented generation architectures, and various bias mitigation techniques. Additional tools such as robustness bonds (used to reduce offensive content and prevent 'jailbreak' attempts), team diversity (to improve fairness), and watermarking (to

31 The goal is to create an AI constitution that governs the training of both public and private AI models. Key stages of this process would involve public education, participation, deliberation, and ratification, as well as the development of case law by so-called AI courts. These courts would provide judicial oversight and interpretation of the AI constitution, serving as a mechanism for the ongoing public contestation and refinement of AI ethics to ensure they stay aligned with evolving societal norms and values. Following Abiri (2024), a public constitutional AI regime offers several advantages. It can help address the twofold legitimacy deficit (i.e., the opacity and the political community deficits) by increasing transparency and ensuring broader political engagement. This approach also fosters public understanding and involvement, creating a shared sense of ownership and investment in AI ethics principles. By grounding legitimacy in popular authorship, the AI constitution would emerge from public discourse rather than being a market-driven invention, significantly enhancing trust in the system. Additionally, the process ensures human oversight and accountability through a collaborative, hybrid, multi-stakeholder governance model, where both public and private, state and non-state actors work together to develop AI systems that serve the common good.

address privacy and copyright concerns) further support the safe and ethical deployment of AI systems.[32]

Like other soft law initiatives, constitutional AI and AI guardrails offer several advantages, including greater flexibility, cost-effectiveness, and efficiency, since the institutions responsible for rulemaking, enforcement, and dispute resolution are typically less expensive. They also allow for more adaptability in setting and revising rules and frameworks. Through multi-stakeholder approaches, these initiatives can harness non-state, non-coercive forces and draw on the expertise of a diverse range of actors, including those with high technological capacity. They benefit from tools, institutions, and processes that leverage market and peer pressure, such as voluntary codes shaped by industry associations, standards bodies, civil society, and NGOs, which can help influence behavior and promote internalization of responsibility. However, soft law mechanisms also face notable drawbacks. These include lower visibility and credibility; difficulties in enforcing compliance among unwilling participants[33] (e.g., issues of opportunistic defection and free riding); the risk of adopting weaker standards; uncertain levels of public accountability; and generally weaker enforcement mechanisms (Webb, 2004a, 2004b, 2012; Webb & Morrison, 2004). In the context of AI, insufficient and ineffective governance mechanisms can lead to severe consequences, particularly for vulnerable or marginalized groups, as demonstrated in Section 3.2.

3.3.2 Hard law: E.U. versus U.S. regulation

Bradford's (2023) analysis of global regulatory approaches highlights two primary models in the Global North: the U.S.' market-driven regulatory model rooted in techno-libertarianism[34] and the E.U.'s rights-driven regulatory model (besides these Western models, there is also China's state-driven regulatory model, characterized by surveillance capitalism or digital authoritarianism). The United States emphasizes political and economic freedom, championing a free market ideology that relies on minimal government intervention, predominantly relying on laissez-faire economics and a deep faith in markets over state regulation. This model reflects a mistrust in govern-

32 Constitutional AI aims to align AI systems with public values and ethical principles by involving a broad range of stakeholders in shaping its ethical framework. It focuses on embedding societal norms into AI's decision-making process through participatory methods. In contrast, AI guardrails focus on ensuring safety by using technical measures to prevent harmful outputs, such as bias or misinformation, without emphasizing public involvement. While constitutional AI seeks to promote ethical behavior, AI guardrails are more about risk mitigation and protecting users from harmful consequences.

33 Note that unlike Microsoft, Meta has decided not to sign the E.U.'s Code of Practice for providers of general-purpose AI (Reuters, 2025).

34 Barbrook and Cameron (1995), Borsook (2000), Gilder (2012), Hill (2023), Mother Jones (2025), Oreskes and Conway (2023), Slobodian (2025), and The Guardian (2025c).

ment regulation, with a preference for self-regulation, and promotes ideals such as free speech and an open Internet, which are conducive to innovation. At the same time, the United States exhibits weakly enforced antitrust laws, an absence of federal data privacy law, and permissive content moderation rules, shielding tech companies from liability. Additionally, the United States displays a techno-optimism and a focus on national and cyber security. In contrast, the E.U. follows a (more) human-centric and (fundamental) rights-driven approach to digital regulation, where principles like dignity, privacy/data protection, and addressing dangerous/hate speech and disinformation (via content moderation) are central (i.e., it also aims to balance market interests and fundamental rights). Their regulatory focus also includes competition, which favors small and medium enterprises and consumers, ensuring that technologies and companies are embedded in and align with a democratic and rule-of-law society and social market economy. Consequently, the E.U.'s regulatory landscape incorporates key legislations like the General Data Protection Regulation (GDPR), the Digital Markets Act (DMA), the Digital Services Act (DSA), and the AI Act (AIA), alongside measures such as the digital services tax (under discussion in several member states) and employment protections for platform/gig workers (Bradford, 2020, 2023).[35]

Hard law measures, such as the E.U.'s GDPR, DMA, DSA, and AIA, encounter several challenges and limitations. As highlighted by Webb (2004a, 2004b, 2012) and Webb & Morrison (2004), key drawbacks of the state's traditional 'command and control' regulatory frameworks include rigidity and formalism; high(er) costs associated with development and operation; the risk of creating adversarial dynamics between regulators and those regulated; restricted jurisdictional reach; lack of motivation for innovation or efforts beyond mere compliance; slow and expensive processes for rule-making and amendments; susceptibility to inconsistent enforcement due to budget and staffing reductions; and (possible) unsuitability for rapidly evolving technological and socio-economic environments. Conversely, traditional regulatory or legal

35 Current debates within the E.U. are considering a possible pause or delay in implementing the AIA and/or a reform of the E.U. Data Act (notably, the E.U.'s AI Liability Directive has already been withdrawn) (E.U. AI Champions Initiative, 2025; FAZ, 2025; IAPP, 2025). This move is largely influenced by lobbying from industry groups arguing that such a delay could stimulate the E.U. economy and reduce trade tensions with the Trump administration, particularly regarding tariffs – an argument similar to previous attempts to weaken E.U. or national laws on supply chains, climate change, and other socio-environmental issues (e.g., the Corporate Sustainability Due Diligence Directive) (Business and Human Rights Resource Center, 2025a; Council of the E.U., 2025; European Commission, 2025a; New York Times, 2025h). Alongside these moratorium or reform discussions, the E.U. Commission has introduced a voluntary code of practice for providers of general-purpose AI, which addresses transparency, copyright protection, and public safety and security. This soft law initiative aims to assist the industry in aligning with the AIA's standards (European Commission, 2025b). However, it is subject to the limitations previously noted – for example, it remains uncertain whether voluntary codes can adequately protect vulnerable and marginalized populations. Therefore, the current trend toward 'softening' E.U. regulations should be reconsidered and (ideally) reversed.

frameworks offer several advantages, including enhanced visibility, credibility, and accountability; mandatory enforcement across the board; a stronger tendency to establish stringent standards; shared costs of implementation; and access to a range of sanctions. These advantages are particularly crucial in the context of AI technologies, especially for safeguarding vulnerable and marginalized communities.

3.3.3 Reform measures

The reform measures outlined in this section are divided into general and more specific categories.[36] General proposals include the introduction of an AI Bill of Rights and efforts to strengthen existing AI regulations, e.g., to enhance oversight, transparency, and accountability. More specific reforms address key impact areas: tackling labor market disruptions through education reform and UBI; improving privacy and data protection via frameworks like the GDPR and CCPA; regulating harmful online content through a (strengthened) DSA; and reinforcing business and human rights through conflict minerals regulations, human rights due diligence, and corporate human rights advocacy. Additional proposals aim to curb the unchecked power of big tech through enhanced antitrust measures and call for ethical guidelines in the development and deployment of military robotics, among other initiatives. The specific reform proposals follow the structure of AI ethics issues outlined in Section 3.2.

36 This paper primarily addresses the regulation of big tech within the context of the United States, the - E.U., and other industrialized nations, while also offering sector-specific guidance, particularly in areas such as competition policy and antitrust reform. Initial reform proposals for AI legislation tend to focus on industrialized countries due to their leading roles in AI development and deployment, as well as their access to the necessary financial, human, and infrastructural resources to tackle AI's ethical challenges. This approach parallels arguments in climate ethics, where nations most responsible for environmental harm – often those hosting multinational corporations such as big oil or big tech – are expected to lead remediation efforts. Ideally, a global AI regulatory framework would be shaped by ordoliberal 2.0 principles of AI ethics, as discussed below. However, implementing such a framework in emerging markets and developing countries may require adaptations to accommodate cultural, economic, political, and legal differences, particularly in areas like content moderation. While sensitive to local contexts, these adaptations must nonetheless safeguard universal human rights, especially privacy, data protection, and protections against mass surveillance, to ensure these foundational rights remain uncompromised.

3.3.3.1 Excursus: ordoliberalism

Ordoliberalism is a business-ethical framework that laid the intellectual foundations of Germany's – and later the E.U.'s – social market economy, implemented after World War II.[37] It seeks to reconcile economic imperatives such as competition and market freedom with ethical commitments to social justice and human rights. Its central objective is to establish a socio-economic order that is both economically efficient and humane, capable of safeguarding liberal – specifically Kantian – values of freedom, autonomy, and human dignity (Böhm, 1961; Eucken, 1952/2004; Müller-Armack, 1956; Oppenheimer, 1933; Röpke, 1944/1949; Rüstow, 2001; Wörsdörfer, 2013a).

Within classical ordoliberalism, two major strands can be distinguished: the Freiburg School of Law and Economics and sociological neoliberalism. The Freiburg School emerged as an interdisciplinary research group at the University of Freiburg, founded by the economist Eucken and the legal scholars Böhm and Großmann-Doerth. Sociological neoliberalism, by contrast, was primarily represented by Rüstow and Röpke. In addition to classical ordoliberalism, a contemporary variant has developed that bears strong affinities with constitutional economics in the tradition of Buchanan and Hayek. Prominent representatives of modern ordoliberalism include Feld, Goldschmidt, and Vanberg (Feld & Köhler, 2011; Goldschmidt, 2002, 2007; Goldschmidt & Wohlgemuth, 2008; Vanberg, 2004, 2005, 2008, 2013).

As ordoliberalism has been discussed extensively elsewhere (Wörsdörfer, 2020, 2022a), the following discussion focuses on Eucken's contributions, in particular his Constituent and Regulating Principles and his Principles of Economic (State) Policy (see Table 3.1) (Eucken, 1952/2004; Grossekettler, 1994; Meijer, 2007). These principles form the core of ordoliberal theory and are essential for an ordoliberal-inspired competition policy as well as for the subsequent discussion on AI ethics and big tech and antitrust.

Eucken's Constituent Principles (Eucken, 1952/2004) aim at establishing a highly competitive economic order in which market processes and the price mechanism function without distortion. This presupposes the absence of external interference – particularly by the state – in the interaction of supply and demand. Open markets are a central prerequisite of competition: only when firms can enter markets freely can competitive dynamics that foster innovation and prosperity emerge. Equally important are low exit barriers. Insolvent firms should not be artificially sustained through subsidies or bailouts but should exit the market as swiftly as possible. Eucken further emphasizes the importance of private property rights and contractual freedom. However, contractual freedom is not absolute: private contracts are legitimate only to the extent that they conform to the competitive order and do not restrict market access or contribute to monopolization. Moreover, economic policy must be long-term oriented and institutionally stable. Rather than relying on ad hoc, case-by-case interventions or frequent policy shifts, governments should adhere to the principles of predict-

37 The work of Eucken and other ordoliberals not only shaped Germany's socio-economic order in the post-World War II period – most notably the monetary and economic reform of 1948, the establishment of an independent central bank through the Bundesbank Act of 1957, and the introduction of anti-cartel legislation in 1957/1958 (the Law against Restraints of Competition and the Monopolies Commission Act) – but has also played a significant role in the European integration process and left a lasting imprint on European Union institutions and policies. For example, Article 3(3) of the Treaty on European Union, reaffirmed by the Treaty of Lisbon, explicitly commits the E.U. to the establishment of a "highly competitive social market economy." Moreover, ordoliberal ideas have strongly influenced the Maastricht Treaty, particularly the convergence criteria for the introduction of the euro, as well as the institutional design of the European Economic and Monetary Union. The emphasis on price stability, fiscal discipline, and the political independence of the European Central Bank reflects core ordoliberal principles (cf. Claassen et al., 2019; Dold & Krieger, 2020; Lechevalier, 2015).

ability and regularity. Crucially, Eucken stresses the interdependence of all Constituent Principles, which together form an integrated and coherent framework for a sustainable ordoliberal economic policy.

In addition to the Constituent Principles, Eucken formulates four complementary Regulating Principles (Eucken, 1952/2004): the containment and correction of socio-economic power, income redistribution, the correction of negative externalities, and the correction of 'abnormal supply reactions.' These principles are designed to ensure the long-term viability of the competitive order by addressing market failures and providing basic social security. Of particular relevance for the subsequent analyses is the principle of containing socio-economic power, which obliges the state to prevent and correct abuses of market power, especially those arising from cartels, trusts, oligopolies, and monopolies.

Finally, Eucken articulates two overarching Principles of Economic (State) Policy. The first principle, limiting the power of pressure groups, seeks to prevent the monopolization of the economy through political influence. The second calls on governments to prioritize regulatory or ordering policy (*Ordnungspolitik*) over interventionist and privilege-conferring process policy (*Prozesspolitik*) (Eucken, 1950/1965, 1952/2004, 1999, 2001). The ideal ordoliberal state is thus conceived as a strong and independent constitutional state (Röpke, 1942, 1944/1949, 1950; Rüstow, 1955), one that stands above special interests and functions as a 'market police' (Röpke, 1942; Rüstow, 1957, 2001), an 'ordering power,' and a 'guardian of the competitive order' (Eucken, 1952/2004; Röpke, 1944/1949). Such a state must be capable of resisting pressure from special interest groups, adhere to neutrality and impartiality, and focus on rule-setting rather than direct market participation. Its primary task is to establish, monitor, and enforce the rules of the game – the institutional framework within which markets operate – rather than to intervene in market processes themselves. The normative foundations of this ordoliberal vision include equality before the law, the absence of privileges, and non-discrimination, principles that closely parallel those of constitutional economics (Brennan & Buchanan, 1985/2000; Buchanan, 1975/2000; Buchanan & Congleton, 1998; Buchanan & Tullock, 1962/1999; Congleton, 2013; Hayek, 1973; Vanberg, 2008).

Table 3.1: Overview of Eucken's ordoliberal principles.

Constituent Principles	Regulating Principles	Principles of State Policy	Competition Policy Principles (CPPs)
Competitive economy	Correction of market power	Limiting power of rent-seekers	Competition law/policy
Monetary policy Price stability	Income redistribution (distributive justice)	Focus on regulatory policy	Cartel office M&A Commission
Open markets	Correction of negative externalities		Corporate break-up (divestiture)
Property rights	Correction of abnormal supply reactions		
(Non-exclusionary) contracts			
Principle of liability			
Regularity of economic policy			
Interdependency of principles			

To implement Eucken's Constituent, Regulating, and Policy Principles, ordoliberalism emphasizes the central role of legal and politico-economic instruments, most notably competition law and competition policy (see the CPPs listed in the table above). A core purpose of these instruments – and of regulatory policy more generally – is to ensure that markets remain open and that abuses of market power are effectively constrained. Accordingly, the economic power of dominant firms and the political influence of rent-seeking groups must be limited. Cartels, trusts, and other forms of collusion or market coordination are therefore subject to continuous monitoring and, where necessary, sanctioning by independent authorities such as a cartel office. Likewise, M&As must be reviewed and approved by a sovereign and independent commission.

If competition authorities determine that a proposed M&A is likely to result in market monopolization – for example, when a conglomerate exceeds a critical market-share threshold – they are entitled to impose pro-competitive conditions that must be fulfilled before approval. Under certain circumstances, they may also prohibit the transaction altogether. The overarching objective of combating cartels, monopolies, and oligopolies is to prevent the emergence of 'too-big-to-fail' or systemically relevant corporations whose failure could jeopardize the stability of the entire economic system, as recent financial crises have demonstrated. Notably, Eucken and other ordoliberals already identified these dangers in the 1940s, warning against the increasing concentration of economic power in the hands of a few firms. In a post–World War II report prepared for the Allied authorities, Eucken explicitly argued for the dismantling of excessively powerful and dominant enterprises (Eucken, 1946/1999).

The primary aim of ordoliberal competition policy is thus to guarantee equal market access, enabling firms of all sizes to compete on the merits for superior products, services, and ideas. Antitrust policy is therefore understood as the protection of 'competition on the merits' (Böhm, 1961; Lenel & Meyer, 1948) and as a 'discovery procedure' (Hayek, 1968/2002). By preserving competitive rivalry, it fosters innovation and, most importantly, safeguards consumer and citizen sovereignty grounded in Kantian notions of autonomy and freedom. Effective competition benefits consumers through lower prices, higher quality, greater innovation, and increased freedom of choice.

Beyond these economic benefits, ordoliberal antitrust policy is also concerned with economic freedom rights and with the distribution of ownership and control. Its goal is to prevent excessive concentrations of private economic power and the associated risks of abuse. Ordoliberals further feared that concentrated economic power could translate into concentrated political power, thereby generating anti-democratic pressures. Monopolies were thus perceived not merely as an economic problem but as a fundamental threat to personal freedom, the rule of law, and democratic governance. The erosion of political freedoms becomes particularly likely when economic concentration is coupled with lobbying and rent-seeking, allowing special interest groups to dominate political and legislative decision-making processes.

3.3.3.2 AI bill of rights

Following Wörsdörfer (2025b),[38] who applied the business-ethical concepts of ordoliberalism[39] and constitutional economics to AI technologies and introduced the term 'ordoliberalism 2.0,' we can identify nine ordoliberal-inspired AI ethics principles,

38 Some of the proposed reforms, such as AI ethics principles and the AI Bill of Rights, are intentionally broad in scope, aiming to serve as foundational frameworks rather than sector-specific regulations. Their primary purpose is to offer guiding principles for addressing the ethical challenges posed by AI across various domains.

39 In this paper, we adopt Wörsdörfer's ordoliberal-inspired AI ethics principles (i.e., ordoliberalism 2.0), as they provide a comprehensive and coherent framework that incorporates key elements from existing ethical models (Attard-Frost, 2022; Fjeld et al., 2020; Leslie et al., 2021) while extending them

which could form the basis for a proposed Digital Bill of Rights or AI constitution (Abiri, 2024; Wörsdörfer, 2023a): respect for human rights, data protection and privacy, harm prevention and beneficence, non-discrimination and freedom of privileges, fairness and justice, transparency and explainability of AI systems, accountability and responsibility, democracy and the rule of law, and socio-environmental sustainability:[40]

- *Respect for human rights*: The ordoliberal 'program of liberty' is grounded in the Kantian tradition (Wörsdörfer, 2022c). It calls for a human-centered approach to AI that safeguards individual agency, control, and oversight, while promoting responsible business conduct in the digital economy. Key elements include human review of automated decisions, the right to opt out of algorithmic decision-making, assessments of AI's societal impact, and leveraging technologies to benefit the public, thereby enhancing health, safety, and well-being.
- *Data protection and the right to privacy*: From an ordoliberal 2.0 perspective, privacy encompasses six key dimensions: (1) integrity and dignity – privacy as a safeguard of human dignity; (2) personhood and identity – privacy as self-determination; (3) intimacy and anonymity – the 'right to be let alone' (Warren & Brandeis, 1890); (4) data and information control; (5) limited access to the self; and (6) freedom of speech and communication. In the AI context, ordoliberal scholars advocate for rights to data minimization and stewardship, informational self-sovereignty, user control over data processing, the right to correction and erasure, privacy by design and default, data security, and effective legal frameworks protecting privacy as a fundamental right.
- *Harm prevention and beneficence*: Ordoliberal 2.0 ethics stresses the importance of technological robustness, mitigation of malicious uses, reliable and reproducible research, built-in safety mechanisms, and attention to unknown risks and unintended consequences, known as 'security by design.' Ordoliberal 2.0 thinkers call for rigorous safety standards, third-party audits, certifications, and licensing. In addition to the duty to avoid harm, ordoliberalism 2.0 promotes positive duties, ensuring that technologies and markets contribute to human flourishing. Modern ordoliberals argue that digital markets should be embedded in a meta-economic order, where technology serves society rather than vice versa (Gregg, 2010; Wörsdörfer, 2013a).

---

further. Notably, they address socio-environmental sustainability and the democratic and rule-of-law implications of AI technologies (missing in other AI ethics frameworks). The following discussion explores how these principles can be operationalized through hard-law regulation, including antitrust and competition policy.

40 See AlgorithmWatch (2023), Attard-Frost et al. (2022), Daly et al. (2021), Fjeld et al. (2020), Hagendorff (2020), Jobin and Vayena (2019), Khanna (2023), Laux et al. (2023b), Leslie (2019), Leslie et al. (2021), Mittelstadt (2019), Morley et al. (2021), Rieder et al. (2021), Rubenstein (2021), and Smuha (2019), for more information on AI ethics (principles).

- *Non-discrimination and freedom of privileges*: Ordoliberalism (2.0) also emphasizes legal equality and the elimination of rent-seeking, lobbying, and privilege. Applied to AI, this entails combating discrimination, manipulation (e.g., via chatbots and deepfakes), and negative profiling while reducing (agentic) AI biases. This requires high-quality, diverse datasets and inclusive, fair design. Extra protections should be in place for marginalized groups such as children, ethnic minorities, and migrants. The concept of platform neutrality – extending beyond net neutrality – is also essential. While net neutrality addresses data transmission fairness, platform neutrality targets digital gatekeeping by dominant firms, such as search engines and app stores, ensuring fair market access.
- *Fairness and justice*: Classical and modern ordoliberals have emphasized the importance of addressing systemic social inequalities and ensuring equal opportunities. AI fairness can be understood in four areas: data, design, outcomes, and implementation (Leslie, 2019; Alvarez et al., 2024). From an ordoliberal 2.0 standpoint, open innovation, accessibility, inclusion, and especially fair markets are crucial. Market fairness entails preventing monopolistic behavior and ensuring a level playing field for small and medium-sized enterprises. It also calls for regulating harmful business practices like gatekeeping, bundling, self-preferencing, predatory pricing, and 'killer acquisitions' (Wörsdörfer, 2021, 2024b).
- *Transparency and explainability of AI systems*: Transparency in ordoliberal thought helps limit the power of special interests. In the context of AI, it involves explainability, open access to data and algorithms, transparent public procurement, the right to be informed when AI makes decisions, and regular disclosures. Opening black box algorithms enhances public trust (Abiri, 2024). This includes intelligibility, ethical evaluation, and non-harm. Alongside system-level transparency, ordoliberalism 2.0 values institutional and professional integrity – honesty, neutrality, impartiality – and demands transparency in business conduct, such as sharing results and best practices.
- *Accountability and responsibility*: The ordoliberal liability principle holds that market actors must bear the consequences of their actions. Applied to AI, this includes verifiability, reproducibility, oversight mechanisms, rights to appeal, legal responsibility, and regulatory enforcement (Attard-Frost et al., 2022; Fjeld et al., 2020; Kazim & Koshiyama, 2021; Laux, 2023; Morley et al., 2021; Novelli et al., 2023). Public trust depends on strong internal and external oversight. Tools such as human rights due diligence, social impact assessments, ethics boards, worker participation, and independent review are key. 'Accountability by design' (Leslie, 2019) and 'ethics-based auditing' (Mökander & Floridi, 2021) – covering code, function, and impact – are essential instruments.
- *Democracy and the rule of law*: The ordoliberal vision of a Kantian-inspired 'private law society' aims to replace privilege-based systems with legal equality and public interest. In the AI realm, this requires embedding technologies within democratic institutions and rule-of-law frameworks. Judicial and legislative oversight,

inclusive participation, and public dialogue are essential. Based on Habermasian discourse ethics, scholars propose a community-in-the-loop model integrating stakeholder engagement in AI governance (Abiri, 2024; Häußermann & Lütge, 2022).
- *Socio-environmental responsibility*: The ordoliberal principle of internalizing externalities requires mitigating ecological harm. For AI, this includes reducing the carbon footprint and energy consumption of data centers, addressing e-waste, and promoting sustainable or green technologies. Social sustainability, likewise, demands human rights impact assessments, support for worker training, and contributions to education and long-term development goals.

3.3.3.3 Strengthening existing AI regulations

To strengthen existing AI regulation, such as the AIA, several reform measures could be implemented (Wörsdörfer, 2024a, 2024c, 2025a), including the introduction or enhancement of the following:[41]
- *Conformity assessment procedures*: The AIA should move beyond the current flawed system of provider self-assessment and adopt mandatory third-party audits for all high-risk AI systems. The existing governance framework, which grants substantial discretion to AI providers and standard-setting bodies, could be replaced by legally mandated external oversight from an independent agency equipped with investigatory and enforcement powers (AlgorithmWatch, 2021; Ebers et al., 2021; EPRS, 2022a; Floridi et al., 2022; Gstrein, 2022; Kop, 2021; Laux et al., 2023a).
- *Democratic accountability and judicial oversight*: All affected stakeholders must be actively involved, including consumers and social partners such as workers and their unions. Public representation should be embedded in the standardization and certification of AI technologies. From an ordoliberal 2.0 perspective, this approach helps ensure that groups with limited bargaining power are represented and their voices heard (Ebers et al., 2021; EPRS, 2022a, 2022b; Gstrein, 2022).
- *Redress and complaint mechanisms*: In addition to participation rights, experts advocate for clear information rights and accessible, affordable legal remedies. Both individuals and groups should be able to challenge AI decisions. Those who feel

41 While the previous section focused on identifying broad AI ethics principles that could serve as guiding principles for an AI Bill of Rights (as well as other relevant legislative frameworks, such as environmental laws), this paragraph shifts its focus to the enhancement of existing AI regulations, particularly the AIA. It provides a comprehensive overview of specific measures that could address the current shortcomings of the AIA and similar regulations. The aim is to propose concrete steps that would not only rectify these flaws but also enhance the overall effectiveness of AI governance, ensuring that such regulations are both adaptable to rapid technological advancements and capable of safeguarding public interests in the long term (these reform measures are grounded in the ordoliberal-inspired AI ethics principles discussed earlier, offering a clear pathway for their practical implementation).

their rights violated must have legal avenues to contest harmful or unlawful outcomes (AlgorithmWatch, 2021; EPRS, 2022a, 2022b; Smuha et al., 2021).

- *Worker protection*: Experts emphasize the involvement and protection of workers and their representatives in the deployment of AI. This may involve classifying more workplace AI systems as high-risk or prohibiting specific tools altogether. Workers should participate in decisions about AI adoption, especially where it may negatively impact their roles, and have the right to object and file complaints (AlgorithmWatch, 2021; Cefaliello & Kullmann, 2022; EPRS, 2022b; Smuha et al., 2021).
- *Governance structure*: Effective enforcement of the AIA depends on strong institutions. The European AI Board and Office could fulfill this role if it is equipped with sufficient expertise (in both technology, ethics, and fundamental rights), resources, and political independence. To ensure transparency, the E.U.'s AI database should list not only high-risk systems but all AI tools used by public and private entities, along with information on algorithmic risk and human rights impacts, presented in an accessible manner (AlgorithmWatch, 2021; Ebers et al., 2021; Smuha et al., 2021).
- *Funding and staffing of market surveillance authorities*: Regulatory bodies must be strengthened financially and staffed with more experts. The AIA's allocation of just 25 full-time equivalent positions for oversight is inadequate, and significantly greater investment in personnel and budgets is required (AlgorithmWatch, 2021; EPRS, 2022b; Smuha et al., 2021).
- *Sustainability considerations*: To address AI's environmental impacts, experts advocate for mandatory sustainability requirements for AI providers, including measures to limit energy consumption and reduce electronic waste. These obligations should go beyond voluntary codes and support the development of green AI (AlgorithmWatch, 2021; Ebers et al., 2021; EPRS, 2022a).

3.3.3.4 Specific reform proposals

3.3.3.4.1 Mitigating the labor market impacts of AI

A reform[42] of the educational system is needed to better prepare future generations for the rapidly changing job market driven by automation and AI technologies (see Sections 3.2.1 and 3.2.2). One key aspect of this reform is expanding access to higher education, particularly in STEM disciplines, with an emphasis on affordability and, ideally, offering free access. The focus should not only be on technical skills but also

42 Having discussed the ordoliberal-inspired principles of AI ethics and potential ways to strengthen the AIA, we now turn to sector- (e.g., education, labor, and antitrust) and industry-specific (e.g., social media, and big tech) laws and regulations that could further address the ethical challenges posed by AI. These reform proposals are structured according to the categories of AI ethics issues outlined in Section 3.2.

on creative and social skills, such as interpersonal communication, cross-cultural competency, new media literacy, critical and analytical thinking, and interdisciplinary research (New York Times, 2025c; World Economic Forum, 2023, 2025). In addition, fostering a culture of lifelong learning will be crucial, enabling individuals to continually adapt to evolving technologies. Other measures to support this transformation include the creation of digital grant colleges (similar to land-grant universities), a national digital corps, and making computer science education (K–12) available to all, alongside vocational training options such as apprenticeships and internships, similar to Germany's dual education system. To support rural communities, governments can implement tech-related hiring incentives, provide fast-speed Internet and laptop access, invest in public infrastructure, and promote technology hubs through venture capital funding. Equally important is ensuring equal access to education and technology for marginalized communities, including girls and women and Black, Latino, and Indigenous peoples, through targeted initiatives that provide greater access to education, technology, and capital (Wörsdörfer, 2018).

Moreover, a UBI may also provide a pathway to address some of the adverse impacts of automation and AI technologies. UBI proposes that every individual, including the wealthy, receive a set amount, such as $1,000 per person per month, unconditionally and without means testing. This would replace government transfers and subsidies, such as social security, Medicare, Medicaid, and food stamps. One of the main advantages of UBI is its simplicity in administration, as it reduces bureaucracy and ensures poverty reduction, especially in the face of technological unemployment. UBI could also boost self-employment, entrepreneurship, and creativity by offering people financial security and support, particularly for unpaid care workers, which could empower women by recognizing and compensating their often-invisible labor. Furthermore, UBI could decrease the need for other forms of social security, providing a more universal safety net. However, critics argue that UBI could decrease work incentives, potentially slowing economic growth and making implementation expensive, which could result in higher taxes or inflation. Additionally, it might exacerbate inequality or fail to address the needs of special populations, e.g., people with disabilities (Hasdell, 2020; Wörsdörfer, 2018).

3.3.3.4.2 Safeguarding privacy in the digital age

To address growing concerns over privacy and data protection (see Section 3.2.4), various reform measures should be implemented across the corporate, governmental, and civil society spheres. Companies must adopt robust corporate due diligence practices that directly address the human rights implications of big data. Core principles such as privacy by design and default should guide product development, complemented by privacy-enhancing technologies like anonymization and encryption. Transparency must be improved through clear and accessible privacy policies, while opt-in consent systems – grounded in Free, Prior, and Informed Consent (Wörsdörfer,

2014) – should replace the prevailing opt-out models. Furthermore, third-party certification schemes and independent auditing mechanisms can help verify compliance, alongside non-judicial grievance mechanisms that provide users with accessible forms of redress. From the consumer and civil society side, efforts should promote digital literacy and raise user awareness of their privacy rights and associated risks. Individuals must be guaranteed the right to access, correct, or amend their data, as well as the right to delete it upon termination of a relationship with a company. Users should also be able to easily adjust their privacy settings on major platforms, such as TikTok. Privacy-respecting tools should be actively encouraged, including alternative non-tracking search engines like DuckDuckGo, anonymity networks like TOR, privacy-focused browsers like Ghostery and Privacy Badger, and VPNs. Finally, governments must play a central role by ending indiscriminate and suspicionless mass surveillance and establishing and enforcing strong privacy laws and data protection regulations. This includes establishing independent regulatory agencies to oversee corporate and state data practices, particularly those of data brokers, and ensuring effective judicial remedies through bodies such as privacy commissions or ombudspersons. Together, these reforms can help rebalance the power asymmetry between data collectors and individuals and uphold basic (digital) rights (Wörsdörfer, 2018).

3.3.3.4.3 Regulating harmful online content

Unlike the United States, several other countries have implemented stringent laws to combat dangerous and hate speech (Bradford, 2023; Carlson, 2021, see Section 3.2.5). Germany's *Network Enforcement Act* requires social media platforms to remove illegal content within 24 h of receiving a user complaint or face significant fines. The *Law Against Hate Crime* takes this further by obligating platforms to report hate speech to the federal police and hold users criminally responsible (Wörsdörfer, 2018). The *Digital Services Act* (DSA) (European Parliament & Council of the E.U., 2022), which applies to major platforms like Meta, X, YouTube, and TikTok, seeks to standardize E.U. regulations on illegal content (including dangerous and hate speech), disinformation, and targeted ads, while strengthening content moderation across social media platforms. Under the DSA, platforms are not automatically responsible for user-generated content, but they must act once they become aware of illegal material (the DSA introduces a conditional liability exemption for intermediaries, in contrast to the broad immunities provided to platforms under Section 230 of the *Communications Decency Act*). Major obligations for companies include transparency in content removal decisions, disclosure of algorithmic processes, accountability in ad and user targeting, mandatory notification and choice requirements, robust risk management and auditing frameworks, and user rights to appeal content removal decisions (Wörsdörfer, 2025d).

Critics of the DSA (and similar laws) argue that its implementation could lead to high administrative costs and increased bureaucracy, making online content regulation more complex and resource-intensive. There is also concern that laws like the DSA might lead to over-blocking or censorship, potentially infringing on freedom of speech. Privacy and data protection issues may emerge, particularly concerning how platforms manage personal data while enforcing the DSA. Additionally, by shifting the responsibility of content removal and law enforcement to platforms, concerns arise about accountability and consistency in enforcement. Further criticisms of the DSA, as noted by Loi et al. (2025), include a lack of a clear definition for systemic risk (i.e., no unified theory), opacity in enforcement (i.e., no publicly available information about DSA cases and investigations), the presence of normative judgments (i.e., subjective decisions), and over-reliance on company self-regulation (i.e., giving platforms discretionary power to assess risks). According to Loi et al. (2025), these issues contribute to a lack of transparency and accountability in DSA enforcement, commonly referred to as the convergence problem.

To address the convergence problem and associated governance concerns, Loi et al. (2025) propose a dual-track approach to systemic risk assessment, combining both research and compliance standards. This framework encourages diverse methodologies and accountability by systematically documenting the risk assessment process (thus enhancing transparency and closing the accountability gap). Loi et al. (2025) emphasize that making this documentation publicly accessible by default is critical. This should include records of discussions between platforms and the Digital Services Coordinator, risk assessments, research methods, and the rationale behind decisions. A public database that tracks methodologies, findings, and decisions would promote collective learning while ensuring confidentiality. The goal of the proposed compliance standard is to establish consistent principles for documenting and evaluating systemic risks, provide a structured method for comparing different approaches, and ensure transparency and traceability in risk assessment processes. Loi et al. (2025) also propose an update process to track changes in platform risks over time: "By systematically documenting, comparing and communicating diverse methodological approaches, our envisaged process creates a longitudinal knowledge base that enables regulators to observe how platform risks emerge, mutate, and reconfigure, thereby transforming methodological pluralism from a potential regulatory challenge into a structured learning mechanism for continuous regulatory adaptation." Key to this process is an engagement forum with stakeholders, similar to what has been suggested for the AIA (Wörsdörfer, 2024a, 2024c, 2025a). In addition to the reforms proposed by Loi et al. (2025), the DSA could be strengthened by establishing or enhancing independent (third-party) conformity assessments, democratic accountability and judicial oversight, governance structures (including enforcement and sanctioning), redress and complaint mechanisms, and adequate funding and staffing (see Wörsdörfer, 2024a, 2024c, 2025a for more details).

3.3.3.4.4 CSR in the digital era

A multi-pronged approach[43] is essential to address the business and human rights challenges arising from the global expansion of AI and related technologies (see Section 3.2.6). First, fostering union activities and supporting worker movements can empower labor forces, particularly in sectors most vulnerable to exploitation, such as data annotation and content moderation centers in developing countries and warehouses in industrialized nations. Strengthening labor laws is crucial to enhancing working conditions and preventing exploitation. Establishing a level playing field by enforcing minimum international standards, such as those outlined in ILO Conventions and OECD Guidelines, can help prevent a global race to the bottom in labor rights. Promoting workplace democracy is another key component, whether through co-determination governance models, co-management structures, works councils, worker cooperatives, or employee ownership schemes. As Muldoon et al. (2025) and Chandler (2024) discuss, these mechanisms help ensure that workers have a meaningful voice in decision-making processes and a stake in the technologies they help build and operate. Moreover, legal frameworks like Germany's *Supply Chain Act* (Federal Ministry of Labor and Social Affairs, 2021), which mandates corporate risk and impact assessments along the supply chain, and human rights due diligence laws, such as the U.S. *Dodd-Frank Act* (Nest, 2013; Wörsdörfer, 2018), the *Uyghur Forced Labor Prevention Act* (Australian Strategic Policy Institute, 2020; Murphy et al., 2022; U.S. Congress, 2021), and the E.U.'s *Corporate Sustainability Due Diligence Directive* (European Parliament & Council of the European Union, 2024; see also European Commission, 2017), further institutionalize responsibility for ethical business conduct. Together, these strategies aim to align technological advancement with social justice and human dignity.

Reform measures at the *micro level*, whether at the management or company level, are essential for creating lasting change. A shift in corporate (tech) culture is critical, with companies adopting a stronger focus on human rights advocacy and activism (see below). Human rights due diligence should be a core part of business operations, ensuring that companies actively monitor and assess their supply chains for any signs of exploitation (Wörsdörfer, 2015). Project- or company-level grievance mechanisms should be established to provide workers and communities with a clear and accessible means of voicing their concerns. Engaging in ongoing stakeholder dialogue is also vital to ensure that all parties are heard and their interests addressed. Finally, implementing impact–benefit agreements between companies and local communities can help ensure that business operations (e.g., in the mining sector) bring tangible benefits to those most affected by the industry's activities.

---

43 The following reform proposals aim to address certain business and human rights concerns outlined in Section 3.2.6 (e.g., supply chain issues, conflict minerals, digital colonialism, and extractivism). Additional justice-related issues, such as those related to the digital and global divide, are discussed further below.

At the *meso level*, involving tech industry associations and CSR initiatives, several key reform measures are necessary to strengthen the protection of human rights and ensure responsible corporate practices. A solid commitment to human rights principles should be established, underpinned by an enforcement pyramid that includes automatic sanctions for non-compliance, such as delisting or excluding non-compliant member institutions. Introducing performance standards – clear, verifiable, and independently monitored metrics – will help assess member institutions' socio-environmental impact. Additionally, minimum entry requirements must be established for membership, ensuring that entities meet criteria such as human rights due diligence, grievance mechanisms, and stakeholder dialogue before joining a CSR initiative or industry association. Reforming tech industry associations and CSR initiatives is also essential, with enhanced funding, staffing, and the creation of a stakeholder forum, advisory group, or ombudspersons to foster collaboration and accountability (Martens et al., 2019; Wörsdörfer, 2015, 2017).

At the *macro level*, nation-states play a critical role in ensuring that tech companies adhere to human rights, environmental, and social standards. Regulatory measures and strong government oversight are necessary to enforce compliance, including denying market access by entities such as the SEC and excluding tech companies from sustainability indexes for failing to meet required standards. Shareholder pressure can also be a powerful tool, with divestment campaigns targeting tech companies that consistently violate socio-environmental and human rights standards, alongside shareholder lawsuits against CEOs and senior management for their roles in these violations (and a possible violation of their fiduciary duties). Third-party beneficiary rights should be established, allowing project- or company-affected communities to have legal recourse. For example, the Alien Tort Claims Act in the United States provides a theoretical pathway for communities to sue parent companies in their home countries for wrongdoings committed by subsidiaries or business partners in host countries (e.g., Meta could face legal action in the United States over the business practices of outsourcing partners such as Sama). This legal framework empowers affected populations (e.g., data annotators and content moderators in the Global South) and can pressure companies to uphold higher accountability standards. Market regulation pressure and shareholder activism thus form an interconnected strategy to hold corporations accountable for their actions on a global scale (Wörsdörfer, 2018).

Corporate human rights advocacy involves several critical strategies to address and mitigate human rights violations within a (tech) company's supply chains. One of the main components is supply chain screening and monitoring, including covenants and divestment strategies. One way to exert leverage-influence over business partners in global (tech) supply chains (Wörsdörfer, 2015) is via business contracts or covenants: Through their contractual business relationships, (tech) companies can easily integrate human rights requirements such as human rights due diligence, human rights impact assessment and action plans, stakeholder dialogue, impact–benefit agreements as well as grievance, complaint, and remedy mechanisms into their supply chain management systems. If these human rights clauses (part of the covenants) are breached, the company may withdraw its funds, terminate the business relationship, or initiate legal action against the client. Divestment also serves as a powerful means of exerting pressure. Tech companies can disengage and divest from those that repeatedly violate international socio-environmental and human rights standards (e.g., Meta and OpenAI could choose to end their business relationships with Sama, Scale AI, and Remotasks, considering these companies' poor human rights records). By terminating direct and indirect business relationships with corporations notorious for harmful practices, companies send a strong message against such violations. This 'exit option' helps hold businesses accountable and reinforces the importance of upholding human rights standards in global supply chains. Human rights lobbyism is another key aspect of corporate advocacy. Tech companies can speak out against ongoing, systematic, and severe human rights abuses and/or engage in public human rights discourses. This involves collaborating with NGOs, civil society organizations, and governments from both the home and host countries, utilizing diplomatic channels to exert influence. Additionally, (tech) companies can advocate for more robust industry and governmental standards (e.g., concerning the working conditions in the data annotation and content moderation industries) to help ensure that human rights are upheld across all levels of operation (Wörsdörfer, 2015).

3.3.3.4.5 Ensuring fair competition in the age of big tech

To improve existing antitrust frameworks, researchers have proposed several reform measures:[44]

- *Modernizing antitrust laws for the digital economy*: This entails introducing new rules tailored explicitly to digital platforms, revising market definitions and concepts, and developing analytical tools to address new forms of market power, such as data power, digital nudging power, bottleneck power, strategic market status, and gatekeeping or rule-setting authority (see Section 3.2.8).
- *Shifting the burden of proof to merging firms*: Under this approach, the parties involved in M&A would be responsible for proving that their transactions do not harm competition or, alternatively, that any adverse effects are offset by public-interest efficiencies. This would lower the threshold for initiating and winning antitrust cases in the tech industry.
- *Establishing a presumption against M&As*: Mergers leading to greater market concentration would be presumed unlawful unless the merging parties demonstrate otherwise. This is particularly relevant in the case of dominant digital platforms and gatekeepers, where such transactions would be assumed to be anti-competitive unless societal benefits are clearly demonstrated.

44 Baer et al. (2020), Commission 'Competition Law 4.0' (2019), Furman Report (2019), Klobuchar (2021), Petit (2020), Stigler Report (2019), Subcommittee on Antitrust (2020), and Wörsdörfer (2022b).

- *Updating merger guidelines and introducing ex-post merger review*: Currently lacking in both the E.U. and the United States, retrospective reviews of past mergers should be implemented to assess long-term market effects. Antitrust agencies would evaluate whether previous M&As harmed competition or served the public interest. If harm is found, remedies such as demergers or reversing approvals should be possible.
- *Making greater use of behavioral and structural remedies*: Behavioral remedies may include ensuring data portability and interoperability, banning predatory pricing, tying, bundling, and self-preferencing. Structural remedies, such as separating business units, unbundling, or organizational restructuring, should be considered as a last resort.
- *Ensuring platform neutrality similar to net neutrality*: This would require dominant platforms to provide equal and fair access to all service providers on non-discriminatory terms. Such a neutrality rule would prevent companies from favoring their own products and uphold competitive fairness in digital markets.
- *Improving funding and staffing of antitrust authorities*: Stronger enforcement requires independent agencies that are better resourced and staffed with experts, such as data scientists, AI researchers, and independent analysts, to effectively oversee digital ecosystems.
- *Raising penalties for anti-competitive practices*: Meaningful deterrents are needed alongside monitoring and enforcement. Substantially higher fines for cartel behavior or exclusionary conduct, combined with structural and behavioral remedies, could be preventive tools.
- *Strengthening whistleblower protections*: Insider information is crucial for uncovering anti-competitive behavior. Providing better protections and incentives, such as bounty or reward programs, could encourage whistleblowers to share valuable information with regulators.
- *Promoting international collaboration*: National-level reforms should be complemented by a global strategy for digital competition. This includes coordination between antitrust authorities, governments, and international bodies (e.g., OECD, G7, G20) to share best practices and avoid regulatory fragmentation. The goal should be harmonization and (ideally) a 'race to the top,' which is especially important in the context of emerging AI regulation.

3.3.3.4.6 Robot military ethics

As AI increasingly influences modern warfare (see Section 3.2.10), there is a growing awareness of the urgent need to establish a framework for robot military ethics. The goal is to provide autonomous weapons – often called warbots – with ethical guidelines, effectively programming rules of engagement into their systems. This prompts important questions: How can this be accomplished, and which ethical principles should govern their behavior? A widely accepted basis is the *Just War* doctrine, which plays a central role in contemporary international law (Walzer, 2015). It forbids atrocities such as genocide and torture, requires a legitimate cause for war (like self-defense), and emphasizes the need to distinguish between combatants and civilians. However, in practice, these distinctions can become unclear, particularly in guerrilla warfare, where civilians are sometimes used as shields. The challenges of real-world combat situations pose severe difficulties for AI systems, which may lack the nuanced contextual understanding to make morally sound judgments in ambiguous scenarios. The *Just War* theory also calls for humane treatment of adversaries – providing care to the injured, respecting those who surrender, and minimizing unnecessary harm – and stresses the importance of justice after conflict, including accountability and rehabilitation. While well-established in human warfare, these principles become harder to translate into machine-executable rules, especially when ethical decisions must be made in real-time and under extreme conditions. Groups such as the *International Committee for Robot Arms Control* and the *Campaign to Stop Killer Robots* advocate for regulatory oversight through international treaties or industry (self-)regulation. A primary concern is preserving meaningful human control over critical, life-or-death decisions, addressing what is known as the control problem in fully autonomous weapons. Critics argue that delegating lethal authority to machines risks eroding moral responsibility and undermining the principles of humanitarian law. There is also concern about a potential AI arms race, which could lower the threshold for conflict by making warfare more automated, rapid, and politically palatable. Nonetheless, several challenges persist: defining what qualifies as military AI (*the definition problem*), managing technologies with both civilian and military applications (*the dual-use problem*), and ensuring adherence to regulations worldwide (*the governance problem*). Questions remain about how to monitor compliance and enforce sanctions for violations. This challenge is especially pressing given today's geopolitical landscape, characterized by strained U.S.–China relations and the ongoing fallout from Russia's invasion of Ukraine. In such a volatile context, trust between major powers is limited, raising concerns about transparency, verification, and the risk of defection from agreements. Some experts, including Payne (2021), suggest adapting Asimov's laws of robotics for battlefield use: warbots should only target authorized individuals, act with humanity, follow their commander's intentions, and protect allied personnel – even at their own risk, so long as it does not jeopardize the mission. These proposals aim to reconcile technical feasibility with moral responsibility; however, significant work remains to bridge the gap between theoretical frameworks and practical implementation. Ultimately, human accountability is paramount, making it critical to integrate ethical considerations throughout R&D and the deployment of military AI systems. As technology evolves, so must our moral and legal frameworks, ensuring that autonomous weapons are firmly grounded in human values and international humanitarian norms.

3.3.3.4.7 Other reform steps

Digital and global divide: To address the digital and global divide (see Section 3.2.2) and counteract winner-takes-all dynamics in the tech industry, several reform measures are essential (Desmond, 2023; Piketty, 2015, 2017, 2020; Saez & Zucman, 2019). Progressive taxation, including wealth and inheritance taxes, can reduce excessive competition for a limited number of highly rewarded positions by redistributing wealth from the top to the bottom (implementing digital services taxes could also be beneficial in this respect). This redistribution helps to level the playing field and create broader economic opportunities. Additionally, combating politico-economic lobbying and rent-seeking is critical (it is worth noting that tech companies rank among the top lobbying spenders in both the E.U. and the United States [Taplin, 2018; Wörsdörfer, 2021, 2022a, 2022b]); measures such as overcoming the 'revolving door' phenomenon (seen in the tech and finance industries) and curbing Wall Street and big tech's influence on legislative decision-making can help ensure fairer policies. Campaign finance reform, including overturning decisions like *Citizens United*, would diminish the disproportionate political power held by the wealthiest 1%, who currently control a significant amount of total wealth. Finally, a comprehensive educational reform – offering full coverage and free or open access – is vital to empower the poor and underprivileged, enabling them to participate fully in the digital economy and reduce systemic inequalities.

AI biases and discrimination: Several critical changes are needed across the AI development pipeline to better address (agentic) AI biases and discrimination (see Section 3.2.3). A major issue lies in the selection of training data, which is often unrepresentative or incomplete, such as datasets that heavily reflect the experiences of the white male U.S. population, leading to cultural and ethnic biases. Algorithms trained on too little data or flawed correlations risk making problematic generalizations, especially when they fail to account for underlying causations. Additionally, the lack of diversity among AI developers and data scientists, with teams often dominated by white, Western men aged 20–40, amplifies the risk of embedding personal beliefs, stereotypes, and societal biases into AI systems. To combat this, we must prioritize inclusive data practices, ensure diverse representation in tech teams, and build systems that reflect the realities and needs of BIPOC, women, disabled and elderly individuals, people from developing countries, and LGBTQ+ communities.

(Socio-)environmental impacts: The ordoliberal (2.0) principle of internalizing externalities underscores the responsibility to address the social and ecological costs of economic activity (see Section 3.2.7). Applied to AI, this means tackling the environmental toll of data centers, such as high energy consumption and carbon emissions, managing electronic waste, and promoting the development of sustainable or green AI technologies. Social sustainability, in turn, involves conducting human rights impact assessments, investing in workforce training, and supporting education and long-term social development. To more effectively curb AI's environmental footprint, many experts advocate for binding sustainability requirements for AI providers.

These would go beyond non-binding codes of conduct by enforcing limits on energy use and e-waste while encouraging the creation of environmentally responsible AI systems. Such regulatory measures would help safeguard the planet and ensure that AI contributes to societal well-being without compromising the prospects of future generations. Embedding sustainability into AI governance frameworks would also enhance transparency and accountability throughout the sector.

Democracy and the rule of law: A Kantian-inspired vision of a private law society seeks to replace systems rooted in privilege with those grounded in legal equality and the public interest. In the context of AI, this translates into embedding technological systems within democratic institutions and the rule of law, supported by strong judicial and legislative oversight, inclusive stakeholder engagement, and sustained public discourse (see Section 3.2.9). Drawing on Habermasian discourse ethics, scholars advocate for a community-in-the-loop governance model that ensures meaningful participation from affected groups, including consumers, workers, and trade unions. Democratic accountability also demands public representation in AI standardization and certification processes to protect stakeholders with limited bargaining power. However, participation alone is insufficient. Effective governance requires accessible mechanisms for redress and transparent information rights that allow individuals to challenge harmful or unjust AI decisions. Worker protection is particularly urgent, with growing calls to classify more workplace AI systems as high-risk or to prohibit specific tools altogether. Ensuring workplace democracy means empowering workers to influence how AI is adopted and used – through institutional mechanisms such as co-determination, works councils, and worker cooperatives – so that those who interact with AI systems have a voice (Abiri, 2024; Chandler, 2024; Häußermann & Lütge, 2022; Muldoon et al., 2025).

3.4 Concluding remarks

In recent months, there has been a discernible move toward deregulating AI technologies and relying on soft law, particularly in the United States, highlighted by Trump's repeal of Biden's EO, and, to a lesser extent, in the E.U., where a voluntary code of conduct for general-purpose AI providers has been introduced. This paper has challenged these deregulatory trends, arguing that the profound risks associated with AI demand stronger, more enforceable governance frameworks. It has outlined ten compelling reasons why comprehensive AI regulation is imperative: the technology's disruptive effects on labor markets and social equity; embedded (agentic) AI biases and systemic discrimination; threats to individual privacy; the spread of harmful online content, including dangerous/hate speech and disinformation; concerns surrounding corporate accountability and human rights; environmental impacts; the unchecked influence of powerful tech corporations; vulnerabilities within democratic systems and the rule of law; and the military and national security risks posed by advanced AI systems. The paper has also examined future regulatory pathways, such as soft versus hard law and concepts like constitutional AI versus AI guardrails, and proposed concrete strategies to strengthen and expand existing frameworks, including the E.U.'s AIA and antitrust laws.

Although the current political environment, particularly in the United States, poses significant challenges to adopting effective hard law measures for AI regulation, this should not diminish our commitment to pursuing a robust and comprehensive regulatory framework. Recognizing these challenges underscores the need for a multifaceted approach, as the ethical issues raised by AI are complex and cannot be addressed by a single solution or silver bullet. Instead, an effective response requires a diverse toolbox of complementary reform measures that combine formal regulations with informal practices where appropriate. This approach requires active engagement from all sectors of society, encompassing individuals, grassroots civil society movements, corporations, municipalities, nation-states, and international organizations. Central to this effort are public education and awareness-raising initiatives, which are critical to informing and sensitizing the broader population about the urgency and importance of AI ethics. To be truly effective, reform must occur across multiple levels of society. At the micro-level, individuals can make informed decisions and advocate for the ethical use of AI; at the meso-level, cities, corporations, and industries must adopt responsible AI governance; and at the macro-level, nation-states and international institutions are accountable for enacting binding policies and fostering cross-border cooperation. Thus, meaningful AI governance requires a balanced combination of top-down strategies, such as legislation and regulation, and bottom-up initiatives driven by civic participation and community involvement. To further support and guide these efforts, future research should undertake cross-country comparative analyses highlighting how different nations address AI's ethical challenges. Developing a database of lessons learned and best practice guidelines would also provide invaluable resources for policymakers, stakeholders, and advocates striving to build more equitable, transparent, and accountable AI governance worldwide.[45]

References

Abiri, G. (2024). Public Constitutional AI. https://arxiv.org/pdf/2406.16696 (last accessed: December 30, 2025).

AI4SDGs Think Tank. (2020/2025). Website. https://ai-for-sdgs.academy/ (last accessed: December 30, 2025).

AlgorithmWatch. (2021). Draft AI Act. https://algorithmwatch.org/en/wp-content/uploads/2021/08/EU-AI-Act-Consultation-Submission-by-AlgorithmWatch-August-2021.pdf (last accessed: December 30, 2025).

45 While this paper focuses primarily on big tech regulation in the context of the United States, the E.U., and other industrialized nations, future research could also build on these general frameworks to develop more tailored, sector-specific proposals.

AlgorithmWatch. (2023). Global Inventory of AI Ethics Guidelines. https://algorithmwatch.org/en/ai-ethics-guidelines-global-inventory/ (last accessed: December 30, 2025).

AI Multiple. (2025). When Will AGI/Singularity Happen? https://research.aimultiple.com/artificial-general-intelligence-singularity-timing/#easy-footnote-bottom-2-583 (last accessed: December 30, 2025).

AI Now Institute. (2025). Artificial Power 2025 Landscape Report. https://ainowinstitute.org/wp-content/uploads/2025/06/FINAL-20250609_AINowLandscapeReport_Full.pdf (last accessed: December 30, 2025).

AI Red Lines. (2025). Global Call for AI Red Lines. https://red-lines.ai/#call (last accessed: December 30, 2025).

Alvarez, J.M. et al. (2024). Policy Advice and Best Practices on Bias and Fairness in AI. Ethics and Information Technology 26:31. 1–26.

American Sunlight Project. (2025). Russian Propaganda May Be Flooding AI Models. https://www.americansunlight.org/updates/new-report-russian-propaganda-may-be-flooding-ai-models (last accessed: December 30, 2025).

Amnesty International. (2019). Surveillance Giants. https://www.amnesty.org/en/documents/pol30/1404/2019/en/ (last accessed: December 30, 2025).

Amnesty International. (2023). DRC: Powering Change or Business as Usual? https://www.amnesty.org/en/documents/AFR62/7009/2023/en/ (last accessed: December 30, 2025).

Association for the Advancement of Artificial Intelligence (AAAI). (2025). AAAI 2025 Presidential Panel on the Future of AI Research. https://aaai.org/wp-content/uploads/2025/03/AAAI-2025-PresPanel-Report-Digital-3.7.25.pdf (last accessed: December 30, 2025).

Ash, T.G. (2016). Free Speech. London, Atlantic Books.

Attard-Frost, B., De Los Rios, A., & Walter, D. (2022). The Ethics of AI Business Practices. AI and Ethics. https://doi.org/10.1007/s43681-022-00156-6 (last accessed: December 30, 2025).

Australian Energy Council. (2023). Data Centers: A 24-Hour Power Source? https://www.energycouncil.com.au/analysis/data-centres-a-24hr-power-source/ (last accessed: December 30, 2025).

Australian Strategic Policy Institute. (2020). Uyghurs for Sale. https://ad-aspi.s3.ap-southeast-2.amazonaws.com/2022-10/Uyghurs_for_sale-11OCT2022.pdf?VersionId=N2JQOako7S4OTiSb6L7kKE5nY2d_LD25 (last accessed: December 30, 2025).

Ayyamperumal, S.G. & Ge, L. (2024). Current State of LLM Risks and AI Guardrails. https://arxiv.org/pdf/2406.12934 (last accessed: December 30, 2025).

Badea, L. & Mungiu-Pupăzan, M. (2021). The Economic and Environmental Impact of Bitcoin. IEEE Access 9. 48091–48104.

Baer, B., Baker, J., Kades, M., Scott Morton, F., Rose, N., Shapiro, C., & Wu, T. (2020). Restoring Competition in the United States. https://equitablegrowth.org/research-paper/restoring-competition-in-the-united-states/ (last accessed: December 30, 2025).

Bai, Y., Kadavath, S., Kundu, S., . . . (2022). Constitutional AI. https://doi.org/10.48550/ARXIV.2212.08073 (last accessed: December 30, 2025).

Barbrook, R. & Cameron, A. (1995). The Californian Ideology. https://www.metamute.org/editorial/articles/californian-ideology (last accessed: December 30, 2025).

BBC. (2025). Meta Scientist Yann LeCun Says AI Won't Destroy Jobs Forever. https://www.bbc.com/news/technology-65886125 (last accessed: December 30, 2025).

Bender, E. & Hanna, A. (2025). The AI Con. London, Harper.

Bender, E., Gebru, T., McMillan-Major, A., & Shmitchell, S. (2021). On the Dangers of Stochastic Parrots. FAccT'21. 610–623.

Bentham, J. (1843). The Works of Jeremy Bentham Vol. 4. Indianapolis, Liberty Fund.

Biden White House. (2022a). Blueprint for an AI Bill of Rights. https://bidenwhitehouse.archives.gov/wp-content/uploads/2022/10/Blueprint-for-an-AI-Bill-of-Rights.pdf (last accessed: December 30, 2025).

Biden White House (2022b). Fact Sheet. https://bidenwhitehouse.archives.gov/ostp/news-updates/2022/09/08/fact-sheet-climate-and-energy-implications-of-crypto-assets-in-the-united-states/ (last accessed: December 30, 2025).

Biden White House. (2023a). Fact Sheet. https://bidenwhitehouse.archives.gov/briefing-room/statements-releases/2023/10/30/fact-sheet-president-biden-issues-executive-order-on-safe-secure-and-trustworthy-artificial-intelligence/ (last accessed: December 30, 2025).

Biden White House. (2023b). Executive Order on the Safe, Secure, and Trustworthy Development and Use of Artificial Intelligence. https://bidenwhitehouse.archives.gov/briefing-room/presidential-actions/2023/10/30/executive-order-on-the-safe-secure-and-trustworthy-development-and-use-of-artificial-intelligence/ (last accessed: December 30, 2025).

Böhm, F. (1961). Demokratie und ökonomische Macht. In Institut für ausländisches und internationales Wirtschaftsrecht (ed.). Kartelle und Monopole im modernen Recht. Karlsruhe, Müller. 1–24.

Borsook, P. (2000). Cyberselfish. New York. PublicAffairs.

Bostrom, N. (2014). Superintelligence. Oxford, Oxford University Press.

Bradford, A. (2020). The Brussels Effect. Oxford, Oxford University Press.

Bradford, A. (2023). Digital Empires. Oxford, Oxford University Press.

Brennan, G. & Buchanan, J. (1985/2000). The Reason of Rules. Indianapolis, Liberty Fund.

Brynjolfsson, E. & McAfee, A. (2016). The Second Machine Age. New York, Norton.

Buchanan, J. (1975/2000). The Limits of Liberty. Indianapolis, Liberty Fund.

Buchanan, J. & Congleton, R. (1998). Politics By Principle, Not Interest. Cambridge, Cambridge University Press.

Buchanan, J. & Tullock, G. (1962/1999). The Calculus of Consent. Indianapolis, Liberty Fund.

Buolamwini, J. (2016). How I'm Fighting Bias in Algorithms. https://www.ted.com/talks/joy_buolamwini_how_i_m_fighting_bias_in_algorithms (last accessed: December 30, 2025).

Buolamwini, J. (2023). Unmasking AI. New York, Random House.

Buolamwini, J. & Gebru, T. (2018). Gender Shades. Proceedings of Machine Learning Research 81. 1–15.

Business and Human Rights Resource Center. (2025a). E.U. Halt Talks on Anti-Greenwashing Law. https://www.business-humanrights.org/en/latest-news/eu-commission-and-council-halt-talks-on-anti-greenwashing-law/ (last accessed: December 30, 2025).

Business and Human Rights Resource Center. (2025b). Kenyan Data Labelers Make Modern Slavery Allegations Against AI Company Appen. https://www.business-humanrights.org/en/latest-news/australia-kenyan-data-labellers-make-modern-slavery-allegations-against-ai-company-appen/ (last accessed: December 30, 2025).

Carlson, C.R. (2021). Hate Speech. Cambridge. MIT Press.

Carney, M. (2021). Value(s). New York, Public Affairs.

Cefaliello, A. & Kullmann, M. (2022). Offering False Security. European Labor Law Journal 13(4). 542–562.

Center for AI Safety. (2023). Statement on AI Risk. https://www.safe.ai/statement-on-ai-risk (last accessed: December 30, 2025).

Chandler, D. (2024). Free and Equal. New York, Knopf.

China Labor Watch. (2019). iPhone 11 Illegally Produced in China. https://chinalaborwatch.org/wp-content/uploads/2021/06/Zhengzhou-Foxconn-English-09.06.pdf (last accessed: December 30, 2025).

Claassen, R., Gerbrandy, A., Princen, S., & Segers, M. (2019). Rethinking the European Social Market Economy: Introduction to the Special Issue. Journal of Common Market Studies 57(1). 3–12.

CNN. (2025). Tesla Proposes Elon Musk Pay Package That Could Make Him the World's First Trillionaire. https://edition.cnn.com/2025/09/05/business/elon-musk-tesla-new-pay-package (last accessed: December 30, 2025).

CompaniesMarketCap.com. (2025). Largest Companies by Marketcap. https://companiesmarketcap.com/ (last accessed: December 30, 2025).

Commission 'Competition Law 4.0.' (2019). A New Competition Framework for the Digital Economy. www.bmwi.de/Redaktion/EN/Publikationen/Wirtschaft/a-new-competition-framework-for-the-digital-economy.pdf?__blob=publicationFile&v=3 (last accessed: December 30, 2025).

Congleton, R. (2013). The Contractarian Constitutional Political Economy. http://papers.ssrn.com/sol3/papers.cfm?abstract_id=2327665 (last accessed: December 30, 2025).

Couldry, N. & Mejias, U. (2019). Data Colonialism. Television & New Media 20(4). 336–349.

Council of the E.U. (2025). Council Agrees Position on Sustainability Reporting and Due Diligence Requirements to Boost E.U. Competitiveness. https://www.consilium.europa.eu/en/press/press-releases/2025/06/23/simplification-council-agrees-position-on-sustainability-reporting-and-due-diligence-requirements-to-boost-eu-competitiveness/?utm_id=3318 (last accessed: December 30, 2025).

Dachwitz, I. & Hilbig, S. (2025). Digitaler Kolonialismus. Munich. C.H. Beck.

Daly, A., Hagendorff, T., Li, H., Mann, M., Marda, V., Wagner, B., & Wang, W. (2021). AI, Governance, and Ethics. In: Micklitz, H., Pollicino, O., Reichman, A., Simoncini, A., Sartor, G., & De Gregorio, G. (eds.). Constitutional Challenges in the Algorithmic Society. Cambridge, Cambridge University Press. 182–201.

Desmond, M. (2023). Poverty, By America. New York, Crown.

Dold, M. & Krieger, T. (eds.). (2020). Ordoliberalism and European Economic Policy. New York, Routledge.

Dong, Y., Mu, R., Jin, G., Qi, Y., Hu, J., Zhao, X., Meng, J., Ruan, W., & Huang, X. (2024). Building Guardrails for Large Language Models. PMLR 235. 11375–11394.

Dou, E. (2025). House of Huawei. New York, Penguin.

Ebers, M., Hoch, V., Rosenkranz, F., Ruschemeier, H., & Steinrötter, B. (2021). The European Commission's Proposal for an Artificial Intelligence Act – A Critical Assessment. J Multidisciplinary Scientific Journal 4(4). 589–603.

Economic Policy Institute. (2022). CEO Pay Has Skyrocketed 1,460% Since 1978. https://www.epi.org/publication/ceo-pay-in-2021/ (last accessed: December 30, 2025).

E.U. AI Champions Initiative. (2025). Stop the Clock – Open Letter. https://aichampions.eu/#stoptheclock (last accessed: December 30, 2025).

Eucken, W. (1946/1999). Über die Verstaatlichung der privaten Banken. In W. Eucken, Ordnungspolitik. Münster, LIT. 38–58.

Eucken, W. (1950/1965). Die Grundlagen der Nationalökonomie. Berlin, Springer.

Eucken, W. (1952/2004). Grundsätze der Wirtschaftspolitik. Tübingen, Mohr Siebeck.

Eucken, W. (1999). Ordnungspolitik. Münster, LIT.

Eucken, W. (2001). Wirtschaftsmacht und Wirtschaftsordnung. Münster, LIT.

European Commission. (2017). Conflict Minerals Regulation. https://policy.trade.ec.europa.eu/development-and-sustainability/conflict-minerals-regulation_en (last accessed: December 30, 2025).

European Commission. (2025a). E.U.'s Climate Law Presents a New Way to Get to 2040. https://ec.europa.eu/commission/presscorner/detail/en/ip_25_1687 (last accessed: December 30, 2025).

European Commission. (2025b). The General-Purpose AI Code of Practice. https://digital-strategy.ec.europa.eu/en/policies/contents-code-gpai (last accessed: December 30, 2025).

European Parliament & Council of the E.U. (2022). Digital Services Act. https://eur-lex.europa.eu/eli/reg/2022/2065/oj/eng (last accessed: December 30, 2025).

European Parliament & Council of the E.U. (2024). Corporate Sustainability Due Diligence Directive. https://eur-lex.europa.eu/eli/dir/2024/1760/oj (last accessed: December 30, 2025).

European Parliamentary Research Service (EPRS). (2022a). Artificial Intelligence Act. www.europarl.europa.eu/RegData/etudes/BRIE/2021/698792/EPRS_BRI(2021)698792_EN.pdf (last accessed: December 30, 2025).

European Parliamentary Research Service (EPRS). (2022b). AI and Digital Tools in Workplace Management and Evaluation. www.europarl.europa.eu/RegData/etudes/STUD/2022/729516/EPRS_STU(2022)729516_EN.pdf (last accessed: December 30, 2025).
FAZ. (2025). "Europa muss Innovationen fördern statt verhindern." https://www.faz.net/aktuell/wirtschaft/unternehmen/sap-und-siemens-fordern-neue-ki-regulierung-110588444.html (last accessed: December 30, 2025).
Federal Ministry of Labor and Social Affairs. (2021). Act on Corporate Due Diligence Obligations in Supply Chains. https://www.csr-in-deutschland.de/SharedDocs/Downloads/EN/act-corporate-due-diligence-obligations-supply-chains.pdf?__blob=publicationFile#linkicon/ (last accessed: December 30, 2025).
Feld, L. & Köhler, E. (2011). Ist die Ordnungsökonomik zukunftsfähig? zfwu 12(2). 173–195.
Field, S. (2025). Why Do Experts Disagree on Existential Risk and P(Doom)? https://arxiv.org/pdf/2502.14870 (last accessed: December 30, 2025).
Fjeld, J., Achten, N., Hilligoss, H., Nagy, A., & Srikumar, M. (2020). Principled Artificial Intelligence. https://dash.harvard.edu/bitstream/handle/1/42160420/HLS%20White%20Paper%20Final_v3.pdf (last accessed: December 30, 2025).
Floridi, L. (2023). The Ethics of Artificial Intelligence. Oxford, Oxford University Press.
Floridi, L., Holweg, M., Taddeo, M., Silva, J., Mökander, & Wen, Y. (2022). capAI. https://papers.ssrn.com/sol3/papers.cfm?abstract_id=4064091 (last accessed: December 30, 2025).
Forbes. (2023). Millions of Americans Are Still Missing Out on Broadband Access and Leaving Money on the Table – Here's Why. https://www.forbes.com/advisor/personal-finance/millions-lack-broadband-access/ (last accessed: December 30, 2025).
Forbes. (2024). Elon Musk's $20 Billion Net Worth Jump Leads Billionaire Surge After Trump's Win. https://www.forbes.com/sites/antoniopequenoiv/2024/11/06/elon-musks-20-billion-net-worth-jump-leads-billionaire-surge-after-trumps-win-fortunes-of-bezos-buffett-and-more-swell/ (last accessed: December 30, 2025).
Foucault, M. (1995). Discipline and Punish. New York, Vintage.
Foucault, M. (2000). Power. New York, The New Press.
Frank, R. & Cook, P. (1996). The Winner-Take-All Society. New York, Penguin Books.
Frankfurt, H. (2005). On Bullshit. Princeton, Princeton University Press.
Fratzscher. M. (2017). Verteilungskampf. Munich, Hanser.
Frey, C.B. & Osborne, M. (2013/2017). The Future of Employment. Technological Forecasting and Social Change 114. 254–280.
Friedman, B. & Nissenbaum, H. (1996). Bias in Computer Systems. ACM Transactions on Information Systems 14(3). 330–347.
Furman, J., Coyle, D., Fletcher, A., Marsden, P. & McAuley, D. (2019). Unlocking Digital Competition ('Furman Report'). www.gov.uk/government/publications/unlocking-digital-competition-report-of-the-digital-competition-expert-panel (last accessed: December 30, 2025).
Future of Life Institute. (2023). Pause Giant AI Experiments: An Open Letter. https://futureoflife.org/open-letter/pause-giant-ai-experiments/ (last accessed: December 30, 2025).
Ganz, A., Camellini, M., Hine, E., Novelli, C., Roberts, H., & Floridi, L. (2024). Submarine Cables and the Risks to Digital Sovereignty. Minds & Machines 34. Article 31.
Gellman, B. (2021). Dark Mirror. New York, Penguin Books.
Gilder, G. (2012). Wealth and Poverty. Washington, Regnery.
Goldman Sachs. (2023). The Potentially Large Effects of Artificial Intelligence on Economic Growth. https://www.key4biz.it/wp-content/uploads/2023/03/Global-Economics-Analyst_-The-Potentially-Large-Effects-of-Artificial-Intelligence-on-Economic-Growth-Briggs_Kodnani.pdf (last accessed: December 30, 2025).
Goldschmidt, N. (2002). Entstehung und Vermächtnis ordoliberalen Denkens. Münster, LIT.

Goldschmidt, N. (2007). Walter Eucken's Place in the History of Ideas. www.gmu.edu/centers/publicchoice/HES%202007/papers/6d%20goldschmidt.pdf (last accessed: December 30, 2025).

Goldschmidt, N. & Wohlgemuth, M. (eds.). (2008). Grundtexte zur Freiburger Tradition der Ordnungsökonomik. Tübingen, Mohr Siebeck.

Grace, K., Stewart, H., Sandkühler, J.F., Thomas, S., Weinstein-Raun, B., & Brauner, J. (2024). Thousands of AI Authors on the Future of AI. https://arxiv.org/abs/2401.02843 (last accessed: December 30, 2025).

Gray, M. & Suri, S. (2019). Ghost Work. Boston, Houghton Mifflin Harcourt.

Greenwald, G. (2015). No Place to Hide. New York, Picador.

Gregg, S. (2010). Wilhelm Röpke's Political Economy. Cheltenham, Edward Elgar.

Grossekettler, H. (1994). On Designing an Institutional Infrastructure for Economies. The Freiburg Legacy after 50 Years. Journal of Economic Studies 21(4). 9–24.

Gstrein, O. (2022). European AI Regulation: Brussels Effect versus Human Dignity. Zeitschrift für Europarechtliche Studien 04/2022. 755–772.

Hagendorff, T. (2020). The Ethics of AI Ethics. Minds and Machines 30. 99–120.

Hagey, K. (2025). The Optimist. NY, Norton.

Hayek, F.A. (1968/2002). Competition as a Discovery Procedure. Quarterly Journal of Austrian Economics 5 (3). 9–23.

Hayek, F.A. (1973). Law, Legislation and Liberty Vol. 1. London, Routledge.

Haidt, J. (2024). The Anxious Generation. New York, Penguin Press.

Hao, K. (2025). Empire of AI. New York, Penguin.

Harari, Y. (2017). Homo Deus. London, Vintage.

Harari, Y. (2019). 21 Lessons for the 21st Century. New York, Random House.

Hasdell, R. (2020). What We Know About Universal Basic Income. https://basicincome.stanford.edu/research/papers/what-we-know-about-universal-basic-income/ (last accessed: December 30, 2025).

Haugen, F. (2023). The Power of One. New York, Little, Brown, and Company.

Häußermann, J., & Lütge, C. (2022). Community-in-the-Loop. AI and Ethics 2(2). 341–362.

Hill, K. (2023). Your Face Belongs to Us. New York, Random House.

Huang, S., Siddarth, D., Lovitt, L., Liao, T. I., Durmus, E., Tamkin, A., & Ganguli, D. (2024). Collective Constitutional AI. The 2024 ACM Conference on Fairness, Accountability, and Transparency, 1395–1417.

Huynh, A., Duong, D., Burggraf, T., Luong, H., & Bu, N. (2022). Energy Consumption and Bitcoin Market. Asia-Pacific Financial Markets 29. 79–93.

IAPP. (2025). Potential E.U. AI Act Pause Opens New Questions on Approach to Global Regulation. https://iapp.org/news/a/navigate-2025-potential-eu-ai-act-pause-opens-new-questions-on-approach-to-global-regulation/ (last accessed: December 30, 2025).

Institute for Human Rights and Business. (2016). Data Brokers and Human Rights. Big Data, Big Business. https://www.ihrb.org/resources/data-brokers-big-data-big-business (last accessed: December 30, 2025).

Internet Watch Foundation. (2025). IWF Annual Data & Insights Report 2024.

ITU. (2025). Facts and Figures 2024. https://www.itu.int/itu-d/reports/statistics/facts-figures-2024/index/ (last accessed: December 30, 2025).

Jobin, A., Ienca, M., & Vayena, E. (2019). The Global Landscape of AI Ethics Guidelines. Nature Machine Intelligence 1. 389–399.

Josephson, P. (2025). Totalitarian Science in the White House. https://www.commondreams.org/opinion/trump-totalitarian-science (last accessed: December 30, 2025).

Kaplan, J. (2016). Artificial Intelligence: What Everyone Needs to Know. Oxford, Oxford University Press.

Kaplan, J. (2024). Generative Artificial Intelligence: What Everyone Needs to Know. Oxford, Oxford University Press.

Kara, S. (2023). Cobalt Red. New York, St. Martin's Press.

Kazim, E. & Koshiyama, A. (2021). A High-Level Overview of AI Ethics. Patterns 2(9). 1–12.
Khanna, R. (2023). Progressive Capitalism. New York, Simon & Schuster.
Klobuchar, A. (2021). Antitrust. New York, Knopf.
Kohli, V., Chakravarty, S., Chamola, V., Singh Sangwan, K., & Zeadally, S. (2023). An Analysis of Energy Consumption and Carbon Footprints of Cryptocurrencies and Possible Solutions. Digital Communications and Networks 9(1). 79–89.
Kop, M. (2021). E.U. Artificial Intelligence Act: The European Approach to AI. https://futurium.ec.europa.eu/sites/default/files/2021-10/Kop_EU%20Artificial%20Intelligence%20Act%20-%20The%20European%20Approach%20to%20AI_21092021_0.pdf (last accessed: December 30, 2025).
Kurzweil, R. (2000). The Age of Spiritual Machines. New York, Penguin.
Kurzweil, R. (2005). The Singularity is Near. London, Penguin.
Kurzweil, R. (2024). The Singularity is Nearer. New York, Viking.
Küster, A. & Wörsdörfer, M. (2025). Exploring Laws of Robotics. Digital Society 4. Article 46.
Kwet, M. (2022). Digital Colonialism and Infrastructure-as-Debt. https://papers.ssrn.com/sol3/papers.cfm?abstract_id=4004594 (last accessed: December 30, 2025).
Lanier, J. (2013). Who Owns the Future? New York, Simon & Schuster.
Laux, J. (2023). Institutionalized Distrust and Human Oversight of Artificial Intelligence. https://papers.ssrn.com/sol3/papers.cfm?abstract_id=4377481 (last accessed: December 30, 2025).
Laux, J., Wachter, S., & Mittelstadt, B. (2023a). Three Pathways for Standardization and Ethical Disclosure by Default Under the European Union Artificial Intelligence Act. https://papers.ssrn.com/sol3/papers.cfm?abstract_id=4365079 (last accessed: December 30, 2025).
Laux, J., Wachter, S., & Mittelstadt, B. (2023b). Trustworthy Artificial Intelligence and the European Union AI Act. Regulation and Governance, February 6, 2023. 1–30.
Lechevalier, A. (2015). Eucken Under the Pillow: The Ordoliberal Imprint on Social Europe. In: Lechevalier, A. & Wielghos, J. (eds.). Social Europe: The Dead End. Copenhagen, Djoef. 49–102.
Lee, K.-F. (2018). AI Superpowers. Boston, Houghton Mifflin Harcourt.
Lenel, H.O. & Meyer, F. (1948). Vorwort. Die Aufgabe des Jahrbuchs. ORDO 1. VII-XI.
Leslie, D. (2019). Understanding Artificial Intelligence Ethics and Safety. https://www.turing.ac.uk/sites/default/files/2019-06/understanding_artificial_intelligence_ethics_and_safety.pdf (last accessed: December 30, 2025).
Leslie, D., Burr, C., Aitken, M., Cowls, J., Katell, M., & Briggs, M. (2021). Artificial Intelligence, Human Rights, Democracy, and the Rule of Law. www.turing.ac.uk/sites/default/files/2021-03/cahai_feasibility_study_primer_final.pdf (last accessed: December 30, 2025).
Li, F.-F. (2023). The Worlds I See. New York. Flatiron Books.
Li, P., Yang, J., Islam, M., & Ren, S. (2025). Making AI Less 'Thirsty.' https://arxiv.org/pdf/2304.03271 (last accessed: December 30, 2025).
Loi, M., Fabbri, M., & Ferrario, A. (2025). Regulating the Undefined: Addressing Systemic Risks in the Digital Services Act. Philosophy & Technology 38. Article 82.
Luccioni, A., Viguier, S., & Ligozat, A.-L. (2022). Estimating the Carbon Footprint of BLOOM, A 176B Parameter Language Model. https://arxiv.org/pdf/2211.02001 (last accessed: December 30, 2025).
Martens, W., Linden, B., & Wörsdörfer, M. (2019). How to Assess the Democratic Qualities of a Multi-Stakeholder Initiative from a Habermasian Perspective? Journal of Business Ethics 155. 1115–1133.
McIntyre, L. (2018). Post-Truth. Cambridge, MIT Press.
McKinsey. (2015). Four Fundamentals of Workplace Automation. https://www.mckinsey.com/capabilities/mckinsey-digital/our-insights/four-fundamentals-of-workplace-automation (last accessed: December 30, 2025).
McKinsey & Company. (2023). Investing in the Rising Data Center Economy. https://www.mckinsey.com/~/media/mckinsey/industries/technology%20media%20and%20telecommunications/high%20tech/our

%20insights/investing%20in%20the%20rising%20data%20center%20economy/investing-in-the-rising-data-center-economy_final.pdf (last accessed: December 30, 2025).

Meijer, G. (2007). Value and Exchange in Economic Theorizing. The Contribution of the Freiburg School. Review of Austrian Economics 20. 171–185.

Mejias, U. & Couldry, N. (2024). Data Grab. Chicago. Chicago University Press.

Microsoft AI. (2025). The Path to Medical Superintelligence. https://microsoft.ai/new/the-path-to-medical-superintelligence/ (last accessed: December 30, 2025).

Mittelstadt, B. (2019). Principles Alone Cannot Guarantee Ethical AI. Nature Machine Intelligence 1. 501–507.

Mökander, J., & Floridi, L. (2021). Ethics-Based Auditing to Develop Trustworthy AI. Minds and Machines 31 (2). 323–327.

Morley, J., Elhalal, A., Garcia, F., Kinsey, L., Mökander, J., & Floridi, L. (2021). Ethics as a Service. Minds and Machines 31. 239–256.

Mother Jones. (2025). The Shocking Far-Right Agenda Behind the Facial Recognition Tech Used by ICE and the FBI. https://www.motherjones.com/politics/2025/04/clearview-ai-immigration-ice-fbi-surveillance-facial-recognition-hoan-ton-that-hal-lambert-trump/ (last accessed: December 30, 2025).

Müller-Armack, A. (1956). Soziale Marktwirtschaft. In Handwörterbuch der Sozialwissenschaften. Stuttgart, Fischer. 390–392

Muldoon, J., Graham, M., & Cant, C. (2025). Feeding the Machine. Edinburgh, Canongate.

Murphy, L., Salcito, K., Uluyol, Y., & Rabkin, M. (2022). Driving Force. https://www.shuforcedlabour.org/drivingforce/ (last accessed: December 30, 2025).

Mwema, E. & Birhane, A. (2024). Undersea Cables in Africa. First Monday, 29(4). 1 April 2024.

Narayanan, A. & Kapoor, S. (2024). AI Snake Oil. Princeton, Princeton University Press.

Nest, M. (2013). Coltan. Cambridge, Polity.

Neuralink. (2025). Company Website. https://neuralink.com/ (last accessed: December 30, 2025).

NewsGuard's Reality Check. (2025). A Well-Funded Moscow-Based Global 'News' Network Has Infected Western Artificial Intelligence Tools Worldwide with Russian Propaganda. https://www.newsguardrealitycheck.com/p/a-well-funded-moscow-based-global (last accessed: December 30, 2025).

New York Times. (2017). Peter Thiel, Trump's Tech Pal, Explains Himself. https://www.nytimes.com/2017/01/11/fashion/peter-thiel-donald-trump-silicon-valley-technology-gawker.html (last accessed: December 30, 2025).

New York Times. (2018). Germany Acts to Tame Facebook, Learning from Its Own History of Hate. https://www.nytimes.com/2018/05/19/technology/facebook-deletion-center-germany.html (last accessed: December 30, 2025).

New York Times. (2020). The Secretive Company That Might End Privacy As We Know It. https://www.nytimes.com/2020/01/18/technology/clearview-privacy-facial-recognition.html (last accessed: December 30, 2025).

New York Times. (2024). A.I. Beings Ushering in an Age of Killer Robots. https://www.nytimes.com/2024/07/02/technology/ukraine-war-ai-weapons.html (last accessed: December 30, 2025).

New York Times. (2025a). The Global A.I. Divide. https://www.nytimes.com/interactive/2025/06/23/technology/ai-computing-global-divide.html (last accessed: December 30, 2025).

New York Times. (2025b). Trump Taps Palantir to Compile Data on Americans. https://www.nytimes.com/2025/05/30/technology/trump-palantir-data-americans.html (last accessed: December 30, 2025).

New York Times. (2025c). How Do You Teach Computer Science in the A.I. Era? https://www.nytimes.com/2025/06/30/technology/computer-science-education-ai.html (last accessed: December 30, 2025).

New York Times. (2025d). A.I. Is Getting More Powerful, But Its Hallucinations Are Getting Worse. https://www.nytimes.com/2025/05/05/technology/ai-hallucinations-chatgpt-google.html (last accessed: December 30, 2025).

New York Times. (2025e). A.I. Is Starting to Wear Down Democracy. https://www.nytimes.com/2025/06/26/technology/ai-elections-democracy.html (last accessed: December 30, 2025).

New York Times. (2025f). The A.I. Frenzy Is Escalating. Again. https://www.nytimes.com/2025/06/27/technology/ai-spending-openai-amazon-meta.html (last accessed: December 30, 2025).

New York Times. (2025g). In Pursuit of Godlike Technology, Mark Zuckerberg Amps Up the A.I. Race. https://www.nytimes.com/2025/06/27/technology/mark-zuckerberg-meta-ai.html (last accessed: December 30, 2025).

New York Times. (2025h). European Union Unveils Rules for Powerful A.I. Systems. https://www.nytimes.com/2025/07/10/business/ai-rules-europe.html (last accessed: December 30, 2025).

New York Times. (2025i). Elon Musk's Grok Chatbot Shares Antisemitic Posts on X. https://www.nytimes.com/2025/07/08/technology/grok-antisemitism-ai-x.html (last accessed: December 30, 2025).

Norris, P. (2001). Digital Divide. Cambridge, Cambridge University Press.

Novelli, C., Taddeo, M., & Floridi, L. (2023). Accountability in Artificial Intelligence. AI and Society 7 February 2023. 1–12.

OECD. (2016). The Risk of Automation for Jobs in OECD Countries. https://www.oecd.org/en/publications/the-risk-of-automation-for-jobs-in-oecd-countries_5jlz9h56dvq7-en.html (last accessed: December 30, 2025).

O'Neil, C. (2016). Weapons of Math Destruction. New York, Penguin.

Oppenheimer, F. (1933). Weder so – noch so. Der Dritte Weg. Potsdam, Protte.

Oreskes, N. & Conway, E. (2023). The Big Myth. New York, Bloomsbury.

Owusu-Sekyere, K., Batteiger, A., Afoblikame, R., Hafner, G., & Kranert, M. (2022). Assessing Data in the Informal E-Waste Sector: The Agbogbloshie Scrapyard. Waste Management 139. 158–167.

Oxfam. (2017). Just 8 Men Own Same Wealth as Half the World. https://www.oxfam.org/en/press-releases/just-8-men-own-same-wealth-half-world (last accessed: December 30, 2025).

Pasquale, F. (2016). The Black Box Society. Cambridge, Harvard University Press.

Patterson, D., Gonzalez, J., Le, Q., Liang, C., Munguia, L.-M., Rothchild, D., So, D., Texier, M., & Dean, J. (2021). Carbon Emissions and Large Neural Network Training. https://arxiv.org/abs/2104.10350 (last accessed: December 30, 2025).

Payne, K. (2021). I, Warbot. Oxford, Oxford University Press.

Petit, N. (2020). Big Tech and the Digital Economy. Oxford, Oxford University Press.

Piketty, T. (2015). The Economics of Inequality. Cambridge. Belknap Press.

Piketty, T. (2017). Capital in the Twenty-First Century. Cambridge. Belknap Press.

Piketty, T. (2020). Capital and Ideology. Cambridge. Belknap Press.

Politico. (2025). Victory for Trump as E.U. Backs Down on Digital Taxes in Next Budget. https://www.politico.eu/article/victory-eu-donald-trump-meta-tax-digital/ (last accessed: December 30, 2025).

PwC. (2018). Will Robots Really Steal Our Jobs? An International Analysis of the Potential Long-Term Impact of Automation. https://www.pwc.com/hu/hu/kiadvanyok/assets/pdf/impact_of_automation_on_jobs.pdf (last accessed: December 30, 2025).

Quinn, M. (2024). Ethics for the Information Age. Hoboken, Pearson.

Ressa, M. (2023). How to Stand Up to a Dictator. New York, Harper.

Reich, R. (2015a). Saving Capitalism for the Many, Not the Few. New York, Knopf.

Reich, R. (2015b). In Sharing Economy, Workers Get Stuck with the Scraps. www.sfgate.com/opinion/reich/article/In-sharing-economy-workers-get-stuck-with-the-6063555.php (last accessed: December 30, 2025).

Reuters. (2025). Microsoft Likely to Sign E.U. AI Code of Practice, Meta Rebuffs Guidelines. https://www.reuters.com/sustainability/boards-policy-regulation/microsoft-likely-sign-eu-ai-code-practice-meta-rebuffs-guidelines-2025-07-18/ (last accessed: December 30, 2025).

Rieder, G., Simon, J., & Wong, P.-H. (2021). Mapping the Stony Road Toward Trustworthy AI. In: Pelillo, M. & Scantamburlo, T. (eds.). Machines We Trust. Cambridge, MIT Press. 27–42.

Rifkin, J. (2014). The Zero Marginal Cost Society. New York, Palgrave.
Risen, C. (2025). Red Scare. New York, Scribner.
Röpke, W. (1942). Die Gesellschaftskrise der Gegenwart. Erlenbach, Rentsch.
Röpke, W. (1944/1949). Civitas Humana. Erlenbach, Rentsch.
Röpke, W. (1950). Mass und Mitte. Erlenbach, Rentsch.
Rubenstein, D. (2021). Acquiring Ethical AI. Florida Law Review 73. 747–819.
Rüstow, A. (1955). Wirtschaftsethische Probleme der sozialen Marktwirtschaft. In P. Boarman (ed.). Der Christ und die soziale Marktwirtschaft. Stuttgart, Kohlhammer. 53–74.
Rüstow, A. (1957). Ortsbestimmung der Gegenwart III. Erlenbach, Rentsch.
Rüstow, A. (2001). Die Religion der Marktwirtschaft. Münster, LIT.
Saez, E. & Zucman, G. (2019). The Triumph of Injustice. New York, Norton.
Schumpeter, J. (1942/2008). Capitalism, Socialism, and Democracy. New York, Harper.
Schwab, K. (2016). The Fourth Industrial Revolution. Geneva, World Economic Forum.
Slobodian, Q. (2025). Hayek's Bastards. London, Penguin.
Smart, J.M. (2003). Acceleration Watch. https://accelerationwatch.com/index.html (last accessed: December 30, 2025).
Smuha, N. (2019). The E.U. Approach to Ethics Guidelines for Trustworthy Artificial Intelligence. Computer Law Review International 20(4). 97–106.
Smuha, N., Ahmed-Rengers, E., Harkens, A., Li, W., MacLaren, J., Piselli, R., & Yeung, K. (2021). How the E.U. Can Achieve Legally Trustworthy AI. https://papers.ssrn.com/sol3/papers.cfm?abstract_id=3899991 (last accessed: December 30, 2025).
Snowden, E. (2019). Permanent Record. New York, Metropolitan Books.
Snyder, T. (2017). On Tyranny. New York, Tim Duggan Books.
Stanford University Human-Centered Artificial Intelligence. (2025). The 2025 AI Index Report. https://hai.stanford.edu/assets/files/hai_ai_index_report_2025.pdf (last accessed: December 30, 2025).
Statista. (2025a). Bitcoin Energy Consumption Worldwide from February 2017 to May 19, 2025. https://www.statista.com/statistics/881472/worldwide-bitcoin-energy-consumption/ (last accessed: December 30, 2025).
Statista. (2025b). Average Annual CEO Compensation Worldwide in 2017, By Country. https://www.statista.com/statistics/424154/average-annual-ceo-compensation-worldwide/ (last accessed: December 30, 2025).
Statista. (2025c). Google, Amazon, Meta, Apple, and Microsoft (GAMAM) – Statistics & Facts. https://www.statista.com/topics/4213/google-apple-facebook-amazon-and-microsoft-gafam/#topicOverview (last accessed: December 30, 2025).
Steinberger, M. (2025). The Philosopher in the Valley: Alex Karp, Palantir, and the Rise of the Surveillance State. New York, Simon & Schuster.
Stigler Center for the Study of the Economy and the State. (2019). Report of the Committee for the Study of Digital Platforms. Market Structure and Antitrust Subcommittee ('Stigler Report'). https://research.chicagobooth.edu/-/media/research/stigler/pdfs/market-structure–report-as-of-15-may-2019.pd (last accessed: December 30, 2025).
Stiglitz. J. (2015). The Great Divide. New York, Norton.
Strubell, E., Ganesh, A., & McCallum, A. (2019). Energy and Policy Considerations for Deep Learning in NLP. https://arxiv.org/abs/1906.02243 (last accessed: December 30, 2025).
Subcommittee on Antitrust, Commercial and Administrative Law of the Committee on the Judiciary. (2020). Investigation of Competition in Digital Markets. https://judiciary.house.gov/news/documentsingle.aspx?DocumentID=3429 (last accessed: December 30, 2025).
Taplin, J. (2018). Move Fast and Break Things. New York, Back Bay Books.

Taylor, M. (2017). Good Work. https://assets.publishing.service.gov.uk/media/5a82dcdce5274a2e87dc35a4/good-work-taylor-review-modern-working-practices-rg.pdf (last accessed: December 30, 2025).
The Citizen Lab. (2025). Citizen Lab Research. https://citizenlab.ca/category/research/ (last accessed: December 30, 2025).
The Guardian. (2019). Revealed: Google Made Large Contributions to Climate Change Deniers. https://www.theguardian.com/environment/2019/oct/11/google-contributions-climate-change-deniers (last accessed: December 30, 2025).
The Guardian. (2023a). US Air Force Denies Running Simulation in Which AI Drone 'Killed' Operator. https://www.theguardian.com/us-news/2023/jun/01/us-military-drone-ai-killed-operator-simulated-test (last accessed: December 30, 2025).
The Guardian. (2023b). OpenAI CEO Calls for Laws to Mitigate 'Risks of Increasingly Powerful' AI. www.theguardian.com/technology/2023/may/16/ceo-openai-chatgpt-ai-tech-regulations (last accessed: December 30, 2025).
The Guardian. (2024). Companies Paid Top Executives More Than They Paid in U.S. Taxes – Report. https://www.theguardian.com/business/2024/mar/13/top-us-executives-salaries-versus-tax-payments (last accessed: December 30, 2025).
The Guardian. (2025a). Soldier Who Exposed Cybertruck in Las Vegas Used ChatGPT to Plan Attack. https://www.theguardian.com/us-news/2025/jan/07/las-vegas-cybertruck-explosion-chatgpt (last accessed: December 30, 2025).
The Guardian. (2025b). UK Creating 'Murder Prediction' Tool to Identify People Most Likely to Kill. https://www.theguardian.com/uk-news/2025/apr/08/uk-creating-prediction-tool-to-identify-people-most-likely-to-kill (last accessed: December 30, 2025).
The Guardian. (2025c). 'Headed for Technofascism.' https://www.theguardian.com/technology/ng-interactive/2025/jan/29/silicon-valley-rightwing-technofascism (last accessed: December 30, 2025).
The Guardian. (2025d). Trump's New 'Gold Standard' Rule Will Destroy American Science As We Know It. https://www.theguardian.com/commentisfree/2025/may/29/trump-american-science (last accessed: December 30, 2025).
The Independent. (2024). Elon Musk's Wealth Jumps By $170bn Since Election After He Backed Trump With $277m. https://www.independent.co.uk/news/world/americas/elon-musk-net-worth-trump-b2665395.html (last accessed: December 30, 2025).
The Influence Industry Project. (2025). Resources. https://influenceindustry.org/en/explorer/ (last accessed: December 30, 2025).
The January 6th Committee. (2022). The January 6 Report. New York, Harper.
Thiel, D. (2023). Identifying and Eliminating CSAM in Generative ML Training Data and Models. https://purl.stanford.edu/kh752sm9123 (last accessed: December 30, 2025).
Thiel, P. (2009). The Education of a Libertarian. https://archive.ph/p2yrX (last accessed: December 30, 2025).
Thiel, P. (2014). Zero to One. Notes on Startups, Or How to Build the Future. New York, Crown Business.
Trump White House. (2025a). Removing Barriers to American Leadership in Artificial Intelligence. https://www.whitehouse.gov/presidential-actions/2025/01/removing-barriers-to-american-leadership-in-artificial-intelligence/ (last accessed: December 30, 2025).
Trump White House. (2025b). White House Unveils America's AI Action Plan. https://www.whitehouse.gov/articles/2025/07/white-house-unveils-americas-ai-action-plan/ (last accessed: December 30, 2025).
Trump White House. (2025c). Winning the Race. America's AI Action Plan. https://www.whitehouse.gov/wp-content/uploads/2025/07/Americas-AI-Action-Plan.pdf.
Trump White House. (2025d). AI.Gov. https://www.ai.gov/#home-services-anchor (last accessed: December 30, 2025).
Tubaro, P., Casilli, A., & Coville, M. (2020). The Trainer, the Verifier, the Imitator. Big Data & Society 7(1).

UNICEF. (2023). Bridging the Gender Digital Divide. https://data.unicef.org/resources/ictgenderdivide/ (last accessed: December 30, 2025).
United Nations Human Rights Council. (2018). Report of Independent International Fact-Finding Mission on Myanmar. https://www.ohchr.org/en/hr-bodies/hrc/myanmar-ffm/reportofthe-myanmar-ffm (last accessed: December 30, 2025).
U.S. Congress. (2021). Uyghur Forced Labor Prevention Act. https://www.govinfo.gov/content/pkg/PLAW-117publ78/pdf/PLAW-117publ78.pdf (last accessed: December 30, 2025).
U.N. Trade and Development. (2024). U.N. Digital Economy Report 2024. https://unctad.org/publication/digital-economy-report-2024 (last accessed: December 30, 2025).
Vaidhyanathan, S. (2020). Antisocial Media. Oxford, Oxford University Press.
Vanberg, V. (2004). The Freiburg School – Walter Eucken and Ordoliberalism. www.eucken.de/publikationen/04_11bw.pdf (last accessed: December 30, 2025).
Vanberg, V. (2005). Market and State: The Perspective of Constitutional Political Economy. Journal of Institutional Economics 1(1). 23–49.
Vanberg, V. (2008). Wettbewerb und Regelordnung. Tübingen, Mohr Siebeck.
Vanberg, V. (2013). James M. Buchanan's Contractarianism and Modern Liberalism. www.eucken.de/fileadmin/bilder/Dokumente/DP2013/Diskussionspapier_1304.pdf (last accessed: December 30, 2025).
Vinge, V. (1993). The Coming Technological Singularity. https://ntrs.nasa.gov/api/citations/19940022856/downloads/19940022856.pdf (last accessed: December 30, 2025).
Walzer, M. (2015). Just and Unjust Wars. New York, Basic Books.
Warren, S.D. & Brandeis, L.D. (1890). The Right to Privacy. Harvard Law Review 4(5). 193–220.
Washington Post. (2021). The Billionaire Boom. https://www.washingtonpost.com/technology/2021/03/12/musk-bezos-zuckerberg-gates-pandemic-profits/ (last accessed: December 30, 2025).
Washington Post. (2023). Despite Reforms, Mining for EV Metals in Congo Exacts Steep Cost on Workers. https://www.washingtonpost.com/world/interactive/2023/ev-cobalt-mines-congo/ (last accessed: December 30, 2025).
Washington Post. (2024). Israel Built an 'AI Factory' for War: It Unleashed It in Gaza. https://www.washingtonpost.com/technology/2024/12/29/ai-israel-war-gaza-idf/ (last accessed: December 30, 2025).
Webb, K. (2004a). Understanding the Voluntary Codes Phenomenon. In: Webb, K. (ed.). Voluntary Codes. Ottawa, Carleton Research Unit for Innovation, Science, and Environment. 3–31.
Webb, K. (2004b). Voluntary Codes. In: Webb, K. (ed.). Voluntary Codes. Ottawa, Carleton Research Unit for Innovation, Science, and Environment. 379–402.
Webb, K. (2012). From De-Responsibilization to Re-Responsibilization. https://librarysearch.georgebrown.ca/discovery/fulldisplay/alma991004604479707310/01OCLS_BROWN:BROWN (last accessed: December 30, 2025).
Webb, K. & Morrison, A. (2004). The Law and Voluntary Codes. In: Webb, K. (ed.). Voluntary Codes. Ottawa, Carleton Research Unit for Innovation, Science, and Environment. 97–174.
Wired. (2023). ICE Records Reveal How Agents Abuse Access to Secret Data. https://www.wired.com/story/ice-agent-database-abuse-records/ (last accessed: December 30, 2025).
World Economic Forum. (2023). The Future of Jobs Report 2023. https://www.weforum.org/publications/the-future-of-jobs-report-2023/in-full/ (last accessed: December 30, 2025).
World Economic Forum. (2025). The Future of Jobs Report 2025. https://www.weforum.org/publications/the-future-of-jobs-report-2025/digest/ (last accessed: December 30, 2025).
World Health Organization. (2021). Children and Digital Dumpsites. https://www.who.int/publications/i/item/9789240023901 (last accessed: December 30, 2025).
Wörsdörfer, M. (2013a). Individual versus Regulatory Ethics: An Economic-Ethical and Theoretical-Historical Analysis of German Neoliberalism. OEconomia 3–4. 523–557.
Wörsdörfer, M. (2013b). Von Hayek and Ordoliberalism on Justice. Journal of the History of Economic Thought 35(3). 291–317.

Wörsdörfer, M. (2014). 'Free, Prior, and Informed Consent' and Inclusion: Nussbaum, Ostrom, Sen, and the Equator Principles Framework. Transnational Legal Theory 5(3). 464–488.

Wörsdörfer, M. (2015). The Equator Principles and Human Rights Due Diligence – Towards a Positive and Leverage-Based Concept of Corporate Social Responsibility. Philosophy of Management 14(3). 193–218.

Wörsdörfer, M. (2017). The Equator Principles and the 'Business and Human Rights Debate': Hype or Hope? In: De Jonge, A. & Tomasic, R. (eds.). Research Handbook on Transnational Corporations. Cheltenham, Elgar. 139–168.

Wörsdörfer, M. (2018). Engineering and Computer Ethics. Dubuque, Great River Learning.

Wörsdörfer, M. (2020). Ordoliberalism 2.0: Towards a New Regulatory Policy for the Digital Age. Philosophy of Management 19(2). 191–215.

Wörsdörfer, M. (2021). Digital Platforms and Competition Policy: A Business-Ethical Assessment. Journal for Markets and Ethics 9(2). 97–119.

Wörsdörfer, M. (2022a). What Happened to 'Big Tech' and Antitrust? And How to Fix Them! Philosophy of Management 21(3). 345–369.

Wörsdörfer, M. (2022b). Big Tech and Antitrust: An Ordoliberal Analysis. Philosophy & Technology 35. Article 85.

Wörsdörfer, M. (2022c). Walter Eucken: Foundations of Economics. In: Biebricher, T., Nedergaard, P., & Bonefeld, W. (eds.). The Oxford Handbook of Ordoliberalism. Oxford, Oxford University Press. 91–107.

Wörsdörfer, M. (2023). The Digital Markets Act and E.U. Competition Policy: A Critical Ordoliberal Evaluation. Philosophy of Management 22(1). 149–171.

Wörsdörfer, M. (2024a). Mitigating the Adverse Effects of AI With the European Union's Artificial Intelligence Act – Hype or Hope? Global Business and Organizational Excellence 43(3). 106–126.

Wörsdörfer, M. (2024b). Apple's Antitrust Paradox. European Competition Journal 20(1). 113–146.

Wörsdörfer, M. (2024c). Biden's Executive Order on AI and the E.U.'s AI Act – A Comparative Computer- and Business-Ethical Analysis. Philosophy & Technology 37. Article 74.

Wörsdörfer, M. (2024d). 'Datafeudalism: The Domination of Modern Societies by Big Tech Companies': A Commentary. Philosophy & Technology 37. Article 86.

Wörsdörfer, M. (2025a). The E.U.'s Artificial Intelligence Act – An Ordoliberal Assessment. AI and Ethics 5 (1). 263–278.

Wörsdörfer, M. (2025b). AI Ethics and Ordoliberalism 2.0: Towards a 'Digital Bill of Rights.' AI and Ethics 5 (1). 507–525.

Wörsdörfer, M. (2025c). Biden's Executive Order on AI: Strengths, Weaknesses, and Possible Reform Steps. AI and Ethics 5(2). 1669–1683.

Wörsdörfer, M. (2025d). 'Regulating the Undefined: Addressing Systemic Risks in the Digital Services Act' – A Commentary. Philosophy & Technology 38. Article 76.

Wynn-Williams, S. (2025). Careless People. New York, Flatiron Books.

Wu, T. (2003). Network Neutrality, Broadband Discrimination. Journal of Telecommunications and High Technology Law 2. 141–179.

Zuboff, S. (2015). Big Other: Surveillance Capitalism and the Prospects of an Information Civilization. Journal of Information Technology 30. 75–89.

Zuboff, S. (2019). The Age of Surveillance Capitalism. New York. Public Affairs.

Chapter 4
Computer ethics in the age of Trump: the politics of AI and tech governance

Abstract: This chapter contrasts key policy shifts under the second Trump administration with those of his predecessor(s), highlighting notable differences in policy style and direction. It focuses on Trump-era policies related to computer ethics, exploring critical areas such as changes in academia and science, big data ethics, industry deregulation, and the evolving landscape of social media platforms like TikTok and X, particularly regarding content moderation and fact-checking. Additionally, it examines the intersection of military and surveillance technologies, and privacy and data protection in the context of government surveillance and partnerships with companies like Palantir, as well as developments in cryptocurrency regulation, deep-sea mining legislation, and conflict minerals. By addressing these issues, this chapter explores the broader ethical implications of Trump's policymaking for AI and digital governance, shedding light on how political shifts influence ongoing debates in technology ethics. The primary aim is to provide a comprehensive overview of recent developments, assess their relevance to computer ethics, and raise awareness of emerging ethical challenges in technology and society.

Keywords: Trump administration, policy initiatives, AI and computer ethics, AI governance and regulation

4.1 Introduction

The inauguration of Trump in January 2025 represents a significant caesura in recent American political history, marking a distinct shift in leadership style and policy direction. The event became the most well-funded inauguration in U.S. history, with the inaugural committee raising an unprecedented $245 million, more than doubling the $88 million raised for Trump's 2017 inauguration. A remarkable share of the funding came from the tech industry's most influential leaders and corporations, many of whom also attended the ceremony. Among the high-profile business attendees were Altman (OpenAI), Bezos (Amazon), Brin (Alphabet), Chew (TikTok), Cook (Apple), Khosrowshahi (Uber), Musk (Tesla, SpaceX, X), Pichai (Microsoft), and Zuckerberg (Meta). Altman and Zuckerberg announced personal donations of $1 million each. Bezos went further, offering a $1 million cash donation and an additional $1 million in-kind donation by streaming the inauguration live on Amazon Prime Video. Apple CEO Cook personally donated $1 million, as did Uber's CEO, Khosrowshahi, who also committed $1 million individually. Alphabet contributed $1 million and promoted the event through a livestream link on YouTube's homepage. Microsoft, Adobe, and Per-

 | https://doi.org/10.1515/9783112245958-005

plexity AI each contributed an additional $1 million to the inauguration fund. Beyond the tech world, (digital) financial services firms and figures also made significant contributions, including some of the most prominent players in the crypto industry, such as Coinbase and Kraken.[1]

The 2025 inauguration not only set a new fundraising benchmark but also symbolized a renewed, and in some cases unexpected, alliance between Trump and the business world's most influential players, including two of the world's wealthiest individuals, Musk and Bezos (Brennan Center for Justice, 2025; Joint Congressional Committee on Inaugural Ceremonies, 2025; Trump/Vance Inaugural Committee, 2025). This event also marked the beginning of a new phase in Trump's political agenda, during which he swiftly reversed several key policy initiatives of his predecessors. Among the most significant of these actions were his decisions to overturn Biden's executive order (EO) on AI, launch the public-private AI partnership Stargate, and unveil a comprehensive AI Action Plan.

This chapter examines the significant policy shifts enacted during the second Trump administration, with a particular focus on their impact on computer ethics.[2] The analysis spans key areas, including academia and science (e.g., budget cuts, science denial, and the rise of post-truth politics), diversity, equity, and inclusion (DEI) (and their possible effects on algorithmic biases and discrimination), industry (de-) regulation (e.g., the repeal of Biden's AI guidelines and the introduction of new policy initiatives), and social media (e.g., the planned TikTok sale and changes to content moderation and fact-checking policies on Meta and X). It also explores military and surveillance technologies (e.g., NSA surveillance programs), privacy and data protection (e.g., government partnerships with Palantir), cryptocurrencies (e.g., attempts at industry deregulation), and environmental issues, including deep-sea mining and conflict minerals. By evaluating these domains, this chapter sheds light on the broader implications of Trump-era policies for AI ethics and digital governance, offering a nuanced understanding of how political shifts shape ethical discussions in technology. The primary aim of this chapter is to provide a comprehensive overview of recent policy developments and their significance for the field of computer ethics. Beyond mapping these developments, this chapter serves as a political commentary grounded in the philosophy of technology, providing critical reflections on how policy shifts shape ethical discourse across technology, governance, and society. Through this dual focus, it seeks to engage with the deeper implications of these transformations for our understanding of technology's role in a democratic society.

This chapter is structured as follows: Section 4.2 examines major policy domains and shifts with direct relevance to computer and AI ethics. Section 4.3 discusses addi-

1 Many of the above companies also donated money to the planned White House ballroom (Politico, 2025c).

2 Note: This chapter analyzes the first 9 months of the second Trump administration, spanning January 20 to October 20, 2025.

tional policy areas, including conflict minerals and supply chain legislation, which may be impacted in the near future. This chapter concludes with a summary of its main findings and an outlook on future research directions.

4.2 Evaluation of policies under the Trump administration

4.2.1 Trump, science, and academia

4.2.1.1 Budget cuts

Trump has cut science funding related to computer science (and ethics) and beyond to its lowest level in decades, with average annual funding from 2015 to 2024 at $2 billion, dropping to less than $1 billion in 2025 (notably, computer science will receive only $192 million). He also canceled funding for in-progress grants, including cuts to STEM education (−$656 million), computer science (−$47 million), technology (−$38 million), and engineering (−$36 million), to name a few related to computer science (and ethics). The decline in new grant funding in 2025 includes STEM education (−$223 million), engineering (−$127 million), computer science (−$85 million), and technology (−$18 million). Funding through May 21 shows sharp reductions in STEM education (−80%), engineering (−57%), computer science (−31%), and technology and innovation (−17%). Changes in National Science Foundation (NSF) grant funding reflect similar declines: education (−80%), engineering (−57%), and computer science (−31%) (New York Times, 2025a).

Trump's proposed budget for fiscal year 2026 would result in a significant reduction in federal science funding, with basic research particularly affected, according to an analysis by the American Association for the Advancement of Science. Funding for basic research is projected to decrease by 34%, dropping from $45 billion to $30 billion. Overall science funding, which includes basic, applied, and developmental research, would fall by 22%, from $198 billion to $154 billion, marking the lowest federal investment in science this century when adjusted for inflation. Agencies such as the NSF face deep cuts, with proposed funding reduced by more than 55%, from $8.8 billion to $3.9 billion (for computer science, there would be a 65% reduction). The expected number of awards is 2,300, down from 9,600 in 2024, with an expected acceptance rate of just 7%, compared to 26% in 2024. The number of supported Ph.D. students is projected to fall to 12,400, down from 41,500 in 2024. Critics argue these cuts could seriously undermine U.S. scientific leadership and economic competitiveness. More importantly, it could lead to long-lasting and pervasive effects on public health, safety, and well-being (e.g., by impeding the advancement of computer ethics research on algorithmic biases and discrimination), not to mention that the reductions could accelerate a brain drain and allow China to overtake the United States in global research investment (American Association for the Advancement of Science, 2025; Executive Office of the President/Office of Management and Budget, 2025; National Science Foundation, 2025).

In July 2025, more than 140 NSF employees signed an open letter denouncing severe proposed budget cuts, exceeding 70% in some disciplines such as biology, engineering, and STEM education, that they warned would cripple American science. The letter condemned the abrupt termination of over 1,600 active research awards without lawful or transparent justification, the political review of scientific grants, and the withholding of $2.2 billion from the agency's $9 billion appropriation. It also cited the unlawful dismissal and threatened mass reduction in staff – over 10% of NSF's workforce has already been terminated – the coerced resignations and resulting loss of expertise (e.g., the number of rotating scholars is being reduced from 330 to 70), and the unplanned, unannounced eviction from NSF headquarters amid a forced relocation. Most urgently, the employees decried what they described as the agency's betrayal of scientific and ethical integrity through politicized probation policies (American Federation Government Employees, 2025).

4.2.1.2 Science denial and post-truth

Reductions in research funding not only constrain the capacity of scientific institutions but also contribute to a broader erosion of public trust in expertise, creating fertile ground for science denial. This erosion of trust has become a defining challenge in contemporary societies – particularly in the United States, where a long-standing tradition of anti-intellectualism fosters skepticism toward science, higher education, and perceived elites, thereby blurring the boundaries between science and pseudoscience, and fact and fiction (Oreskes, 2021; Oreskes & Conway, 2011).[3] Against this backdrop, a pressing research-ethical question arises: are we witnessing a crisis of public trust and legitimacy in the scientific community? The emergence of so-called 'post-truth' or 'post-factual' societies, where science denial thrives, underscores the urgency of this question. Within these contexts, movements such as Holocaust denial, climate change denial, antivaccination campaigns, the flat-earth theory, creationism (i.e., 'intelligent design'), and coronavirus conspiracy theories have proliferated – each directly challenging the scientific consensus. These developments are often fueled by the politicization of science, whereby facts are distorted or dismissed to advance ideological agendas, further deepening public mistrust in objective, evidence-based knowledge.

Science denial often manifests through five key tropes, as identified by McIntyre (2021). First, there is a widespread belief in conspiracy theories, where complex scien-

3 Critics warn that the Trump administration's suppression of experts – through tactics such as repression, threats, budget cuts, and surveillance – combined with the promotion of pseudoscience, the purging of government scientists, and the censorship of scientific work and free speech, could pave the way for a form of 'state-controlled' or even 'totalitarian science.' Notably, *Project 2025* has explicitly called for the dismantling of the administrative state and declared a 'war on science' and the federal bureaucracy (Josephson, 2025; Prescott, 2024; The Guardian, 2025d).

tific issues are reduced to deliberate plots. Second, cherry-picking evidence – also known as selection bias – enables deniers to reinforce their preferred narrative while ignoring contradictory data. Third, science denial frequently involves the reliance on fake experts, who are elevated over legitimate scientists, to discredit established knowledge and brand real experts as biased or politically motivated. Fourth, logical errors – such as straw man arguments, red herrings, false analogies, false dichotomies, and jumping to conclusions – are often employed to undermine scientific reasoning. Finally, science denial sets impossible expectations for what science can achieve, demanding that science be perfect and free from uncertainty, when, in reality, scientific inquiry inherently involves dealing with complexities and unknowns. These tropes all serve to sow confusion and undermine public trust in science (McIntyre, 2021).

The roots of science denial are complex, involving motivational and psychological factors. A key driver is ideology-based reasoning, where individuals adopt beliefs that protect their ideology, a process known as identity-protective cognition (Kahan, 2013). This means that identity and values play a crucial role in shaping how people form beliefs, with specific positions becoming deeply intertwined with one's personal or social identity. Additionally, special interests, such as corporate or political entities, often contribute to science denial through rent-seeking behavior and lobbying efforts. A prime example is the fossil fuel industry, which has historically funded campaigns to cast doubt on climate science (McIntyre, 2021; Oreskes, 2021; Oreskes & Conway, 2011, 2023).

Science denial exists along a spectrum and comes in varying degrees, ranging from soft to hard-core denial, which requires a nuanced approach to counter effectively. Moreover, science denial is not confined to one side of the political spectrum; both right- and left-wing movements can harbor science denial, seen in phenomena like antivaccination or anti-GMO movements. Mis- and disinformation, amplified on social media platforms and by generative AI tools such as chatbots and deepfakes, further exacerbate the problem, spreading false or misleading narratives widely. This is compounded by the politicization of science, which is deeply connected to the broader polarization and fragmentation of society and politics, where scientific consensus becomes another battleground in ideological conflict (McIntyre, 2021).

Post-truth refers to a cultural shift in which facts are abandoned, and truth becomes irrelevant, often leading to a denial of reality. In post-truth environments, objective facts are diminished in shaping public opinion, while appeals to personal beliefs and emotions become more influential. This phenomenon is closely linked to science denial, where individuals reject scientific facts in favor of beliefs that align with their identity or political views (McIntyre, 2018).[4] Several factors contribute to the rise of the post-truth era. Cognitive biases, such as cognitive dissonance, social conformity, and confirmation bias, make it easier for individuals to reject information that contradicts their worldview. This is amplified by (extreme) partisan bias, where people are more likely to accept information that supports their side, regardless of its accuracy. Social media, which has become the dominant source of news for many, exacerbates the issue by creating news and information silos. These echo chambers, together with filter bubbles (Pariser, 2011), perpetuate polarization and fragmentation, ensuring that individuals are exposed only to information that reinforces their existing beliefs (McIntyre, 2018). Other causes include the decline of traditional media, which has been replaced by social media, talk radio, and cable news, and has shifted from fact-based investigative reporting to opinion-driven, partisan (or pundit-driven) coverage. The result is a blurred line between news and opinion, leading to the spread of fake news – deliberately false or misleading information, often in the form of clickbait or disinformation. The primary motives behind this are financial gain and political manipulation (Oreskes, 2021; Oreskes & Conway, 2011; Wörsdörfer, 2018). This post-truth environment has become a fertile ground for authoritarian politics, as historian Snyder (2017) suggests, arguing that "post-truth is pre-fascism," implying that the rejection of objective truth can pave the way for more authoritarian forms of governance (a situation where society is not able to hold people in power accountable and speaking truth to power) (McIntyre, 2018).

The work of Oreskes and Conway (2023) is particularly insightful in the context of science denial and the post-truth era. The two researchers highlight how influential organizations, such as the National Association of Manufacturers, the National Electric Light Association, and the Foundation for Economic Education, helped shape a robust ideological framework rooted in libertarian and neoliberal thought. Drawing on thinkers such as Mises and Hayek, as well as cultural figures like Lane, Wilder (author of the *Little House* series), and Fifield Jr., who promoted Christian libertarianism through Spiritual Mobilization, this framework also found expression in Hollywood libertarian filmmaking, inspired by Rand and Reagan. The Chicago School of Economics, with leaders like Director Friedman, Stigler, and Bork, advanced concepts such as the consumer welfare standard (Wörsdörfer, 2022a, 2022b) while corporations like GE, through figures like Boulware, aligned with Reagan's economic policies. This ideological foundation fueled Carter's deregulation and the Reagan Revolution, characterized by trickle-down economics, tax cuts, budget deficits, deregulation (including the underfunding and understaffing of government agencies, such as those related to antitrust), and shareholder value maximization, all of which contributed to socioeco-

4 In August 2025, Trump dismissed the Bureau of Labor Statistics commissioner after a disappointing employment report. In an effort to secure more favorable economic data, he appointed a new statistics chief with strong ties to the Heritage Foundation (Politico, 2025b).

nomic inequalities, antienvironmentalism, and antiscience attitudes. Think tanks promoting antigovernment views reinforced these trends, underpinning the so-called 'Tripod of Freedom' – representative democracy, political freedom, and free enterprise – as core U.S. building blocks. The Clinton administration and the 'New Democrats' continued this trajectory through 'neo-neoliberal' policies (according to Oreskes & Conway [2023], Carter started the Reagan Revolution, and Clinton completed it), including deregulation of telecommunications and financial markets, culminating in the repeal of the Glass-Steagall Act, which contributed to the 2007/08 financial market crisis. The Trump administration intensified antiscience and antigovernment sentiments, especially evident in climate science denial, pandemic response, and industry/tech deregulation. Central to this ideology is the indivisibility thesis, which conflates economic and political freedom, alongside a 'magic of the marketplace' or market fundamentalism, fostering mistrust in government, unwavering trust in markets, and opposition to regulation and science – factors that have exacerbated crises in finance, climate, public health, and social welfare (see, for example, the COVID-19 pandemic, the opioid epidemic, the healthcare crisis, and the gun violence epidemic). The latest example is the push for deregulation in the tech/crypto sector (see below).

The Environmental Protection Agency (EPA)'s antiscience stance – evident during the 2017–2021 period and again beginning in 2025 – fits within a broader pattern of undermining scientific integrity in U.S. federal agencies.[5] This includes the censorship and removal of content from the EPA's and other scientific websites, the dismissal of climate science advisors, and significant cuts to research funding, particularly in climate and clean energy programs (see, for example, Trump's 'Big, Beautiful Tax Bill'). In addition to dismantling institutional support for science, the EPA and other agencies under the Trump administration frequently promoted bogus studies characterized by methodological flaws and pseudo-scientific approaches. These sources often presented misleading or decontextualized data and disregarded inconvenient evidence. This posture was further codified in a controversial rule on 'scientific transparency,' ostensibly intended to end so-called 'secret science,' but widely criticized as a means to disqualify valid research. Overall, the agency adopted a stance that was antiscience and overtly pro-business, as reflected in the frequent meetings and business connections between former (and current) EPA Administrator Pruitt (and Zeldin) and industry executives and lobbyists (Wörsdörfer, 2018).

In addition to the EPA, several other U.S. government agencies have experienced significant changes in both policy directions and leadership styles (some of which might impact the work of computer ethicists) – these include the Centers for Disease Control and Prevention (CDC), the Department of Education, the National Institutes of

5 The EPA's antiscience stance may also hinder the work of AI ethicists, particularly those investigating the environmental impacts (i.e., the greenhouse gas emissions and water consumption) of cryptocurrencies, data centers, and generative AI technologies.

Health, the National Oceanic and Atmospheric Administration (NOAA), the NSF, and the U.S. Agency for International Development. Under the Trump administration, these changes have involved the mass firing or reassigning of government employees, including scientists and researchers. For instance, the EPA's scientific research arm will be eliminated, potentially resulting in the dismissal of more than 1,150 biologists, chemists, toxicologists, and other researchers (some of whom are researching the carbon footprint of AI technologies); Trump also called for eliminating NOAA's scientific research division. The administration has also imposed funding freezes, budget cuts, and grant cancellations – some of which directly endanger global health efforts (Callaway, 2025). Additional actions have included revoking laws and regulations, as well as withdrawing from international treaties and agreements, such as the Paris Climate Accord and the World Health Organization. Funding and staffing for major climate reports have been drastically reduced, authors of government climate reports have been dismissed, and scientific reports have either not been published on government websites or entire websites have been shut down – practices that amount to censorship, as discussed below (Columbia University, 2025; New York Times, 2025b).

In the area of health and human services, the Trump administration, primarily through RFK Jr., has canceled scientific meetings, delayed the release of health data, and established the Make America Healthy Again Commission, led by an antivaxxer and conspiracy theorist. It has gutted the National Institutes of Health and training programs at the CDC, fired health inspectors, blocked funds for biomedical research, terminated contracts related to Ebola, eliminated advisory committees focused on food safety,[6] and announced a CDC investigation into the long-debunked link between vaccines and autism.[7] The administration has repeatedly strayed from mainstream science and public health messaging, such as during the 2025 measles outbreak in West Texas. Other actions include replacing the FDA's chief counsel, considering the shutdown of the CDC's HIV prevention division, canceling funding for dozens of studies aimed at developing vaccines and treatments for COVID-19 and other infectious diseases, and other plans to lay off 10,000 employees at the Department of Health and Human Services. Funding and staffing at the CDC have been drastically reduced, states have been urged to ban fluoride in drinking water, and the administration has promoted the false claim that autism is preventable, contradicting federal researchers. Parents of newborns were even advised to 'do your own research' before vaccinating their infants, undermining evidence-based medical guidance (New York Times, 2025b).

6 The Trump administration also eliminated the advisory panels on vaccines, the environment, and AI.

7 Note that both the CDC and NIH have funded research at the intersection of AI and health (data), such as public health surveillance, health equity, clinical practices, and algorithmic fairness or bias mitigation – all of which are relevant from a computer ethics perspective.

4.2.2 Trump and DEI

The broader consequences of budget cuts and antiscience positions within the government sector have not only eroded scientific integrity but also undermined initiatives aimed at promoting social justice. This erosion is increasingly visible in the growing political backlash against DEI efforts, particularly under the influence of figures like Trump and other prominent Republican lawmakers and 'influencers.' Amid this climate of heightened scrutiny, DEI initiatives have faced significant cutbacks,[8] with some organizations, including research and funding agencies, even banning DEI-related terminology altogether (see below). This broader trend was recently mirrored by Meta, which relocated its remaining content moderation team from California to Texas, home to the headquarters of Tesla and SpaceX, while simultaneously discontinuing its DEI hiring and training programs (Zuckerberg, 2025). Such moves reflect a broader shift among multinational corporations away from progressive social policies, which carry significant implications for AI ethics. These developments resonate with longstanding concerns raised by researchers like Buolamwini (2016, 2023) and O'Neil (2016), who have warned about the ethical risks of biases and discrimination in technology and the societal implications of unchecked algorithmic decision-making in environments lacking inclusive oversight.

4.2.2.1 Biases and discrimination

Human biases often shape decision-making, leading individuals to make poor choices by prioritizing emotions over logic, relying excessively on others' opinions, or overlooking important information (Kahneman, 2011; Thaler & Sunstein, 2008/2009). Although automated systems are designed to enhance decision-making by being faster, cheaper, more objective, and data-driven, they can still produce flawed results due to biases inherent in their design. As defined by Friedman and Nissenbaum (1996), algorithmic biases refer to computer systems that unfairly deny opportunities or impose adverse outcomes based on unreasonable or inappropriate criteria. These biases are

8 For example, the Trump administration has announced plans to recruit federal workers based on 'merit' and to prohibit hiring decisions based on race, sex, or religion. It has also mandated that the federal government recognize only two sexes; terminated DEI programs, policies, and related initiatives across federal agencies (including those addressing LGBTQ+ issues and cultural or religious observances); and removed documents and webpages referencing DEI. In addition, the administration has paused federal grants, active research awards, and loans, and withheld funding from schools and universities (e.g., Columbia and Harvard); rolled back protections for LGBTQ+ students; required federal employees to remove pronouns from email signatures; and ordered investigations into DEI practices in schools and corporations. Further actions include moves to phase out gender-affirming medical care for veterans, the removal of hundreds of books from government libraries, lawsuits against states over transgender athletes, and the reinstatement of a ban on transgender troops in the military (New York Times, 2025c, 2025x).

manifested in various ways, including preexisting, technical, and emergent biases (Quinn, 2024; see also Floridi, 2023).

Preexisting biases are embedded in society before the system's development and are rooted in historical inequalities such as patriarchy, White supremacy, and ableism. These 'power shadows' are reflected in the data used to train AI systems, especially when datasets are incomplete or unrepresentative of the broader population. For example, facial recognition systems trained predominantly on datasets featuring White men tend to have higher error rates when applied to darker-skinned women. Research by Buolamwini (2016, 2023) and colleagues (Bender et al, 2021; Buolamwini & Gebru, 2018; Li, 2023) shows that over 80% of faces in widely used training sets were White, with more than 75% being male. These disparities result in higher error rates for darker-skinned women, reaching 35%, which can lead to real-world consequences such as false arrests or denied access to public spaces.

Technical biases stem from limitations in the design of computer systems. A prime example is Google Search, where the algorithm prioritizes the top search results, with the first result receiving approximately 27.6% of click-throughs, while the tenth result gets only 2.5% (Quinn, 2024). Less than 1% of users navigate to the second page of results. This algorithmic ranking can inadvertently introduce bias by giving more visibility to specific sources or viewpoints that may not reflect a balanced perspective, thereby shaping the information users encounter.

Emergent biases develop over time as systems interact with external users. A well-known case of emergent bias occurred with Microsoft's chatbot Tay, which was designed to adapt its responses based on user input. Unfortunately, malicious users fed Tay offensive language, causing the chatbot to generate inappropriate responses, including misogynistic and racist slurs (a similar incident recently occurred involving Musk's chatbot, Grok). Within 24 h, Microsoft took Tay offline, demonstrating the risks of emergent biases in AI systems. This incident highlights how external interactions can cause systems to evolve in unexpected and harmful ways (Quinn, 2024).

Machine learning systems, such as those used in image recognition, have also been shown to perpetuate preexisting and emergent biases. In 2015, Google Photos came under fire when its image recognition software misidentified Black men as gorillas. In response, Google disabled visual searches for primates. This incident underscored how the data used to train machine learning systems, often drawn from photo collections, can reflect and amplify societal stereotypes. For instance, machine-learning models frequently associate certain activities with specific genders – cooking and shopping with women, and coaching and shooting with men – reinforcing societal biases (Narayanan & Kapoor, 2024; Quinn, 2024).

Biases are also present in speech recognition systems, which are critical for accessibility but are often trained on nonrepresentative datasets, such as the Corpus of Regional African American Language and Voices of California. Studies show that commercial speech recognition systems tend to perform better with White speakers than Black speakers, revealing the limitations of these systems. To address this, machine learning must be trained on more diverse datasets, ensuring that speech recognition technology works equitably for all users, regardless of ethnicity or accent (Quinn, 2024).

The biases in big data and algorithmic systems stem primarily from two interrelated issues: the quality of training data and the lack of diversity among the teams that design AI systems. One significant concern is the use of unrepresentative or incomplete datasets. When data primarily reflects a narrow demographic, such as White males, it introduces cultural and ethnic biases that undermine accuracy and fairness for other groups. Moreover, flawed generalizations based on insufficient data or unexamined causal relationships often result in skewed outcomes. These problems are further exacerbated by the homogeneity of many AI development teams, which are often dominated by young White males from Western countries. Their limited perspectives can (unconsciously) embed societal stereotypes and cultural blind spots into the systems they create. The underrepresentation of BIPOC (Black, Indigenous, and People of Color), women, people with disabilities, older individuals, and LGBTQ+ communities contributes to the development of technologies that fail to serve, or even harm, diverse populations.[9]

The consequences of these design flaws extend beyond individual errors – they reflect the 'dark side' of big data analytics, as described by O'Neil (2016). AI systems increasingly shape decisions about education, employment, housing, and criminal justice, often reinforcing existing power structures and social hierarchies. Operating within opaque 'black box' frameworks (Pasquale, 2016), these algorithms disproportionately impact marginalized and/or vulnerable groups, exacerbating discrimination, racism, and systemic inequality. Left unchecked, such systems generate harmful feedback loops, such as the poverty trap or algorithmic redlining, that entrench disadvantage and erode democratic values (Institute for Human Rights and Business, 2016). A key issue is the lack of transparency and accountability, which allows for manipulation without oversight. In an unregulated data economy, data brokers commodify individuals by transforming personal information into marketable products, thereby amplifying existing inequalities.

These structural and systemic issues manifest in harmful ways across various sectors. In advertising, targeted or predatory marketing utilizes data, such as ZIP codes, to exploit vulnerable populations, as seen in the promotion of high-interest loans to low-income communities. In healthcare, wellness apps and fitness trackers often double as tools of workplace surveillance, posing privacy risks and potentially discriminating against those with chronic illnesses or disabilities. In the financial sector, algorithmic tools such as redlining restrict access to credit and insurance for

9 It is important to note that the Trump administration's ongoing efforts to undermine DEI policies at both the federal and corporate levels are likely to exacerbate the underlying causes of algorithmic biases and discrimination.

marginalized groups, reinforcing structural exclusion. Hiring systems that rely on personality tests and credit scores may penalize those already disadvantaged, creating cycles where unemployment leads to poor credit, which in turn reduces job prospects. In law enforcement, predictive policing software like PredPol has been criticized for perpetuating racial profiling and reinforcing patterns of overpolicing. Finally, in politics, cases like the Cambridge Analytica scandal have revealed how big data enables digital voter manipulation, distorting public discourse and undermining democratic trust (Haugen, 2023; O'Neil, 2016; Wynn-Williams, 2025). Given the Trump administration's ongoing efforts to dismantle DEI initiatives, these issues will likely persist or may even intensify.

4.2.2.2 (Self-)censorship

Beyond algorithmic biases and discrimination, another critical concern in the digital sphere is the regulation and restriction of information itself. Censorship, broadly defined, is the attempt to restrict, block, or regulate public access to offline and online content and material considered dangerous, harmful, critical, or offensive, and it often impedes freedom of information, expression, and speech. In the information age, censorship takes on various forms, ranging from self-censorship to direct, i.e., government or corporate, censorship (Wörsdörfer, 2018).[10]

Self-censorship occurs when journalists, political opponents, researchers, scientists, and artists suppress critical work out of fear – real or perceived – of punishment or sanction (for example, in academic settings, particularly in Republican-leaning states, some instructors increasingly avoid politically sensitive topics such as climate science, abortion, LGBTQ+ issues, and specific AI ethical topics, e.g., biases and discrimination). Direct censorship, on the other hand, might include government monopolization (i.e., restricting Internet access or blocking/censoring web content), prepublication review (e.g., in academia), and licensing and registration (which serves as an additional form of media control) (Wörsdörfer, 2018, see also the section on Foucault's panopticon below).

Information and communication technologies have enabled governments and corporations to more easily block Internet content and restrict fundamental freedoms, i.e., filtering and surveillance of Internet content are key tools in enforcing such control. In extreme cases like North Korea, the Internet is virtually inaccessible, while Saudi Arabia operates a centralized control center to monitor and filter online material. China is known for blocking Internet access during social unrest and maintaining a vast web filtering system, the 'Great Firewall of China.' Even democratic countries engage in forms of censorship. For example, Germany prohibits access to neo-Nazi websites, while the United States has repeatedly sought to restrict minors'

10 Note that the distinction between self-censorship and direct censorship, as well as between government and corporate censorship, as seen on social media platforms, is increasingly blurred.

access to pornography, faced the NSA mass surveillance scandal, which has intensified self-censorship, and witnessed a surge in book bans across states and counties (Wörsdörfer, 2018).

The Trump administration's latest efforts include banning specific keywords in grant proposals, publications, and related academic or research documents, particularly in fields such as computer and AI ethics – a move that constitutes a troubling form of censorship, both direct and self-imposed. Especially concerning is the removal of (AI ethics-related) terms such as bias(es)/biased, BIPOC, Black, DEI, discrimination, ethnicity, hate speech, Indigenous community, inequality/inequity, injustice, LGBTQ (+), marginalize(d), mental health, minorities, Native American, polarization, prejudice, privilege(s), race/racial (identity), social justice, stereotype(s), underprivileged/underrepresented/underserved, and vulnerable populations, to name a few. These and other keywords are essential to discussions surrounding social media platforms, where effective content moderation, the spread of dangerous or hate speech, and the mental health of teens remain pressing concerns. They are equally critical in the analysis of algorithmic biases and discrimination, which disproportionately affect marginalized and vulnerable groups, including ethnic minorities and Indigenous communities. The removal or suppression of such terms hinders vital conversations around algorithmic fairness, justice, transparency, and accountability. Moreover, this shift raises concerns that the NSF and other federal funding agencies may reduce financial support for specific AI ethics projects (New York Times, 2025d).

Censorship is also apparent in other research and policy areas: as in his first term, Trump has once again ordered the removal of documents and government webpages.[11] For example, the EPA is censoring and deleting content from federal climate science websites (in addition to dismissing or silencing climate science advisors and making deep cuts to research funding and programs related to climate and clean energy). For instance, NASA has announced it will not publish the National Climate Assessment (NCA) on its website, citing no legal obligation to do so. This decision reverses a previous commitment made by the White House to host the report on NASA's platform after the closure of the original site, globalchange.gov. The NCA is a congressionally mandated, peer-reviewed report produced every four years, detailing the impacts of climate change across the United States. NASA's move has raised concerns among scientists and policymakers about the accessibility of critical climate data (data which might also be relevant for computer ethicists working on the ecological footprint of AI technologies). While past reports remain accessible through NOAA, the future of the NCA's dissemination is uncertain. Critics argue that this action under-

11 In mid-2025, Trump ordered a thorough review of all Smithsonian exhibitions, giving museums 120 days to remove 'divisive or ideologically driven' language and replace it with more 'patriotic content' (Trump White House, 2025l).

mines public access to essential climate information and may hinder efforts to address climate-related challenges (Associated Press, 2025a).

4.2.3 Trump and industry (de)regulation

4.2.3.1 Biden's executive order on AI

Questions of control and accountability that emerge in debates over censorship are equally central to the governance of AI. Seeking to address these challenges, the Biden administration advanced initiatives such as the *Blueprint for an AI Bill of Rights* (2022) and the EO *Ensuring Safe, Secure, and Trustworthy AI* (2023), which articulated core principles for responsible innovation (Biden White House, 2022a, 2023a, 2023b): ensuring AI safety and security, fostering innovation and competition, supporting workers, advancing equity and civil rights, protecting consumers, safeguarding privacy, promoting responsible federal AI use, and strengthening U.S. leadership on the global stage while encouraging international collaboration. Despite some flaws, the EO represented a positive step forward in terms of AI ethics and ordoliberalism 2.0 (Wörsdörfer, 2024a, 2025a).

The EO's primary strength lay in its focus on public safety, worker and consumer protections (e.g., protecting the rights of patients, passengers, and students), advancing social equity and civil rights, and safeguarding privacy and sensitive data. Additionally, its shift from soft to semihard law was noteworthy. However, the EO also had notable shortcomings, including a lack of legally binding provisions, insufficient monitoring and enforcement mechanisms, limited democratic oversight, and inadequate attention to broader AI ethics issues such as transparency and accountability. These gaps could have been addressed by bolstering governance structures, incorporating third-party audits, engaging more stakeholders, ensuring judicial oversight, and establishing clear legal rights and complaint systems. Creating an AI board or public database for technologies, similar to the E.U.'s AI Act, could have also been beneficial. Moreover, the EO would have been strengthened with greater consideration of socioenvironmental sustainability (Wörsdörfer, 2024a, 2025a).

However, in early 2025, the Biden administration's AI EO was overturned (Trump White House, 2025a). In its place, Trump signed EO 14179, *Removing Barriers to American Leadership in Artificial Intelligence*, which reversed key AI safety regulations from the prior administration. This new EO, alongside other economic policies of the Trump administration, emphasizes deregulation, or free markets, to foster innovation and U.S. dominance in AI research and development. It removes AI safety standards, content watermarking, and measures to mitigate national security risks. Critics argue that these changes might exacerbate the risks of disinformation, biased AI systems, and vulnerabilities in critical infrastructure.

4.2.3.2 Stargate and AI action plan

Overall, the Trump administration's approach to technology industry regulation reflects a Friedman- or Chicago School-inspired economic philosophy that emphasizes deregulation, privatization, and corporate self-regulation. For example, in August 2025, Trump revoked a Biden-era EO aimed at curbing anticompetitive business practices (e.g., in the tech industry [Wörsdörfer, 2022b]) and replaced it with an 'America First Antitrust' agenda prioritizing 'free markets' (The Globe and Mail, 2025).[12] In line with this philosophy, the administration also supported policies favorable to big business, including low capital gains taxes and broad corporate tax cuts, exemplified by Trump's 'Big, Beautiful Tax Bill.' While the administration strongly promoted U.S. leadership in AI, it largely left ethical oversight, including the development of frameworks and guidelines, to the private sector. This approach created a significant gap in comprehensive, government-led regulation and governance of AI ethics.

A prominent example of this vision is the launch of Stargate on January 21, 2025, a $500 billion AI infrastructure initiative involving OpenAI (Hao, 2025), Oracle, SoftBank, and investment firm MGX, and with the support of the Trump administration (other core partners include Microsoft, Nvidia, and ARM) (Stargate Project, 2025). Stargate aims to build up to 20 data centers nationwide over the next 4 years to support advanced AI systems, including artificial general intelligence, and is projected to generate over 100,000 jobs. The public-private partnership is set to begin with a $100 billion investment, with plans to expand to $500 billion, positioning it as the largest AI infrastructure project in history. While the administration touts Stargate as a strategic move to strengthen national security and U.S. leadership in AI, critics have raised concerns about its financial viability and environmental costs, especially its energy demands and potential reliance on fossil fuels for power generation.

In July 2025, Trump announced a sweeping plan to accelerate AI development in the United States, emphasizing deregulation, reduced oversight, and eliminating what he called 'partisan bias' in AI systems. He signed three EOs and released an *AI Action Plan* to promote infrastructure, limit federal restrictions, and encourage the export of AI technologies. Key actions include banning federal purchases of AI tools deemed ideologically biased; fast-tracking permits for AI data center construction; promoting U.S. AI exports and reducing environmental and DEI-related regulations; and prioritizing contracts for companies that align with his administration's ideological views on freedom of speech. In his remarks, Trump also repeated conservative concerns about 'woke' influence in AI models and vowed to fight China's AI advancement (Trump tends to frame the AI arms race between China and the United States as a

12 A notable exception is the Trump administration's acquisition of a 10% stake in Intel, valued at $10 billion – one of the largest government interventions in a U.S. company since the 2008 financial crisis (Reuters, 2025b) – as well as the proposed TikTok deal discussed below.

zero-sum game and contest for geopolitical dominance) (Trump White House, 2025h, 2025i, 2025j).

This deregulatory (and antiordoliberal) agenda also extended to legislative efforts – House Republicans included a controversial provision in their major tax bill that would have banned state and local governments from regulating AI for a decade (Associated Press, 2025b; New York Times, 2025e).[13] Though the Senate later voted 99-1 to strike the amendment (Business and Human Rights Resource Centre, 2025a), the proposal sparked criticism for undermining democratic oversight.[14]

The current trend toward deregulation, privatization, and soft law initiatives offers several advantages, including greater flexibility, cost-effectiveness, and efficiency, since the institutions responsible for rulemaking, enforcement, and dispute resolution are typically less expensive. They also allow for more adaptability in setting and revising rules and frameworks. Through multistakeholder approaches, these initiatives can harness nonstate, noncoercive forces and draw on the expertise of a diverse range of actors, including those with high technological capacity. They benefit from tools, institutions, and processes that leverage market and peer pressure, such as voluntary codes shaped by industry associations, standards bodies, civil society, and NGOs, which can help influence behavior and promote internalization of responsibility. However, soft law mechanisms also face notable drawbacks. These include lower visibility and credibility; difficulties in enforcing compliance among unwilling participants (e.g., issues of opportunistic defection and free riding);[15] the risk of adopting weaker standards; uncertain levels of public accountability; and generally weaker enforcement mechanisms (Webb, 2004a, 2004b, 2012; Webb & Morrison, 2004). In the context of AI, insufficient and ineffective governance mechanisms can lead to severe consequences, particularly for vulnerable or marginalized groups (e.g., through algorithmic biases and discrimination or the spread of harmful Internet content). In short,

---

13 In December 2025, Trump signed the executive order *Ensuring a National Policy Framework for Artificial Intelligence*, which preempts state-level AI legislation (Trump White House, 2025n). The order has raised significant legal and constitutional questions and is widely expected to face judicial challenges. Any resulting litigation may further complicate the AI regulatory landscape by introducing uncertainty over the division of federal and state authority, potentially delaying the development, adoption, and enforcement of coherent (e.g., ordoliberal-inspired) AI governance frameworks.

14 Trump's broader economic policies – including tariffs targeting allies such as the E.U., trade conflicts with adversaries like China, and immigration crackdowns affecting international students and skilled tech workers (e.g., revoking or denying visas for STEM students and tech employees, or drastically increasing H-1B visa fees) – have negatively impacted major companies such as Apple and Nvidia, fueling concerns about a potential brain drain to countries like Canada, China, and the E.U. Additionally, the administration established the Department of Government Efficiency to oversee federal technology and operational initiatives. While the restructuring aims to streamline government operations, it has also raised privacy concerns due to the increasing centralization of data and the associated risks to data protection and security.

15 Notably, unlike Microsoft, Meta has chosen not to sign the recently announced (voluntary) E.U. Code of Practice for general-purpose AI providers (European Commission, 2025; Reuters, 2025a).

company self-regulation and soft laws tend to be ineffective, especially when corporations face inherent conflicts of interest (e.g., between company self-interest and the common good), prioritize profit over public safety, and lack transparency, accountability, and democratic legitimacy.

4.2.4 Trump and social media

4.2.4.1 ByteDance and TikTok

The administration's broader commitment to deregulation and minimal corporate oversight extends into the realm of social media, shaping policies and actions that target platforms like TikTok and X while prioritizing market-driven mechanisms and executive actions over comprehensive regulatory oversight.

This deregulatory stance sets the stage for high-profile controversies, such as the debate over TikTok, which illustrates a complex intersection of national security, free speech, privacy, and corporate accountability. In 2024, Congress labeled the app's Chinese ownership a national security risk and passed a law requiring TikTok to be sold by January 19, 2025, or face a nationwide ban. While TikTok and its creators argue that the law violates First Amendment rights, raising the ethical dilemma of national security vs. free speech, the Supreme Court upheld the law's constitutionality in a January 17, 2025, decision. Following the ruling, TikTok briefly went dark on January 19 but later restored services, signaling either defiance or uncertainty, as Biden declared he would not enforce the ban, while Trump proposed a 75-day extension to allow time for a potential sale (which he later extended several times) (U.S. Congress, 2024; U.S. Supreme Court, 2025).

Beyond legal challenges, TikTok has faced numerous political controversies that have fueled calls for stricter oversight. National security concerns focus on allegations that the app is used for spying and sharing data with Chinese authorities, prompting ongoing investigations and security reviews in the U.S. Privacy and security issues have also raised alarm, particularly following incidents of hackers accessing user accounts and exposing minors to sexual predators (i.e., cyber-grooming), as well as the FTC's $5.7 million fine for illegally collecting children's data in violation of COPPA (FTC, 2019, 2024). The platform has been criticized for enabling cyberbullying, fostering addictive behaviors, and suppressing content from disabled, LGBTQ+, and racially marginalized users – who often face racial abuse. TikTok has additionally been accused of censoring videos addressing China's human rights abuses, as well as facilitating the spread of dangerous content, hate speech, mis- and disinformation, and government propaganda.

These issues present ethical questions about whether a ban is justified and the balance between individual freedoms and national interests. While a ban could protect sensitive data and national infrastructure, it risks stifling expression and setting a dangerous precedent for state control over digital platforms. Alternative solutions –

such as increased transparency, stronger regulatory oversight, independent data audits, or requiring local data storage – might better balance security with civil liberties, thereby avoiding the blunt instrument of an outright ban.

The proposed TikTok deal illustrates how these controversies intersect with corporate restructuring and the concentration of economic and political power. The agreement involves a consortium comprising Oracle (led by Larry Ellison), Silver Lake (a private equity firm), Andreessen Horowitz (a prominent Silicon Valley venture capital firm), and MGX (an Abu Dhabi investment firm), as well as possibly Michael Dell (CEO of Dell Technologies) and the Murdochs. This group will control approximately 80% of the company, while ByteDance and other Chinese investors retain the remaining 20%. Oracle will play a central role in overseeing the security of American user data and monitoring any changes to TikTok's powerful recommendation algorithm – the core technology behind the app's addictive short-video feed. A copy of this algorithm will be licensed from China to a U.S. investor group, ensuring localized oversight of the platform's operations. The governance structure will also shift significantly: six out of seven board seats will be held by U.S. interests, including one reserved for the U.S. government, which is reportedly set to receive a billion-dollar payment from the involved companies. The seventh seat will go to ByteDance. This arrangement has raised concerns that the app may become a form of state-run/influenced media. Notably, Ellison – one of the world's richest individuals, nearly as wealthy as Musk – will emerge as a central figure in the new TikTok. Ellison is also the majority shareholder in Paramount/Skydance and may gain control of Warner Bros. Discovery, bringing major media outlets like CBS, CNN, HBO, and now TikTok under his influence. His son, David, currently serves as CEO and chairman of Paramount Pictures and Skydance Media. The deal also underscores the impact of figures closely tied to the Trump administration – not only Ellison, but also Andreessen and the Murdochs – highlighting growing concerns about the concentration of media power among a politically connected elite (The Wall Street Journal, 2025b; Trump White House, 2025m).

4.2.4.2 Content moderation and fact-checking

While the TikTok deal highlights concerns over corporate control, national security, and algorithmic oversight, similar ethical and political challenges are emerging across other social media platforms. Meta, for example, has ended its third-party fact-checking program (Zuckerberg, 2025) and implemented significant changes to content moderation ahead of the second Trump term, illustrating how major tech companies navigate the complex intersection of political influence, free expression, and platform governance. Its platforms – Threads, Facebook, and Instagram – will now prioritize political content recommendations and replace traditional fact-checking with a system similar to X's Community Notes. The company cites freedom of speech ('no more censorship') and concerns about political bias as the rationale, explicitly referencing sensitive topics such as migration and gender. Reflecting a political realignment, Meta has appointed several Trump allies and Republicans to its board and contributed $1 million to Trump's inaugural fund. It has also relocated its remaining content moderation team from California to Texas and discontinued DEI hiring and training programs (Wörsdörfer, 2025b).

While this move supports freedom of speech and First Amendment rights, it carries significant drawbacks, including a potential rise in dangerous and hate speech, fake news, and conspiracy theories (e.g., experts caution that X's growing reliance on chatbots and other AI tools for fact-checking amplify harmful Internet content, including disinformation [Business and Human Rights Resource Centre, 2025b]). Meta's political shift toward the right appears aimed at appealing to the 'MAGA universe' for company gains (i.e., profits), raising concerns about possible violations of the E.U.'s Digital Services Act and resulting layoffs among fact-checking companies. Analysts warn this is a risky strategy, especially given how Musk's takeover of Twitter led to an advertiser exodus (initially) and damaged brand reputation (among specific demographics) (note that Meta heavily relies on advertising revenue). This situation also raises important questions about the sociopolitical responsibility of big tech platforms and whether social media should function as neutral platforms or act as editors and publishers (Wörsdörfer, 2025b).

The two Trump administrations have also significantly influenced two closely related issues – content moderation and free speech, as well as misinformation and public trust. During his first term in office, Trump repeatedly accused social media platforms like Twitter and Facebook of bias against conservatives (i.e., censoring and suppressing 'alternative worldviews'). In response, the administration proposed changes to Section 230 of the Communications Decency Act, which shields online platforms from liability for user-generated content. This sparked ethical discussions about platform responsibility, the balance between censorship and free speech, and the algorithmic amplification of misinformation. The second Trump administration now blames the previous administration for "trampling free speech rights," "censoring Americans' speech on online platforms," and "exerting substantial coercive pressure on third parties, such as social media companies, to moderate, deplatform, or otherwise suppress speech that the Federal Government did not approve" over the past several years (Trump White House, 2025b).[16] In 2025, Trump signed EO 14149, ti-

16 The Trump administrations have promoted a highly selective interpretation of the First Amendment, particularly regarding free speech and freedom of the press. This stance was evident in reactions to high-profile media controversies, such as the suspension of Jimmy Kimmel and the cancellation of Stephen Colbert, which were framed as examples of censorship and the silencing of government critics. Similarly, Trump pursued legal action against major social media platforms – Meta, X, and YouTube – after his accounts were blocked following the January 6 insurrection, ultimately reaching settlements that highlighted ongoing tensions over content moderation, political expression, and the boundaries of platform governance.

tled *Restoring Freedom of Speech and Ending Federal Censorship*, aimed at reducing government involvement in content moderation. This could significantly impact efforts to combat online mis-/disinformation and other harmful Internet content. Notably, the rhetoric of the Trump administration, particularly regarding the COVID-19 pandemic (i.e., science denial and anti-vaccination movement)[17] and the 2020 election (i.e., election denial movement), played a central role in spreading disinformation and conspiracy theories. Some of these narratives culminated in violent events, including the January 6 insurrection (in light of this, many argue that the current administration, along with certain advisors and allies, is among the primary sources of the spread of online disinformation). This raises critical concerns about the public's trust in digital platforms, information systems, and government institutions, as well as the role and accountability of social media companies.

4.2.4.2.1 Excursus: Trump and Musk

The shifts in content moderation and fact-checking across major platforms also set the stage for Elon Musk's high-profile interventions in the social media landscape. As X's leader, where he maintains close political and personal ties to Trump, Musk has intensified debates over free speech, platform governance, and the intersection of technology and political influence.

Beyond his role at X, Musk is a central figure in technology, business, and politics today (Isaacson, 2023; Siddiqui, 2025), serving as CEO of Tesla and SpaceX, owner, CTO, and Executive Chairman of X, co-founder of Neuralink and OpenAI, founder and CEO of xAI and The Boring Company, and president of the Musk Foundation. As of fall 2025, he is the world's wealthiest person. Known for his controversial personality and leadership style, Musk is often labeled a disruptor and visionary. However, his approach has been marred by allegations of micromanagement, workplace misconduct, mass layoffs, and the dissolution of Twitter's ethics, human rights, and privacy teams. Politically, Musk is a vocal advocate for free speech, demonstrated by reactivating Trump's X account, and known for spreading disinformation, hate speech, conspiracy theories, and 'anti-woke' and right-wing ideologies such as Bolsonaro's, contributing to the erosion of democracy and the rule of law (The Guardian, 2025c). Musk supports pro-natalism, promoting the reproduction of human life as an essential objective of humanity and therefore advocates for high birthrates, especially among White populations, to counter the decline of the aging (White) population; notably, he has 14 children himself. He advocates voting for Republican politicians and actively endorses Trump's campaigns (and policies), including a $277 million contribution to his 2024 presidential campaign (The Independent, 2024). In the first half of 2025, he headed the Department of Government Efficiency (DOGE), which had access to the Treasury's payment system and Internal Revenue Service (IRS) taxpayer data. He also actively supports right-wing politicians and parties, such as Farage, Poilievre, Meloni, and the German AfD, while opposing democratic leaders like Scholz and Starmer – all of this questions the political neutrality of platforms such as X. Musk wields significant geopolitical influence and power, e.g., by commenting on issues like the China-Taiwan conflict and providing Internet access through Starlink to Ukrainians and Iranians. Especially problematic from a computer-/business-ethics point of view is the extreme concentration of economic (wealth), political (DOGE), and (social) media

17 Note: The current HHS Secretary is known for promoting conspiracy theories and holding antivaccination views.

power of Musk and other (tech) billionaires (besides Musk, other influential tech and media figures include Zuckerberg, owner of Meta; Bezos, owner of The Washington Post; Ellison, a major (future) investor in TikTok; and Murdoch, owner of Fox News). This concentration of power and ownership of critical infrastructure presents numerous conflicts of interest.

For example, the government cuts and layoffs implemented by Musk and the DOGE team are financially benefiting multiple private firms – his own included – through lucrative government contracts. This reflects a broader shift toward privatization and deregulation, as well as a fundamental restructuring of the welfare state that primarily favors large industry players, particularly in sectors such as defense and intelligence (The Guardian, 2025a). In addition, personnel changes, such as the dismissal of several high-ranking officials, have impacted various federal agencies involved in investigations or regulatory disputes with Musk's companies, including SpaceX, Tesla, and X. Affected agencies include several government departments, the National Highway Traffic Safety Administration, the National Labor Relations Board, the Equal Employment Opportunity Commission, the Consumer Financial Protection Bureau, the Securities and Exchange Commission, the Federal Election Commission, and the Office of Government Ethics (New York Times, 2025f). It is also noteworthy that Starlink now provides the White House with a separate high-speed Internet access, while SpaceX has secured multibillion-dollar federal contracts (New York Times, 2025g). Finally, even Musk's platform X is reaping benefits – both in terms of increased ad revenue and being used as an official channel for government communications – while Musk plays an ([un]official) advisory role in the Trump administration (New York Times, 2025h).

4.2.5 Trump and the military

Musk's (and others') close ties to Trump highlight the broader entanglement of political influence, technology, and defense interests, setting the stage for examining the administration's approach to the military and the rise of autonomous combat systems.

In the emerging age of AI-driven warfare – often referred to as 'i-battle' or 'i-war' – nations are heavily investing in advanced weapons and autonomous systems, including unmanned drones and fully autonomous lethal weapons, also known as warbots. At the core of this transformation lies the military-industrial complex, long shaped by influential entities like DARPA and the CIA, which not only played pivotal roles in developing the Internet but has also funded cutting-edge AI research.[18]

18 The latest developments in tech-military collaboration highlight a growing trend of Silicon Valley firms deepening ties with the U.S. defense sector. OpenAI is now working with the Department of Defense (and its Defense Advanced Research Projects Agency) to develop advanced cybersecurity software to protect military systems and support veteran services (Bloomberg, 2025). At the same time, Meta has partnered with defense contractor Anduril Industries to create augmented and virtual reality headsets designed for combat use by the U.S. Army (The Wall Street Journal, 2025a). Notably, Google, Meta, and OpenAI – companies that once included explicit bans on the military use of AI in their mission and vision statements – have since removed such language from their corporate policies (Hao, 2025; New York Times, 2025y). At the same time, the Trump administration has allocated a record $1 trillion to defense spending for 2026, with significant investments in technologies such as autonomous drones. One of Trump's executive orders (Trump White House, 2025k) directs the U.S. military to modernize its technology acquisition systems – measures that will benefit Silicon Valley companies, particularly defense-

As the United States, China, and to a certain extent, Russia, intensify their pursuit of AI dominance, an AI arms race has emerged – one that could shape global power dynamics. This competition extends beyond military concerns, impacting economic and technological spheres as nations impose export restrictions, vie for critical resources such as semiconductors and rare earth minerals, and even enforce bans on certain minerals (Muldoon et al., 2025).[19] The rise of lethal autonomous weapons has spurred urgent ethical and regulatory debates, with groups like the Campaign to Stop Killer Robots calling for strict regulations or a ban on such weapons. These discussions may necessitate revisiting foundational ethical frameworks, including updating Asimov's laws of robotics, to ensure AI is used to serve humanity rather than threaten it.

The increasing role of AI in military decision-making carries significant implications for the future of warfare. As both a tool and an agent, AI introduces nonhuman decision-making into military operations, fundamentally altering the nature of war. This shift raises ethical questions surrounding accountability, human judgment, and the intrinsic value of life in automated conflict scenarios. Furthermore, the evolving skill set of modern soldiers reflects this transformation: traditional virtues like courage, leadership, and command presence are increasingly being supplemented – and at times replaced – by technical expertise, STEM skills, and advanced strategic thinking. These developments necessitate a thoughtful reevaluation of how we engage with warfare in the era of intelligent machines (Payne, 2021).

AI weapon systems are rapidly reshaping the landscape of modern warfare. Semi-autonomous helicopters and drones, such as unmanned combat air vehicles, are already used for tactical surveillance and precision strikes. The Predator drone, for instance, is a remotely piloted air vehicle equipped with missiles and stealth technology. Autonomous submarines and marine vessels are also being developed for tasks like minesweeping and antisubmarine warfare (see New York Times [2024] and Washington Post [2024] for examples of AI weapons in the Ukraine war and Israel's conflict with Gaza). Looking to the near future, military innovation is leaning toward human-machine collaboration, with AI systems working closely alongside human soldiers. AI swarms – networks of weaponized robots or drones – are being designed using swarm intelligence, which enables rapid learning and decision-making through the collective

---

oriented startups. Among those poised to gain are firms like Anduril – which partners with Meta, OpenAI, and the Department of Defense, and was previously backed by Vice President Vance during his time as a venture capitalist – alongside Palantir (cofounded by Karp and Thiel [Steinberger, 2025]), and investment firms such as Andreessen Horowitz. The resurgence of interest from Silicon Valley in the defense sector is driven by several factors: the ongoing wars in Ukraine and Gaza, intensifying technological rivalry with China, and a broader political realignment, with major tech players openly embracing right-wing politics.

19 In August 2025, Trump imposed export fees on Nvidia and AMD's chips following negotiations with Nvidia CEO Huang regarding chip export licenses to China (New York Times, 2025z).

coordination of information. The concept of 'enhanced soldiers' is emerging, integrating brain-computer interfaces and AI-driven biotechnology. In some visions, entirely robot-led armies capable of autonomous ground combat might become a reality, reminiscent of scenarios seen in science fiction films like *The Terminator*. Early examples of such systems include warbots such as the Tomahawk cruise missile, Joint Directed Attack Munition, and acoustic torpedoes. Military robots already perform vital tasks, including search-and-rescue missions, bomb disposal, equipment transport, and surveillance, further blurring the lines between combat and support roles in AI-driven warfare (Payne, 2021).

Cyber warfare is also profoundly shaped by AI, as cybersecurity and AI technologies become increasingly intertwined. AI systems can automate cyberattacks and defensive responses, introducing new dimensions of threat and protection for national security. For example, AI could be used to disrupt critical infrastructure, such as power grids, or hijack enemy healthcare systems. It could also execute sophisticated attacks aimed at degrading advanced military systems. This new cyber battlefield mirrors the historical tension between encryption and codebreaking, as seen in Turing's (and others') work. Today, AI tools can scan code for vulnerabilities, exploit weaknesses, or generate security patches. As AI capabilities continue to advance, the speed at which cyber flaws are detected and addressed may determine the success or failure of cyber operations in future conflicts (Payne, 2021).

During the two Trump administrations, national defense policy has shifted toward prioritizing technological dominance in both military and space. A central initiative was the formal establishment of the U.S. Space Force in 2019, which became the sixth branch of the U.S. Armed Forces. Tasked with organizing, training, and equipping personnel – known as Guardians – the Space Force is responsible for securing American interests in, from, and to space. Its duties include missile warning, satellite operations, global positioning, and maintaining space superiority against growing threats from adversaries like China and Russia (U.S. Space Force, 2025). In 2025, Trump unveiled the Golden Dome, an ambitious and costly missile defense project aimed at shielding the entire United States from ballistic, hypersonic, cruise, and space-based missile threats. The system aims to use satellite constellations, space-based and ground-based interceptors, directed-energy weapons, and AI-powered command systems to create a multilayered shield (Lockheed Martin, 2025). While praised by advocates as a bold vision for modern warfare, critics have raised concerns about its technical feasibility, the estimated cost (which is expected to exceed $500 billion), and the potential to accelerate a global arms race (New York Times, 2025i). The expansion of the Space Force, the development of the Golden Dome, and the integration of AI (and bolstering the military-industrial complex) reflect Trump's push to transform U.S. defense into a space-age, technologically superior force.

AI-powered weapon systems offer several advantages that are transforming military operations. One of the most notable benefits is the enhanced speed and accuracy in decision-making. AI can rapidly process vast amounts of data, improving performance in critical tasks such as precision shooting and maneuvering in combat. AI systems can also support commanders by providing real-time intelligence and situational awareness through big data analysis, pattern recognition, and correlation identification. Surveillance footage captured by unmanned aerial vehicles, combined with facial recognition technology and sensors, enables the precise identification of targets. Furthermore, AI is revolutionizing military training, with immersive simulation systems, such as augmented and virtual reality tools, being utilized for flight simulations, battlefield scenarios, and medical training (The Guardian, 2023). Perhaps most significantly, AI systems could save human lives by reducing the number of soldiers deployed on the battlefield and potentially lowering the rates of PTSD, drug abuse, and suicide by minimizing direct exposure to combat (Payne, 2021).

Despite these tactical advantages, AI weapon systems raise significant ethical concerns. A key limitation is their lack of common-sense understanding. AI systems often misinterpret context, leading to dangerous errors, such as confusing a person surrendering with someone picking up a weapon, which could have tragic consequences. Furthermore, AI lacks emotional intelligence and empathy, making it incapable of understanding human suffering or responding appropriately in morally complex situations. These systems are also limited in creativity and imagination – essential qualities for adapting to unpredictable combat situations and developing unconventional strategies (Payne, 2021).

The deployment of autonomous weapons introduces numerous ethical challenges that challenge traditional moral frameworks of warfare. One significant concern is automation bias, where human operators overly rely on machines, potentially accepting flawed outputs without question. The delegation of life-and-death decisions to algorithms – the act of automating killing – raises profound moral issues, as it may strip victims of their dignity and lead to dehumanization. Furthermore, by abdicating responsibility for lethal actions to machines that lack personhood, we risk eroding accountability for violence. AI systems are also prone to escalatory dynamics, where misinterpreted data could lead to unintended and disproportionate escalation, resulting in indiscriminate killings. While 'killer robots' may improve the combat effectiveness of attacking forces, they could also increase civilian casualties (if used recklessly). In the chaotic, unpredictable battlefield environment, where smoke, dust, and fire obscure sensors, it is doubtful that autonomous systems can consistently identify targets or make the complex ethical judgments that warfare demands. Replacing human soldiers with machines may lower the threshold for war, shifting the burden of conflict onto civilians, who will inevitably bear the brunt of its consequences. A further concern is the potential normalization of autonomous weapons in military operations, which could lead to their adoption in policy decisions, private security firms, or even fall into the hands of criminals or terrorists. The pressing issue is maintaining human control and accountability in an age when machines dominate the battlefield (Payne, 2021).

As AI continues to transform modern warfare, there is an increasing recognition of the urgent need to establish a framework for the ethics of military robots. The goal is to embed an ethical code into warbots, essentially programming them with rules and guidelines for combat (i.e., 'uploading' ethical instructions). This raises several complex questions: how can this be accomplished, and which norms and values should be integrated? One proposed foundation is the 'Just War' doctrine, which is enshrined in modern international law (Walzer, 2015). The doctrine prohibits atrocities like genocide and torture, mandates a just cause (such as self-defense) for initiating war, and insists on a clear distinction between combatants, who can be targeted, and civilians, wounded soldiers, or prisoners, who must not be harmed. However, in practice, these distinctions are often blurred (e.g., guerrilla forces using civilians as shields). Just War theory also stresses humane treatment of the enemy, including offering medical aid to casualties, ceasing hostilities with those who surrender, and minimizing unnecessary suffering. Restorative justice, through accountability, punishment, and rehabilitation, is also a key principle (Walzer, 2015). Advocacy groups, such as the International Committee for Robot Arms Control and the Campaign to Stop Killer Robots, call for robust ethical oversight and stringent regulatory measures. This could include international treaties and (self-)regulation by/of corporations and AI researchers to ensure that human oversight remains integral to decision-making – an essential safeguard against the 'control problem' – and to prevent the development of fully autonomous AI weapons.[20] Nonetheless, several challenges persist. These include defining what qualifies as military AI (i.e., 'definition problem'), addressing the dual-use nature of many technologies (i.e., 'dual-use problem'), and managing the risks of nations defecting from international agreements (i.e., 'governance problem'). How do we monitor compliance, and what sanctions should be applied for violations? The debate continues whether to ban killer robots outright or impose stricter regulations (and, if so, how). Payne (2021) suggests revising or updating Asimov's laws of robotics to fit the battlefield context: a warbot should only kill those it is authorized to target, do so with the utmost humanity, understand the commander's intentions, and act creatively to fulfill them. It should also protect human allies, even at the cost of its existence, so long as doing so does not jeopardize the mission. Ultimately, humans must (ideally) remain accountable for the machines they create, making the incorporation of ethical reasoning at every stage of military AI development imperative (however, the Trump administration's rollback of AI safeguards and other AI ethics-related policies has made achieving these goals increasingly difficult).

---

20 Given the Trump administration's emphasis on deregulation, privatization, and its reluctance toward international collaboration, such multilateral treaties and safeguards are unlikely to materialize in the near future.

4.2.6 Trump, ICE, and the NSA

The Trump administration's emphasis on AI-driven military capabilities and national security, combined with its ideological agenda, also extended into domestic surveillance and law enforcement. Agencies such as Immigration and Customs Enforcement (ICE) and the NSA leveraged these technological advances, further normalizing mass data collection and undermining established privacy norms.

The twenty-first century, fueled by breakthroughs in information and communication technologies, is often viewed as the 'golden age' of mass surveillance and espionage. Smartphones with their location tracking, social media platforms' social graphs, and AI-driven big data analytics contribute to creating detailed digital profiles that increase individuals' visibility and transparency, transforming them into 'glass people.' The collection, aggregation, and distribution of personal data for commercial purposes, such as targeted advertising, has never been more seamless, leading to a significant erosion of privacy. However, privacy threats extend beyond the realm of commercial surveillance – often referred to as 'surveillance capitalism' or 'dataveillance' (Zuboff, 2015, 2019) – to include covert government spying, which is justified as a means to protect public safety and national security (Gellman, 2021; Greenwald, 2015; Snowden, 2019). The merging of public and private mass surveillance poses a serious threat to privacy and fundamental human rights, including those safeguarded by international law (Amnesty International, 2019). This danger is further exacerbated by shifts in power dynamics, where individuals are increasingly outmatched by both 'big government' and 'big business.' These unprecedented challenges have the potential to fundamentally undermine democracy and the rule of law (Wörsdörfer, 2018).

Foucault's (1995, 2000) concept of the Panopticon serves as a foundational mechanism for understanding modern state control and surveillance. Originally a prison design, the Panopticon becomes a metaphor for how state programs monitor and record individuals, creating what Foucault calls 'imaginary prisons.' In such systems, people begin to restrict their behavior out of fear of being observed by those in power, turning surveillance into a powerful instrument of social control and self-censorship. This ubiquitous surveillance does more than merely empower authorities and compel compliance – it induces individuals to 'internalize their watchers,' meaning that those who believe they are being watched will instinctively act in ways that conform to expected norms, often without realizing they are being controlled. As a result, surveillance creates an 'illusion of freedom,' where individuals feel autonomous even as their actions are subtly dictated by the (imagined) presence of oversight (Wörsdörfer, 2018).

Today's digital environment functions as a digital panopticon or cryptopticon – a ubiquitous system of surveillance that creates an atmosphere of uncertainty, where the possibility of electronic mass surveillance looms over everyone. The knowledge that one's words and actions are susceptible to monitoring, and that one can be watched at any time by unseen authorities, is a constant undercurrent in modern life.

This pervasive surveillance has the disturbing ability to get inside a person's mind, influencing their thoughts and behaviors. The consequences are profound: mass surveillance keeps people in line, as seen in systems like China's Social Credit System, fostering conformity, obedience, and passivity. It not only stifles dissent in public spaces but also in private thoughts, where individuals begin to think only in ways that align with societal expectations. The feeling of being watched leads to oppressive self-censorship (as discussed above), particularly affecting journalists and researchers, whose freedom of speech and academic inquiry can be severely hindered. Furthermore, such surveillance instills anxiety, suspicion, and mistrust among citizens, reminiscent of the McCarthy-era 'Red Scare' (Risen, 2025). Political dissent is crushed, with individuals labeled as potential threats to national security or terrorists, further enabling discrimination against marginalized or minority groups. This widespread abuse of power and unchecked government overreach compromises personal freedoms and deepens societal divisions (Wörsdörfer, 2018, 2024b).

Building on Foucault's concepts of the panopticon and cryptopticon, which illustrate how surveillance shapes behavior and conceals power, these theoretical frameworks become particularly tangible in contemporary policy. During the first Trump administration, the rollback of FCC privacy rules in 2017 eliminated requirements for Internet service providers to obtain consumer consent before sharing browsing data. This move sparked ethical concerns over informed consent and individuals' control over their personal information. Additionally, the administration's immigration and law enforcement policies heightened fears about expanding government surveillance, particularly through the use of AI and facial recognition technologies. These developments raised serious ethical questions regarding (informed) consent, fairness, privacy, and data protection.

The second Trump administration has taken a (much) more aggressive stance on policing and surveillance. One of its early actions included firing key NSA leadership, including General Haugh, who also headed U.S. Cyber Command (besides the NSA). Trump also removed several inspectors general tasked with overseeing technologies like Clearview AI (Hill, 2023; Mother Jones, 2025; Narayanan & Kapoor, 2024; New York Times, 2020; Wired, 2023) and Palantir (and preventing their misuse [see below]), signaling a disregard for legal, congressional, and constitutional checks that had previously restrained executive overreach of prior presidents and administrations (Mother Jones, 2025; New York Times, 2025w). The current administration has expanded the government's responsibilities and increasingly outsourced them to private tech firms, forming public-private surveillance partnerships (similar to the NSA's cooperation with Booz Allen Hamilton and other companies) that some experts argue are leading toward a surveillance or police state – ideas echoed in Zuboff's theory of surveillance capitalism (Zuboff, 2015, 2019).

In March 2025, Trump issued an EO titled *Stopping Waste, Fraud, and Abuse by Eliminating Information Silos*, requiring all federal agencies and departments to share data on Americans (Trump White House, 2025c). To carry out this plan, the administration selected Palantir Technologies (Amnesty International, 2019; New York Times, 2025j), a big data and software company specializing in data analysis and surveillance tools with close connections to the NSA and ICE (Steinberger, 2025). Palantir, founded by Trump ally Thiel (New York Times, 2017; Thiel, 2009, 2014), has been one of the biggest winners of Trump's presidency. According to the New York Times (2025), the organization has received over $113 million in federal funds since Trump returned to office in early 2025, including additional funding from new and existing contracts with the Department of Homeland Security, ICE, and the Pentagon. This figure excludes a $795 million contract recently awarded by the Department of Defense (or War) that remains unspent (New York Times, 2025j). In the summer of 2025, Palantir secured a new $10-billion contract with the U.S. Army (Washington Post, 2025).

Palantir representatives are also in discussions with the Social Security Administration and the IRS, as well as reportedly with the Department of Education, regarding the potential purchase or expansion of its technology. Its software, Foundry, is already used by at least four federal agencies, including Department of Homeland Security and Health and Human Services, to merge information and data across various government agencies and build detailed digital profiles of individuals. These profiles could be used for immigration enforcement efforts, including carrying out deportations, policing migrants, and even for the suppression of political dissent, prompting concerns about a further erosion of privacy or even a path toward techno-authoritarianism. Reports from CNN (2025) and Wired (2025) reveal that DOGE[21] – the Trump administration's cost-saving task force – is building a centralized database to surveil immigrants with the help of Palantir. This effort is supported by a $30 million ICE contract awarded in April to develop a platform capable of tracking migrant movements in real time (see also Reich, 2025; The Guardian, 2025e).

Beyond immigration, Palantir also works with the CDC to collect disease data, raising further (patient) privacy concerns. The aggregation of sensitive health information, especially concerning gender-affirming care, reproductive services, and disability status, could place vulnerable groups at increased risk of exposure and harm (New York Times, 2025k).

21 Noteworthy is that Palantir's selection as chief vendor was heavily influenced by DOGE, whose membership includes at least three former Palantir employees and two others connected to companies funded by Thiel. Thiel also mentored JD Vance, who previously worked at one of Thiel's venture capital firms. Thiel later bankrolled Vance's 2022 Senate run, introduced him to Trump, and helped secure his nomination as vice president.

4.2.7 Trump and the crypto-industry

Although AI technologies and cryptocurrencies have a significant environmental footprint[22] and raise ethical concerns (Lewis, 2023), including high energy and water consumption, greenhouse gas emissions, and growing e-waste, the Trump administration has actively promoted the crypto industry and advocated for its products. While such actions may position the United States as a global leader in digital finance, ethics experts have raised alarms about potential conflicts of interest, as the Trump family holds substantial investments in various crypto-related businesses.

In 2024, Trump, who had previously been a critic of Bitcoin, began earning a significant income from cryptocurrency ventures, including a $57 million stake in World Liberty Financial and $1.2 million from non-fungible token licensing. The First Lady also earned from crypto-related licensing. Since starting his second presidential term, Trump's crypto wealth (Forbes, 2025) has increased significantly through new business deals, including the launch of a personal memecoin called $TRUMP, which could be worth billions. Trump's recent financial disclosure (U.S. Office of Government Ethics, 2025) reveals that crypto is now one of his most lucrative businesses, alongside his real estate and media holdings (his properties, including Mar-a-Lago and overseas real estate deals, continue to generate millions in revenue, although exact profits remain undisclosed). Trump's expanding role as a major crypto operator and top policymaker raises unprecedented concerns about conflicts of interest. At several events, including a 'Crypto Dinner,' Trump promised to ease regulations on the crypto industry, aligning his political agenda with his growing crypto interests (New York Times, 2025l).

As Truth Social continues to struggle financially, posting a $31 million loss in Q1 2025 and never turning a profit since its initial public offering, Trump Media & Technology Group is pivoting into cryptocurrency. The company has raised $2.5 billion in investment in Bitcoin and is working with Crypto.com to launch several crypto-related ETFs (exchange-traded funds), including Truth Social-branded Bitcoin and Ethereum ETFs. Despite having no formal role, Trump is the company's largest shareholder, and he and his family have become vocal advocates for the industry (New York Times, 2025m).[23] Note that Truth Social faces several ongoing challenges: low ad revenue, lim-

22 Australian Energy Council, 2023; Badea & Mungiu-Pupăzan, 2021; Biden White House, 2022b; Dachwitz & Hilbig, 2025; Huynh et al., 2022; Kohli et al., 2023; Li et al., 2025; Luccioni et al., 2022; McKinsey & Company, 2023; Muldoon et al., 2025; Owusu-Sekyere et al., 2022; Patterson et al., 2021; Statista, 2025; U.N. Trade and Development, 2024; World Health Organization, 2021.

23 Eric Trump has launched a new cryptocurrency venture, American Bitcoin, in partnership with crypto firm Hut 8, focusing on Bitcoin mining. He claims the Trump administration's pro-crypto and low-cost energy policies will give the company a significant edge. American Bitcoin holds over $22 million in Bitcoin and is preparing to go public. A business entity controlled by Eric and Don Jr. owns 20% of the company (note that Trump's two sons were also involved in the founding of the World Liberty Financial crypto firm) (Forbes, 2025; New York Times, 2025p).

ited user growth beyond Trump's political base, and reliance on Trump's content to drive traffic (which accounts for about 80% of visits). The company has just 29 employees and a minimal advertising infrastructure. Critics argue this move deepens potential conflicts of interest, especially given Trump's deregulatory approach to crypto as president (see below).[24] Analysts see the new ETFs as leveraging the Trump brand more than offering unique financial products. Trump Media's economic health remains uncertain, though the company could become one of the largest public holders of Bitcoin. Some investors view the pivot as a survival strategy for Truth Social, although even supporters acknowledge Trump's ultimate focus: financial gain (New York Times, 2025n).

From a regulatory (i.e., ordoliberal) standpoint, it is worth noting that the SEC has scaled back its specialized crypto enforcement unit, which previously had over fifty lawyers focused on regulating digital assets (New York Times, 2025o; Securities and Exchange Commission, 2025a). This move aligns with Trump's push to reduce regulatory oversight of cryptocurrencies (and other tech products), following his EO to promote crypto growth and limit what he calls 'regulatory overreach' (Trump White House, 2025d, 2025e).

Coinbase recently announced that the SEC has agreed in principle to drop its 2023 lawsuit against the company without any financial penalty (Coinbase, 2025; Securities and Exchange Commission, 2025b). The lawsuit accused Coinbase of selling unregistered securities through its crypto platform. If finalized, this settlement would mark a significant regulatory retreat for the SEC and a major win for the crypto industry, which has faced intense scrutiny under the Biden administration. The SEC's legal push, led by former chair Gensler, sought to classify most cryptocurrencies as securities requiring strict regulation. Coinbase and other crypto firms challenged these actions, arguing the rules were outdated and harmful to innovation. After a lengthy and complex legal battle and amid growing crypto lobbying (New York Times, 2025q) and political support for deregulation under Trump, the SEC has scaled back enforcement efforts and is set to dismiss the case. While Coinbase praised the settlement as a 'complete win,' critics warn it undermines the SEC's authority and investor protections. The move reflects a shift in Washington toward a more laissez-faire regulatory environment for digital assets, influenced by the crypto industry's political investments and the new administration's policy direction.

Trump also appointed a 'crypto czar' and signed an EO to establish a national cryptocurrency reserve, starting with $17 billion worth of Bitcoin previously seized by the U.S. government (notably, only Bitcoin will be actively purchased for the reserve; other cryptocurrencies will be limited to those seized in legal actions). The order directs federal agencies to explore buying more Bitcoin, provided it does not increase

24 Crypto firms, including Crypto.com, donated millions to Trump's inaugural committee, and under his administration, the SEC has closed or dropped several investigations into crypto companies.

taxpayer costs, and prohibits selling any of the holdings, likening the reserve to a 'digital Fort Knox' (Trump White House, 2025f). This move is part of a broader pro-crypto shift under Trump, including dropping lawsuits or halting investigations against major crypto firms (such as Binance,[25] Coinbase, and Kraken) and hosting a crypto summit at the White House. While proponents say the reserve could reduce national debt and boost U.S. leadership in digital finance, others call it risky due to crypto's volatility and its potential to enrich existing investors (and benefit the Trump family).

As part of the self-declared 'Crypto Week' (the week of July 14, 2025), the U.S. Congress passed three major pieces of legislation under Trump to turn the United States into a global crypto stronghold: the GENIUS Act, the Clarity Act, and the Anti-CBDC Surveillance State Act. *The Guiding and Establishing National Innovation for US Stablecoins* (GENIUS) Act (Congress.gov, 2025) is a bipartisan bill that marks a pivotal shift in Washington's approach to cryptocurrency regulation. Its passage represents the first time the Senate and House have approved primary crypto legislation. The bill follows an intense lobbying campaign by crypto firms and super PACs, which spent over $130 million influencing key congressional races (New York Times, 2025q). The GENIUS Act establishes a unified legal framework for stablecoins – digital assets pegged to the U.S. dollar to minimize volatility, aiming to integrate them more fully into the financial system. It is expected to improve payment efficiency (by making them faster and cheaper), strengthen U.S. Treasury markets, and reinforce the dollar's global dominance.[26] Notably, the Trump family has already launched its own stablecoin, USD1. While many Republicans and several Democrats supported the bill, progressive Democrats raised concerns over its lack of anticorruption safeguards, particularly considering Trump's financial interests. Republican lawmakers blocked proposed amendments that would have barred government officials from profiting. Critics have also warned that the bill offers only superficial oversight, with some arguing it is too favorable to large tech firms, while others see it as overly burdensome for crypto startups (New York Times, 2025r). The *Clarity Act* classifies digital assets as securities or commodities, thereby creating greater legal certainty. However, this reclassification shifts oversight from the (more) crypto-skeptical SEC to the Commodity Futures Trading Commission (CFTC), which regulates commodities and derivatives markets. The *Anti-CBDC Surveillance State Act* prohibits the introduction of a central bank digital currency (CBDC) in the United States. As a result, the Federal Reserve is not permitted to issue its own digital currency (New York Times, 2025v).

---

25 Trump also granted a pardon to Changpeng Zhao, the cofounder and former CEO of Binance, who had been convicted on money laundering charges and served several months in prison.

26 The value of stablecoins is pegged to a stable underlying asset, such as the U.S. dollar. Issuers of stablecoins will be required to prove full 1:1 backing with U.S. dollars or short-term U.S. Treasury bonds. The industry expects a boom in new stablecoins due to the Genius Act, while the heavily indebted U.S. government is hoping for increased demand for its bonds.

4.2.7.1 Excursus: Bankman-Fried and FTX

Sam Bankman-Fried (SBF) is the founder and former CEO of FTX, a cryptocurrency exchange, and Alameda Research, its sister hedge fund, launched in 2019. Born in 1992 to well-known Stanford professors, SBF studied physics at MIT, where he developed a utilitarian philosophy inspired by Singer and MacAskill's concept of effective altruism. This philosophy led him to donate millions to political campaigns, including significant contributions to the Biden campaign and Democratic causes, raising questions about political lobbying and rent-seeking behaviors. SBF was deeply interested in games, puzzles, and mathematics, which led him to a career in high-frequency trading. He worked for Jane Street Capital, where his trading skills were honed, eventually transitioning from intern to a full-time ETF trader in 2014. Despite being a brilliant finance strategist, he struggled with social intelligence and interpersonal skills (Lewis, 2023).

SBF cofounded the cryptocurrency trading firm Alameda Research in 2017 alongside MacAulay, and the firm played a central role in the broader operations of FTX. Alameda traded FTX's own token, FTT, which helped bolster the exchange's liquidity. Over time, Alameda received significant funding from hundreds of venture capitalists, solidifying its position in the largely unregulated world of cryptocurrencies. This lack of (ordoliberal-style) regulation, a hallmark of the techno-libertarian ideology, meant that traditional financial institutions, such as governments and real banks, had little to no involvement. Instead, the system was dominated by 'pseudo-banks' and decentralized entities, often creating opportunities for regulatory arbitrage/capture, revolving doors, lobbying, rent-seeking, and conflicts of interest. FTX, initially incorporated in Antigua, operated in Hong Kong and later headquartered in the Bahamas, strategically placed itself beyond the reach of U.S. regulatory bodies, including the SEC and the CFTC. The CFTC oversees U.S. derivatives markets, including futures and swaps, but FTX could operate without much scrutiny due to its international structure. The overlap between Alameda and FTX was significant, with questions surrounding where one company ended and the other began. Although they were legally separate entities, they were controlled by SBF, who owned 90% of Alameda and more than half of FTX. This created an inherent conflict of interest, as the exchange and the trading firm were effectively controlled by the same person, allowing for potential market manipulation. Furthermore, SBF and Ellison, the business partner and co-CEO of Alameda, were in a romantic/sexual relationship, which compounded the concerns about conflicts of interest within their operations (Lewis, 2023).

FTX quickly became the fastest-growing cryptocurrency exchange, positioning itself as the main competitor to Binance, the world's largest crypto exchange, founded by Changpeng Zhao (CZ). This rivalry between SBF and CZ was intense, with both men emerging as key figures in the crypto world, yet deeply antagonistic toward each other. Despite cutthroat competition, FTX built a substantial public profile, attracting high-profile spokespersons such as Curry, James, Ohtani, and O'Neal. FTX also entered lucrative business partnerships, including deals with the Miami Heat, MLB, Formula 1, and even the Coachella music festival. Brady signed an ad deal with FTX, further boosting the exchange's visibility. By 2021, FTX's business was valued at $40 billion, and SBF's net worth reached $22.5 billion. His rapid rise led to widespread media coverage, with Time magazine even including him in their annual list of the world's 100 most influential people. SBF became a media sensation, often hailed as the 'crypto wunderkind' and compared to financial legends like Morgan and Buffett. In many ways, he was seen as the face of the future of finance, embodying the promise of crypto as the next revolutionary wave in financial technology (Lewis, 2023).

The 2022 crypto crisis marked a turning point for the industry, with two high-profile crypto banks, BlockFi and Voyager Digital, collapsing, sending shockwaves through the market. The panic quickly spread, triggering a 'bank run' on FTX, ultimately leading to a massive liquidity crisis. At the heart of FTX's downfall was its enormous debt – SBF's exchange owed a staggering $8.7 billion to account holders and customers. Behind the scenes, FTX's financial mismanagement became apparent, with SBF's private investments and spending totaling $4.4 billion, including controversial loans from the company to SBF himself, amounting to $1 billion, which were allegedly used for political donations and funding of his effective altruism initiatives. Moreover, the company lost over $1 billion in funds to hackers, further deepening the crisis. To add to the financial turmoil, Alameda Research, the trading firm closely linked to FTX, suffered significant losses in the 2022 crypto market crash. The underlying problems within FTX were severe: a lack of an organizational chart, unclear financial and governance structures, and a complete failure of corporate controls and governance. Conflicts of interest, particularly with SBF's dual role at FTX and Alameda, added to the instability. Amid the chaos, Binance, the world's largest cryptocurrency exchange and a former rival, considered acquiring FTX but ultimately backed out due to reports of mishandled customer funds and ongoing investigations by U.S. agencies. Ultimately, both Alameda and FTX filed for bankruptcy in 2022, marking the most significant crash in the history of cryptocurrency to date (Lewis, 2023).

In 2022, the legal fallout from FTX's collapse began to unfold, with former Alameda Research CEO Ellison pleading guilty to two counts of wire fraud and five conspiracy charges, including wire, securities, commodities fraud, and money laundering. Her guilty plea set the stage for the FTX executives' legal challenges. Later that year, SBF was arrested in the Bahamas and extradited to the United States. Once in U.S. custody, SBF faced an indictment on seven criminal charges, including wire fraud, commodities fraud, securities fraud, money laundering, and violations of campaign finance laws. The legal battle reached a significant milestone in November 2023 when SBF was convicted on all seven charges in the case of *U.S. v. Bankman-Fried*. The court found him guilty of orchestrating a complex fraud scheme that ultimately led to the collapse of FTX and Alameda Research, resulting in billions of dollars in lost customer funds. A second trial for SBF took place in March 2024, during which he faced five additional charges, including bank fraud and bribery. This trial culminated in a 25-year prison sentence (Lewis, 2023).

In 2021, Binance, the world's largest cryptocurrency exchange, faced significant legal challenges when the CFTC filed a lawsuit against both the platform and its founder, CZ. This legal action was further complicated by investigations from the Department of Justice and the IRS, which probed Binance for alleged money laundering and tax offenses. These investigations came amid growing concerns over Binance's role in facilitating illicit financial activities. By 2023, Binance was forced to confront the full extent of its legal issues, as it paid over $4.3 billion in fines for violations related to providing financial services for terrorists and criminals, as well as enabling the circumvention of international sanctions, particularly those targeting Iran. To resolve the charges, CZ agreed to plead guilty to violating money laundering rules. As part of the settlement, Zhao was ordered to pay a $50 million fine, step down from his position as CEO, and serve a 4-month prison sentence (in 2025, he was pardoned by Trump).

4.2.8 Trump and deep-sea mining

Beyond cryptocurrencies, the Trump administration's policies have also influenced other high-stakes domains, such as deep-sea mining, where regulatory rollbacks and environmental oversight decisions carry significant ethical and ecological implications.

Deep-sea mining is the extraction of minerals and metals from the ocean floor, primarily targeting polymetallic nodules, cobalt, lithium, manganese, nickel, and rare earth elements. It matters to businesses because these minerals are essential for producing electronics, such as laptops and smartphones, as well as electric vehicle (EV) batteries and renewable energy technologies like wind and solar power. It is seen as a solution to reduce reliance on terrestrial mining and diversify supply chains, particularly given the increasing demand for these materials. Currently, most exploratory activity is focused on discovering resource-rich areas, with high-potential regions, such as the Clarion-Clipperton Zone between Hawaii and Mexico, drawing attention. However, regulatory barriers still limit commercial mining (Standing, 2023).

Governance and regulation are dominated by the International Seabed Authority (ISA), which was established under the U.N. Convention on the Law of the Sea (UNCLOS) in 1994. While more than 165 countries have ratified the ISA, the United States has not ratified the treaty (the same applies to the global High Seas Treaty, aimed at protecting marine biodiversity, which was recently ratified by the 60th nation, surpassing the threshold required for U.N. treaties to take effect). The ISA organizes, regulates, and controls mineral-related activities in seabed areas beyond national jurisdiction, i.e., in international waters, which cover approximately half of the world's oceans. Despite its role, the ISA has faced severe challenges, mainly due to its limited annual budget of roughly $9 million and a consensus-based decision-making model, which often favors industrialized nations and sidelines developing countries, Indigenous communities, and local fishermen (note that the low amount is indicative of the low priority given to the issues the ISA is supposed to regulate and leads to insufficient governance mechanisms; together with the consensus-based decision-making, they make it difficult to monitor and enforce environmental safeguards and sanction noncompliance) (Feichtner, 2019; Feichtner & Ranganathan, 2019; ISA, 2025a, 2025b).

In 2023, the ISA failed to adopt a mining code to regulate deep-sea mining, with a tentative decision timeline set for 2025 to determine if and how mining in international waters may proceed. However, a legal loophole exists, allowing for provisional approval of mining applications submitted before the mining code is in place (critics fear this might be the start of unregulated mining). As a result, companies like the Metals Company are planning to submit more applications soon (although ISA's new secretary-general urges a delay until the regulations are fully defined). So far, more than 30 exploration permits covering approximately 1 million km^2 (roughly the size of Egypt) have been issued since 2001; however, these permits do not yet permit for-profit (i.e., commercial) activities. Noteworthy is also that more than thirty countries oppose the fast-tracking of deep-sea mining, with opposition growing significantly in recent years (other countries, including the United States, however, support the unregulated deep-sea mining) (Standing, 2023).

New leadership at the ISA, with Secretary-General Carvalho, a Brazilian oceanographer, appointed in 2024, has renewed hope for more socioenvironmental sustainability. Her background suggests a shift toward stronger ecological safeguards and scientific rigor in deep-sea mining regulations. She has committed herself to increased transparency and stakeholder engagement, aiming to address concerns over marine conservation (note that under the previous leadership, the licensing process was opaque with [almost] no independent environmental impact assessment; another big problem was regulatory capture and the revolving door phenomenon, especially given that the ISA is dominated by representatives of American and European multinational mining companies; the former ISA leader, Lodge, also faced scrutiny over his alleged financial misconduct and ties to pro-mining interests, fueling calls for change). With 32 nations now backing the precautionary[27] pause on mining, Carvalho may encourage a more cautious and research-driven decision-making process (ISA, 2025a).

Recent developments, however, have raised significant concerns. The Trump administration, along with certain members of Congress, is reportedly being urged by the Vancouver-based Metals Company and its CEO, Gerard Barron, to bypass regulations set by the ISA and authorize deep-sea mining as early as 2027 (New York Times, 2025s). Such a move would effectively sidestep international law, prompting growing legal and environmental scrutiny over its long-term sustainability. Adding to these concerns, Commerce Secretary Lutnick – formerly CEO of Cantor Fitzgerald, the financial firm that served as lead banker for Metals Company – is now playing a central role in shaping U.S. mining policy. This connection underscores the increasing influence of private economic interests on public decision-making. Further intensifying the situation is Metals Company's severe financial distress, including declining cash reserves and limited access to capital. These pressures have reportedly added urgency to the push for regulatory approval. In a more worrying turn, Trump signed an EO in April 2025 authorizing deep-sea mining in international waters (New York Times, 2025t; Trump White House, 2025g), signaling a dramatic policy shift favoring commercial extraction. At the same time, the Interior Department is reviewing a separate request from California-based Impossible Metals to begin mining operations off the coast of American Samoa in May 2025 (New York Times, 2025u). This push for commercial deep-sea mining stands in stark contrast to intensifying international calls for a moratorium. Environmental organizations and several ISA member states are urging the adoption of stricter protections and a temporary halt to mining until more comprehensive scientific assessments can be conducted. Critics caution that moving forward without adequate safeguards could cause irreversible harm to fragile marine ecosystems.

As pointed out by the Trump administration, the business case for deep-sea mining remains strong due to its economic and strategic benefits, such as access to minerals in high demand for green technologies and the potential to reduce the reliance on mineral-rich nations, especially China, which currently controls a large share of rare earth processing. The resource necessity for the energy transition is undeniable, as green energy technologies require metals like copper, nickel, cobalt, and other critical minerals, many of which are found in large quantities on the seabed. With the increasing demand for EVs and battery storage systems, it has become clear that land-based resources alone will not be sufficient to meet future needs. This creates a strong case for deep-sea mining, which is seen as a potential solution to bridge the gap in

27 The precautionary principle advocates for erring on the side of caution when scientific knowledge is incomplete, as is the case for deep-sea mining; it also calls for the ISA to restrict or closely monitor activities that could have an irreversible impact on deep-sea ecosystems.

mineral supply. However, alternative solutions could alleviate some of the pressure on mining. For instance, increasing recycling efforts for materials like lithium-ion batteries could help reduce the demand, though less than 5% of these batteries are currently recycled. Additionally, resource shortages might inspire lifestyle changes that reduce excessive consumption of mineral-dependent technologies, helping to mitigate some of the environmental and ethical concerns. The global demand for minerals like cobalt and lithium is projected to rise significantly, driven by the growing reliance on wind and solar energy, EVs, batteries, and other low-carbon technologies (International Energy Agency, 2025). This surge in demand underscores the urgency of securing a stable and diverse supply chain. As of 2024, China dominates the global processing and refining of critical minerals, handling approximately two-thirds of the world's total capacity. It is responsible for more than half of the worldwide refining of aluminum, lithium, and cobalt, nearly 90% of rare earth metals, and almost all of the global processing of natural graphite. Additionally, China processes over a third of the world's copper and nickel, making it a dominant player in the global supply chain (Statista, 2024). Reducing dependence on such a concentrated source is crucial to ensure a more resilient and diversified supply chain, and deep-sea mining could play a significant role in that diversification. Proponents also argue that deep-sea mining might have a smaller ecological footprint than terrestrial mining and is therefore more environmentally sustainable (though these claims are disputed, especially given the remaining knowledge gaps and uncertainties) (Miller et al., 2018; Standing, 2023).

Numerous compelling arguments, however, exist against deep-sea mining, mainly due to its significant socioenvironmental and ethical risks. One of the primary concerns is the destruction of seabed landscapes and ecosystems, leading to an unavoidable loss of biodiversity. The disruption caused by mining operations could also impair the ocean's vital role as a carbon sink, which helps store carbon and regulate the global climate through the biological pump. Additionally, the noise generated by underwater mining equipment can disrupt the migration patterns and reproductive behaviors of marine mammals, resulting in long-term impacts on aquatic life. The risks are amplified by the fact that 85% of the seabed remains unmapped, with large sections of the ocean, particularly the abyssal and hadal zones, still unexplored. This creates uncertainty about the potential ecological consequences, as species and ecosystems may be harmed before they are understood. In particular, the microbes attached to polymetallic nodules could hold the potential to form the basis for new medicines and antibiotics, making their destruction a potential loss for medical science. Deep-sea mining also threatens habitats that have taken millions of years to form, causing irreversible and irreparable damage to seabed ecosystems. The risk of 'anonymous extinctions' – the loss of species unknown to science – is a profound concern. Furthermore, local fishing industries could be severely impacted as mining operations disrupt fish populations, thereby harming the livelihoods and food sources of communities that depend on them for sustenance. Culturally, deep-sea mining poses a threat to Indigenous communities that have sacred ties to marine resources. For these communities, mining is not just an environmental concern but an infringement on their cultural identity and way of life, as expressed in the statement, 'when they mine, they mine our culture.' Extracting resources from the ocean violates their sacred connection to the seas, further fueling opposition to the practice. Lastly, the impact of deep-sea mining raises significant questions about the global commons: does any organization have the right to exploit ocean resources? The oceans, as a shared resource, should be protected for the benefit of all humanity. However, deep-sea mining threatens to cause irreparable damage to ecosystems, with potentially unknown effects on global marine biodiversity. The destruction of habitats and species that play vital roles in maintaining ocean health may have far-reaching and irreversible consequences. Moreover, there is a responsibility to future generations under the common heritage of humankind principle set out in UNCLOS. This principle emphasizes intergenerational equity, meaning that current generations must manage ocean resources to preserve them for the benefit of future generations (Feichtner, 2019; Feichtner & Ranganathan, 2019; Miller et al., 2018; Standing, 2023).

4.3 Outlook

Looking ahead, there are indications that the current administration may pursue the reform or repeal of key regulatory frameworks, including the Dodd-Frank Act, as part of a broader agenda focused on financial market deregulation. Such changes could have profound implications for the conflict minerals industry, particularly in regions like the Democratic Republic of the Congo (DRC), where mining practices are closely linked to human rights concerns. Similarly, potential reforms to the Uyghur Forced Labor Prevention Act could weaken protections related to forced labor (and other business ethics issues) and have significant consequences for the tech supply chain, e.g., concerning key minerals used in electronics. These possible policy shifts raise critical questions about the future of corporate accountability, business and human rights, and the ethical sourcing of raw materials.

The U.S. Conflict Minerals Law, under Section 1502 of the Dodd-Frank Wall Street Reform and Consumer Protection Act, utilizes domestic law to regulate global supply chains, with a focus on human rights, particularly concerning minerals sourced from conflict zones. This section requires companies listed on U.S. stock markets to conduct country-of-origin inquiries for '3Ts' (tin, tungsten, and tantalum) and gold, and to implement human rights due diligence measures if minerals from the DRC are involved. Companies must submit an annual Conflict Minerals Report to the SEC, undergo independent private sector audits, and make public disclosures. A product labeling system also emerged, indicating whether products are DRC conflict-free.

The impacts of Dodd-Frank have been significant in raising awareness and sensitizing companies and customers about the ethical sourcing of minerals. It has helped increase supply chain transparency and accountability, fostering changes in business practices and influencing consumer behavior, particularly through the rise of ethical consumerism. The law has made illegal and uncertified mining less profitable and less attractive for armed groups. As a result, the market for minerals with unclear origin has shrunk substantially, leading to a price drop for uncertified minerals. This shift has also contributed to the fact that armed groups are now present in only one-third of all mines in the Eastern DRC, compared to almost all mines before the Dodd-Frank Act, thus promoting the transition to a more peaceful and legal use of mineral resources. However, the issues of Dodd-Frank cannot be ignored. One problem is its narrow geographical and content scope, as the law only addresses the 3Ts and gold and applies solely to the DRC, leaving substantial loopholes. Additionally, the definition of armed groups under the law excludes the DRC army, which has been a significant issue, especially given the army's involvement in the conflict minerals trade. The complexity and volatility of global supply chains also present a challenge, particularly regarding traceability of conflict minerals, due to a lack of reliable data (e.g., related to minerals mapping) (Nest, 2013; Kara, 2023; Wörsdörfer, 2018).

Regarding reform measures, suggestions include extending the regional and content-related scope beyond the 3Ts and gold, and incorporating other countries or regions affected by conflict minerals. A critical question is whether auditing, reporting, and disclosure alone are sufficient or if more vigorous enforcement, monitoring, and sanctioning mechanisms should exist. Additionally, the future of the Dodd-Frank Act remains unclear, as the Trump administration may attempt to repeal parts or all of the law, much like the Consumer Financial Protection Bureau (Nest, 2013; Kara, 2023; Wörsdörfer, 2018).[28]

This broader deregulatory stance could also impact labor-related legislation, such as the Uyghur Forced Labor Prevention Act, which came into effect in mid-2022. This law requires companies importing goods from China's Xinjiang region to provide 'clear and convincing evidence' that forced labor was not used in their production, effectively imposing a ban on such imports (U.S. Congress, 2021). Should the Trump administration pursue further deregulation, it might challenge or attempt to roll back parts of this law as well.

Additional issues of concern include Trump's demand that iPhones be produced in the United States, a move that could address various human rights issues within Apple's supply chain (see the discussion surrounding the working conditions at Foxconn) but would likely lead to significantly higher production costs – costs that would most likely be passed on to consumers. Another major topic is the ongoing debate around digital services taxes. Both Canada and the E.U. have proposed such taxes to ensure big tech companies pay their fair share (and contribute to the public good,

---

28 The same applies to the E.U.-U.S. Data Privacy Framework – a transatlantic agreement that replaced the Privacy Shield and the International Safe Harbor Privacy Principles – aimed at protecting E.U. citizens from broad U.S. government surveillance programs, which could also be revoked by the Trump administration.

e.g., by maintaining public infrastructure), as many currently do not (The Guardian, 2025b; Wörsdörfer, 2018). However, these proposals are temporarily on hold due to ongoing tariff disputes and trade deal negotiations with the Trump administration (Politico, 2025a).[29]

4.4 Concluding remarks

This chapter has provided an overview and critical analysis of the Trump administration's policies and their profound impact on computer and AI ethics. Key areas of focus include: academia and science, addressing issues such as budget cuts, science denial, and the rise of post-truth politics; DEI, with an emphasis on big data ethics and the pressures of self-censorship; industry deregulation, highlighted by the repeal of the Biden-era AI EO and other major policy shifts; social media platforms like TikTok and X, examining content moderation, fact-checking, and political influence; military and surveillance technologies, with attention to their ethical implications; privacy and data protection, exploring government surveillance and the roles of companies like Palantir; cryptocurrencies, particularly in relation to the business-ethical challenges, such as concerns about financial transparency, security, and possible conflicts of interest; and environmental concerns, including legislation on deep-sea mining and conflict minerals. Through these analyses, this chapter underscores the complex intersection of politics, technology, and ethics in the Trump era.

By examining these domains, this chapter has explored the broader ethical implications of Trump's AI and digital governance policies. It offers a nuanced perspective on how political developments intersect with ongoing computer and AI ethics debates. It also aims to raise awareness and sensitize readers to the evolving ethical challenges in the tech landscape and their broader societal ramifications.

It is essential to note that we are only slightly more than nine months into the second Trump administration, meaning that more than three years remain, with the potential for an even longer tenure if Republicans win the next presidential election. As such, further disruptions and unforeseen developments are likely to occur. This highlights the importance of ongoing vigilance and the necessity of developing proactive risk mitigation and adaptation strategies. While this chapter has offered a high-level overview, future research should explore these issues in greater depth – for example, by examining the specific impacts of Trump-era policies on AI regulation and governance and proposing concrete mitigation and adaptation strategies.

---

29 Note that Trump is threatening tariffs and restrictions on countries perceived to be unfairly regulating U.S. tech firms, citing measures such as the DSA, DMA, and digital services taxes as examples (Trump, 2025).

References

American Association for the Advancement of Science. (2025). FY 2026 R&D Appropriations Dashboard. https://www.aaas.org/news/fy-2026-rd-appropriations-dashboard (last accessed: December 30, 2025).

American Federation Government Employees. (2025). Appeal to Defend Civil Service Protections and the Mission of the National Science Foundation. https://democrats-science.house.gov/imo/media/doc/AFGE_Local_3403_NSF_Letter_to_RM_Lofgren_REDACTED_Redacted.pdf (last accessed: December 30, 2025).

Amnesty International. (2019). Surveillance Giants. https://www.amnesty.org/en/documents/pol30/1404/2019/en/ (last accessed: December 30, 2025).

Associated Press. (2025a). Trump Administration Says It Won't Publish Major Climate Change Reports on NASA Website As Promised. https://apnews.com/article/climate-change-nasa-reports-trump-hidden-doc-1ade1eb89bb4785f7cdd6e1d6ba31a21 (last accessed: December 30, 2025).

Associated Press. (2025b). House Republicans Include a 10-Year Ban on US States Regulating AI in 'Big, Beautiful' Bill. https://apnews.com/article/ai-regulation-state-moratorium-congress-39d1c8a0758ffe0242283bb82f66d51a (last accessed: December 30, 2025).

Australian Energy Council. (2023). Data Centers: A 24-Hour Power Source? https://www.energycouncil.com.au/analysis/data-centres-a-24hr-power-source/ (last accessed: December 30, 2025).

Badea, L. & Mungiu-Pupăzan, M. (2021). The Economic and Environmental Impact of Bitcoin. IEEE Access 9. 48091–48104.

Bender, E., Gebru, T., McMillan-Major, A., & Shmitchell, S. (2021). On the Dangers of Stochastic Parrots. FAccT'21: Proceedings of the 2021 ACM Conference on Fairness, Accountability, and Transparency. 610–623.

Biden White House. (2022a). Blueprint for an AI Bill of Rights. https://bidenwhitehouse.archives.gov/wp-content/uploads/2022/10/Blueprint-for-an-AI-Bill-of-Rights.pdf (last accessed: December 30, 2025).

Biden White House (2022b). Fact Sheet. https://bidenwhitehouse.archives.gov/ostp/news-updates/2022/09/08/fact-sheet-climate-and-energy-implications-of-crypto-assets-in-the-united-states/ (last accessed: December 30, 2025).

Biden White House. (2023a). Fact Sheet. https://bidenwhitehouse.archives.gov/briefing-room/statements-releases/2023/10/30/fact-sheet-president-biden-issues-executive-order-on-safe-secure-and-trustworthy-artificial-intelligence/ (last accessed: December 30, 2025).

Biden White House. (2023b). Executive Order on the Safe, Secure, and Trustworthy Development and Use of Artificial Intelligence. https://bidenwhitehouse.archives.gov/briefing-room/presidential-actions/2023/10/30/executive-order-on-the-safe-secure-and-trustworthy-development-and-use-of-artificial-intelligence/ (last accessed: December 30, 2025).

Bloomberg. (2025). OpenAI Is Working With US Military on Cybersecurity Tools. https://www.bloomberg.com/news/articles/2024-01-16/openai-working-with-us-military-on-cybersecurity-tools-for-veterans (last accessed: December 30, 2025).

Brennan Center for Justice. (2025). Million-Dollar Donors Flooded Trump's Second Inauguration. https://www.brennancenter.org/our-work/research-reports/million-dollar-donors-flooded-trumps-second-inauguration (last accessed: December 30, 2025).

Buolamwini, J. (2016). How I'm Fighting Bias in Algorithms. https://www.ted.com/talks/joy_buolamwini_how_i_m_fighting_bias_in_algorithms (last accessed: December 30, 2025).

Buolamwini, J. (2023). Unmasking AI. New York, Random House.

Buolamwini, J. & Gebru, T. (2018). Gender Shades. Proceedings of Machine Learning Research 81. 1–15.

Business and Human Rights Resource Centre. (2025a). USA: Senate Votes 99-1, Rejecting a 10-Year Ban on AI Regulation. https://www.business-humanrights.org/en/latest-news/usa-senate-votes-99-1-rejecting-a-10-year-ban-on-ai-regulation/ (last accessed: December 30, 2025).

Business and Human Rights Resource Centre. (2025b). Experts Warn X's AI Fact-Checkers Could Fuel Misinformation. https://www.business-humanrights.org/en/latest-news/experts-warn-xs-ai-fact-checkers-could-fuel-misinformation/ (last accessed: December 30, 2025).

Callaway, E. (2025). 'It is Chaos': US Funding Freezes Are Endangering Global Health. Nature. 6 February 2025. https://www.nature.com/articles/d41586-025-00385-9 (last accessed: December 30, 2025).

CNN. (2025). DOGE is Building a Master Database for Immigration Enforcement, Sources Say. https://www.cnn.com/2025/04/25/politics/doge-building-master-database-immigration/index.html (last accessed: December 30, 2025).

Coinbase. (2025). Righting a Major Wrong. https://www.coinbase.com/en-ca/blog/righting-a-major-wrong (last accessed: December 30, 2025).

Columbia University. (2025). Climate Backtracker. https://climate.law.columbia.edu/content/climate-backtracker (last accessed: December 30, 2025).

Congress.Gov. (2025). GENIUS Act. https://www.congress.gov/bill/119th-congress/senate-bill/394/text (last accessed: December 30, 2025).

Dachwitz, I. & Hilbig, S. (2025). Digitaler Kolonialismus. Munich. C.H. Beck.

European Commission. (2025). The General-Purpose AI Code of Practice. https://digital-strategy.ec.europa.eu/en/policies/contents-code-gpai (last accessed: December 30, 2025).

Executive Office of the President/Office of Management and Budget. (2025). Discretionary Funding Levels for Fiscal Year 2026. https://www.whitehouse.gov/wp-content/uploads/2025/05/Fiscal-Year-2026-Discretionary-Budget-Request.pdf (last accessed: December 30, 2025).

Federal Trade Commission/FTC. (2019). Video Social Networking App Musical.ly Agrees to Settle FTC Allegations That It Violated Children's Privacy Law. https://www.ftc.gov/news-events/news/press-releases/2019/02/video-social-networking-app-musically-agrees-settle-ftc-allegations-it-violated-childrens-privacy (last accessed: December 30, 2025).

Federal Trade Commission/FTC. (2024). FTC Investigation Leads to Lawsuit Against TikTok and ByteDance for Flagrantly Violating Children's Privacy Law. https://www.ftc.gov/news-events/news/press-releases/2024/08/ftc-investigation-leads-lawsuit-against-tiktok-bytedance-flagrantly-violating-childrens-privacy-law (last accessed: December 30, 2025).

Feichtner. I. (2019). Sharing the Riches of the Sea. European Journal of International Law 30(2). 601–633.

Feichtner. I. & Ranganathan, S. (2019). International Law and Economic Exploitation in the Global Commons: Introduction. European Journal of International Law 30(2). 541–546.

Floridi, L. (2023). The Ethics of Artificial Intelligence. Oxford, Oxford University Press.

Forbes. (2025). Here's How Much the Trump Kids Have Made Because of the Presidency. https://www.forbes.com/sites/danalexander/2025/09/22/heres-how-much-the-trump-kids-have-made-because-of-the-presidency/?ctpv=searchpage (last accessed: December 30, 2025).

Foucault, M. (1995). Discipline and Punish. New York, Vintage.

Foucault, M. (2000). Power. New York, The New Press.

Friedman, B. & Nissenbaum, H. (1996). Bias in Computer Systems. ACM Transactions on Information Systems 14(3). 330–347.

Gellman, B. (2021). Dark Mirror. New York, Penguin Books.

Greenwald, G. (2015). No Place to Hide. New York, Picador.

Haugen, F. (2023). The Power of One. New York, Little, Brown, and Company.

Hao, K. (2025). Empire of AI. New York, Penguin.

Hill, K. (2023). Your Face Belongs to Us. New York, Random House.

Huynh, A., Duong, D., Burggraf, T., Luong, H., & Bu, N. (2022). Energy Consumption and Bitcoin Market. Asia-Pacific Financial Markets 29. 79–93.

Institute for Human Rights and Business. (2016). Data Brokers and Human Rights. https://www.ihrb.org/resources/data-brokers-big-data-big-business (last accessed: December 30, 2025).

International Energy Agency. (2025). Global Critical Minerals Outlook 2025. https://www.iea.org/reports/global-critical-minerals-outlook-2025 (last accessed: December 30, 2025).

International Seabed Authority (ISA). (2025a). The Secretary General. https://www.isa.org.jm/the-secretary-general/ (last accessed: December 30, 2025).

International Seabed Authority (ISA). (2025b). About ISA. https://www.isa.org.jm/about-isa/ (last accessed: December 30, 2025).

Isaacson, W. (2023). Elon Musk. New York, Simon & Schuster.

Joint Congressional Committee on Inaugural Ceremonies. (2025). 60th Inaugural Ceremonies. https://www.inaugural.senate.gov/60th-inaugural-ceremonies/ (last accessed: December 30, 2025).

Josephson, P. (2025). Totalitarian Science in the White House. https://www.commondreams.org/opinion/trump-totalitarian-science (last accessed: December 30, 2025).

Kahan. D. (2013). Ideology, Motivated Reasoning, and Cognitive Reflection. Judgment and Decision Making 8(4). 407–424.

Kahneman, D. (2011). Thinking, Fast and Slow. London, Allen Lane.

Kara, S. (2023). Cobalt Red. New York, St. Martin's Press.

Kohli, V., Chakravarty, S., Chamola, V., Singh Sangwan, K., & Zeadally, S. (2023). An Analysis of Energy Consumption and Carbon Footprints of Cryptocurrencies and Possible Solutions. Digital Communications and Networks 9(1). 79–89.

Lewis, M. (2023). Going Infinite. New York, Norton.

Li, F.-F. (2023). The Worlds I See. New York. Flatiron Books.

Li, P., Yang, J., Islam, M., & Ren, S. (2025). Making AI Less 'Thirsty': Uncovering and Addressing the Secret Water Footprint of AI Models. https://arxiv.org/pdf/2304.03271 (last accessed: December 30, 2025).

Lockheed Martin. (2025). Golden Dome for America. https://www.lockheedmartin.com/en-us/capabilities/missile-defense/golden-dome-missile-defense.html (last accessed: December 30, 2025).

Luccioni, A., Viguier, S., & Ligozat, A.-L. (2022). Estimating the Carbon Footprint of BLOOM, A 176B Parameter Language Model. https://arxiv.org/pdf/2211.02001 (last accessed: December 30, 2025).

McIntyre, L. (2018). Post-Truth. Cambridge, MIT Press.

McIntyre, L. (2021). How to Talk to a Science Denier. Cambridge, MIT Press.

McKinsey & Company. (2023). Investing in the Rising Data Center Economy. https://www.mckinsey.com/~/media/mckinsey/industries/technology%20media%20and%20telecommunications/high%20tech/our%20insights/investing%20in%20the%20rising%20data%20center%20economy/investing-in-the-rising-data-center-economy_final.pdf (last accessed: December 30, 2025).

Miller, K., Thompson, K., Johnston, P., & Santillo, D. (2018). An Overview of Seabed Mining Including the Current State of Development, Environmental Impacts, and Knowledge Gaps. Frontiers in Marine Science 4. 418.

Mother Jones. (2025). The Shocking Far-Right Agenda Behind the Facial Recognition Tech Used by ICE and the FBI. https://www.motherjones.com/politics/2025/04/clearview-ai-immigration-ice-fbi-surveillance-facial-recognition-hoan-ton-that-hal-lambert-trump/ (last accessed: December 30, 2025).

Muldoon, J., Graham, M., & Cant, C. (2025). Feeding the Machine. Edinburgh, Canongate.

Narayanan, A. & Kapoor, S. (2024). AI Snake Oil. Princeton, Princeton University Press.

National Science Foundation. (2025). FY 2026 Budget Request to Congress. https://nsf-gov-resources.nsf.gov/files/00-NSF-FY26-CJ-Entire-Rollup.pdf (last accessed: December 30, 2025).

Nest, M. (2013). Coltan. Cambridge, Polity.

New York Times. (2017). Peter Thiel, Trump's Tech Pal, Explains Himself. https://www.nytimes.com/2017/01/11/fashion/peter-thiel-donald-trump-silicon-valley-technology-gawker.html (last accessed: December 30, 2025).

New York Times. (2020). The Secretive Company That Might End Privacy As We Know It. https://www.nytimes.com/2020/01/18/technology/clearview-privacy-facial-recognition.html (last accessed: December 30, 2025).

New York Times. (2024). A.I. Beings Ushering in an Age of Killer Robots. https://www.nytimes.com/2024/07/02/technology/ukraine-war-ai-weapons.html (last accessed: December 30, 2025).
New York Times. (2025a). Trump Has Cut Science Funding to Its Lowest Level in Decades. https://www.nytimes.com/interactive/2025/05/22/upshot/nsf-grants-trump-cuts.html (last accessed: December 30, 2025).
New York Times. (2025b). All of the Trump Administration's Major Moves in the First 100 Days – Climate, Education, and Health Sections. https://www.nytimes.com/interactive/2025/us/trump-agenda-2025.html?categories=Health%2CEducation%2CClimate (last accessed: December 30, 2025).
New York Times. (2025c). All of the Trump Administration's Major Moves in the First 100 Days – DEI Section. https://www.nytimes.com/interactive/2025/us/trump-agenda-2025.html?categories=D.E.I (last accessed: December 30, 2025).
New York Times. (2025d). These Words Are Disappearing in the New Trump Administration. https://www.nytimes.com/interactive/2025/03/07/us/trump-federal-agencies-websites-words-dei.html (last accessed: December 30, 2025).
New York Times. (2025e). Blackburn Backs Down on A.I. Moratorium Compromise. https://www.nytimes.com/2025/06/30/us/politics/senates-new-ai-moratorium-proposal-draws-fresh-criticism.html (last accessed: December 30, 2025).
New York Times. (2025f). Elon Musk's Business Empire Scores Benefits Under Trump Shake-Up. https://www.nytimes.com/2025/02/11/us/politics/elon-musk-companies-conflicts.html (last accessed: December 30, 2025).
New York Times. (2025g). Musk Is Positioned to Profit Off Billions in New Government Contracts. https://www.nytimes.com/2025/03/23/us/politics/spacex-contracts-musk-doge-trump.html (last accessed: December 30, 2025).
New York Times. (2025h). How X is Benefiting as Musk Advises Trump. https://www.nytimes.com/2025/04/07/technology/elon-musk-x-trump.html (last accessed: December 30, 2025).
New York Times. (2025i). Trump Unveils Plans for 'Golden Dome' Missile Defense System. https://www.nytimes.com/2025/05/20/us/politics/trump-golden-dome.html?searchResultPosition=2 (last accessed: December 30, 2025).
New York Times. (2025j). Trump Taps Palantir to Compile Data on Americans. https://www.nytimes.com/2025/05/30/technology/trump-palantir-data-americans.html (last accessed: December 30, 2025).
New York Times. (2025k). Palantir's Collection of Disease Data at C.D.C. Stirs Privacy Concerns. https://www.nytimes.com/2025/06/06/health/cdc-data-privacy-palantir.html (last accessed: December 30, 2025).
New York Times. (2025l). Even Before His Return to the White House, Trump Was Becoming a Crypto Czar. https://www.nytimes.com/2025/06/13/us/politics/trump-disclosure-cryptocurrency.html (last accessed: December 30, 2025).
New York Times. (2025m). Secret Deals, Foreign Investments, Presidential Policy Changes: The Rise of Trump's Crypto Firm. https://www.nytimes.com/2025/04/29/us/politics/trump-crypto-world-liberty-financial.html (last accessed: December 30, 2025).
New York Times. (2025n). As Truth Social Business Struggles, Trump Media Goes Big on Crypto. https://www.nytimes.com/2025/07/09/business/truth-social-trump-media-crypto.html (last accessed: December 30, 2025).
New York Times. (2025o). S.E.C. Moves to Scale Back Its Crypto Enforcement Efforts. https://www.nytimes.com/2025/02/04/business/sec-crypto-task-force.html (last accessed: December 30, 2025).
New York Times. (2025p) Trump Family Bitcoin Company Announces Plan to Go Public. https://www.nytimes.com/2025/05/12/business/trump-american-bitcoin-crypto.html (last accessed: December 30, 2025).
New York Times. (2025q). The 'Trump Pump': How Crypto Lobbying Won Over a President. https://www.nytimes.com/2025/07/09/us/politics/trump-crypto-lobbying.html (last accessed: December 30, 2025).

New York Times. (2025r). Senate Passes Cryptocurrency Bill, Handing Industry a Victory. https://www.nytimes.com/2025/06/17/us/politics/senate-cryptocurrency-bill.html?smid=url-share (last accessed: December 30, 2025).

New York Times. (2025s). Mining Company Seeks Trump Support to Shortcut Access to Seabed Metals. https://www.nytimes.com/2025/03/27/climate/mining-company-seeks-trump-support-to-shortcut-access-to-seabed-metals.html (last accessed: December 30, 2025).

New York Times. (2025t). Trump Takes a Major Step Toward Seabed Mining in International Waters. https://www.nytimes.com/2025/04/24/climate/trump-seabed-mining.html (last accessed: December 30, 2025).

New York Times. (2025u). U.S. Takes Another Step Toward Opening the Seabed for Mining. https://www.nytimes.com/2025/05/21/climate/trump-seabed-mining-impossible-metals-american-samoa.html (last accessed: December 30, 2025).

New York Times. (2025v). What to Know About the Three Crypto Regulation Bills in Congress. https://www.nytimes.com/2025/07/17/us/politics/crypto-regulation-bills-explainer.html (last accessed: December 30, 2025).

New York Times. (2025w). In the Trump Administration, Watchdogs Are Watching Their Backs. https://www.nytimes.com/2025/07/17/us/politics/inspectors-general-trump.html (last accessed: December 30, 2025).

New York Times. (2025x). As Trump Attacks Universities, Some Are Agreeing to Negotiate. https://www.nytimes.com/article/trump-university-college.html?searchResultPosition=1 (last accessed: December 30, 2025).

New York Times. (2025y). The Militarization of Silicon Valley. https://www.nytimes.com/2025/08/04/technology/google-meta-openai-military-war.html (last accessed: December 30, 2025).

New York Times. (2025z). Trump Has Made Himself Commander-in-Chief of the Chip Industry. https://www.nytimes.com/2025/08/13/technology/trump-chips-nvidia-intel.html (last accessed: December 30, 2025).

O'Neil, C. (2016). Weapons of Math Destruction. New York, Penguin.

Oreskes, N. (2021). Why Trust Science? Princeton, Princeton University Press.

Oreskes, N. & Conway, E. (2011). Merchants of Doubt. New York, Bloomsbury.

Oreskes, N. & Conway, E. (2023). The Big Myth. New York, Bloomsbury.

Owusu-Sekyere, K., Batteiger, A., Afoblikame, R., Hafner, G., & Kranert, M. (2022). Assessing Data in the Informal E-Waste Sector: The Agbogbloshie Scrapyard. Waste Management 139. 158–167.

Pariser, E. (2011). The Filter Bubble. New York, Penguin Press.

Pasquale, F. (2016). The Black Box Society. Cambridge, Harvard University Press.

Patterson, D., Gonzalez, J., Le, Q., Liang, C., Munguia, L.-M., Rothchild, D., So, D., Texier, M., & Dean, J. (2021). Carbon Emissions and Large Neural Network Training. https://arxiv.org/abs/2104.10350 (last accessed: December 30, 2025).

Payne, K. (2021). I, Warbot. Oxford, Oxford University Press.

Politico. (2025a). Victory for Trump as EU Backs Down on Digital Taxes in Next Budget. https://www.politico.eu/article/victory-eu-donald-trump-meta-tax-digital/ (last accessed: December 30, 2025).

Politico. (2025b). Trump Fires Statistics Chief After Soft Jobs Report. https://www.politico.com/news/2025/08/01/trump-firing-bureau-labor-statistics-chief-jobs-report-00488960 (last accessed: December 30, 2025).

Politico. (2025c). Tech, Crypto, Tobacco, Other Companies Fund Trump's White House Ballroom. https://www.politico.com/news/2025/10/23/trump-ballroom-donors-list-00620230?nid=0000015a-dd3e-d536-a37b-dd7fd8af0000&nname=playbook-pm&nrid=d7cb7e15-6d6b-4706-953a-6b30edf4c64f (last accessed: December 30, 2025).

Prescott, J. (2024). Project 2025. Washington, Heritage Foundation.

Quinn, M. (2024). Ethics for the Information Age. Hoboken, Pearson.

Reich, R. (2025). Peter Thiel's Palantir Poses a Grave Threat to Americans. https://www.theguardian.com/commentisfree/2025/jun/30/peter-thiel-palantir-threat-to-americans (last accessed: December 30, 2025).

Reuters. (2025a). Microsoft Likely to Sign EU AI Code of Practice, Meta Rebuffs Guidelines. https://www.reuters.com/sustainability/boards-policy-regulation/microsoft-likely-sign-eu-ai-code-practice-meta-rebuffs-guidelines-2025-07-18/ (last accessed: December 30, 2025).

Reuters. (2025b). Trump Says Intel Has Agreed to Deal for US to Take 10% Equity Stake. https://www.reuters.com/business/trump-says-intel-has-agreed-deal-us-take-10-equity-stake-2025-08-22/ (last accessed: December 30, 2025).

Risen, C. (2025). Red Scare. New York, Scribner.

Securities and Exchange Commission. (2025a). The Journey Begins. https://www.sec.gov/newsroom/speeches-statements/peirce-journey-begins-020425 (last accessed: December 30, 2025).

Securities and Exchange Commission. (2025b). SEC Report Coinbase Global, Inc. https://www.sec.gov/ix?doc=/Archives/edgar/data/1679788/000119312525031346/d857645d8k.htm (last accessed: December 30, 2025).

Siddiqui, F. (2025). Hubris Maximus. New York, St. Martin's Press.

Snowden, E. (2019). Permanent Record. New York, Metropolitan Books.

Snyder, T. (2017). On Tyranny. New York, Tim Duggan Books.

Standing, G. (2023). The Blue Commons. London, Pelican Books.

Stargate Project. (2025). Shaping the Future of AI Infrastructure. https://stargateprojects.net/ (last accessed: December 30, 2025).

Statista. (2024). China Leads Critical Minerals Production. https://www.statista.com/chart/32748/top-countries-processing-critical-minerals/ (last accessed: December 30, 2025).

Statista. (2025). Bitcoin Energy Consumption Worldwide from February 2017 to May 19, 2025. https://www.statista.com/statistics/881472/worldwide-bitcoin-energy-consumption/ (last accessed: December 30, 2025).

Steinberger, M. (2025). The Philosopher in the Valley: Alex Karp, Palantir, and the Rise of the Surveillance State. New York, Simon & Schuster.

Thaler, R. & Sunstein, C. (2008/2009). Nudge. London, Penguin.

The Globe and Mail. (2025). Trump Revokes Biden-Era Order Which Aimed to Combat Anti-Competitive Practices. https://www.theglobeandmail.com/business/article-trump-revokes-biden-era-order-which-aimed-to-combat-anti-competitive/ (last accessed: December 30, 2025).

The Guardian. (2023). US Air Force Denies Running Simulation in Which AI Drone 'Killed' Operator. https://www.theguardian.com/us-news/2023/jun/01/us-military-drone-ai-killed-operator-simulated-test (last accessed: December 30, 2025).

The Guardian. (2025a). Elon Musk's Mass Government Cuts Could Make Private Companies Millions. https://www.theguardian.com/technology/2025/feb/16/elon-musk-doge-government-privatization (last accessed: December 30, 2025).

The Guardian. (2025b). 'Silicon Six' Accused of Avoiding Almost $278bn in US Corporation Taxes Over 10 Years. https://www.theguardian.com/us-news/2025/apr/15/silicon-six-accused-of-avoiding-almost-278bn-in-us-corporation-taxes-over-10-years (last accessed: December 30, 2025).

The Guardian. (2025c). 'Headed for Technofascism': The Rightwing Roots of Silicon Valley. https://www.theguardian.com/technology/ng-interactive/2025/jan/29/silicon-valley-rightwing-technofascism (last accessed: December 30, 2025).

The Guardian. (2025d). Trump's New 'Gold Standard' Rule Will Destroy American Science As We Know It. https://www.theguardian.com/commentisfree/2025/may/29/trump-american-science (last accessed: December 30, 2025).

The Guardian. (2025e). Documents Offer Rare Insight On ICE's Close Relationship With Palantir. https://www.theguardian.com/us-news/ng-interactive/2025/sep/22/ice-palantir-data (last accessed: December 30, 2025).

The Independent. (2024). Elon Musk's Wealth Jumps By $170bn Since Election After He Backed Trump With $277m. https://www.independent.co.uk/news/world/americas/elon-musk-net-worth-trump-b2665395.html (last accessed: December 30, 2025).

The Wall Street Journal. (2025a). Meta Fired Palmer Luckey. Now, They're Teaming Up on A Defense Contract. https://www.wsj.com/tech/meta-army-vr-headsets-anduril-palmer-luckey-142ab72a?st=AFcxj5&reflink=desktopwebshare_permalink (last accessed: December 30, 2025).

The Wall Street Journal. (2025b). U.S. Investors, Trump Close In On TikTok Deal With China. https://www.wsj.com/tech/details-emerge-on-u-s-china-tiktok-deal-594e009f (last accessed: December 30, 2025).

Thiel, P. (2009). The Education of a Libertarian. https://archive.ph/p2yrX (last accessed: December 30, 2025).

Thiel, P. (2014). Zero to One. New York, Crown Business.

Trump/Vance Inaugural Committee. (2025). Inauguration of the 45th and 47th President of the United States of America. https://web.archive.org/web/20250130012456/https://t47inaugural.com/ (last accessed: December 30, 2025).

Trump, D. (2025). Truth Social Post, August 26, 2025. https://truthsocial.com/@realDonaldTrump/posts/115092243259973570 (last accessed: December 30, 2025).

Trump White House. (2025a). Removing Barriers to American Leadership in Artificial Intelligence. https://www.whitehouse.gov/presidential-actions/2025/01/removing-barriers-to-american-leadership-in-artificial-intelligence/ (last accessed: December 30, 2025).

Trump White House. (2025b). Restoring Freedom of Speech and Ending Federal Censorship. https://www.whitehouse.gov/presidential-actions/2025/01/restoring-freedom-of-speech-and-ending-federal-censorship/ (last accessed: December 30, 2025).

Trump White House. (2025c). Stopping Waste, Fraud, and Abuse by Eliminating Information Silos. https://www.whitehouse.gov/presidential-actions/2025/03/stopping-waste-fraud-and-abuse-by-eliminating-information-silos/ (last accessed: December 30, 2025).

Trump White House. (2025d). Strengthening American Leadership in Digital Financial Technology. https://www.whitehouse.gov/presidential-actions/2025/01/strengthening-american-leadership-in-digital-financial-technology/ (last accessed: December 30, 2025).

Trump White House. (2025e). Fact Sheet. https://www.whitehouse.gov/fact-sheets/2025/01/fact-sheet-executive-order-to-establish-united-states-leadership-in-digital-financial-technology/ (last accessed: December 30, 2025).

Trump White House. (2025f). Establishment of the Strategic Bitcoin Reserve and United States Digital Asset Stockpile. https://www.whitehouse.gov/presidential-actions/2025/03/establishment-of-the-strategic-bitcoin-reserve-and-united-states-digital-asset-stockpile/ (last accessed: December 30, 2025).

Trump White House. (2025g). Unleashing America's Offshore Critical Minerals and Resources. https://www.whitehouse.gov/presidential-actions/2025/04/unleashing-americas-offshore-critical-minerals-and-resources/ (last accessed: December 30, 2025).

Trump White House. (2025h). White House Unveils America's AI Action Plan. https://www.whitehouse.gov/articles/2025/07/white-house-unveils-americas-ai-action-plan/ (last accessed: December 30, 2025).

Trump White House. (2025i). Winning the Race. America's AI Action Plan. https://www.whitehouse.gov/wp-content/uploads/2025/07/Americas-AI-Action-Plan.pdf.

Trump White House. (2025j). AI.Gov. https://www.ai.gov/#home-services-anchor (last accessed: December 30, 2025).

Trump White House. (2025k). Fact Sheet. https://www.whitehouse.gov/fact-sheets/2025/04/fact-sheet-president-donald-j-trump-modernizes-defense-acquisitions-and-spurs-innovation-in-the-defense-industrial-base/ (last accessed: December 30, 2025).
Trump White House. (2025l). Letter to the Smithsonian: Internal Review of Smithsonian Exhibitions and Materials. https://www.whitehouse.gov/briefings-statements/2025/08/letter-to-the-smithsonian-internal-review-of-smithsonian-exhibitions-and-materials/ (last accessed: December 30, 2025).
Trump White House. (2025m). Saving TikTok While Protecting National Security. https://www.whitehouse.gov/presidential-actions/2025/09/saving-tiktok-while-protecting-national-security/ (last accessed: December 30, 2025).
Trump White House. (2025n). Ensuring a National Policy Framework for Artificial Intelligence. https://www.whitehouse.gov/presidential-actions/2025/12/eliminating-state-law-obstruction-of-national-artificial-intelligence-policy/ (last accessed: December 30, 2025).
U.N. Trade and Development. (2024). U.N. Digital Economy Report 2024. https://unctad.org/publication/digital-economy-report-2024 (last accessed: December 30, 2025).
U.S. Office of Government Ethics. (2025). Executive Branch Personnel Public Financial Disclosure Report. https://oge.app.box.com/s/k0hxcezgk7j1cyqoue16cillsi9srmfu (last accessed: December 30, 2025).
U.S. Congress. (2021). Uyghur Forced Labor Prevention Act. https://www.govinfo.gov/content/pkg/PLAW-117publ78/pdf/PLAW-117publ78.pdf (last accessed: December 30, 2025).
U.S. Congress. (2024). Protecting Americans from Foreign Adversary Controlled Applications Act. https://www.congress.gov/bill/118th-congress/house-bill/7521 (last accessed: December 30, 2025).
U.S. Space Force. (2025). About Us. https://www.spaceforce.mil/About-Us/ (last accessed: December 30, 2025).
U.S. Supreme Court. (2025). TikTok v. Garland. https://www.supremecourt.gov/opinions/24pdf/24-656_new_3dq3.pdf (last accessed: December 30, 2025).
Walzer, M. (2015). Just and Unjust Wars. New York, Basic Books.
Washington Post. (2024). Israel Built an 'AI Factory' for War: It Unleashed It in Gaza. https://www.washingtonpost.com/technology/2024/12/29/ai-israel-war-gaza-idf/ (last accessed: December 30, 2025).
Washington Post. (2025). Palantir Gets $10 Billion Contract from U.S. Army. https://www.washingtonpost.com/technology/2025/07/31/palantir-army-contract-10bn/ (last accessed: December 30, 2025).
Webb, K. (2004a). Understanding the Voluntary Codes Phenomenon. In: Webb, K. (ed.). Voluntary Codes. Ottawa, Carleton Research Unit for Innovation, Science, and Environment. 3–31.
Webb, K. (2004b). Voluntary Codes: Where to from here? In: Webb, K. (ed.). Voluntary Codes. Ottawa, Carleton Research Unit for Innovation, Science, and Environment. 379–402.
Webb, K. (2012). From De-Responsibilization to Re-Responsibilization. https://librarysearch.georgebrown.ca/discovery/fulldisplay/alma991004604479707310/01OCLS_BROWN:BROWN (last accessed: December 30, 2025).
Webb, K. & Morrison, A. (2004). The Law and Voluntary Codes: Examining the "Tangled Web." In: Webb, K. (ed.). Voluntary Codes. Ottawa, Carleton Research Unit for Innovation, Science, and Environment. 97–174.
Wired. (2023). ICE Records Reveal How Agents Abuse Access to Secret Data. https://www.wired.com/story/ice-agent-database-abuse-records/ (last accessed: December 30, 2025).
Wired. (2025). DOGE is Building a Master Database to Surveil and Track Immigrants. https://www.wired.com/story/doge-collecting-immigrant-data-surveil-track/ (last accessed: December 30, 2025).
World Health Organization. (2021). Children and Digital Dumpsites. https://www.who.int/publications/i/item/9789240023901 (last accessed: December 30, 2025).
Wörsdörfer, M. (2018). Engineering and Computer Ethics. Dubuque, Great River Learning.
Wörsdörfer, M. (2022a). What Happened to 'Big Tech' and Antitrust? And How to Fix Them! Philosophy of Management 21(3). 345–369.

Wörsdörfer, M. (2022b). Big Tech and Antitrust: An Ordoliberal Analysis. Philosophy & Technology 35. Article 85.
Wörsdörfer, M. (2024a). Biden's Executive Order on AI and the E.U.'s AI Act – A Comparative Computer- and Business-Ethical Analysis. Philosophy & Technology 37. Article 74.
Wörsdörfer, M. (2024b). 'Datafeudalism: The Domination of Modern Societies by Big Tech Companies': A Commentary. Philosophy & Technology 37. Article 86.
Wörsdörfer, M. (2025a). Biden's Executive Order on AI: Strengths, Weaknesses, and Possible Reform Steps. AI and Ethics 5(2). 1669–1683.
Wörsdörfer, M. (2025b). 'Regulating the Undefined: Addressing Systemic Risks in the Digital Services Act' – A Commentary. Philosophy & Technology 38. Article 76.
Wynn-Williams, S. (2025). Careless People. New York, Flatiron Books.
Zuboff, S. (2015). Big Other: Surveillance Capitalism and the Prospects of an Information Civilization. Journal of Information Technology 30. 75–89.
Zuboff, S. (2019). The Age of Surveillance Capitalism. New York. Public Affairs.
Zuckerberg, M. (2025). Meta Announcement. https://www.instagram.com/reel/DEhf2uTJUs0/?igsh=dHVxbmdrbW9xMzg (last accessed: December 30, 2025).

Chapter 5
California's AI Act versus the E.U.'s AI Act: a comparative ordoliberal analysis

Abstract: This chapter provides a comparative analysis of two prominent artificial intelligence (AI) regulatory frameworks: the E.U.'s AI Act (AIA) and California's Transparency in Frontier AI Act (TFAIA). Against the backdrop of a deregulatory, market-driven federal approach in the United States, California has adopted a precautionary, governance-focused model aligned with E.U. standards, highlighting the global challenge of balancing innovation, safety, accountability, and ethics in AI regulation. While the AIA has been extensively studied, scholarly analysis of the TFAIA remains limited. Drawing on an ordoliberal-inspired framework ('ordoliberalism 2.0') and comparative approaches used in prior studies of U.S. AI executive orders, this chapter examines the strengths and weaknesses of both frameworks, comparing their scope, governance mechanisms, and ethical safeguards. It further explores potential reforms to 'harden' AI governance, offering insights for policymakers, researchers, and industry stakeholders seeking effective strategies to manage AI risks while promoting responsible technological innovation.

Keywords: California's Transparency in Frontier AI Act, E.U.'s AI Act, ordoliberalism 2.0, AI ethics

5.1 Introduction

In early 2025, Biden's AI Executive Order (Wörsdörfer, 2024b, 2025c) was revoked and replaced with Executive Order 14179, *Removing Barriers to American Leadership in AI* (Trump White House, 2025a). This directive rolled back prior safety regulations, prioritizing innovation, entrepreneurial activity, and U.S. leadership in AI over mandates on safety standards, content watermarking, and national security risk assessments. By summer 2025, the administration launched a broader initiative emphasizing market liberalization, reduced federal oversight, and the removal of what it described as partisan bias in AI systems. Measures included banning federal procurement of ideologically biased AI tools, fast-tracking AI data center permits, promoting AI exports, and relaxing environmental and DEI regulations – framed publicly as efforts to counter perceived 'woke' influences and secure U.S. dominance over China in AI development (Trump White House, 2025b, 2025c, 2025d).

Against this backdrop of a deregulatory, market-driven federal approach, California has pursued a markedly different strategy, favoring a risk-aware/sensitive, governance-focused model more closely aligned with European regulatory frameworks

 | https://doi.org/10.1515/9783112245958-006

(Wörsdörfer, 2024a, 2024b, 2025a), as exemplified by its Transparency in Frontier Artificial Intelligence Act (TFAIA). This contrast underscores a broader challenge in global AI governance: designing legislative frameworks that simultaneously foster innovation and safeguard public interests, including safety, accountability, and democratic values. By diverging from federal priorities, California demonstrates how subnational actors can adopt precautionary measures to manage AI risks while continuing to promote technological development.

California's approach also exemplifies the broader, global discourse on AI governance: As AI increasingly influences economic, social, and political domains, policymakers internationally are compelled to establish regulatory frameworks that reconcile technological innovation with ethical and societal responsibility. Among the most prominent examples are the E.U.'s Artificial Intelligence Act (AIA) and California's TFAIA. While the AIA has received substantial scholarly attention, with numerous studies assessing its strengths and proposing ways to 'harden' its governance framework, analysis of the TFAIA remains limited, primarily confined to journalistic and popular sources (Freedman & Patel, 2025; Hunton Andrews Kurth, 2025; NBC News, 2025; New York Times, 2025; Vox, 2025). This chapter seeks to fill that gap by providing a systematic comparative analysis of both legislative instruments from the perspectives of computer and AI ethics, as well as business ethics, drawing on an ordoliberal-inspired framework (termed 'ordoliberalism 2.0') and approaches similar to prior comparative studies of Biden's AI executive orders and the AIA (Wörsdörfer, 2023, 2025a, 2025b).

This chapter addresses three central research questions: What are the key strengths and weaknesses of the AIA and the TFAIA? How do these two regulatory frameworks compare in terms of scope, governance mechanisms, and ethical safeguards? And, finally, what measures could be adopted to enhance or 'harden' AI governance frameworks to better manage emerging risks while promoting responsible innovation? By exploring these questions, this chapter contributes to ongoing debates on AI ethics, policy, and regulation, highlighting areas of convergence and divergence between U.S. (state-level) and E.U. approaches.

This chapter is structured as follows. It begins with a summary of the AIA and TFAIA, highlighting their legislative objectives, governance mechanisms, and risk management provisions (Section 5.2). This is followed by a critical evaluation (Section 5.3) and a comparative analysis (Section 5.4) that identify strengths and weaknesses, as well as parallels and differences in scope, regulatory design, and ethical orientation. Building on this analysis, this chapter proposes potential reform measures to strengthen both frameworks (Section 5.5). The study concludes with a discussion of the broader implications for AI ethics and governance, offering insights for policymakers, researchers, and industry stakeholders seeking to navigate the rapidly evolving landscape of AI regulation (Section 5.6).

5.2 Key characteristics of the AI governance frameworks

The primary goal of the 2024 AIA is to establish a legal framework for secure, trustworthy, and ethical AI in the E.U., ensuring that AI systems are human-centric, safe, law-compliant, and respectful of fundamental rights (European Parliament & Council of the European Union, 2024). The Act builds on extensive stakeholder consultation, including the work of the High-Level Expert Group on AI's Ethics Guidelines for Trustworthy AI (2019) and the European Commission's White Paper on AI (2020), and forms part of the E.U.'s digital single market strategy and New Legislative Framework. It complements existing legislation such as the General Data Protection Regulation (GDPR), the Digital Services Act, the Digital Markets Act, and various sectoral regulatory initiatives.

The AIA applies to both private and public actors within and outside the E.U. if their AI systems have an impact on E.U. citizens. AI systems are broadly defined to include machine/deep learning, logic- and knowledge-based systems, and statistical approaches, with a technology-neutral, future-proof approach. The regulation distinguishes between three risk categories: prohibited, high-risk, and low- or minimal-risk AI systems. Prohibited systems pose unacceptable risks or violate fundamental rights (e.g., manipulative, exploitative, or social scoring systems, and specific biometric surveillance applications) (Title II, AIA). High-risk systems, such as AI for critical infrastructure, education, employment, essential public services, law enforcement, migration, and justice, must comply with strict ex ante requirements (i.e., risk management, data governance, transparency, human oversight, robustness, and cybersecurity), undergo conformity assessment, and be registered in an E.U.-wide public database (Title III). Low- or minimal-risk systems must meet general safety and transparency obligations, such as informing users when interacting with AI systems.

Governance is based on the ordoliberal principle of subsidiarity, with responsibilities shared between the Commission and national competent authorities (Title VI). The newly established AI Office and European Artificial Intelligence Board (EAIB) coordinate national authorities, provide guidance, and promote best practices in the field of AI. Both ex ante conformity assessments and post-market monitoring are required, with providers obliged to report incidents and grant authorities access to data, as well as, under specific circumstances, source code. Noncompliance can result in fines of up to €35 million or 7% of global annual turnover (Title VIII).

The TFAIA, by contrast, was signed into law in 2025 (California State Legislature, 2025; Governor Newsom, 2025; see also Joint California Policy Working Group on AI Frontier Models, 2025). It establishes a comprehensive framework for the governance, oversight, and transparency of advanced AI systems, with a particular focus on foundation and especially frontier models – highly capable AI systems at the cutting edge of development. The legislation positions California as a leader in AI (governance), recognizing both the societal and economic opportunities presented by frontier AI and the potential catastrophic risks arising from its misuse, malfunctions, or loss of control. Transparency, whistleblower protections, incident reporting, governance, and precautionary measures are emphasized as essential for public trust and AI safety. The Act is specifically designed to focus on frontier developers without imposing undue burdens on smaller entities operating below frontier thresholds (Section 1, TFAIA).

Under the TFAIA, large frontier developers – those with annual revenues exceeding $500 million – are required to publish a publicly accessible frontier AI framework that details governance structures, risk and impact assessments, and mitigation strategies, as well as third-party review processes, cybersecurity measures, and internal oversight and due diligence mechanisms. Developers must also submit transparency reports before or concurrent with deploying new or substantially modified frontier models, including summaries of catastrophic risk assessments, third-party evaluations, and mitigation efforts. Critical safety incidents, such as loss of control resulting in harm or deceptive model behavior, must be reported to the Office of Emergency Services (OES) or relevant authorities within 15 days. If there is an imminent risk of serious injury or death, the incident must be reported within 24 h. The California Department of Technology (CDT) is responsible for periodically updating definitions and standards to keep pace with technological advancements. Violations of the Act may incur civil penalties of up to $1 million per occurrence (Section 2).

The Act also establishes a public AI computing consortium within the Government Operations Agency (GovOps) to develop CalCompute, a public cloud cluster supporting safe, ethical, equitable, and sustainable AI research. The consortium, comprising representatives from universities, labor organizations, public-interest groups, and AI experts, is tasked with submitting a comprehensive report to the Legislature by 2027, addressing infrastructure, governance, funding, workforce development, and potential partnerships (Section 3).

Finally, the TFAIA includes robust whistleblower protections, safeguarding employees involved in AI risk assessment and safety from retaliation when reporting potential catastrophic risks or violations. Developers are required to maintain internal mechanisms for anonymous reporting and to ensure that employees are informed of their rights and the confidentiality of disclosures. Overall, the TFAIA establishes a governance-/due diligence and transparency-driven framework that promotes accountability, public safety, and responsible innovation in frontier AI (Section 4).

5.3 Critical evaluation

5.3.1 Strengths of the AIA

Among the key ordoliberal strengths of the AIA are its legally binding nature, its extraterritorial scope and potential to expand the so-called 'Brussels effect,' its capacity to address data quality and discrimination risks, and its institutional innovations, such as the creation of the EAIB and the establishment of publicly accessible logs and databases for AI systems (Wörsdörfer, 2024a, 2024b, 2025a).

5.3.1.1 Legally binding framework

The AIA (European Parliament & Council of the European Union, 2024) represents the first comprehensive government initiative worldwide aimed at mitigating the potential negative impacts of AI systems. It is widely regarded as a milestone in the regulation of advanced computer technologies. What sets the AIA apart from earlier initiatives is its legally binding – i.e., hard law – character, imposing mandatory obligations on AI developers, operators, and users. This marks a decisive shift away from prior self-regulatory or soft law approaches to AI ethics (Attard-Frost et al., 2022; EPRS, 2022a; Fjeld et al., 2020; Häußermann & Lütge, 2022; Khanna, 2022; Leslie, 2019; Leslie et al., 2021; Mittelstadt, 2019; Rubenstein, 2021).

Such a legally binding framework is particularly significant given the inherent challenges posed by (generative) AI systems. Scholars such as Ebers (2022) highlight these systems' complexity, interconnectivity, reliance on correlation over causation, capacity for continuous adaptation, (semi-)autonomous behavior, and opacity, or black-box nature. These characteristics generate diverse ethical and societal concerns, including labor displacement, human enhancement via brain-computer interfaces, safety risks, accountability gaps, privacy violations, and algorithmic manipulation or discrimination (e.g., through profiling, political microtargeting, nudging, or the spread of disinformation) (Ebers, 2020; Wörsdörfer, 2025e). In light of these profound implications, regulatory intervention appears both necessary and overdue, particularly as many jurisdictions continue to face a regulatory vacuum. The AIA's central objective is to address these gaps and align ordoliberal-inspired governance structures with the rapid pace of technological advancement (Ebers, 2022).

Initially, the E.U. pursued a soft law approach through its nonbinding *Ethics Guidelines for Trustworthy AI and Policy and Investment Recommendations* (High-Level Expert Group on AI, 2019). However, the recognition of AI's complex societal and ethical challenges prompted a shift toward a hard law legislative strategy, culminating in a comprehensive, binding regulatory framework. These rules complement the E.U.'s existing product safety and consumer protection legislation while introducing provisions specific to AI. In contrast, the United States (at least at the federal level) and other countries have generally adopted a more laissez-faire approach, emphasizing voluntary standards and self-regulation (Trump White House, 2025a, 2025b, 2025c, 2025d).

5.3.1.2 Extraterritorial reach

Another commendable strength of the AIA is its acknowledgment of a post-Westphalian world order (Kobrin, 2009; Scherer & Palazzo, 2007, 2008; Scherer et al., 2014; Zumbansen, 2010a, 2010b, 2010c), as well as its explicit extraterritorial reach. Under Article 2, the AIA applies irrespective of where an AI system provider or operator is based, so long as their products or services affect E.U. citizens. This design prevents regulatory arbitrage, such as companies relocating to jurisdictions with weaker oversight, and ensures consistent protection across member states, a principle central to ordoliberalism 2.0 (AlgorithmWatch, 2021).

In doing so, the AIA has the potential to extend the 'Brussels effect' (Bradford, 2020; Petit, 2020) into the AI domain. This effect suggests that global companies often choose to comply with E.U. regulations, such as the GDPR – and potentially the AIA – even outside the E.U., as harmonized compliance across markets is more practical than maintaining divergent standards. Through this mechanism, the E.U. exerts de facto global regulatory influence, promoting its standards beyond its borders. Ideally, the AIA's leadership-by-example model could inspire similar AI legislation worldwide (besides the TFAIA), much as the GDPR influenced instruments such as the California Consumer Privacy Act (CCPA) and the California Privacy Rights Act (CPRA; Floridi, 2021).

The AIA also envisions an AI ecosystem that is ethically sound, legally acceptable, socially equitable, and environmentally sustainable, promoting AI as a force to serve the economy and society (Floridi, 2021). This vision aligns with the broader ordoliberal 2.0 idea that ethical conduct can strengthen markets rather than hinder them. Nonetheless, scholars caution that the AIA could go further in safeguarding consumer and fundamental rights, as well as in establishing mechanisms to redress harms caused by (generative) AI systems (see below) (Floridi, 2021).

5.3.1.3 Addressing data quality, discrimination, and innovation risks

The AIA's potential to mitigate key risk categories – data quality, discrimination, and innovation risks – is another notable strength (Hacker, 2021). It places particular emphasis on data quality by mandating that training datasets must be relevant, representative, error-free, and complete, and that protected groups be adequately represented. This establishes a foundation for an independent (and quasi-ordoliberal) data quality regime, a crucial step toward the responsible development of AI. However, as discussed later, further improvements could be made to strengthen the AIA's provisions against algorithmic bias and discrimination (Hacker, 2021).

5.3.1.4 Institutional innovation and transparency mechanisms

Finally, the establishment of the EAIB (Title VI) and the creation of a publicly accessible database for high-risk AI systems (Title VII) represent a significant step toward transparency and accountability. Under certain conditions, AI providers must grant authorities access to system logs and, if necessary, source code. These measures aim to enhance the understanding of AI's black box operations and echo calls by AlgorithmWatch (2021) and ordoliberalism 2.0 scholars (Wörsdörfer, 2023, 2025a, 2025b) for the establishment of public registers and improved data access for research in the public interest. If endowed with sufficient independence and transformed into a stakeholder forum, as proposed by the Council of the European Union (2022a, 2022b), the EAIB could become a cornerstone institution in the governance of AI within the E.U. and beyond.

5.3.2 Weaknesses of the AIA

Ordoliberal critics of the AIA highlight several weaknesses in its governance framework. Their main concerns relate to ineffective enforcement, limited oversight and control mechanisms, insufficient procedural and workers' rights, unclear institutional structures, inadequate funding and staffing, and the limited consideration of sustainability issues (Wörsdörfer, 2024a, 2024b, 2025a).[1] The following analysis discusses these limitations, beginning with governance and enforcement deficiencies.

5.3.2.1 Ineffective enforcement

A fundamental weakness of the AIA, as seen from an ordoliberal 2.0 perspective, lies in its (over-)reliance on self-assessment and standardization processes. In its current form, the AIA's governance model depends heavily on providers' self-monitoring – most notably through the ex ante conformity assessment procedure. This process is conducted by the provider itself rather than an independent third party, while state authorities intervene only ex post. As a result, AI providers retain significant discretion to determine whether a system qualifies as AI, whether it poses high risks, and how to comply with the AIA's mandatory requirements (Castets-Renard & Besse, 2022; Smuha et al., 2021). This discretion even allows them, at least in theory, to classify high-risk technologies as compliant under self-assessment procedures (EPRS, 2022a). Critics thus fear that the AIA's provisions on prohibited and high-risk AI practices could remain largely ineffective in the absence of independent monitoring.

1 Other notable points of criticism concern the AIA's overarching orientation and conceptual foundations. Ordoliberal and other critics argue that the Act tends to prioritize economic growth, business interests, and innovation over moral and ethical considerations, thereby de-prioritizing human rights and fundamental freedoms. Moreover, the definition of AI systems remains overly broad and imprecise, resulting in an unclear regulatory scope. The risk-based framework – central to the AIA's architecture – has also been criticized as conceptually flawed, featuring an incomplete list of prohibited AI practices and insufficient regulation of non-high-risk systems. Finally, the AIA has been called out for its failure to adequately address the specific challenges posed by generative AI, such as issues of content authenticity, disinformation, and accountability (Wörsdörfer, 2024a, 2024b, 2025a).

In addition to these discretionary powers, the AIA grants considerable leeway to standardization[2] and notified bodies.[3] Standardization – one of the Act's central provisions – requires providers to follow 'harmonized standards' developed by European standardization organizations such as CEN and CENELEC. However, delegating regulatory authority to such private associations raises ordoliberal 2.0 concerns about regulatory capture (Ebers, 2022). Notified bodies, which charge fees to providers for certification, may lack sufficient independence and impartiality (Cefaliello & Kullmann, 2022). The dominance of large AI providers, particularly big tech, further exacerbates capture risks (Laux et al., 2023a). Overall, the heavy reliance on self-regulation and corporate self-assessment could lead to under-regulation or circumvention of the Act's goals. This risk is amplified by the AIA's use of soft law instruments, such as voluntary codes of conduct (Title IX), for low-risk AI systems (Biber, 2021; Ebers et al., 2021; Stuurman & Lachaud, 2022).[4]

5.3.2.2 Limited oversight and control mechanisms

The delegation of rule-making powers to standardization organizations also raises ordoliberal 2.0 concerns regarding democratic legitimacy and judicial accountability (Castets-Renard & Besse, 2022; Ebers et al., 2021; Smuha et al., 2021).

- *Insufficient stakeholder participation*: Standardization processes often exclude or inadequately involve civil society and consumer representatives (Castets-Renard & Besse, 2022). Limited financial resources, expertise, and representation at the E.U. level further marginalize these actors (AlgorithmWatch, 2021; Micklitz & Gestel, 2013; Schepel, 2005; Veale & Zuiderveen Borgesius, 2021), resulting in weak democratic (input) legitimacy (Laux et al., 2023b).
- *Power asymmetries*: Industry actors typically exert significant influence in standard-setting, while civil society voices remain underrepresented, particularly given the lack of E.U.-level advocacy infrastructure for such groups (Castets-Renard & Besse, 2022).

2 Standardization bodies are responsible for developing harmonized, voluntary technical standards, for example, in fields such as electrical engineering.

3 Notified bodies (e.g., TÜV and other technical organizations) are designated and accredited by the notifying authorities of member states. They are responsible for conducting and verifying conformity assessments under the AIA. In principle, their activities should be independent, objective, and impartial; however, this is not always ensured in practice, as these bodies often receive commissions or fees from the AI providers they evaluate. Moreover, they are subject to specific information and reporting obligations as outlined in Articles 30–39 and 46 of the AIA.

4 The Commission has also introduced a voluntary code of practice for general-purpose AI providers, addressing transparency, copyright protection, and public safety. While nonbinding, it aims to guide industry actors in aligning with current/upcoming AIA obligations and is considered a form of soft law (European Commission, 2025).

- *Lack of transparency*: Many standardization and notified bodies operate with limited public visibility, often outsourcing testing and certification tasks to private third parties, thereby weakening independent oversight (Veale & Zuiderveen Borgesius, 2021).
- *Consensus challenges*: AI regulation inevitably entails normative debates, such as defining fairness, equality, and transparency, that require explicit value judgments. As Laux et al. (2023b) argue, these politically sensitive determinations should rest with democratically accountable institutions, such as the Commission and Parliament, rather than with technical standardization organizations lacking democratic oversight.
- *Techno-paternalism*: The AIA risks conflating trustworthiness with acceptability, effectively delegating ethical evaluation to technocratic experts and conformity assessors. This top-down model reinforces paternalism and technocracy, with limited public engagement and accountability, and, as a result, runs counter to the principles of ordoliberalism 2.0 (Laux et al., 2023a).

5.3.2.3 Shortcomings in legal recourse

Another significant shortcoming from an ordoliberal 2.0 perspective concerns the lack of procedural and judicial redress mechanisms. Individuals adversely affected by (generative) AI systems have no right to file complaints with market surveillance authorities, unlike the rights afforded under the GDPR, which allow individuals to lodge complaints and seek judicial remedies against supervisory authorities. In other words, the AIA does not create a legal avenue to sue providers, operators, or users for failures of AI systems – there is no mechanism to contest decisions or obtain redress. Similarly, civil rights organizations, consumer advocacy groups, and other interested parties lack the ability to submit representative complaints, as is possible under existing data protection law. Only entities subject to obligations under the AIA may challenge regulators' decisions, leaving those whose fundamental human rights are negatively impacted without recourse.

Given these inadequate complaint and judicial redress mechanisms, the AIA lacks a bottom-up force capable of holding providers or regulators accountable for weak enforcement, a deficiency particularly significant considering ordoliberalism 2.0's emphasis on liability. Put differently, the Act provides (almost) no effective means of private enforcement (i.e., individual enforcement rights) to compensate for the shortcomings of public enforcement (Castets-Renard & Besse, 2022; Ebers et al., 2021; EPRS, 2022a; Smuha et al., 2021; Veale & Zuiderveen Borgesius, 2021).

5.3.2.4 Inadequate safeguards for workers' rights

AI systems are increasingly used in human resource management for recruitment, task allocation, performance evaluation, and disciplinary procedures. While such applications can enhance efficiency and workplace safety, they also pose serious ethical risks, including privacy intrusions, algorithmic discrimination, and 'digital Taylorism' or techno-paternalism (Klump & Wörsdörfer, 2015). Continuous monitoring via wearables or Internet of Things devices can heighten stress and undermine autonomy, while potentially restricting workers' rights and union activities (Cefaliello & Kullmann, 2022; EPRS, 2022b).

Ordoliberal 2.0 critics argue that, compared with the GDPR and related E.U. instruments, the AIA offers weaker protection for workers' rights. The list of prohibited workplace AI practices remains narrow, and neither human oversight mechanisms nor standardization processes mandate the involvement of workers or social partners. The result is a regulatory imbalance that fails to counteract the power asymmetries between employers and employees (Cefaliello & Kullmann, 2022).[5]

5.3.2.5 Unclear institutional structure

The AIA's implementation involves seven(!) oversight institutions – market surveillance authorities, national supervisory authorities, notified authorities, notified bodies, conformity assessment bodies, post-market monitoring agencies, and the EAIB (Biber, 2021). While multilevel governance can enhance inclusivity, the AIA's institutional architecture remains fragmented and ambiguous, violating key ordoliberal 2.0 principles. Responsibilities overlap, coordination mechanisms are unclear, and procedural consistency is lacking (EPRS, 2022a). Moreover, the interaction between the AIA and existing regimes such as the GDPR, the Digital Services Act, and the Digital Markets Act remains undefined (Gstrein, 2022).

5 It is important to note that deployers of high-risk AI systems are required to conduct a *Fundamental Rights Impact Assessment (FRIA)*. According to Article 29a of AIA, the FRIA must include:

> (a) a description of the deployer's processes in which the high-risk AI system will be used [. . .]; (b) a description of the period of time and frequency in which each [. . .] system is intended to be used; (c) the categories of natural persons and groups likely to be affected by its use [. . .]; (d) the specific risks of harm likely to impact the categories [. . .] or group of persons [. . .]; (e) a description of the implementation of human oversight measures [. . .]; (f) the measures to be taken in case of the materialization of these risks, including their arrangements for internal governance and complaint mechanisms (European Parliament & Council of the European Union, 2024).

If properly implemented and effectively monitored, the FRIA could strengthen the protection of workers and other vulnerable groups affected by high-risk AI systems. However, doubts remain regarding its effectiveness. The AIA explicitly describes the FRIA as a 'light version' of an impact assessment – 'relatively easy to comply with' – and specifies that it needs to be carried out only for aspects not already covered by other legal obligations, such as the *Data Protection Impact Assessment* under the GDPR. The stated aim, therefore, is to 'eliminate any overlap and additional burden' (European Parliament & Council of the European Union, 2024, pp. 4–5). Open questions also persist concerning the FRIA's scope and implementation, including who is responsible for conducting the assessment, how it should be performed in practice, and whether it should evaluate all fundamental rights or only those most likely to be affected (Waem et al., 2024).

Although the EAIB and public AI databases could enhance enforcement and transparency, the EAIB currently lacks substantive powers and independence. Its reliance on the Commission, which chairs the Board and holds veto power over its rules of procedure, raises significant ordoliberal 2.0 concerns regarding political influence and the prioritization of process policy over substantive ordering or regulatory policy. The mechanisms for cooperation between the EAIB, national authorities, and affected individuals also remain to be clarified (Ebers et al., 2021).

5.3.2.6 Underfunding and understaffing

Effective implementation of the AIA – and compliance with ordoliberal 2.0 principles – requires adequate financial and human resources. Yet, the Commission's Impact Assessment (Annex 3) estimates that only 25 additional full-time staff per member state will be needed (European Commission, 2021) – a figure widely regarded as insufficient (Veale & Zuiderveen Borgesius, 2021). Many standardization and surveillance bodies also lack the technical expertise to match the sophistication of AI providers, often relying on outsourcing and private actors to fill this gap. This dependence undermines transparency and accountability and heightens capture risks. Ordoliberal 2.0 scholars therefore call for substantial increases in funding and staffing, including the recruitment of data analysts, AI specialists, and independent researchers (Almada & Petit, 2023; Wörsdörfer, 2024a, 2024b, 2025a).

5.3.2.7 Weak sustainability provisions

Finally, the AIA falls short from an ordoliberal 2.0 perspective in addressing environmental and sustainability concerns. Despite growing recognition of AI's ecological footprint – including high energy and water consumption, greenhouse gas emissions from data centers, and the generation of electronic waste – the AIA makes only cursory references to sustainability, climate change, or environmental protection, primarily through voluntary codes (EPRS, 2022a; Ebers et al., 2021). This limited attention to (socio-)environmental impacts reflects a broader anthropocentric orientation in the E.U.'s AI governance, which Floridi (2021) critiques for prioritizing human needs while largely overlooking systemic ecological consequences. The absence of binding sustainability requirements means that AI providers are under little obligation to account for the environmental and social costs of their operations, which could potentially exacerbate climate and resource pressures. Consequently, environmentalists and scholars call for the integration of sustainability principles into AI regulation, advocating for mechanisms that require providers to internalize ecological impacts, promote energy efficiency, and adopt environmentally responsible practices.

5.3.3 Strengths of the TFAIA

Among the principal strengths of the TFAIA – as seen from an ordoliberal 2.0 perspective – are its hard law nature, its targeted focus on frontier models and high-impact developers, its strong emphasis on transparency, accountability, and whistleblower protection, its investment in public infrastructure and institutional capacity, its legal coherence through statewide harmonization, and its potential to serve as a (inter-)national role model for responsible AI governance (Wörsdörfer, 2024a, 2024b, 2025a, 2025b).

5.3.3.1 Hard law and regulatory leadership

Like the AIA, the TFAIA stands out as a pioneering example of hard law in the field of AI ethics and governance. Unlike voluntary frameworks, soft-law initiatives, or federal measures such as Biden's *Executive Order on AI* and the *Blueprint for an AI Bill of Rights* (Wörsdörfer, 2024b, 2025b, 2025c), the TFAIA establishes binding legal obligations for AI developers and operators. This represents a significant departure from the U.S. tradition of self-regulation and industry-led governance (Wörsdörfer, 2025e). By embedding enforceable requirements, the law counteracts broader trends toward laissez-faire, hands-off approaches that have characterized federal policies, particularly those implemented under the Trump administrations (Wörsdörfer, 2025d).

California's transition from nonbinding ethical principles to a comprehensive hard-law framework reflects its historical role as a regulatory innovator in the United States (and beyond) – a state-level laboratory for policy experimentation and a 'norm entrepreneur' in global AI governance (Kobrin, 2009; Scherer & Palazzo, 2007, 2008; Scherer et al., 2014; Zumbansen, 2010a, 2010b, 2010c). In the spirit of ordoliberalism 2.0, the TFAIA aims to restore balance between markets and moral order by integrating ethical and safety obligations into market structures. Given California's centrality to the global AI ecosystem – hosting major research laboratories and leading technology firms – the law possesses significant potential to influence regulatory practices beyond state borders. By mandating responsible governance practices, it may shape both national and international norms, promoting transparency, accountability, and ethical alignment across the AI industry.

5.3.3.2 Scope and focus on frontier models

The TFAIA's targeted scope represents another significant strength. It specifically regulates frontier models – those exceeding 10^{26} operations – and large frontier developers, defined as firms with annual revenues above \$500 million (Section 2, TFAIA). This focus mirrors the ordoliberal-inspired E.U.'s Digital Markets Act, which addresses the concentrated power of gatekeeper platforms (Wörsdörfer, 2023, 2025d). By focusing on the most capable and potentially hazardous AI systems, the TFAIA prioritizes high-stakes and catastrophic risks, defined as incidents likely to result in death or serious injury to more than 50 individuals or economic damage exceeding \$1 billion

(Section 2). This differentiated approach recognizes that not all AI risks are equivalent: while bias, discrimination, and disinformation are serious, existential and systemic threats demand specialized governance tools.

At the same time, the TFAIA maintains a pro-innovation orientation, identifying innovation as one of its core objectives alongside transparency, safety, and effective governance. Similar to the AIA, it promotes regulatory experimentation through mechanisms akin to regulatory sandboxes (Title V, AIA), facilitating safe testing environments for small and medium-sized enterprises (SMEs). In doing so, it strikes a careful balance between risk mitigation and innovation support, embodying the ordoliberal 2.0 principle that regulation and competition are mutually reinforcing rather than mutually exclusive.

5.3.3.3 Transparency, accountability, and whistleblower protections

Transparency and accountability form a central pillar of the TFAIA (and ordoliberalism 2.0). The law requires large frontier developers to publish and regularly update frameworks for assessing and mitigating catastrophic risks. It also mandates incident reporting to OES, including a 24-h notification window for imminent threats. These obligations substantially enhance public and governmental oversight of an industry that has historically been characterized by a lack of transparency.

Equally crucial from an ordoliberal 2.0 perspective are the whistleblower protections embedded in the law (Section 4, TFAIA). Employees who raise safety concerns are protected from retaliation, and contractual provisions restricting disclosure are rendered void. The inclusion of internal anonymous reporting mechanisms and anti-retaliation safeguards marks a significant advance over the AIA, which lacks comparable provisions. By empowering employees to act as moral agents within AI firms, the TFAIA fosters internal accountability and helps surface potential safety issues before they escalate into systemic failures.

5.3.3.4 Public infrastructure and state capacity

Another notable innovation is the establishment of CalCompute, a state-backed public cloud computing cluster. CalCompute represents a significant investment in public-interest AI infrastructure, designed to democratize access to computational resources, particularly for smaller developers and research institutions. By offering shared computing power and promoting ethical, equitable, and safe AI development, CalCompute seeks to reduce dependence on dominant private-sector platforms and foster a more inclusive innovation ecosystem – an approach that aligns closely with ordoliberalism 2.0 and its support for SMEs (and independent research/science as a potential 'ordering power'). It also strengthens California's institutional capacity for AI oversight and governance, thereby enhancing the state's long-term resilience. However, the full realization of these goals depends on future budget appropriations and sustained political commitment.

5.3.3.5 Legal clarity and statewide harmonization

The TFAIA introduces a preemption clause that prevents local jurisdictions from adopting rules conflicting with statewide catastrophic risk management standards. This harmonization creates a unified regulatory framework across California, thereby reducing legal uncertainty and streamlining compliance for developers (note that the state is the largest subnational economy in the world; if it were an independent country, its economy would rank fourth globally in nominal terms, trailing Germany and surpassing Japan). Such consistency reflects the principles of ordoliberalism 2.0, emphasizing the importance of clear and predictable regulatory environments. Nevertheless, this approach may also constrain local regulatory experimentation and limit opportunities for municipalities to pilot alternative AI governance models.

5.3.3.6 TFAIA as a potential role model

Beyond California, the TFAIA may serve as a template for other U.S. states and potentially for federal AI regulation targeting advanced and frontier systems. Historically, California has played a pivotal role in translating European regulatory principles into the U.S. context. The GDPR, for example, inspired the CCPA and CPRA, setting in motion a pattern of regulatory diffusion from the E.U. to California and then across U.S. states.

Similarly, the AIA – a key reference point for the TFAIA's design – demonstrates how ambitious regional regulation can shape global standards. In this sense, the TFAIA could generate a 'California effect' analogous to Bradford's (2020, 2023) 'Brussels effect,' exporting its standards through market influence and policy emulation. As such, the TFAIA not only strengthens AI governance within California but also has the potential to catalyze a broader shift toward ethical, transparent, and accountable AI practices across the United States and beyond.

5.3.4 Weaknesses of the TFAIA

While the TFAIA marks a significant step forward in AI governance, especially in the United States, it is not without significant shortcomings. Ordoliberal 2.0 critics have identified several limitations (some of which are similar to the AIA's), including its narrow scope, risk gaps, definitional ambiguities, insufficient accountability mechanisms, weak procedural rights, inadequate governance structures, and limited worker protection. Further concerns relate to compliance burdens, environmental shortcomings, and implementation uncertainties. The following subsections examine these weaknesses in turn.

5.3.4.1 Narrow scope and risk gaps

One of the most frequently cited weaknesses of the TFAIA concerns its deliberately narrow scope, which confines regulatory obligations to large frontier developers and frontier models exceeding defined compute and revenue thresholds. By focusing almost exclusively on catastrophic risks, critical safety incidents, and high-impact systems, the law leaves numerous AI-related harms unregulated – particularly those emerging from smaller-scale models or novel applications that fall below the prescribed thresholds.

This limited scope creates significant risk gaps, especially in areas such as algorithmic bias, discrimination, and privacy violations, which disproportionately affect marginalized and vulnerable populations (Bender & Hanna, 2025; Buolamwini, 2023; Buolamwini & Gebru, 2018; Dachwitz & Hilbig, 2025; Muldoon et al., 2025; O'Neil, 2016). From an ordoliberal 2.0 perspective, these unaddressed harms represent negative externalities – social costs that the market fails to internalize due to insufficient regulation.

The law's lack of a tiered or risk-based regulatory pyramid, as adopted in the artificial intelligence act (AIA), undermines its fairness and equity dimensions. By targeting only a narrow segment of AI activity, the TFAIA fails to protect individuals and communities affected by lower-impact systems. Its limited jurisdictional reach also constrains its effectiveness: as a state law, it applies primarily to entities under California's authority, whereas the E.U.'s ordoliberal-inspired framework applies extraterritorially to all AI systems entering the E.U. market, regardless of their origin (Wörsdörfer, 2024a, 2024b, 2025a).

5.3.4.2 Ambiguities and regulatory lag

A further weakness, as seen from an ordoliberal 2.0 perspective, lies in the fluidity of key definitions – including frontier models, large frontier developers, catastrophic risks, and critical safety incidents. These categories are inherently dynamic and evolve in tandem with technological innovation, creating interpretive uncertainty. Although the TFAIA mandates annual reassessments beginning in 2027, developers and regulators alike may struggle to operationalize these terms in practice.

This regulatory indeterminacy risks producing grey areas, regulatory arbitrage, and inconsistent enforcement. Loopholes are particularly evident in the reporting regime, which "encourages but does not mandate" (California State Legislature, 2025) disclosures for foundation models that do not meet frontier thresholds, rendering such reporting effectively voluntary. Similarly, the law permits flexibility in internal reporting schedules – for example, allowing developers to submit safety assessments every three months or on another "reasonable schedule" (California State Legislature, 2025) – which may dilute the frequency and rigor of (ordoliberal) oversight.

5.3.4.3 Transparency without accountability

Although transparency is one of the TFAIA's cornerstones, ordoliberal 2.0 critics argue that transparency alone is insufficient to guarantee meaningful accountability. Mandatory disclosures, risk frameworks, and incident reports can easily devolve into performative or symbolic acts – forms of window dressing or ethics washing (Metzinger, 2019) – if not paired with independent verification and enforcement.

From an ordoliberal 2.0 perspective, effective governance requires accountability mechanisms that correct market failures through enforceable oversight. Yet the TFAIA lacks strong provisions for third-party auditing, external monitoring, or substantive sanctions for noncompliance. Without these, transparency risks functioning as a procedural formality rather than a substantive safeguard, allowing firms to project ethical responsibility without materially changing their practices.

5.3.4.4 Insufficient procedural rights

The TFAIA – same as the AIA – affords only minimal procedural rights and provides limited avenues for individuals adversely affected by AI systems to seek redress. In contrast to the GDPR and the CCPA/CPRA, which effectively confer the right to lodge complaints and pursue judicial remedies, the TFAIA contains no comparable mechanisms. Consequently, individuals experiencing harm from AI deployment encounter significant impediments when attempting to challenge decisions, contest adverse outcomes, or obtain legal remedies.

This absence of robust bottom-up enforcement mechanisms centralizes accountability almost exclusively within regulatory authorities, effectively constraining the capacity of individuals and civil society organizations to function as corrective agents. From an ordoliberal 2.0 perspective, this arrangement manifests a pronounced imbalance between public and private enforcement: the TFAIA relies solely on the former, and even that is circumscribed. As a result, the Act risks operating primarily as a top-down governance instrument, with limited responsiveness to the very citizens and workers it is intended to safeguard (Castets-Renard & Besse, 2022; Ebers et al., 2021; Smuha et al., 2021; Veale & Zuiderveen Borgesius, 2021).

5.3.4.5 Missing governance mechanisms

Compared with the AIA (Title VI), the TFAIA lacks institutional depth and participatory governance structures. It does not establish a dedicated AI office, advisory board, or scientific panel of independent experts, nor does it create a public AI database similar to that envisioned under the E.U. framework (AlgorithmWatch, 2021; Ebers et al., 2021; Smuha et al., 2021).

Furthermore, opportunities for stakeholder consultation and participation are minimal (and mostly limited to the definition review and update process as well as CalCompute). Consumer and civil society organizations – often constrained by limited financial and technical resources – face considerable barriers to engagement (Castets-

Renard & Besse, 2022; Micklitz & Gestel, 2013; Veale & Zuiderveen Borgesius, 2021). Consequently, the TFAIA risks reproducing deficits in input, throughput, and output legitimacy (Laux et al., 2023b). It neither ensures participatory input from affected stakeholders, guarantees transparent and accountable processes, nor adequately aligns its outcomes with societal needs.

In addition, the law does little to empower SMEs or promote competition, thereby weakening one of the central ordoliberal 2.0 goals of fostering fair and open markets. By failing to counterbalance the dominance of large technology firms, the TFAIA risks entrenching existing power asymmetries instead of correcting them.

5.3.4.6 Inadequate worker protection

A further notable limitation of the TFAIA pertains to its inadequate protection of workers' rights. Aside from provisions for whistleblowers, the legislation provides few safeguards for employees interacting with AI systems in the workplace. Similar to the AIA, the Act does not sufficiently address issues such as algorithmic management, digital monitoring, or intrusions into worker privacy, nor does it establish explicit rights for employees to object, submit complaints, or participate in oversight processes. From an ordoliberal 2.0 perspective, this gap compromises the law's social justice function. Classical and contemporary ordoliberals emphasize the centrality of labor protections and collective worker representation as counterweights to the concentration of economic and managerial power among employers, thereby promoting fairness and stability within the market order (Wörsdörfer, 2023, 2025a, 2025b). In the absence of structured mechanisms for worker consultation or union participation, the TFAIA fails to mediate the asymmetry of technological authority between employers and employees, undermining the equitable distribution of rights and safeguards in the workplace (Cefaliello & Kullmann, 2022).

5.3.4.7 Compliance burdens and innovation risks

Ironically, while the TFAIA aims to regulate large technology firms, its compliance obligations – including mandatory risk frameworks, incident reporting, and disclosures – may reinforce the dominance of those very actors. Major companies (i.e., big tech) are generally best positioned to absorb the associated administrative and financial costs, whereas some start-ups (e.g., the so-called unicorns) and medium-sized developers – those exceeding the TFAIA's revenue threshold but falling short of the largest tech firms – may face challenges in meeting these requirements. This dynamic risks stifling innovation and limiting market entry, running counter to the ordoliberal 2.0 goal of sustaining fair competition. (Smaller and) medium-sized entities may relocate or exit the market entirely, while established firms consolidate their dominance, undermining the Act's intended corrective function.[6]

5.3.4.8 Enforcement and penalty limitations

The TFAIA authorizes civil penalties of up to $1 million per violation, enforceable by the California Attorney General. However, these amounts are modest compared to the potential scale of catastrophic harms, which may reach billions of dollars. The resulting deterrence gap weakens the law's effectiveness, particularly given the immense resources of major AI firms. Without proportionate sanctions, compliance may be viewed as merely a cost of doing business rather than a binding legal obligation.

Effective enforcement also depends on adequate institutional resources and technical expertise. Yet, the TFAIA presumes that existing state agencies (e.g., CDT, GovOps, and OES) oversee compliance without a significant expansion of personnel or budgets. This assumption overlooks the high degree of specialization required to assess AI systems, monitor safety risks, and investigate violations. Scholars argue that underfunded and understaffed regulators are vulnerable to regulatory capture and dependency on private-sector expertise (Almada & Petit, 2023; Veale & Zuiderveen Borgesius, 2021). From an ordoliberal 2.0 perspective, this lack of state capacity undermines the ability to enforce fair competition and correct market failures (Wörsdörfer, 2024a, 2025a). Strengthening regulatory bodies through targeted recruitment of AI specialists, data scientists, and independent researchers – as well as substantial budget increases – is therefore essential for meaningful oversight.

5.3.4.9 Environmental shortcomings

From an environmental and sustainability standpoint, the TFAIA provides minimal attention to the ecological externalities associated with AI development and deployment. The Act does not adequately address the substantial energy and water demands of data centers, the associated greenhouse gas emissions, or the increasing challenge of electronic waste (Bender & Hanna, 2025; EPRS, 2022a; Muldoon et al., 2025). References to ecological sustainability or 'green AI' are sparse and largely indirect. This anthropocentric orientation – prioritizing human and economic interests – stands in

6 It may thus be worth considering a staged or tiered approach to regulation, in which different types of businesses – large tech companies, SMEs, and start-ups – are subject to tailored requirements based on factors such as revenue thresholds, market impact, or the level of risk posed by their AI systems. Such a differentiated framework could help ensure that compliance burdens are proportionate to a company's size and capacity, preventing smaller firms from being disproportionately disadvantaged while maintaining robust oversight of high-risk or high-impact AI systems. This approach aligns with the AIA (and ordoliberalism 2.0), which impose stricter obligations on higher-risk systems and larger operators, illustrating how risk- and scale-sensitive regulation can balance innovation, fairness, and safety.

tension with ordoliberal 2.0 principles, which emphasize the internalization of social and environmental costs in governance frameworks. By neglecting these considerations, the TFAIA – same as the AIA – fails to integrate AI regulation with broader environmental and climate imperatives, thereby missing a critical opportunity to ensure that technological innovation is both socially responsible and ecologically sustainable.

5.3.4.10 Fragmentation and implementation uncertainty

Finally, the TFAIA faces implementation and coordination challenges. Despite its preemption clause, national regulatory fragmentation persists, as other states may enact laws that diverge from California's standards. This patchwork could complicate compliance for multi-jurisdictional firms.[7] Moreover, while the Act mandates transparency, it allows for redactions in cases involving trade secrets, cybersecurity, and public safety, thereby limiting public access to critical information. The future of CalCompute, one of the TFAIA's most ambitious public-interest initiatives, remains uncertain pending budgetary approval. Should funding not materialize, the law's potential to strengthen public infrastructure and oversight capacity would be significantly diminished.

5.4 Comparative analysis

The following section presents a comparative analysis of the AIA and TFAIA from an ordoliberal 2.0 perspective, highlighting key parallels – including their focus on advanced AI systems and foundation models, transparency and risk management obligations, accountability mechanisms, and dynamic, adaptive regulatory design – while also examining critical differences in scope, focus, definitions, obligations, enforcement, implementation timeframes, and orientations toward innovation versus safety, as well as the broader implications for global AI governance.

5.4.1 Parallels

5.4.1.1 Targeting advanced AI systems and foundation models

Both the TFAIA and AIA represent comprehensive regulatory hard-law responses to the rapid development of large-scale AI systems. Each framework acknowledges that

7 An additional source of implementation uncertainty stems from the Trump administration's executive order *Ensuring a National Policy Framework for Artificial Intelligence*, which preempts state-level AI legislation (Trump White House, 2025e). This directive has raised significant legal questions, and it is expected that the executive order will be challenged in court. The resulting litigation could further complicate the regulatory landscape for AI by creating ambiguity around federal versus state authority, potentially delaying the adoption and enforcement of AI governance measures.

once AI models surpass a specific computational scale, measured by floating-point operations (FLOPs), they may pose systemic or catastrophic risks that necessitate heightened governance and oversight. The TFAIA (Section 2) applies to frontier models trained on more than 10^{26} FLOPs (including fine-tuning), while the AIA presumes systemic risk for general-purpose AI (GPAI) models trained above 10^{25} FLOPs (Title VIIIA). Thus, both regimes adopt compute-based thresholds as proxies for capability and potential societal impact,[8] though California's threshold is notably higher and therefore applies to a smaller subset of models.

5.4.1.2 Transparency and risk management obligations

In both jurisdictions, transparency and risk management form the foundation of governance obligations. Under the TFAIA, large frontier developers – defined partly by revenue exceeding $500 million – must publicly disclose a frontier AI framework outlining their approaches to catastrophic risk and impact assessment, mitigation, and deployment governance (Section 2). Similarly, the AIA imposes comprehensive transparency and documentation requirements on high-risk and GPAI systems, mandating that deployers understand model limitations, interpret outputs, and maintain detailed logs (they must also maintain documentation, human oversight, and other relevant safeguards) (Title III). Both frameworks establish mechanisms for incident/critical risk reporting: California requires notification of critical safety incidents to state authorities (Sections 1 and 2), whereas the E.U. mandates reporting of 'serious incidents' related to high-risk systems (Titles III and VIII [Chapter 2]).

5.4.1.3 Accountability mechanisms

Accountability is enforced through penalties and compliance structures. California's TFAIA provides whistleblower protections (i.e., internal reporting channels and anti-retaliation measures), and civil penalties for noncompliance of up to $1 million per violation, enforceable by the State Attorney General (Sections 2 and 4). In contrast, the E.U. regime introduces more substantial sanctions – up to €35 million or 7% of global annual turnover (Title X) – underscoring its supranational reach and deterrent focus. The E.U.'s enforcement powers are delegated to national competent authorities (Title 6, Chapter 2), while California's are centralized at the state level (Section 2).

5.4.1.4 Dynamic and adaptive design

Both regimes include mechanisms for adaptability. California's law mandates an annual review of key definitions, such as frontier models and developers, by the CDT starting in 2027 (Section 2), while the AIA allows for the adjustment of thresholds (e.g.,

8 That is, both regimes acknowledge that once models reach a sufficiently large scale/capability, additional governance obligations come into effect.

compute thresholds for GPAI/systemic risk) and technical specifications through delegated acts (AIA, pages 64–65). This dynamic design reflects a shared recognition of the rapid evolution of AI capabilities and the need for regulatory flexibility.[9]

5.4.2 Differences

While both the AIA and TFAIA seek to promote trustworthy, transparent, and accountable AI, they differ markedly in scope, design, and underlying regulatory philosophy. From an ordoliberal 2.0 perspective, these differences illustrate two distinct approaches to balancing innovation with governance: California's more market-oriented, innovation-driven framework versus the E.U.'s rule-based, precautionary model, which emphasizes institutional oversight and the public interest, e.g., through the protection of consumer rights, the support of SMEs, and the maintenance of fair and competitive markets.[10]

5.4.2.1 Scope and focus

The TFAIA adopts a narrow and targeted approach, focusing on the development of frontier AI models – very large general-purpose systems trained above a compute threshold of 10^{26} FLOPs and developed by entities earning over $500 million annually. Its provisions concentrate primarily on the developmental stage, emphasizing transparency, internal governance, and reporting of catastrophic or critical safety incidents. In contrast, the AIA takes a comprehensive, lifecycle-based approach that governs both development and deployment across diverse sectors and risk levels. It applies to developers, providers, and deployers, extending its reach to various contexts, including employment, healthcare, and law enforcement.

5.4.2.2 Risk classification and thresholds

The TFAIA and AIA differ fundamentally in their treatment of risk. The TFAIA adopts a minimalist and quantitative approach,[11] defining catastrophic risk as the foreseeable potential for more than 50 deaths or property damage exceeding $1 billion. It es-

9 As the preceding critical analysis of the AIA and TFAIA demonstrates, both AI governance frameworks exhibit comparable shortcomings, particularly concerning inadequate procedural rights, limited worker protections, and insufficient environmental provisions.

10 Note that the AIA demonstrates a markedly broader regulatory ambition, extending to roughly 270 pages across 12 titles and several annexes, and covering a wide array of provisions and mechanisms. The TFAIA, by contrast, is far more concise, containing only six sections and around ten pages.

11 Moreover, California's framework combines this compute threshold with a revenue-based criterion – defining a large frontier developer as an entity generating annual revenue exceeding $500 million. In contrast, the AIA does not employ financial metrics as part of its regulatory classification.

tablishes a high computational threshold for coverage and omits a structured taxonomy of risk or prohibitions on harmful AI practices. The AIA, by contrast, develops a multi-tiered classification framework that distinguishes between prohibited, high-risk, limited-risk, and minimal-risk systems. Within this framework, general-purpose models exhibiting systemic risk – typically those trained with over 10^{25} FLOPs[12] – are subject to enhanced obligations, including conformity assessments, human oversight, and traceability requirements. From an ordoliberal 2.0 standpoint, the AIA's structured differentiation exemplifies the principle of proportional regulation: calibrating state intervention according to systemic risk and ensuring that private actors internalize the potential social costs of their technologies.

5.4.2.3 Obligations and regulatory design

Another area of divergence is the nature and design of regulatory obligations. The TFAIA primarily emphasizes disclosure and internal governance, requiring large frontier developers to publish transparency frameworks, report incidents, implement mitigation strategies, and establish due diligence mechanisms, including risk and impact assessments. However, it does not, in its current form, mandate comprehensive conformity assessments or impose extensive deployment restrictions. Notably, California's framework incorporates explicit whistleblower protections – including safeguards against retaliation and provisions for internal reporting – which are largely absent from the E.U.'s regime (note that there is only one AIA reference to whistleblowers on page 90). In contrast, the AIA imposes a far more detailed and prescriptive set of obligations for high-risk systems and general-purpose AI models with systemic risk. These include stringent requirements for data governance, human oversight, documentation, pre-market conformity assessments, continuous logging, user information and transparency, and system registration. Furthermore, the E.U. framework explicitly prohibits certain AI practices deemed to present unacceptable risks, such as social scoring and emotion recognition in sensitive contexts – areas that California's TFAIA does not currently regulate.

5.4.2.4 Enforcement and penalties

Enforcement mechanisms further illustrate the institutional and jurisdictional differences between the two frameworks. The TFAIA authorizes civil penalties of up to $1 million per violation for large frontier developers, reflecting a state-level enforcement model confined to California's territorial jurisdiction. Its sanctioning authority is vested primarily in the California Attorney General, emphasizing a domestic compliance regime oriented toward entities with a nexus to the state. By contrast, the AIA

12 The E.U. sets a lower compute threshold for systemic-risk general-purpose AI models at 10^{25} FLOPs, with supplementary guidance identifying GPAI systems at levels as low as 10^{22}–10^{23} FLOPs, depending on the version or interpretation. By contrast, California's higher threshold of 10^{26} FLOPs encompasses far fewer models, concentrating regulatory attention on only the most advanced systems.

establishes a markedly more stringent and comprehensive enforcement regime, permitting administrative fines of up to €35 million or 7% of a company's global annual turnover for the most serious infringements. This approach not only introduces a significantly higher deterrent effect but is also embedded within a multi-level institutional architecture comprising the AI Office, the EAIB, and the E.U.-wide AI database. Collectively, these ordoliberal-like mechanisms ensure coordinated supervision, monitoring, and sanctioning across member states, thereby reinforcing regulatory coherence and institutional accountability at the supranational level.

From a jurisdictional standpoint, the AIA exhibits a pronounced extraterritorial dimension: it applies to any AI system placed on, or whose output is used within, the E.U. market, regardless of the developer's domicile or the system's geographic origin. This expansive scope extends the E.U.'s normative influence far beyond its borders, shaping global compliance behavior through what has been termed the 'Brussels effect' (Bradford, 2020, 2023). It also reflects the E.U.'s ordoliberal 2.0 tradition of embedding market activity within a legal and moral framework that safeguards both competition and social welfare. In contrast, California's TFAIA remains territorially bounded as a state-level instrument, formally applying only to developers and entities under California's legal authority – though, given the concentration of major AI firms within the state, its practical reach may prove broader than its formal jurisdiction suggests.

5.4.2.5 Innovation and research support

The AIA and TFAIA also diverge in their orientation toward innovation and market development. The TFAIA incorporates a distinctly innovation-oriented component through the establishment of the CalCompute public computing cluster consortium, which is designed to support safe, ethical, equitable, and sustainable AI R&D. This initiative exemplifies California's dual focus on advancing technological innovation while maintaining robust safety governance. By contrast, the AIA adopts a more precautionary and regulatory stance, emphasizing risk mitigation, compliance, and accountability rather than providing direct support for innovation. Nevertheless, the E.U. framework embeds complementary economic objectives, particularly by promoting competition and mitigating market concentration, thereby aiming to level the playing field between large technology firms and SMEs. Mechanisms such as regulatory sandboxes and other SME support measures facilitate experimentation and compliance within a controlled environment (Title V). Overall, while both frameworks aim to ensure trustworthy and responsible AI, California's law explicitly integrates innovation facilitation with safety, whereas the E.U.'s approach prioritizes regulatory oversight, equitable market participation, and the protection of consumer rights,[13] reflecting principles of ordoliberalism 2.0.

13 That is, upholding or advancing the ordoliberal principle of consumer or citizen sovereignty (Vanberg 2005, 2013).

5.4.2.6 Implementation timeline

The TFAIA will take effect on January 1, 2026, with its definitions subject to annual review, ensuring adaptability to rapid technological evolution. The AIA follows a phased implementation schedule, with specific provisions, such as transparency obligations for general-purpose AI, entering into force in 2025, and others, including high-risk system requirements, to follow (the provisions concerning prohibited practices are also already in effect).

5.4.2.7 Implications for global AI governance

The differing thresholds and regulatory scopes of the TFAIA and the AIA carry significant implications for AI developers operating across jurisdictions. California's higher compute threshold narrows the law's application, targeting only the most advanced frontier models and a limited number of large developers. By contrast, the E.U.'s lower thresholds and broader coverage capture a wider range of AI systems and applications, classifying many as high-risk or GPAI. As a result, more organizations must evaluate whether their systems trigger compliance obligations – even when those systems would not qualify as frontier models under California's framework. For global developers, this divergence creates the possibility of (costly) dual compliance regimes: a model built in California but deployed in Europe may need to satisfy both sets of requirements. To manage this complexity, companies are increasingly advised to design integrated AI governance programs that align with both local and international standards.[14]

A potential interplay between the TFAIA and AIA may signal the E.U.'s regulatory spillover effect (Bradford, 2020, 2023) – its capacity to set de facto global benchmarks through the external influence of its internal market rules. Because the AIA applies beyond the E.U.'s territorial boundaries to any AI system placed on or used within its market, companies worldwide may feel compelled to align with E.U. requirements to maintain access and competitiveness. In practice, even California-based developers may preemptively adopt E.U.-aligned compliance measures, harmonizing their operations with European regulatory expectations. Combined with California's own emerging state-level rules, this convergence creates overlapping obligations that encourage firms to adhere to the stricter or more comprehensive regime. The result is a gradual globalization of regulatory norms, where the E.U.'s high-standard, rights-based approach could indirectly shape industry practices and promote a shared commitment to safer, more transparent, and accountable AI systems.

14 Given the differing thresholds and obligations, many organizations may adopt a highest common denominator approach to compliance or develop modular governance structures capable of addressing both frameworks simultaneously. This dual approach helps ensure that AI deployment aligns with both California and E.U. requirements while supporting scalable, cross-jurisdictional risk management.

Differences in enforcement, penalties, and transparency requirements further illustrate this dynamic. California emphasizes public disclosure, requiring frontier developers to publish their AI frameworks, while the E.U. focuses more on internal compliance documentation and institutional oversight. The two systems also differ in penalty scale, with the E.U. imposing potentially higher fines and broader enforcement mechanisms. Both frameworks, however, incorporate adaptability: California mandates annual reviews of key definitions, while the AIA allows for adjustable compute thresholds. Together, these mechanisms ensure that both regimes can evolve alongside technological progress. Consequently, AI providers must remain proactive, continuously monitoring and adjusting their practices to navigate a regulatory landscape that is both dynamic and increasingly interconnected.

The following table 5.1 summarizes the key differences between the TFAIA and AIA.

5.5 Summary of findings

Despite their structural and jurisdictional differences, California's TFAIA and the AIA ultimately converge in their objectives: mitigating systemic and catastrophic risks, fostering responsible AI innovation, and ensuring regulatory adaptability amid rapid technological change. Together, they exemplify a broader international movement toward risk-proportionate, capability-based governance of frontier AI systems. To consolidate and extend this convergence, targeted reforms could address the respective weaknesses of both instruments, thereby enhancing – or 'hardening' – their overall regulatory resilience.

To create a robust and stable (ordoliberal 2.0) AI governance framework in the United States, it would be beneficial to enact federal hard law AI legislation that applies across all fifty states and industry sectors, extending beyond the current state-level regime. Such legislation should be designed to provide legal certainty for all stakeholders and ideally be resistant to easy reversal. Crucially, compliance must be actively monitored and noncompliance effectively sanctioned, using both behavioral and structural remedies where appropriate.

This approach requires the establishment of a dedicated federal agency to oversee and implement the legislation. The institution should be politically independent, well-funded, and staffed with a combination of legal experts, economists, and AI specialists. To avoid overburdening the Federal Trade Commission, which primarily focuses on antitrust and consumer protection, AI regulatory responsibilities – including AI-related consumer protection – should be assigned to this separate institution rather than existing agencies.

Beyond the federal institutional framework, the TFAIA should implement a comprehensive stakeholder engagement process, strengthen democratic accountability, and establish information rights, legal remedies, and accessible complaint and redress mechanisms. Drawing on ordoliberal 2.0 elements of the AIA, it could further enhance

Table 5.1: Key differences between TFAIA versus AIA.

Feature	TFAIA	AIA
Scope and focus	– Frontier models (narrower scope): $>10^{26}$ FLOPs – Applies to large developers only (revenue >$500 m)	– Broad coverage: all AI systems with risk-based approach – GPAI models with $>10^{25}$ FLOPs presumed systemic risk – High-risk systems across sectors
Risk classification and thresholds	– Emphasis on development of frontier models, transparency, internal governance, and incident reporting – Catastrophic risk and critical safety incidents – No prohibitions	– Focus on both development *and* deployment of AI systems – Risk-based obligations for providers and deployers (risk pyramid) – Bans on certain practices
Obligations and regulatory design	– Publish public frontier AI framework, transparency reports, and incident reporting – Internal governance (risk and impact assessment) and due diligence – Whistleblower protections	– Transparency, human oversight, data governance, and conformity assessments for high-risk systems – Classification by risk level – Disclosure to authorities and deployers – Lack of whistleblower protection
Enforcement and penalties	– Up to $1 million per violation for large frontier developers – California Attorney General enforcement – Lack of (additional) governance institutions (besides CDT, GovOps, and OES)	– Up to €35 million or 7% of global annual turnover for worst cases – National authorities + E.U. AI Office enforcement – Other governance institutions (board, advisory forum/panel)
Innovation and research support	– Focus on innovation (and safety) – Includes CalCompute consortium for public computing cluster	– Focus on competition, SMEs, and consumer rights – More regulatory in tone – Lesser explicit focus on state-provided innovation infrastructure
Timeline and implications (temporal and geographic reach)	– State law (California) – Effective January 1, 2026 – Definitions reviewed annually	– E.U.-wide regulation – Phased implementation (some rules in force already, full obligations later) – Extraterritorial impact (if placing in E.U. market)

its institutional design by establishing an AI office or advisory board, creating publicly accessible logs, and developing a comprehensive database of AI systems. Moreover, the TFAIA should place greater emphasis on consumer rights (or citizen sovereignty), provide stronger support for SMEs, and promote fair and competitive markets. Conversely, the AIA could be strengthened by adopting a greater focus on R&D and innovation, moving beyond regulatory sandboxes and creating a CalCompute-style research center.

For both the AIA and TFAIA, reform efforts should focus on enhancing oversight, accountability, and the protection of affected stakeholders:

- *Conformity assessment procedures*: The AIA should move beyond self-assessment and provider-led certification or reporting, as in the case of the TFAIA. High-risk AI systems must undergo mandatory third-party audits conducted by independent regulatory bodies with investigative and enforcement powers. This ensures legally binding external oversight rather than discretionary self-certification (AlgorithmWatch, 2021; Ebers et al., 2021; EPRS, 2022a; Floridi et al., 2022; Gstrein, 2022; Kop, 2021; Laux et al., 2023b).
- *Democratic accountability*: Both the AIA and TFAIA should ensure meaningful engagement of all affected groups, including consumers, workers, and unions. Public participation should extend to standardization and certification (and other accountability) processes, ensuring that stakeholders with less bargaining power can influence AI governance (Ebers et al., 2021; EPRS, 2022a, 2022c; Gstrein, 2022).[15]
- *Redress and complaint mechanisms*: AI legislation should explicitly provide information rights, affordable and accessible legal remedies, and individual and collective complaint mechanisms. This ensures that those whose fundamental rights are affected by AI systems can challenge adverse outcomes in court or before relevant authorities (AlgorithmWatch, 2021; EPRS, 2022a, 2022c; Smuha et al., 2021).
- *Worker protection*: Both Acts should better safeguard workers by expanding the classification of AI systems used at work as high-risk, prohibiting the use of harmful systems, and granting workers the right to participate in decisions regarding the deployment of AI. Workers must be able to object to the use of AI and file complaints if technologies adversely affect their working conditions (AlgorithmWatch, 2021; Cefaliello & Kullmann, 2022; EPRS, 2022c; Smuha et al., 2021). The AIA could

15 Experts recommend making the risk classification and standardization process more inclusive and transparent (Ebers, 2022). Achieving this would require granting substantive information rights to affected individuals, expanding public participation rights for citizens, and ensuring that organizations representing public interests – rather than only corporate and expert groups – are actively involved in the classification and standardization process (Smuha et al., 2021). It may also be worthwhile to consider expanding the responsibilities of the EAIB. Currently, the board serves primarily in an advisory capacity, but (ordoliberal critics argue that its mandate should be strengthened to include investigatory and regulatory powers. Additionally, the EAIB could be restructured as a stakeholder forum to address the ongoing shortcomings in consultation, participation, and stakeholder dialogue (Council of the European Union, 2022a, 2022b).

likewise be strengthened by enhancing its whistleblower protections, drawing on the model established under the TFAIA.

- *Governance structure*: Effective ordoliberal enforcement depends on strong,[16] independent institutions with sufficient expertise, resources, and political independence. The (reformed) EAIB offers a model of 'ordering power' (Wörsdörfer, 2023, 2025a, 2025b) that could strengthen oversight. National AI databases should cover all AI systems used by private and public entities, including information on algorithmic risks and human rights impact assessments, presented in accessible formats. TFAIA could benefit from similar structures, including an AI office/board and publicly accessible logs and databases (AlgorithmWatch, 2021; Ebers et al., 2021; Smuha et al., 2021).
- *Funding and staffing*: Supervisory authorities must be adequately funded and staffed. Current allocations under the AIA (e.g., 25 full-time equivalents for national authorities) and TFAIA are insufficient. Both California and E.U. institutions require additional financial and human resources to implement AI regulations effectively (AlgorithmWatch, 2021; EPRS, 2022c; Smuha et al., 2021).
- *Sustainability considerations*: Both Acts should address the socio-environmental impacts of AI systems. This includes mandatory measures to reduce energy consumption, e-waste, and other environmental harms, moving beyond voluntary codes and industry guidelines toward 'green AI' practices (AlgorithmWatch, 2021; Ebers et al., 2021; EPRS, 2022a).
- *International cooperation*: AI legislation at the U.S. state and E.U. levels should be complemented by a coordinated global approach. International collaboration – between jurisdictions such as California and the E.U. (and ideally the United States), as well as multilateral organizations like the OECD, G7, and G20 – can foster the exchange of best practices and harmonized regulatory standards. This approach mitigates the risk of fragmented and incoherent regulations, promoting a race to the top rather than a race to the bottom.

5.6 Concluding remarks

This analysis has examined the AIA and TFAIA through an ordoliberal 2.0 lens, highlighting both their convergences and divergences in approach, scope, and institutional design. Both frameworks share a commitment to legally binding regulation, transparency, accountability, and adaptive governance, reflecting a broader international shift toward risk-proportionate, capability-based oversight of frontier AI systems. At the same time, each exhibits distinctive strengths: the AIA's extraterritorial

16 In the sense of standing above special interest groups and operating with (more) neutrality and impartiality.

reach, institutional innovations, and potential to amplify the 'Brussels effect' position it as a globally influential standard-setter, while the TFAIA's targeted focus on frontier models, robust transparency, and whistleblower protections, and investment in public infrastructure offer a model for practical, state-level implementation.[17]

Nevertheless, both regimes face significant challenges. The AIA contends with governance and enforcement gaps, unclear institutional responsibilities, limited procedural and worker protections, and insufficient attention to sustainability considerations. The TFAIA, while more narrowly focused, exhibits definitional ambiguities, coverage gaps, weak accountability mechanisms, and environmental and implementation shortcomings. These weaknesses point to the importance of ongoing reform, including measures to strengthen institutional capacity, clarify obligations, enhance procedural safeguards, and harmonize approaches across jurisdictions.

The comparative analysis has also revealed that, despite differences in geographic scope, focus, and regulatory philosophy, both frameworks contribute to a gradually converging landscape of AI governance. Targeted reforms – ranging from improved whistleblower protections and expanded oversight mechanisms to more precise definitions and enhanced public infrastructure – could 'harden' these frameworks, ensuring that AI regulation remains robust, adaptive, and socially accountable.

Looking forward, several avenues merit further research and policy attention. First, empirical studies could assess how extraterritorial and state-level AI regulations interact in practice, including their impact on compliance costs, innovation incentives, and the deployment of cross-border AI. Second, comparative work could explore how AI governance frameworks balance safety, accountability, and innovation in different political and economic contexts, and whether these approaches can inform the development of global regulatory norms. Third, research could investigate the role of institutional mechanisms, such as AI offices/boards, public databases, and whistleblower protections, in enhancing both compliance and societal trust. Finally, sustainability, labor, and ethical considerations remain underexplored in both frameworks, raising questions about how AI regulation can better integrate environmental and social welfare objectives alongside technical risk mitigation.

Ultimately, the (likely) interplay between the AIA and TFAIA illustrates the potential for regulatory cross-pollination, where state-level and supranational initiatives mutually inform the evolution of global AI governance. Policymakers and scholars alike will need to closely monitor these developments, ensuring that regulatory frameworks evolve in step with technological advances, societal expectations, and ethical imperatives – striking a durable balance between innovation, safety, and social welfare in a rapidly changing AI landscape.

17 Moreover, while the AIA prioritizes consumer welfare/rights, SME support, and fair competition, the TFAIA places greater emphasis on innovation and safety.

References

AlgorithmWatch. (2021). Draft AI Act: EU Needs to Live Up to Its Own Ambitions in Terms of Governance and Enforcement. https://algorithmwatch.org/en/wp-content/uploads/2021/08/EU-AI-Act-Consultation-Submission-by-AlgorithmWatch-August-2021.pdf (last accessed: December 30, 2025).

Almada, M. & Petit, N. (2023). The E.U. Act: Between Product Safety and Fundamental Rights. https://papers.ssrn.com/sol3/papers.cfm?abstract_id=4308072 (last accessed: December 30, 2025).

Attard-Frost, B., De Los Rios, A., & Walter, D. (2022). The Ethics of AI Business Practices: A Review of 47 AI Ethics Guidelines. AI and Ethics 2022. https://doi.org/10.1007/s43681-022-00156-6 (last accessed: December 30, 2025).

Bender, E. & Hanna, A. (2025). The AI Con. How to Fight Big Tech's Hype and Create the Future We Want. London, Harper.

Biber, S. (2021). Machines Learning the Rule of Law. https://verfassungsblog.de/ai-rol/ (last accessed: December 30, 2025).

Bradford, A. (2020). The Brussels Effect. Oxford, Oxford University Press.

Bradford, A. (2023). Digital Empires. Oxford, Oxford University Press.

Buolamwini, J. (2023). Unmasking AI. My Mission to Protect What is Human in a World of Machines. New York, Random House.

Buolamwini, J. & Gebru, T. (2018). Gender Shades: Intersectional Accuracy Disparities in Commercial Gender Classification. Proceedings of Machine Learning Research 81. 1–15.

California State Legislature. (2025). Senate Bill 53 (Transparency in Frontier Artificial Intelligence Act). https://legiscan.com/CA/text/SB53/2025 (last accessed: December 30, 2025).

Castets-Renard, C. & Besse, P. (2022). Ex Ante Accountability of the AI Act: Between Certification and Standardization, in Pursuit of Fundamental Rights in the Country of Compliance. https://papers.ssrn.com/sol3/papers.cfm?abstract_id=4203925 (last accessed: December 30, 2025).

Cefaliello, A. & Kullmann, M. (2022). Offering False Security: How the Draft Artificial Intelligence Act Undermines Fundamental Workers' Rights. European Labor Law Journal 13(4). 542–562.

Council of the European Union. (2022a). Artificial Intelligence Act: Council Calls for Promoting Safe AI That Respects Fundamental Rights. www.consilium.europa.eu/en/press/press-releases/2022/12/06/artificial-intelligence-act-council-calls-for-promoting-safe-ai-that-respects-fundamental-rights/#:~:text=The%20Council%20has%20adopted%20its,fundamental%20rights%20and%20Union%20values (last accessed: December 30, 2025).

Council of the European Union. (2022b). Artificial Intelligence Act. General Approach. https://data.consilium.europa.eu/doc/document/ST-14954-2022-INIT/en/pdf (last accessed: December 30, 2025).

Dachwitz, I. & Hilbig, S. (2025). Digitaler Kolonialismus. Wie Tech-Konzerne und Großmächte die Welt unter sich aufteilen. Munich. C.H. Beck.

Ebers, M. (2020). Regulating AI and Robotics: Ethical and Legal Challenges. In: Ebers, M. & Navas, S. (eds.). Algorithms and Law. Cambridge, Cambridge University Press. 37–99.

Ebers, M. (2022). Standardizing AI – The Case of the European Commission's Proposal for an Artificial Intelligence Act. In: DiMatteo, L., Poncibo, C., & Cannarsa, M. (eds.). The Cambridge Handbook of Artificial Intelligence. Global Perspectives on Law and Ethics. Cambridge, Cambridge University Press. 321–344.

Ebers, M., Hoch, V., Rosenkranz, F., Ruschemeier, H., & Steinrötter, B. (2021). The European Commission's Proposal for an Artificial Intelligence Act – A Critical Assessment by Members of the Robotics and AI Law Society (RAILS). J Multidisciplinary Scientific Journal 4(4). 589–603.

European Commission. (2020). White Paper on Artificial Intelligence: A European Approach to Excellence and Trust. https://commission.europa.eu/publications/white-paper-artificial-intelligence-european-approach-excellence-and-trust_en (last accessed: December 30, 2025).

European Commission. (2021). Commission Staff Working Document. Impact Assessment. Annexes. https://ec.europa.eu/info/law/better-regulation/have-your-say/initiatives/12527-Artificial-intelligence-ethical-and-legal-requirements_en (last accessed: December 30, 2025).

European Commission. (2025). The General-Purpose AI Code of Practice. https://digital-strategy.ec.europa.eu/en/policies/contents-code-gpai (last accessed: December 30, 2025).

European Parliamentary Research Service. (2022a). Artificial Intelligence Act. www.europarl.europa.eu/RegData/etudes/BRIE/2021/698792/EPRS_BRI(2021)698792_EN.pdf (last accessed: December 30, 2025).

European Parliamentary Research Service. (2022b). Artificial Intelligence Act and Regulatory Sandboxes. www.europarl.europa.eu/RegData/etudes/BRIE/2022/733544/EPRS_BRI(2022)733544_EN.pdf (last accessed: December 30, 2025).

European Parliamentary Research Service. (2022c). AI and Digital Tools in Workplace Management and Evaluation. www.europarl.europa.eu/RegData/etudes/STUD/2022/729516/EPRS_STU(2022)729516_EN.pdf (last accessed: December 30, 2025).

European Parliament & Council of the European Union. (2024). Artificial Intelligence Act. https://eur-lex.europa.eu/eli/reg/2024/1689/oj/eng (last accessed: December 30, 2025).

Fjeld, J., Achten, N., Hilligoss, H., Nagy, A., & Srikumar, M. (2020). Principled Artificial Intelligence: Mapping Consensus in Ethical and Rights-Based Approaches to Principles for AI. https://dash.harvard.edu/bitstream/handle/1/42160420/HLS%20White%20Paper%20Final_v3.pdf (last accessed: December 30, 2025).

Floridi, L. (2021). The European Legislation on AI: A Brief Analysis of Its Philosophical Approach. Philosophy & Technology 34. 215–222.

Floridi, L., Holweg, M., Taddeo, M., Silva, J., Mökander, & Wen, Y. (2022). capAI – A Procedure for Conducting Conformity Assessment of AI Systems in Line with the E.U. Artificial Intelligence Act. https://papers.ssrn.com/sol3/papers.cfm?abstract_id=4064091 (last accessed: 4 February 2026).

Freedman, L. & Patel, R. (2025). AI At the Frontier: What California's SB-53 Means for Large AI Model Developers. https://natlawreview.com/article/ai-frontier-what-californias-sb-53-means-large-ai-model-developers (last accessed: December 30, 2025).

Governor Newsom. (2025). Governor Newsom Signs SB 53, Advancing California's World-Leading Artificial Intelligence Industry. https://www.gov.ca.gov/2025/09/29/governor-newsom-signs-sb-53-advancing-californias-world-leading-artificial-intelligence-industry/ (last accessed: December 30, 2025).

Gstrein, O. (2022). European AI Regulation: Brussels Effect versus Human Dignity. Zeitschrift für Europarechtliche Studien 04/2022. 755–772.

Hacker, P. (2021). A Legal Framework for AI Training Data – From First Principles to the Artificial Intelligence Act. Law, Innovation, and Technology 13(2). 257–301.

Häußermann, J. & Lütge, C. (2022). Community-In-The-Loop: Towards Pluralistic Value Creation in AI, Or – Why AI Needs Business Ethics. AI and Ethics 2. 341–362.

High-Level Expert Group on AI. (2019). Ethics Guidelines for Trustworthy AI. https://digital-strategy.ec.europa.eu/en/library/ethics-guidelines-trustworthy-ai (last accessed: December 30, 2025).

Hunton Andrews Kurth. (2025). California Governor Newsom Signs Groundbreaking AI Legislation Into Law. https://natlawreview.com/article/california-governor-newsom-signs-groundbreaking-ai-legislation-law (last accessed: December 30, 2025).

Joint California Policy Working Group on AI Frontier Models. (2025). The California Report on Frontier AI Policy. https://www.gov.ca.gov/wp-content/uploads/2025/06/June-17-2025-%E2%80%93-The-California-Report-on-Frontier-AI-Policy.pdf (last accessed: December 30, 2025).

Khanna, R. (2022). Dignity in a Digital Age: Making Tech Work for All of Us. New York, Simon & Schuster.

Klump, R. & Wörsdörfer, M. (2015). Paternalist Economic Policies. Foundations, Implications, and Critical Evaluations. ORDO Yearbook of Economic and Social Order 66. 27–60.

Kobrin, S. (2009). Private Political Authority and Public Responsibility: Transnational Politics, Transnational Firms, and Human Rights. Business Ethics Quarterly 19(3). 349–374.

Kop, M. (2021). E.U. Artificial Intelligence Act: The European Approach to AI. https://futurium.ec.europa.eu/sites/default/files/2021-10/Kop_EU%20Artificial%20Intelligence%20Act%20-%20The%20European%20Approach%20to%20AI_21092021_0.pdf (last accessed: December 30, 2025).

Laux, J., Wachter, S., & Mittelstadt, B. (2023a). Trustworthy Artificial Intelligence and the European Union AI Act: On the Conflation of Trustworthiness and Acceptability of Risk. Regulation and Governance 6 (February 2023). 1–30.

Laux, J., Wachter, S., & Mittelstadt, B. (2023b). Three Pathways for Standardization and Ethical Disclosure by Default Under the European Union Artificial Intelligence Act. https://papers.ssrn.com/sol3/papers.cfm?abstract_id=4365079 (last accessed: December 30, 2025).

Leslie, D. (2019). Understanding Artificial Intelligence Ethics and Safety. A Guide for the Responsible Design and Implementation of AI Systems in the Public Sector. www.turing.ac.uk/sites/default/files/2019-06/understanding_artificial_intelligence_ethics_and_safety.pdf (last accessed: December 30, 2025).

Leslie, D., Burr, C., Aitken, M., Cowls, J., Katell, M., & Briggs, M. (2021). Artificial Intelligence, Human Rights, Democracy, and the Rule of Law: A Primer. www.turing.ac.uk/sites/default/files/2021-03/cahai_feasibility_study_primer_final.pdf (last accessed: December 30, 2025).

Metzinger, T. (2019). Ethics Washing Made in Europe. www.tagesspiegel.de/politik/ethics-washing-made-in-europe-5937028.html (last accessed: December 30, 2025).

Micklitz, H. & Gestel, R. (2013). European Integration Through Standardization: How Judicial Review is Breaking Down the Clubhouse of Private Standardization Bodies. Common Market Law Review 50(1). 145–181.

Mittelstadt, B. (2019). Principles Alone Cannot Guarantee Ethical AI. Nature Machine Intelligence 1. 501–507.

Muldoon, J., Graham, M., & Cant, C. (2025). Feeding the Machine: The Hidden Human Labor Powering AI. Edinburgh, Canongate.

NBC News. (2025). California Bill Regulating Top AI Companies Signed Into Law. https://www.nbcnews.com/tech/tech-news/ai-law-california-ca-companies-regulation-newsom-rcna234562 (last accessed: December 30, 2025).

New York Times. (2025). California Governor Signs Sweeping A.I. Law. https://www.nytimes.com/2025/09/29/technology/california-ai-safety-law.html (last accessed: December 30, 2025).

O'Neil, C. (2016). Weapons of Math Destruction. New York, Penguin.

Petit, N. (2020). Big Tech and the Digital Economy. Oxford, Oxford University Press.

Rubenstein, D. (2021). Acquiring Ethical AI. Florida Law Review 73. 747–819.

Schepel, H. (2005). The Constitution of Private Governance. Product Standards in the Regulation of Integrating Markets. Oxford, Hart.

Scherer, A. & Palazzo, G. (2007). Toward a Political Conception of Corporate Responsibility – Business and Society Seen from a Habermasian Perspective. Academy of Management Review 32(4). 1096–1120.

Scherer, A. & Palazzo, G. (2008). Globalization and Corporate Social Responsibility. In: Crane, A. et al. (eds.). The Oxford Handbook of Corporate Social Responsibility. Oxford, Oxford University Press. 413–431.

Scherer, A., Palazzo, G., & Matten, D. (2014). The Business Firm as a Political Actor. A New Theory of the Firm for a Globalized World. Business and Society 53(2). 43–156.

Smuha, N., Ahmed-Rengers, E., Harkens, A., Li, W., MacLaren, J., Piselli, R., & Yeung, K. (2021). How the E.U. Can Achieve Legally Trustworthy AI: A Response to the European Commission's Proposal for an Artificial Intelligence Act. https://papers.ssrn.com/sol3/papers.cfm?abstract_id=3899991 (last accessed: December 30, 2025).

Stuurman, K. & Lachaud, E. (2022). Regulating AI. A Label to Complete the Proposed Act on Artificial Intelligence. Computer Law & Security Review 44 (April 2022). 1–23.

Trump White House. (2025a). Removing Barriers to American Leadership in Artificial Intelligence. https://www.whitehouse.gov/presidential-actions/2025/01/removing-barriers-to-american-leadership-in-artificial-intelligence/ (last accessed: December 30, 2025).

Trump White House. (2025b). White House Unveils America's AI Action Plan. https://www.whitehouse.gov/articles/2025/07/white-house-unveils-americas-ai-action-plan/ (last accessed: December 30, 2025).

Trump White House. (2025c). Winning the Race. America's AI Action Plan. https://www.whitehouse.gov/wp-content/uploads/2025/07/Americas-AI-Action-Plan.pdf.

Trump White House. (2025d). AI.Gov. https://www.ai.gov/#home-services-anchor (last accessed: December 30, 2025).

Trump White House. (2025e). Ensuring a National Policy Framework for Artificial Intelligence. https://www.whitehouse.gov/presidential-actions/2025/12/eliminating-state-law-obstruction-of-national-artificial-intelligence-policy/ (last accessed: December 30, 2025).

Vanberg, V. (2005). Market and State: The Perspective of Constitutional Political Economy. Journal of Institutional Economics 1(1). 23–49.

Vanberg, V. (2013). James M. Buchanan's Contractarianism and Modern Liberalism. www.eucken.de/fileadmin/bilder/Dokumente/DP2013/Diskussionspapier_1304.pdf (last accessed: December 30, 2025).

Veale, M. & Zuiderveen Borgesius, F. (2021). Demystifying the Draft E.U. Artificial Intelligence Act. Computer Law Review International 4/2021. 97–112.

Vox. (2025). This California Law Will Require Transparency From AI Companies. But Will It Actually Prevent Major Disasters? https://www.vox.com/future-perfect/461340/sb53-california-ai-bill-catastrophic-risk-explained (last accessed: December 30, 2025).

Waem, H., Dauzier, J., & Demircan, M. (2024). Fundamental Rights Impact Assessments Under the EU AI Act: Who, What, and How? www.technologyslegaledge.com/2024/03/fundamental-rights-impact-assessments-under-the-eu-ai-act-who-what-and-how/ (last accessed: December 30, 2025).

Wörsdörfer, M. (2023). The Digital Markets Act and E.U. Competition Policy: A Critical Ordoliberal Evaluation. Philosophy of Management 22(1). 149–171.

Wörsdörfer, M. (2024a). Mitigating the Adverse Effects of AI With the European Union's Artificial Intelligence Act – Hype or Hope? Global Business and Organizational Excellence 43(3). 106–126.

Wörsdörfer, M. (2024b). Biden's Executive Order on AI and the E.U.'s AI Act – A Comparative Computer- and Business-Ethical Analysis. Philosophy & Technology 37. Article 74.

Wörsdörfer, M. (2025a). The E.U.'s Artificial Intelligence Act – An Ordoliberal Assessment. AI and Ethics 5(1). 263–278.

Wörsdörfer, M. (2025b). AI Ethics and Ordoliberalism 2.0: Towards a 'Digital Bill of Rights.' AI and Ethics 5(1). 507–525.

Wörsdörfer, M. (2025c). Biden's Executive Order on AI: Strengths, Weaknesses, and Possible Reform Steps. AI and Ethics 5(2). 1669–1683.

Wörsdörfer, M. (2025d). Computer Ethics in the Age of Trump: The Politics of AI and Tech Governance. Orono. University of Maine Working Paper.

Wörsdörfer, M. (2025e). Ten Reasons Why – The Case for More and Better AI Regulation. AI and Ethics 6, Article 62.

Zumbansen, P. (2010a). Corporate Governance, Capital Market Regulation, and the Challenge of Disembedded Markets. Osgoode CLPE 24/2010.

Zumbansen, P. (2010b). Transnational Legal Pluralism. Transnational Legal Theory 1(2). 141–189.

Zumbansen, P. (2010c). Neither 'Public' nor 'Private,' 'National' nor 'International.' Transnational Corporate Governance from a Legal Pluralist Perspective. Osgoode CLPE 22/2010.

Chapter 6
The case for breaking up tech conglomerates

Abstract: This chapter provides a business- and computer-ethical analysis of current antitrust lawsuits, regulatory investigations, and anti-competitive business practices in the United States and E.U., with a focus on the ethical, economic, and societal implications of artificial intelligence (AI) deployment by dominant technology firms. Adopting an interdisciplinary framework that integrates AI ethics and competition policy perspectives, the study examines how corporate concentration in firms such as Alphabet and Meta affects consumer rights/welfare, innovation, market competition, and small and medium-sized enterprises. Drawing on principles of ordoliberalism 2.0, this chapter argues that existing regulatory measures are insufficient to mitigate the economic and political power of big tech. It evaluates policy instruments ranging from automatic sanctions to structured enforcement pyramids, ultimately considering corporate breakups as a measure of last resort to restore competitive balance. By linking ethical considerations with practical regulatory strategies, the study offers actionable insights for enhancing AI governance, promoting fair competition, and safeguarding both consumer and societal interests in increasingly concentrated digital markets.

Keywords: Big tech, antitrust, competition policy, anti-competitive business practices, Digital Markets Act, ordoliberalism 2.0

6.1 Introduction

Recent developments in U.S. antitrust enforcement, exemplified by the lawsuits against Google and Meta, underscore the growing tension between the (socio-)economic power of dominant digital platforms and the (insufficient) legal frameworks designed to regulate them. In Google's landmark search-monopoly case, a judge determined that the company had acted illegally to maintain its dominance in online search, recognizing it as a true monopolist. The DOJ proposed breaking up Google, including the divestiture of Chrome or Android; however, the final ruling imposed significantly narrower remedies. Google was (only) required to share portions of its search index and user-interaction data with competitors and to establish an antitrust technical committee – a five-person group including privacy experts tasked with ensuring that Google complies with the court ruling, sharing appropriate data with competitors, and safeguarding user privacy – while retaining its core business model and a multibillion-dollar default-search agreement with Apple. Under this deal, Google pays Apple approximately $20 billion annually for handling search queries on iPhones, reinforcing its dominance while providing Apple with financial incentives to

 | https://doi.org/10.1515/9783112245958-007

refrain from developing an independent search engine (United States et al. vs. Google LLC, 2020, 2024, 2025).

This pattern of entrenched market power is echoed in the recent Meta case, which highlights the limitations of existing antitrust law when applied to dynamic digital markets. On November 18, 2025, U.S. District Judge Boasberg ruled in favor of Meta, finding that the Federal Trade Commission (FTC) had not demonstrated that the company holds an illegal monopoly in the personal social networking market. While the FTC argued that Meta's acquisitions of Instagram (2012) and WhatsApp (2014) represented a buy-or-bury strategy to suppress potential competition, the court emphasized that current or imminent monopoly power – not past dominance – must be proven. The judge also noted that social media markets have evolved, with algorithm-driven, video-based platforms like TikTok and YouTube intensifying competition and blurring traditional distinctions between social networking and social media. As a result, Meta faced no sanctions, celebrated the ruling as evidence of 'fierce (market) competition,' and underscored the benefits of innovation on its platforms, while the FTC expressed disappointment and indicated it would review its options (Federal Trade Commission vs. Meta Platforms, Inc., 2025; GovInfo.Gov, 2025; Wu, 2025b).

Against this backdrop, this chapter addresses several central research questions: What are the main socioeconomic problems posed by big tech from an antitrust perspective? What measures have been attempted so far? Why have they proven insufficient? What alternative approaches could enhance regulatory effectiveness? The analysis adopts an interdisciplinary approach, integrating AI and business ethics with an ordoliberal 2.0 antitrust perspective that emphasizes consumer sovereignty (i.e., consumer rights/welfare) – understood here in the ordoliberal sense rather than in Bork's or the Chicago School's framework (see below) – alongside product quality, innovation, and the interests of small and medium-sized enterprises (SMEs). From this standpoint, structural remedies, including the potential breakups of dominant firms such as Alphabet and Meta, are not only defensible but necessary to curb the excessive economic and political power of big tech, with benefits extending to consumers, innovation, and investors (e.g., startups and SMEs) alike. Proposed reforms include automatic sanctions, the implementation of an enforcement pyramid, and the strategic use of divestitures as a measure of last resort to restore market contestability and safeguard consumer welfare or (citizen) sovereignty, to use the ordoliberal term. Methodologically, this chapter relies on a qualitative and normative analysis of recent lawsuits and regulatory probes, complemented by a comprehensive review of the relevant academic literature.

This chapter is structured as follows: The next section examines the economic and political power of big tech, including an excursus on anti-competitive business practices. This is followed by an overview of current and recent E.U. and U.S. lawsuits and probes. Subsequent sections assess the shortcomings of existing policies and outline pathways to enhanced regulatory effectiveness. This chapter concludes with a summary of its main findings and an outlook for future antitrust and regulatory approaches to platform-based digital markets.

6.2 The problem: the growing power of big tech

The global reach of major tech companies underscores their substantial dominance across numerous digital sectors. Google, for example, commands over 90% of the search engine market in most countries, while its Chrome browser and Apple's Safari lead the web browser segment. In mobile operating systems, Android maintains a substantial lead over iOS, just as Windows outpaces macOS in desktop OS usage. In social media, Facebook dominates, supported by Instagram and WhatsApp, collectively attracting billions of users and amplifying Meta's market reach. Platforms such as YouTube and TikTok further illustrate the concentration of digital power among a few key players. Across other markets, big tech firms dominate digital advertising (Google and Meta), e-commerce (Amazon), mapping services (Google), voice assistants and smart speakers (Amazon, Apple, and Google), app stores (Apple and Google), cloud computing (Amazon AWS), and generative AI (OpenAI/Microsoft, Gemini/Google, Anthropic/Amazon, and Google). Chinese tech giants, including Alibaba, Baidu, ByteDance, Huawei, and Tencent, exhibit this concentration in their domestic markets (Wörsdörfer, 2020, 2021, 2022a, 2022b, 2023a, 2024).

Financially, these firms are extraordinarily profitable and continue to grow. In 2024, Amazon led in revenue ($638 billion) and total assets ($625 billion). Alphabet topped net income ($100 billion) and total equity ($325 billion), while Apple reported the highest operating income ($123 billion). Collectively, the 'Big Five' generated over $1.5 trillion in revenue (Statista, 2025a). Their market capitalizations place them among the largest companies globally, led by Nvidia,[1] followed by Microsoft, Apple, Amazon, Alphabet, and Meta – all valued at over a trillion dollars as of mid-2025 (CompaniesMarketCap.com, 2025). Mergers and acquisitions (M&As), including 'killer acquisitions,' have been central to their strategies, often targeting intellectual property or potential competitors, with most deals historically unchallenged by U.S. and European regulators (Wörsdörfer, 2020, 2021, 2022a, 2022b, 2023a, 2024).

These firms function as de facto monopolists or oligopolists, exerting near-total control within their sectors. This concentration, often referred to as 'monopoly capitalism,' is reinforced by structural advantages such as economies of scale and strong network effects, where platform value increases with user adoption, further marginalizing competitors. While platform capitalism offers certain consumer benefits, it frequently displaces smaller businesses and limits market diversity. Access to vast quantities of personal data – the so-called 'oil of the twenty-first century' – further strengthens their market dominance. Many digital markets also exhibit winner-takes-all dynamics, where a few firms capture the majority of value (Wörsdörfer, 2020, 2021, 2022a, 2022b, 2023a, 2024).

1 Nvidia commands approximately 95% of the Graphics Processing Unit (GPU) market for machine learning applications (Muldoon et al., 2025).

The consolidation of economic power raises significant political concerns, including lobbying, rent-seeking, and regulatory capture via mechanisms such as revolving doors, campaign contributions, and frequent interactions with government officials (Taplin, 2018). Big tech's anti-competitive practices (see below) intensify these issues. They also contribute to novel consumer harms, including privacy erosion and data exploitation,[2] alongside socio-political risks such as the spread of disinformation and harmful content[3] (Wörsdörfer, 2020, 2021, 2022a, 2022b, 2023a, 2024).

2 Dominant digital platforms can generate *novel forms of consumer harm* through both market and behavioral mechanisms (Petit, 2020; Srinivasan, 2019; Zuboff, 2019). As discussed above, powerful firms often extract monopoly rents while restricting market entry, regulating access to key platforms, or excluding competitors entirely. Strategic M&As can further block potential entrants, reducing venture capital investment in sectors dominated by a single company. These practices collectively slow the pace of innovation, ultimately harming consumers. Beyond innovation suppression, consumers face increased advertising exposure, higher prices for apps, software, and services, fewer choices, and lower service quality. Quality and welfare losses are particularly evident in decreased data security and privacy violations, exemplified by repeated breaches and misuse of personal data by platforms such as Meta. Consumers are also vulnerable to exploitation of cognitive and behavioral biases, including status quo bias, salience bias, and limited self-control, which are leveraged through tools like digital advertising (e.g., subliminal messaging and personalized layouts), captology (persuasive technology), digital nudging via AI algorithms, and gamification (Commission Competition Law 4.0, 2019; Helbing et al., 2017; Klump & Wörsdörfer, 2015; Stigler Center, 2019). The resulting effects include consumer stickiness, discrimination, manipulation, exploitation of personal vulnerabilities, and potential mental health issues, particularly in advertising-supported platforms and online gaming (Haidt, 2024).

3 Big tech also produces *socio-political harm* by shaping the information environment. Algorithmically curated content can create filter bubbles and echo chambers (Ash, 2016; Pariser, 2011), where users' personalized newsfeeds reflect only pre-existing interests and ideologies. This reduces exposure to diverse ideas, reinforces confirmation bias, and diminishes open-mindedness, creativity, and critical thinking. Such dynamics fragment society, weaken social cohesion, and erode the public sphere by reducing bridging social capital (Habermas, 1983, 1991; Putnam, 1993a, 1993b, 2000), while reinforcing ideological subcultures. The spread of misinformation and disinformation, or 'fake news,' compounds these effects, undermining public trust in democratic institutions (Snyder, 2017). Social media platforms, incentivized by attention-driven business models, often amplify false or misleading content because it generates higher engagement and ad revenue than accurate information, with rapid dissemination leaving little opportunity for fact-checking (Frenkel & Kang, 2021). Online platforms can also propagate dangerous and hate speech. Dangerous speech, which presents imminent threats of violence, is legally restricted in both the United States and E.U., whereas hate speech, verbal insults without immediate threat, is treated differently: largely unregulated in the United States under the First Amendment but increasingly restricted in the E.U. via legislation such as Germany's Network Enforcement Act and the E.U.'s Digital Services Act (Ash, 2016). These regulatory differences highlight the discretion of tech companies in controlling content, with platforms in the United States enjoying broad immunity under Section 230 of the Communications Decency Act (Frenkel & Kang, 2021). This legal framework effectively positions firms as neutral intermediaries rather than socially accountable publishers, leaving the moderation of harmful content primarily in the hands of private corporations rather than public institutions (Wörsdörfer, 2025).

6.2.1 Excursus: anti-competitive business practices of big tech

Various forms of anti-competitive business conduct exist in the digital economy, including but not limited to structural dominance, leveraging, gatekeeping, self-preferencing, copycat expropriations, discriminatory platform access, predatory pricing, 'killer acquisitions,' and monopsony power.[4] The following paragraphs provide an overview of these practices, outlining how each contributes to the consolidation of market power and the distortion of competitive dynamics in big tech-dominated ecosystems.

Structural dominance (market power)
Many technology companies command a substantial share of industry output and maintain an outsized corporate footprint – whether measured by product portfolios, market capitalization, or global reach. Big data – often described as the 'new currency' or the 'oil of the twenty-first century' – is a central driver of this structural dominance (and hence market power). From an ordoliberal 2.0 perspective, the problem is not the sheer size of large tech firms per se; rather, it is that many have built 'data-opolies,' conglomerates whose market power is anchored in the control and ownership of vast data reservoirs. This data concentration enables tech firms to entrench dominance and extend their influence across markets and sectors.

Leveraging
Large technology firms routinely leverage their market power in one domain to secure monopoly or oligopoly positions in adjacent markets, thereby contravening ordoliberal 2.0 principles, such as the principles of a competitive economy and open markets. Cross-leveraging of data and financial resources enables them to tilt markets in their favor, rather than 'competing on the merits,' as ordoliberalism 2.0 demands. This power asymmetry also allows them to conduct targeted market research, monitor the performance of competing software, or swiftly replicate successful applications. In doing so, they can overshadow or eliminate rivals with comparatively little effort.

Gatekeeping
Dominant tech companies often act as essential gatekeepers between consumers and digital markets. They mediate – and to a significant extent control – the mechanisms through which users communicate, interact, transact, and access information. Amazon (and Alibaba) serve as primary gateways for online commerce; Facebook (and Tencent) for social networking; Google (and Baidu) for search; and Apple and Google for app distribution on iOS and Android.

Gatekeeping power concentrates control over digital filters in the hands of a few firms, heightening the risk of abuse and thus violating key ordoliberal 2.0 principles. Moreover, companies dependent on these gatekeepers face heightened business risks, as gatekeepers can tax, squeeze, coerce, or expropriate them, according to the Subcommittee on Antitrust (2020). GAFAM (Google, Apple, Facebook, Amazon, and Microsoft) and their Chinese counterparts also occupy a conflicted dual role: they regulate platform access for third parties while simultaneously competing against them. This structural conflict poses significant antitrust concerns, particularly when exploited through sudden changes to terms and conditions, data extraction, technology appropriation, self-preferencing, and other exclusionary practices.

Self-preferencing
Dominant firms can use their entrenched position in 'tipped' markets to favor their own products or services in adjacent 'untipped' markets. Preferential treatment for their own downstream or upstream offerings allows them to extend dominance, entrench market power, and violate ordoliberal 2.0 requirements

4 Baer et al., 2020; Commission 'Competition Law 4.0,' 2019; Furman Report, 2019; Klobuchar, 2021; Petit, 2020; Scott Morton, 2019; Stigler Report, 2019; Subcommittee on Antitrust, 2020.

for non-exclusionary contracts. As shown in the Google Shopping case (Kornelakis, 2021), such conduct can lead to the promotion of inferior products, distort competitive dynamics, and ultimately result in reduced service quality for consumers.

Copycat expropriation

Some major tech firms imitate or replicate products developed by third-party creators. Apple and Google, for example, have copied successful apps created by independent software developers within their app stores, while Amazon has replicated high-selling products offered by third-party sellers on its marketplace. Such copycat strategies exploit information asymmetries and undermine the competitiveness of smaller innovators.

Discriminatory platform access

Exclusionary or discriminatory practices can take various forms, including:
- imposing Most Favoured Nation (MFN) (exclusivity or price-parity) clauses,
- impeding multi-homing,
- preventing switching through bundling and tying,
- restricting data portability, and
- limiting interoperability through technical barriers (Crémer et al., 2019).

These practices prevent independent sellers from offering lower prices elsewhere, hinder users from accessing multiple services simultaneously, raise switching costs, and create data-driven lock-ins. Collectively, they raise market-entry barriers, weaken competitive pressure, and can harm consumer welfare – for example, by preventing access to higher-quality alternatives. Such conduct directly conflicts with ordoliberal 2.0 principles of open markets and non-exclusionary contracts.

Predatory pricing

Companies such as Amazon (e.g., Amazon Echo) and Apple (e.g., Apple TV) have employed below-cost pricing strategies to eliminate potential rivals. By temporarily sacrificing profits in pursuit of scale, they seek to secure market dominance and achieve 'winner-takes-all' or 'winner-takes-most' outcomes. This strategy prioritizes growth – and the entrenchment of power – over sustainable market competition.

'Killer acquisitions'

'Killer M&As' refer to acquisitions in which dominant firms buy promising start-ups to prevent them from emerging as future competitors (Glick et al., 2020; Subcommittee on Antitrust, 2020; Washington Post, 2021).[5] Wu terms this the 'Kronos effect,' whereby dominant firms "consume their potential successors in their infancy" (Wu, 2011, p. 25; see also Wu, 2025a). In some cases, large tech firms have used 'sell-or-be-ruined' threats to pressure start-ups into being acquired. Such acquisitions diminish competitive pressure on incumbents and may impede competition through horizontal, vertical, or conglomerate effects, including increased data concentration, thereby violating core ordoliberal 2.0 principles. They also block future entry by potential rivals, reduce innovation, and discourage the creation and financing of new firms. Ven-

5 Examples of major big tech M&As over the past decade and a half illustrate the continued trend toward large-scale consolidation in digital markets. Notable transactions include Microsoft's acquisition of Skype for $8.5 billion (2011); Facebook's purchase of Instagram for $1 billion (2012); Google's acquisition of Waze for $966 million (2013); Apple's acquisition of Beats for $3 billion (2014); Facebook's acquisition of WhatsApp for approximately $19–22 billion (2014); Google's purchase of Nest for $3.2 billion (2014); Microsoft's acquisition of LinkedIn for roughly $26–27 billion (2016); Amazon's acquisition of Whole Foods Market for $13.7 billion (2017); Microsoft's acquisition of GitHub for $7.5 billion (2018); Google's acquisition of Fitbit for $2.1 billion (2019); Salesforce's acquisition of Slack for $27.7 billion (2020); Amazon's acquisition of MGM for $8.45 billion (2021); and Microsoft's acquisition of Activision Blizzard for $68.7 billion (2022), one of the largest tech acquisitions in history.

ture capitalists, for example, are often reluctant to fund start-ups in market segments dominated by a single powerful player due to the risk of replication or predatory M&A behavior. Areas surrounding dominant platforms – characterized by a near-total absence of viable competition – have become known as 'innovation kill zones' (Commission Competition Law 4.0, 2019). According to the U.S. Subcommittee on Antitrust (2020), such acquisitions have contributed to declining business formation, reduced start-up funding, and lower entrepreneurship and job creation. The dominance of online platforms has therefore weakened innovation ecosystems in the United States.

Monopsony power

Corporate concentration also generates adverse effects in labor markets. Firms with monopsony power, such as Amazon, wield disproportionate bargaining power over their workforce, especially delivery, warehouse, seasonal, and logistics workers. This allows them not only to suppress wages, dictate working conditions, and influence labor standards across entire sectors (Subcommittee on Antitrust, 2020), but also to employ union-busting tactics (as seen at Amazon and Apple), impose non-compete clauses, and rely heavily on subcontracting arrangements that further weaken worker protections. These practices often contribute to inhumane working conditions, exacerbating the 'social question' and the problem of the working poor discussed by Eucken (1952/2004; see Wörsdörfer, 2022c) and other ordoliberals, thereby potentially violating key ordoliberal 2.0 principles.

A list of illustrative examples of big tech's anti-competitive business practices is provided in Table 6.1.

Table 6.1: Illustrative examples of big tech's anti-competitive business practices.

Practice	Description (short)	Illustrative examples
Structural dominance	Power based on scale, data concentration, and multi-market reach.	Amazon's data collection across retail, logistics, and Prime ecosystems. Google's dominance in search (90% + market share). Meta's integration of Facebook, Instagram, and WhatsApp data.
Leveraging	Using dominance in one market to gain advantages in another.	Amazon using marketplace sales data to develop Amazon Basics. Google leveraging Search to strengthen Chrome and Android adoption. Google Maps offering hotel/restaurant reviews, thereby entering TripAdvisor and Yelp's market.
Gatekeeping	Controlling critical access routes between consumers and businesses.	Apple App Store and Google Play controlling mobile app distribution. Amazon Marketplace as the primary retail entry point for small sellers. Google Search determining visibility for firms and websites.
Self-preferencing	Favoring one's own products or services over third-party competitors.	Amazon giving preferential positioning to Basics and private-label brands. Apple pre-installing native apps (Apple Music and Safari) as defaults.

Table 6.1 (continued)

Practice	Description (short)	Illustrative examples
		Apple/Google's app stores promoting their own services. Google promoting its own service in search results (Google Shopping, etc.). Meta replicating Snapchat-like features (e.g., Stories and Reels).
Copycat expropriation	Replicating third-party innovations using privileged platform data.	Amazon copying high-performing third-party products. Apple integrating popular app features into iOS (e.g., parental controls). App store operators spotting and integrating popular products. Meta cloning features from Snapchat and TikTok.
Discriminatory platform access	Practices that restrict competition through exclusive contracts or technical barriers.	Amazon imposing MFN clauses on sellers. Apple limiting alternative payment systems and multi-homing. Google's Android contracts requiring pre-installation of Google apps. Meta restricting API access for competing apps (e.g., Vine). Microsoft tying Internet Explorer to Windows and bundling Office/Teams with Windows.
Predatory pricing	Below-cost pricing to eliminate or weaken rivals.	Amazon selling Echo devices below cost to expand Alexa ecosystem. Apple TV launching with low pricing or free bundles. Lyft and Uber below-cost pricing to dominate ride-hailing.
'Killer acquisitions'	Acquiring potential rivals to prevent future competition.	Amazon acquiring Diapers.com after aggressive price undercutting. Facebook acquiring Instagram and WhatsApp. Google acquiring Waze (navigation) and DoubleClick (ads).
Monopsony power	Dominance in labor markets enabling wage suppression, the weakening of labor protections, and restrictions on worker mobility and bargaining power.	Amazon's influence on logistics and warehouse worker wages (and inhumane working conditions). Apple and Amazon's union-busting tactics (stores, warehouses). Lyft/Uber shaping wage and labor standards for gig workers. Various companies: no-poach wage suppression agreement, non-compete clauses, and sub-contracting

Lanier (2013) critiques this trajectory, arguing that the current information economy resembles a new form of feudalism rather than traditional capitalism. He describes 'Siren Servers' – centralized data systems controlled by a few tech giants – that concentrate wealth, influence, and control over digital identities. According to Lanier, this 'Silicon Age' is a new Gilded Age, benefiting a small number of firms while leaving the majority with minimal gains. When these firms become indispensable to society, they reach a 'too big to fail' status, with potential collapses threatening markets and governments. Lanier warns that the convergence of big tech and government (e.g., via agencies like the NSA) poses a dual threat to personal liberty, undermining privacy, autonomy, and democratic governance.

O'Neil's analysis in *Weapons of Math Destruction* (2016; see Buolamwini, 2023) extends and concretizes these concerns by illustrating how the same concentration of data power enables harmful algorithmic systems that disproportionately impact poor and ethnic minorities. These systems are shown to lead to and enhance discrimination, racism, and entrenched prejudices. The opaque models that underpin them increase inequality, deepen the social divide by reinforcing the status quo, and ultimately harm democratic processes. By creating and amplifying negative feedback loops, such as poverty traps, they lock vulnerable groups into vicious circles with little chance of escape. The primary issues stem from a lack of accountability and transparency, as these algorithms often operate as 'black boxes' that can be manipulated without public oversight. Coupled with minimal monitoring, weak regulatory oversight, and the absence of meaningful complaint mechanisms, this unregulated aspect of the data economy enables data brokers to treat individuals as products, thereby accelerating the commodification of society.

6.3 Actions taken: major lawsuits and regulatory probes

Over the past two decades, major technology companies have faced increasing scrutiny from regulators in both the United States and the E.U., reflecting concerns about their monopolistic and anti-competitive behavior (New York Times, 2025a). In the United States, the Department of Justice (DOJ) has filed lawsuits against Google and Apple. Google is accused of maintaining an illegal monopoly over search[6] and online advertising[7] through exclusive business contracts and unfair dominance in online ad-

---

6 The DOJ, along with a coalition of states, filed a landmark antitrust lawsuit against Google on October 20, 2020, alleging that the company maintained a monopoly over online search, which accounts for roughly 90% of all internet queries in the United States. The suit contended that Google used exclusive contracts with phone makers, including Apple, to make its search engine the default on devices, thereby limiting consumer choice and hindering competition from rivals such as Bing and DuckDuckGo (United States et al. vs. Google LLC, 2020). The trial began on October 2, 2023, with Microsoft CEO Nadella testifying that even his company struggled to compete with Google's search products, while Alphabet CEO Pichai argued that Google's deals benefited consumers. On August 5, 2024, a federal judge ruled in a 277-page decision that Google had acted illegally to maintain its monopoly (United States et al. vs. Google LLC, 2024). Remedies proceedings began on April 21, 2025, culminating in a September 2, 2025 ruling requiring Google to share search results with competitors and prohibiting exclusive deals that make it the default search engine on browsers and smartphones. However, the judge did not order the company to divest its Chrome web browser, falling short of the government's broader breakup request (United States et al. vs. Google LLC, 2025).

7 In January 2024, the DOJ and eight states filed an antitrust lawsuit accusing Google of abusing its monopoly over the technologies used to place digital ads, alleging that the company acquired rivals through anticompetitive mergers and pressured publishers and advertisers into using its ad tech stack (United States et al. vs. Google LLC, 2023). The trial began on September 27, 2024, with the government

vertising, while Apple is charged with preserving its smartphone monopoly by preventing third-party access to its software and hardware.[8] Similarly, the FTC, alongside several states, filed a lawsuit against Meta (formerly Facebook), alleging that the acquisitions of Instagram and WhatsApp created an anti-competitive social networking giant, prompting calls for the breakup of the company.[9] Investigations by the House Judiciary Subcommittee on Antitrust, Commercial, and Administrative Law have drawn comparisons between big tech and the oil barons and railroad tycoons of the First Gilded Age (Subcommittee on Antitrust, 2020). In response, multiple bipartisan reform proposals have been introduced in Congress, and neo-Brandeisian scholars (Wörsdörfer 2023b, 2023c, 2023d), including Khan (2017, 2018) and Wu (2018, 2025), have joined the Biden administration to shape competition policy.

In Europe, regulatory actions have similarly targeted the market practices of dominant tech firms (Wörsdörfer, 2022a, 2022b, 2023a, 2024). Between 2004 and 2007, the European Commission investigated Microsoft and required the company to offer a Windows version without a preinstalled Media Player. In 2015 and 2016, Google was accused of abusing its dominant market position through several anti-competitive practices. The company allegedly leveraged Android to promote its own mobile services, imposed Google Search and Chrome on device manufacturers, and prohibited the pre-installation of competing browsers or applications, thereby restricting consumer choice and limiting market entry. Additionally, Google was accused of using its Search platform to favor its own advertising and shopping services. These combined practices led

---

seeking a breakup of Google's advertising business, while Google argued the market was intensely competitive and that the DOJ overlooked rivals such as Facebook and Amazon. On April 17, 2025, a federal judge ruled in a 115-page decision that Google had illegally maintained a monopoly in parts of the online advertising technology market, marking a major victory for the government's case.

8 The DOJ alleged that Apple leveraged its monopoly in the smartphone market to suppress competition and inflate consumer prices. According to the lawsuit, Apple blocked other companies from offering apps that could compete with its own services, including Messages and Wallet (United States v. Apple Inc., 2024). On August 1, 2024, Apple filed a motion to dismiss the case, which Judge Neals ultimately denied on June 30, 2025. The case is pending as of the time of writing.

9 In December 2020, the FTC and more than 40 states filed suit against Facebook – now Meta – alleging that the company established a social media monopoly by acquiring nascent rivals such as Instagram and WhatsApp, and urging the court to unwind those deals. Although a federal judge dismissed the initial complaints in June 2021 for lack of sufficient factual support, the FTC refiled an expanded and more detailed complaint in August 2021, which the court allowed to proceed in January 2022. Meta moved to dismiss the case again in April 2024, but the judge rejected that motion in November 2024, clearing the way for trial. Proceedings began on April 14, 2025, marking the first major antitrust trial against a tech company under the Trump administration; CEO Zuckerberg was the first witness, and the FTC argued that Meta's acquisitions were part of a broader 'buy-or-bury strategy' to neutralize competitive threats. Meta, for its part, maintained that its purchases were pro-competitive and accompanied by substantial investments in the acquired platforms. On November 18, 2025, U.S. District Judge Boasberg ruled in Meta's favor, finding that the FTC failed to show the company holds a current monopoly in 'personal social networking' and rejecting calls to force a breakup of Instagram or WhatsApp.

to fines totaling €8.2 billion across the Android, Google Shopping, and AdSense investigations (European Commission, 2017–2019). In 2020, Amazon faced antitrust charges in the E.U. for allegedly exploiting its dual role as both a retailer and a marketplace platform. The company was accused of using its market power to disadvantage smaller competitors through self-preferencing and of leveraging data from third-party sellers to identify popular products, replicate them, and sell them – often at lower prices – a practice commonly referred to as copycat appropriation. In 2021, Apple and Google faced antitrust investigations over allegedly unfair terms in the App Store and Google Play. Both companies were criticized for their dual role as platform operators and app providers, engaging in self-preferencing, imposing mandatory use of proprietary payment systems, charging up to 30% commission fees on sales and in-app purchases, and enforcing anti-steering provisions that prevented developers from informing users of cheaper alternatives or payment options available elsewhere. These practices were deemed to limit developer choice and restrict competition in mobile app marketplaces (in 2024, Apple was fined over €1.8 billion for abusive App Store practices affecting music streaming providers [European Commission, 2024]). In 2021, the Commission investigated Meta for allegedly tying its Facebook Marketplace service to its social networking platform, while also probing Google's online ad business for favoring its own display ad technology in the ad tech supply chain at the expense of advertisers and publishers. In 2023, the Commission issued a statement of objections to Google over these alleged abusive practices, with the potential goal of breaking up its ad business (in 2025, the company was fined €2.95 billion for violating E.U. antitrust laws [European Commission, 2025b]). In 2022, Apple faced similar scrutiny for allegedly abusing its dominant position in mobile wallets on iOS devices by restricting third-party access to Near Field Communication (NFC) technology, which is used for contactless payments in stores (Wörsdörfer, 2022a, 2022b, 2023a, 2024; see also Table 6.2. for more information).

Table 6.2: Timeline of select E.U. regulatory actions against major tech firms.

Year(s)	Company	Investigation and action	Key allegations and outcomes
2004–2007	Microsoft	Market dominance investigation	Required to offer Windows version without preinstalled Media Player
2015–2016	Google	Abuse of dominant position via Android and Search	Leveraging Android, imposing Search/Chrome, restricting competing apps, and favoring own services
2017–2019	Google	Android, Google Shopping, and AdSense cases	Continuation and expansion of 2015–2016 abuse cases
2020	Amazon	Antitrust charges (Marketplace)	Self-preferencing, exploiting marketplace/ retailer role, and copying popular products

Table 6.2 (continued)

Year(s)	Company	Investigation and action	Key allegations and outcomes
2021	Apple and Google	App Store and Google Play	Self-preferencing, mandatory payments, 30% commission, anti-steering clauses
2021	Meta	Facebook Marketplace investigation	Tying Marketplace to social network
2021	Google	Ad tech investigation	Favoring own display ad technology, possible breakup
2022	Apple	NFC/mobile wallets	Restricting third-party access to NFC for contactless payments
2024–2025	Apple, Google, and Meta	DMA investigations	Engaging in anticompetitive business conduct and violating DMA

To address these concerns, the E.U. implemented the Digital Markets Act (DMA), an ex-ante, sector-specific regulatory framework complementing existing competition law (European Parliament & Council of the European Union, 2022). The overall goal of this Act is to ensure contestability, fairness of digital markets, and strengthen the internal European market, e.g., by lowering market entry barriers, leveling the playing field, and protecting consumer welfare. The DMA targets gatekeepers – companies that provide core platform services and control key distribution channels between businesses and end-users, such as search engines, social networks, video-sharing platforms, operating systems, cloud computing services, app stores, and advertising platforms. Gatekeepers are defined based on their significant market impact (measured in terms of turnover and market capitalization), control over essential gateways (measured in monthly active business and end users), and entrenched and durable positions maintained over at least three consecutive financial years. The DMA imposes obligations to ensure fairness and contestability, including prohibitions on combining personal data without consent, anti-steering and parity clauses, tying and bundling practices, restrictions on pre-installed software, and limitations on app side-loading. Gatekeepers must ensure interoperability, provide FRAND access to rankings (i.e., no self-preferencing in rankings), allow multi-homing and switching, and offer access to continuous, real-time data portability and ad performance tools. Sanctions for non-compliance can reach 10–20% of a firm's global turnover, with Apple[10] ($570 million) and Meta[11] ($230 million) among the first companies fined (New York Times, 2025b;

10 To comply with the DMA, Apple will introduce alternative app stores and marketplaces for customers in the E.U., as well as expanded options for app distribution and payment processing (Apple, 2024).

11 Meta recently announced plans to allow WhatsApp users to communicate seamlessly across multiple messaging platforms (Meta, 2025).

see also European Commission, 2025a).[12] Repeat violations may not only trigger behavioral but also structural remedies, such as divestiture or spin-offs, while ongoing market investigations allow the Commission to designate additional gatekeepers, expand obligations, or extend the scope of the DMA (Wörsdörfer, 2023a).

Collectively, these U.S. and E.U. regulatory actions demonstrate a global effort to curb anti-competitive behavior by dominant tech firms. From DOJ and FTC lawsuits against Google, Apple, and Meta to E.U. antitrust fines and the DMA, these measures aim to ensure market contestability, consumer welfare, and fairness, while mitigating the concentration of economic and political power in a small number of globally influential digital platforms. The legal and regulatory landscape highlights the challenges posed by firms that simultaneously act as gatekeepers, competitors, and rule-makers, raising persistent questions about the balance between innovation, competition, and market fairness in the digital economy.

6.4 Assessing the shortcomings of existing policies

Despite these efforts, existing antitrust measures in both the United States and the E.U. have increasingly proven inadequate for addressing the concentrated power of today's dominant digital platforms. In the United States, the core problem lies in the continued reliance on the Chicago School's consumer-welfare standard, which requires plaintiffs to demonstrate that anti-competitive behavior will lead to higher prices. This framework is fundamentally incompatible with digital and other zero-price markets, where consumers 'pay' not with money but with data, attention, and market lock-in. As a result, harmful conduct, such as leveraging data advantages, self-preferencing, exclusionary design, or acquiring nascent competitors, often escapes meaningful scrutiny because it does not immediately result in price increases.

6.4.1 Excursus: Bork's consumer welfare standard

Between the early to mid-1980s and 2019/2020, antitrust enforcement in the United States remained relatively moderate, with limited government intervention. Notable tech-related cases during this period included the breakup of AT&T into the 'Baby Bells' in 1982, the abandoned case against IBM that same year,

---

12 The Commission has also launched an antitrust investigation into Google's 'site reputation abuse' policy after publishers claimed it penalizes third-party content and hurts their revenue, especially when they host content from commercial partners. The E.U. suspects Google may be demoting legitimate news-publisher content in its search rankings, undermining a key way they monetize their sites. Ribera, the E.U.'s antitrust chief, said the review will determine whether Google is treating publishers "fairly, reasonably and non-discriminatorily" under the DMA (European Commission, 2025c).

and the Microsoft case, which was ultimately settled in 2004. Experts attribute this largely laissez-faire approach to the influence of the Chicago School of Antitrust, led by Robert Bork.

In his seminal work, *Antitrust Paradox* (Bork, 1978/1993; Bork & Bowman, 1965), Bork argued – contrary to ordoliberal 2.0 principles and the Harvard School of Antitrust[13] – for minimal enforcement of antitrust laws. He posited that the sole legitimate goal of antitrust should be the maximization of 'consumer welfare,' understood primarily in terms of market efficiency and aggregate welfare, including corporate profits (Hovenkamp, 2019). Bork also emphasized market self-regulation, asserting that monopolies and cartels are naturally unstable and will inevitably face competitive disruption over time. From this perspective, government intervention, including antitrust enforcement, was unnecessary: left to themselves, markets would naturally correct imbalances and produce efficient outcomes – a process he described as the 'natural purification' of markets (Bork, 1978/1993; Bork & Bowman, 1965; Hovenkamp, 2019, 2021a; Hovenkamp & Scott Morton, 2020).

The libertarian ideology of Bork and the Chicago School had a significant societal impact, particularly during the Reagan administration and subsequent Republican-led governments (Baer et al., 2020). During this era, the antitrust infrastructure was systematically weakened: agency budgets were cut, merger guidelines became more permissive, and the DOJ and FTC pursued far fewer enforcement actions (DOJ, 2021; Klobuchar, 2021; Petit, 2020). Combined with a pro-business judiciary and favorable case law (Baer et al., 2020; Cohen, 2020; Hovenkamp, 2021a), these developments contributed to increasing corporate consolidation and the emergence of 'superstar firms,' particularly in the digital economy (Baer et al., 2020; Hovenkamp & Scott Morton, 2020; Klobuchar, 2021; Wu, 2018, 2025a).

However, the Chicago School's consumer-welfare standard has proven ill-suited for digital and other zero-price markets. In such environments, plaintiffs must demonstrate that a firm's anti-competitive conduct, such as predatory pricing, will eventually result in higher prices, a requirement that is nearly impossible to satisfy when services are free to users. Moreover, the price-centric focus of the consumer-welfare standard overlooks other critical dimensions of competitive harm, including reduced innovation, diminished consumer choice, degraded product or service quality, and threats to consumer sovereignty in areas such as privacy and data protection. For these reasons, many scholars argue that modern antitrust – especially in the digital context – must adopt a broader framework that moves beyond pricing effects and reflects the structural and societal impacts of platform power.

Exacerbating these conceptual gaps are structural limitations: U.S. antitrust cases are slow, reactive, and highly vulnerable to lobbying (Financial Times, 2025; Issue One, 2025; Statista, 2025b), rent-seeking, the revolving door phenomenon, and judicial resistance rooted in four decades of laissez-faire legal precedent. Even when enforcers win major cases, the remedies are frequently narrow or too late to restore competition.

The recent rulings involving Google highlight the limitations of existing U.S. antitrust enforcement (United States et al. vs. Google LLC, 2025). In the landmark search-monopoly case, a judge determined that Google had illegally maintained its dominance in online search, recognizing the company as a true monopolist and ruling that it had acted unlawfully to preserve its market position. The DOJ had proposed a full

13 For further information on the Chicago School, its distinguishing features compared with the Harvard School of antitrust, and its main representatives, Areeda and Turner, see Hovenkamp (2019), Hovenkamp & Scott Morton (2020), Kovacic (2007), and Wu (2018). For an analysis of the similarities and differences between the Chicago School and ordoliberal thought, see Kornelakis and Hublart (2021) and Wörsdörfer (2022b, 2023a).

breakup of Google, including the potential divestment of Chrome and Android, but the court ultimately imposed far narrower remedies. Instead of forcing divestitures, the ruling required Google to share portions of its search index and user-interaction data with competitors and to establish an antitrust technical committee – a five-person group including privacy experts tasked with ensuring compliance while safeguarding user privacy. Despite these measures, Google retained its core business model, its most valuable assets, and its multibillion-dollar default-search agreement with Apple, which continues to reinforce its dominance; under this deal, Google pays Apple roughly $20 billion annually for handling search queries on iPhones, benefiting both companies while deterring Apple from developing its own search engine (Wu, 2025a). As a result, even a rare government victory produced only incremental change, leaving Google's structural market power largely intact (New York Times, 2025c; United States et al. vs. Google LLC, 2020, 2024, 2025).

The Meta case further demonstrates the limits of existing frameworks. In November 2025, a district judge ruled that Meta did not violate antitrust law through its acquisitions of Instagram and WhatsApp, concluding that the FTC had failed to prove the company held a monopoly in 'personal social networking.' The judge emphasized the growing competition from TikTok and YouTube, noting that digital markets have evolved so dramatically that traditional market definitions no longer apply. Because U.S. antitrust law requires proof of current monopoly power – not past dominance or future harm – the government could not challenge Meta's long-term strategy of buying potential rivals. The ruling highlights the challenges of regulating dominant firms within a legal system that evaluates tech markets using narrow, outdated definitions and short-term price effects, rather than considering long-term innovation, data concentration, or ecosystem control (Federal Trade Commission vs. Meta Platforms, Inc., 2025; GovInfo.Gov, 2025; Wu, 2025b).

Despite adopting a more interventionist approach through the DMA, the E.U. continues to face significant enforcement gaps. Critics argue that implementation has been slow, inconsistent, and susceptible to industry lobbying (Corporate Europe Observatory, 2025). Major gatekeepers often delay compliance, negotiate reduced obligations, or exploit procedural loopholes, underscoring regulators' limited capacity to enforce behavioral and structural remedies on a large scale. These challenges are intensified by the lengthy nature of E.U. antitrust proceedings: many cases take years to resolve, remain pending, and in some instances, initial decisions or fines have been overturned or modified by the courts. As in the United States, regulatory capture and resource constraints hinder effective oversight, leaving enforcement trailing behind rapidly evolving technologies and market structures.

Lastly, the second Trump administration has exerted pressure on the E.U. to relax its digital markets regulations, including the DMA (and the Digital Services Act). This pressure has taken multiple forms, such as the threat of tariffs, leveraging trade deal negotiations, and signaling potential retaliatory measures against European digital regulations perceived as disadvantageous to U.S. tech companies. As a result, the DMA faces an uncertain future, with its implementation and enforcement subject to political negotiations, external pressures, and potential adjustments. These dynamics underscore the geopolitical dimension of digital market governance and the tension between promoting competition in Europe and protecting U.S. commercial interests.

6.4.2 Excursus: critical analysis of the DMA

The DMA represents a noteworthy step toward an ordoliberal-inspired framework for regulating digital gatekeepers, yet its implementation reveals both institutional strengths and significant weaknesses.

The DMA incorporates several core ordoliberal 2.0 principles, including competition as a process, competition on the merits, freedom from privileges and non-discrimination, and consumer sovereignty. A primary objective of the Act is to protect competition as a process: it seeks to ensure contestability in gatekeeper markets and related sectors (Crémer et al., 2021; Schweitzer, 2021). In line with ordoliberalism 2.0, competition is understood not only as an economic mechanism but also as a tool to disempower dominant firms and maintain a level playing field. This is particularly relevant in digital markets, where self-preferencing, platform envelopment, and network effects can entrench dominance and distort competition. The DMA also advances competition on its merits, safeguarding fair intermediation and ensuring that businesses and end-users are treated equitably. Measures such as interoperability, multi-homing, and enhanced data mobility reduce switching costs and promote contestable markets (Petit, 2021). Similarly, consumer sovereignty – central to ordoliberalism 2.0 – guides DMA provisions aimed at increasing user autonomy, from limiting manipulative digital nudging to enhancing data portability and user mobility (Wörsdörfer, 2021). Unlike the Chicago School's consumer welfare approach, which emphasizes aggregated efficiency and self-correcting markets (Bork, 1978/1993; Hovenkamp, 2019), the DMA aligns with the ordoliberal 2.0 vision of consumers as active directors of the economic process. Moreover, the DMA has incorporated several ordoliberal-inspired reform proposals from prior scholarship. These include enforcing self-preferencing bans, prohibiting discriminatory business practices such as tying and bundling, promoting interoperability and data portability, and providing the possibility of structural remedies as a last resort. These measures collectively represent a significant effort to integrate ordoliberal 2.0 values into the E.U.'s digital policy framework.

Despite these advances, the DMA reveals critical weaknesses, particularly in governance, enforcement, and sanctioning mechanisms. First, the Act favors a highly centralized enforcement model, concentrating decision-making powers within the European Commission (Larouche & de Streel, 2021; Leistner, 2021). While centralization offers benefits, such as harmonization across the Digital Single Market and reduced compliance costs, it also risks overloading the Commission, slowing enforcement, and diminishing the role of national competition authorities, which could provide crucial local expertise and monitoring capabilities (CERRE, 2021b). From an ordoliberal 2.0 perspective, this lack of subsidiarity and decentralization undermines regulatory effectiveness and predictability. A coordinated model between the Commission and national authorities, possibly complemented by private enforcement mechanisms, would better align with ordoliberal 2.0 ideals of checks and balances, as well as distributed oversight (Monti, 2021; Podszun, 2021).

Second, the DMA's reliance on discretionary 'process-based' regulation introduces legal uncertainty. Key terms such as contestability, fairness, gatekeeper, and core platform services remain ambiguously defined, opening the door to interpretative discretion, lobbying, and potential politicization of enforcement (Akman, 2021; Crémer et al., 2021; Schweitzer, 2021). Ordoliberals would argue for more self-executing, principle-based rules to enhance legal certainty, reduce reliance on subjective value judgments, and speed up enforcement interventions.

Third, merger control under the DMA is insufficient. While the Act includes provisions for gatekeeper notification of mergers (Art. 12), it lacks a robust ex-ante merger review regime. This gap has allowed 'killer acquisitions' to proliferate, enabling dominant platforms to acquire nascent competitors and suppress potential rivals, thereby weakening market contestability and innovation (Cabral et al., 2021; Franck & Peitz, 2021). Effective DMA enforcement should be complemented by a strengthened, forward-looking merger control policy capable of scrutinizing both past and future acquisitions and imposing divestitures when anti-competitive effects are identified.

Fourth, enforcement and sanctioning mechanisms remain too slow and insufficiently resourced. The DMA relies on an enforcement pyramid beginning with regulatory dialogue and progressing to commitments, fines, and, ultimately, behavioral or structural remedies. While theoretically sound, in practice, market investigations can take years, potentially allowing harm to persist unchecked. Critics recommend accelerated procedures, enhanced interim measures, and expanded financial and technical resources for enforcement teams, including data analysts, AI specialists, and independent researchers (CERRE, 2021a; de Streel & Larouche, 2021).

Finally, structural remedies, which ordoliberals favor as a stronger corrective tool, remain secondary under the DMA. Article 16 reserves structural separations and divestitures as ultima ratio measures, which may be insufficient to counter entrenched dominance in digital markets. Experts suggest that proactive structural interventions, such as unbundling services, separating business units, or adjusting financial structures, should complement behavioral rules to restore competition and foster innovation (CMA et al., 2021; Franck & Peitz, 2021).

In summary, the DMA has made significant progress toward embedding ordoliberal 2.0 principles into E.U. digital policy, particularly in promoting contestable markets, consumer sovereignty, and non-discriminatory platform practices. Nevertheless, several critical weaknesses – centralized enforcement, discretionary process policy, weak merger control, slow sanctioning, and limited structural remedies – undermine its potential to fully realize ordoliberal 2.0 objectives. Addressing these shortcomings through stronger decentralized coordination, principle-based enforcement, robust merger review, and expanded structural remedies would not only enhance the DMA's effectiveness but also align it more closely with the ordoliberal vision of a self-regulating, fair, and competitive digital economy.

Taken together, these developments suggest that existing antitrust measures – whether grounded in the U.S. consumer welfare standard or the E.U.'s still-evolving digital regulation regime – are insufficient for digital markets. The cases of Google and Meta illustrate how current frameworks fail to address structural dominance, data concentration, and long-term competitive harms. What is needed instead is a shift toward frameworks that recognize zero-price and data-driven markets, integrate structural and long-term assessments of market power, and emphasize consumer sovereignty, quality, innovation, and privacy – not just prices. Effective reform would involve modernized legal standards, faster and more proactive enforcement tools, stronger protections against lobbying and regulatory capture, and a willingness to impose structural remedies when dominant platforms engage in exclusionary conduct. Only such comprehensive changes can curb the entrenched power of digital giants and restore fair competition in today's platform-based economy.

6.5 Pathways to enhanced regulatory effectiveness

Policymakers must adopt a multifaceted approach that combines proactive enforcement, clear rules, and structural interventions.[14] By emphasizing long-term market dynamics, empowering regulators with adequate resources, and prioritizing consumer welfare beyond price effects, they can create more resilient and competitive digital markets. This approach moves beyond reactive case-by-case litigation, aiming instead to prevent dominance from becoming entrenched and to ensure that innovation and consumer choice remain central to the platform economy. The discussion below outlines a proposed ordoliberal 2.0 antitrust agenda designed to address these shortcomings and strengthen competition in digital markets.

6.5.1 Reform of the consumer welfare standard

From an ordoliberal 2.0 perspective, one of the most critical reforms is abandoning Bork's consumer welfare standard, which still dominates U.S. antitrust policy and remains influential elsewhere. Antitrust analysis must broaden beyond short- and long-term price and output effects to include competition, innovation, and consumer choice. In digital and zero-price markets, in particular, it is essential to look beyond prices and incorporate concepts such as the ordoliberal 2.0 notion of consumer sovereignty (e.g., regarding personal data and information), as well as product quality, including privacy and data protection.

6.5.2 Updated antitrust laws

In addition to this paradigmatic shift, existing antitrust laws must be updated to reflect the realities of the digital economy (Subcommittee on Antitrust, 2020). This includes adopting new, platform-specific regulations such as the DMA; revising market definitions and analytical tools; and accounting for new forms of power, including data power, digital nudging power, bottleneck power, strategic market status, and gatekeeping or rule-setting power (Commission Competition Law 4.0, 2019; Furman et al., 2019; Hovenkamp, 2021b). The overarching goal is to maintain free and open markets, reduce entry barriers, and promote robust competition. Ideally, antitrust should remain a pro-competition, pro-entry, and pro-small business framework (Furman et al., 2019) aimed at reducing harmful consolidation – monopolies, oligopolies, cartels, and trusts – often resulting from horizontal, vertical, and conglomerate mergers.

14 Cp. for foundation: Wörsdörfer, 2022b, 2023a.

6.5.3 Shifting the burden of proof

In merger control, a key reform is shifting the burden of proof from competition authorities to the merging parties. Under current law, agencies must demonstrate that a merger is likely to be harmful. A reformed regime would require the merging firms to show that their transaction does not substantially lessen competition or that any merger-specific efficiencies outweigh the potential harms. Such a shift would lower the evidentiary threshold for enforcement, enabling agencies to initiate and win antitrust cases more easily.

6.5.4 Antimerger presumption

Experts also advocate for reinstating an antimerger presumption, where mergers that risk increasing market concentration would be considered presumptively illegal unless the parties can prove otherwise (Klobuchar, 2021). This is especially important in digital markets dominated by powerful platforms. Future big tech acquisitions could thus be presumed anti-competitive unless the firms demonstrate significant public benefits. This approach seeks to limit market power by preventing anti-competitive consolidation (Subcommittee on Antitrust, 2020). Notably, neither the DMA nor current U.S. or E.U. frameworks incorporate such a presumption or the burden-shifting mechanism described above.

6.5.5 Revised merger guidelines

Merger guidelines must also be updated (Elhauge, 2018; Klobuchar, 2021). Existing U.S. and E.U. guidelines – including those informed by the DMA – remain ill-suited for evaluating big tech deals. They rely on narrow market definitions, ignore serial acquisitions, and overlook the cumulative, long-term effects of merger strategies (Commission Competition Law 4.0, 2019). They also lack retrospective evaluation mechanisms.[15]

15 Ordoliberals would also call for closer scrutiny of conglomerate M&As, particularly to curb the influence and leverage exercised by large conglomerates. This could include prohibiting mergers once they exceed a certain structural threshold. Hovenkamp (2021b), for example, argues that platform acquisitions of start-ups should be treated as exclusionary practices – given that their primary purpose is often to eliminate potential future competitors – and that such deals should only be approved if accompanied by guaranteed non-exclusive licensing agreements. He further contends that 'killer acquisitions' should be classified as cartel behavior. In cases where an established firm acquires an innovative start-up and subsequently shuts it down to protect its own business, or purchases patents only to shelve them while suing others for infringement, the conduct is functionally equivalent to car-

6.5.6 Ex-post merger control

A crucial but absent component of both U.S. and E.U. regimes is systematic ex-post merger review (Furman et al., 2019; Glick et al., 2020). Agencies should regularly reassess past mergers to evaluate medium- and long-term impacts on prices, product quality, innovation, and consumer choice. If retrospective analysis reveals anti-competitive harm, authorities should have the power to implement remedies, including demergers or unwinding the original transaction. From an ordoliberal 2.0 standpoint, strong post-merger oversight helps ensure that markets remain competitive over time.

6.5.7 Lowering market-entry barriers

Beyond M&As, market entry barriers and strategic exclusion pose significant challenges for effective antitrust enforcement. Specific barriers, such as network effects, economies of scale, and control over data, naturally arise from the characteristics of digital markets. Others, including self-preferencing, switching costs, and limited interoperability or data portability, are artificially created as part of deliberate exclusionary strategies. These strategies often involve identifying and neutralizing emerging rivals through 'killer acquisitions' or copying competitor innovations (i.e., copycat appropriations). Together, these practices reinforce conglomerate structures and entrench market power in digital sectors.

6.5.8 Behavioral remedies

6.5.8.1 Data portability and interoperability

To counter such barriers, behavioral interventions focus on improving data mobility and promoting technical openness. Building on this logic, the Furman Report and the DMA advocate robust data portability and real-time data mobility (Commission Competition Law 4.0, 2019), alongside open standards that ensure interoperability across platforms and services. These measures reduce lock-in effects, facilitate multihoming, and lower switching costs, thereby strengthening competitive pressure. They also enhance user sovereignty and control over personal data. Further recommendations include expanding secure access to non-personal and anonymized data – potentially through data trusts – to lower entry barriers for startups and foster data-driven innovation (Hovenkamp, 2021b; Furman et al., 2019).

---

tel activity. Such 'merger-plus-shutdown' strategies generate no efficiencies; on the contrary, they undermine competition and harm consumer welfare.

6.5.8.2 Predatory pricing claims

Beyond structural and data-related barriers, dominant firms can employ pricing strategies to stifle competition. Accordingly, behavioral rules should address predatory pricing. Companies such as Amazon have used below-cost pricing to eliminate rivals and deter new entrants. To prevent such anti-competitive behavior, the legal threshold for predatory pricing claims – currently based on the recoupment test – should be lowered or replaced. One alternative is to presume that below-cost pricing by dominant firms is anti-competitive unless the firm can demonstrate otherwise (Klobuchar,-buchar, 2021).

6.5.8.3 Ban on tying and bundling

Similarly, behavioral oversight is needed to prevent exclusion through product design and packaging. Practices such as tying and bundling, where customers are required to purchase an additional product as a condition of access, should be presumed anti-competitive when employed by dominant firms unless proven otherwise. This presumption, which the DMA already incorporates, helps prevent dominant players from leveraging their market power across products and services.

6.5.8.4 Self-preferencing ban

Ultimately, effective behavioral remedies are crucial for platforms that serve as gatekeepers. Clear rules of conduct are necessary to prevent unjustified self-preferencing, where a platform favors its own services over those of third parties. Such a ban – also included in the DMA – would stop Amazon from privileging its retail division on its marketplace and curb similar practices by Google Search, Google Shopping, and major app stores. Self-preferencing generates conflicts of interest, undermines platform neutrality, and allows dominant firms to extend their market power into adjacent markets. These practices conflict with ordoliberal 2.0 principles of competition on the merits. Platforms with gatekeeping or rule-setting power must operate impartially and non-discriminatorily, ensuring fair and neutral access for all market participants (Commission Competition Law 4.0, 2019).

6.5.9 Structural remedies

In exceptional cases – and as an *ultima ratio* – structural remedies should complement behavioral obligations to maintain competitive markets. Echoing Eucken's recommendations from the 1940s,[16] such measures can include separating business

16 As early as the 1940s, Eucken and other ordoliberals were already analyzing the risks posed by too-big-to-fail and systemically important corporations, as well as the growing concentration of eco-

units, unbundling companies, horizontally dividing services, or restructuring financial arrangements. When carefully designed and enforced, structural remedies have the power to reshape entire industries, realign incentives, stimulate innovation, and protect both consumers and smaller market participants. For example, divestitures can restore competition, enhance product quality (e.g., through stronger privacy protections), promote consumer rights/welfare, and reduce concentrations of economic and political influence over information flows (Wu, 2018). Potential break-ups might include separating Meta into Facebook, Instagram, and WhatsApp, requiring Google to divest its advertising business, or obligating Amazon to spin off its AWS business. Such measures can also level the playing field for SMEs, allowing new entrants to compete more fairly in markets historically dominated by a few conglomerates.

Beyond restoring competition, merger blocks and structural remedies serve as critical ex-ante deterrents against excessive market concentration (Furman et al., 2019; Shapiro, 2019). Current E.U. policy relies heavily on ex-post fines and behavioral measures, which are often insufficient to prevent the formation of dominant firms with disproportionate economic and political power. An ordoliberal 2.0 approach emphasizes a tiered enforcement framework – an enforcement pyramid – combining monitoring, credible sanctions, and graduated interventions. Under this model, break-ups or divestitures serve as a measure of last resort, applied only when a firm's market power and conduct justify such decisive action. Importantly, this does not imply the automatic dissolution of successful firms or broad de-concentration; instead, each intervention is evaluated individually, weighing its impact on consumer welfare, market fairness, innovation, and the broader socioeconomic and political landscape (Larouche & de Streel, 2021).

6.5.9.1 Excursus: benefits of breaking up tech conglomerates

A breakup of dominant tech conglomerates could yield significant benefits across multiple dimensions, including for consumers, innovation, and investors, by reducing market power concentration and fostering a more competitive ecosystem (Wörsdörfer, 2020, 2021, 2022a, 2022b, 2023a).

Benefits for consumers: Large, consolidated tech firms often face limited competitive pressure, which can lead to higher prices, reduced choice, and slower improvements in product quality or services. By splitting these conglomerates into smaller, independent entities, markets would likely see increased competition, incentivizing firms to offer better products, lower costs, and improved customer service. Additionally, reduced concentration can help prevent exploitative practices such as self-preferencing, discriminatory access, or unfair data collection.

Benefits for innovation and SMEs: Monopolistic or oligopolistic structures can stifle innovation by reducing competition and incentives for firms to experiment or take risks. Smaller, independent companies are often more agile and motivated to differentiate themselves through new products and technologies. A

---

nomic power in the hands of a few dominant firms. In one of his post-World War II reports prepared for the Allied authorities, Eucken explicitly advocated the break-up of excessively powerful companies to safeguard competitive markets (Eucken, 1946/1999).

breakup can create a more dynamic market environment, where multiple firms compete on features, usability, and novel solutions, thereby accelerating technological progress. It also helps level the playing field by giving startups and smaller competitors (and niche players) a fairer chance to enter markets and challenge established players, fostering diversity in ideas and approaches.

Benefits for investors: While large conglomerates may seem stable, extreme market concentration can increase systemic risk. If one dominant firm faces regulatory penalties, technological failure, or reputational damage, the financial impact can ripple across markets. Breaking up such entities can diversify risk and create multiple publicly traded companies with clearer business models, allowing investors to make more targeted decisions. Moreover, smaller, competitive firms may have higher growth potential as they compete more effectively, thereby generating long-term value for their shareholders.[17]

In summary, breaking up tech conglomerates could restore competitive pressure, spur innovation, enhance consumer welfare (i.e., protect consumer rights), and reduce systemic financial risk, thereby creating a healthier and more resilient digital economy, aligned with ordoliberal 2.0 principles.

6.5.10 Platform neutrality

A platform neutrality rule – analogous to net neutrality – would operationalize these ordoliberal 2.0 principles (Wu, 2003). Such a rule would require gatekeepers to provide fair, equal, and non-discriminatory access and terms to all market participants. In practice, this would prevent big tech firms from privileging their own services and help maintain free, open, and competitive platform ecosystems (Khan, 2017).[18]

---

17 Breaking up Alphabet/Google into its constituent divisions could potentially increase the combined market capitalization, for instance, Waymo alone might be valued at approximately $1 trillion, comparable to Tesla (New York Times, 2025d).

18 According to Wu (2025a), big tech is characterized by extensive wealth and resource extraction – including data, attention, and profits (e.g., advertising revenue) – as well as the marginalization and commercialization of people and (small) businesses, contributing to growing socioeconomic inequality. This dynamic has given rise to a two-class digital economy reminiscent of a feudal system: extractors and their agents (AI-driven tech platforms) dominate, while dependent businesses (SMEs), consumers, and employees have limited agency and opportunities. In this context, ensuring platform neutrality (similar to net neutrality and the Open Internet order) and strengthening the middle class are essential objectives for regulatory intervention. To achieve these goals, a multifaceted approach is required. First, renewed anti-monopoly measures can directly challenge dominant firms, rejecting the notion of 'natural monopolies' in digital markets – a concept increasingly difficult to justify given the dynamic and modular nature of technology ecosystems. Second, neutrality rules can prevent platforms from engaging in discriminatory practices that distort competition on the merits or serve as extraction tools against downstream firms. Third, countervailing power can be enhanced by supporting key stakeholders such as journalists, artists, and other copyright holders to ensure fair compensation, as well as workers and unions to improve labor conditions and wages. Fourth, treating major tech platforms as essential utilities and imposing caps on specific services can mitigate the hidden economic 'tax' these platforms extract through data and profit capture, similar to fee caps in sectors such as credit cards. Finally, line-of-business restrictions can separate a platform's monopoly power from other commercial activities, for example, preventing Amazon from selling its own products on its marketplace or barring dominant tech firms from acquiring or controlling emerging AI platforms.

6.5.11 Gatekeeper regulation

Regulatory efforts should focus particularly on gatekeepers – those digital firms with significant user bases, revenues, or control over critical distribution channels. This is the organizing principle of the DMA, which targets platform providers offering core platform services. Gatekeepers can 'pick winners and losers,' impose 'exorbitant fees,' set 'oppressive terms' (e.g., take-it-or-leave-it contracts), and extract valuable data from dependent users and businesses (Subcommittee on Antitrust, 2020). Effective regulation must therefore prioritize constraining the power of gatekeepers.

6.5.12 Antitrust agencies

Effective enforcement requires well-funded, well-staffed, and politically independent antitrust agencies (Baer et al., 2020; Commission Competition Law 4.0, 2019; Furman et al., 2019; Stigler Center, 2019). The U.K.'s Digital Markets Unit offers a potential model. Increased budgets – via direct appropriations or higher filing fees – would enable proactive rather than reactive enforcement, thereby enhancing agencies' ability to deter anti-competitive behavior.[19]

6.5.13 Fines

Robust sanctioning mechanisms are essential to ensure effective antitrust enforcement and deter anti-competitive behavior. Experts recommend significantly increasing penalties for exclusionary conduct and cartel participation, with Klobuchar (2021) suggesting fines of 15–30% of a company's total revenue. In addition, cartel participants could face elevated penalties and temporary bans from operating in the industry, helping to deter white-collar crime and prevent cartel formation. The Furman Report further advocates for accelerated investigations, aiming to resolve cases within months rather than years, alongside interim measures that immediately halt harmful conduct while proceedings are ongoing (Furman et al., 2019). This approach reflects an 'enforcement pyramid' model, beginning with regulatory dialogue between antitrust agencies and gatekeepers, escalating to commitments and fines, and culminating in behavioral or structural remedies (CERRE, 2021b). Successful antitrust plaintiffs should also be allowed to recover both pre- and post-judgment interest (Klobuchar, 2021), which is crucial in multi-year cases where price fixers can retain illegal over-

19 It is worth noting that the DMA does not provide for the establishment of an independent antitrust agency at the European level, nor does it ensure the necessary financial and human resources for effective enforcement, such as increased budgets or sufficient technical expertise, including data analysts, AI specialists, and independent researchers (cp. de Streel & Larouche, 2021).

charges, earn interest, and reinvest the funds. Recovering these amounts ensures that violators bear the full costs of their actions, deters future wrongdoing, and incentivizes earlier settlements, preventing lawsuits from being exploited to maintain the status quo.

6.5.14 Protection of whistleblowers

Successful antitrust enforcement often relies on insider information. Policymakers should therefore strengthen whistleblower protections and adopt incentives such as reward or bounty programs for individuals who disclose cartel activity or exclusionary practices (Klobuchar, 2021).

6.5.15 International cooperation

Finally, national reforms should be supported by an international ordoliberal agenda. Cross-border cooperation among antitrust agencies, governments, and international bodies (e.g., the OECD, G7, and G20) is crucial for developing coherent and harmonized approaches toward digital platforms. A fragmented regulatory landscape risks a 'race to the bottom'; instead, global coordination should aim for harmonization and a 'race to the top.'

6.6 Concluding remarks

This chapter has examined the growing market power of big tech firms and the range of anticompetitive business practices they employ, including structural dominance, gatekeeping, self-preferencing, and predatory strategies. It has analyzed the responses of regulators and policymakers, from major U.S. lawsuits against Google and Meta to regulatory probes targeting Apple, highlighting both the scope and limitations of existing enforcement. In doing so, this chapter has critically assessed the shortcomings of current policies, including the constraints of Bork's consumer welfare standard and the uneven application of instruments such as the DMA.

Building on this ordoliberal 2.0 analysis, this chapter has explored pathways for enhancing regulatory effectiveness in digital markets. These include revising antitrust laws, shifting the burden of proof to merging parties, adopting an antimerger presumption for transactions involving tech conglomerates, and updating merger guidelines and ex-post merger control. It has also argued for a combination of behavioral and structural remedies – including automatic sanctions, a tiered enforcement pyramid, and divestitures as a last resort – as mechanisms to restore competition, limit the concentration of economic and political power, and promote platform neutrality.

This chapter has further examined the potential benefits of structural remedies, particularly the breakup of dominant tech conglomerates, showing how such measures can enhance consumer welfare, stimulate innovation, level the playing field for SMEs, and create new opportunities for investors. In addition, it has highlighted complementary regulatory approaches, including gatekeeper regulation, stronger antitrust agencies, fines for anticompetitive conduct, whistleblower protections, and international cooperation.

Looking ahead, several important research questions remain. Future studies could explore the long-term effects of structural remedies on innovation and market dynamics, assess the effectiveness of enforcement pyramids and automatic sanctions in practice, and evaluate the interplay between domestic and international regulatory frameworks. Additional work is needed to understand how platform neutrality and gatekeeper regulation influence smaller market participants and consumers, as well as how emerging technologies, such as generative AI, digital currencies, and decentralized platforms, may reshape the scope and methods of anticompetitive behavior.

Overall, this study provides a comprehensive ordoliberal 2.0 framework for understanding the challenges posed by big tech and for designing more effective, multidimensional regulatory responses. By integrating legal, economic, and policy perspectives, it demonstrates how behavioral, structural, and systemic reforms can work together to foster competitive, fair, and resilient digital markets.

References

Akman, P. (2021). Regulating Competition in Digital Platform Markets: A Critical Assessment of the Framework and Approach of the E.U. Digital Markets Act. https://papers.ssrn.com/sol3/papers.cfm?abstract_id=3978625 (last accessed: December 30, 2025).

Apple. (2024). Apple Announces Changes to iOS, Safari, and the App Store in the European Union. http://www.apple.com/newsroom/2024/01/apple-announces-changes-to-ios-safari-and-the-app-store-in-the-european-union/ (last accessed: December 30, 2025).

Ash, T.G. (2016). Free Speech. Ten Principles for a Connected World. London, Atlantic Books.

Baer, B., Baker, J., Kades, M., Scott Morton, F., Rose, N., Shapiro, C., & Wu, T. (2020). Restoring Competition in the United States. A Vision for Antitrust Enforcement for the Next Administration and Congress. https://equitablegrowth.org/research-paper/restoring-competition-in-the-united-states/ (last accessed: December 30, 2025).

Bork, R. (1978/1993). The Antitrust Paradox. New York, Free Press.

Bork, R. & Bowman, W. (1965). The Crisis in Antitrust. Columbia Law Review 65(3). 363–375.

Buolamwini, J. (2023). Unmasking AI. My Mission to Protect What is Human in a World of Machines. New York, Random House.

Cabral, L., Haucap, J., Parker, G., Petropoulos, G., Valletti, T., & Van Alstyne, M. (2021). The E.U. Digital Markets Act. A Report from a Panel of Economic Experts. https://papers.ssrn.com/sol3/papers.cfm?abstract_id=3783436 (last accessed: December 30, 2025).

Center on Regulation in Europe/CERRE. (2021a). The European Proposal for a Digital Markets Act. A First Assessment (Assessment Paper). https://cerre.eu/wp-content/uploads/2021/01/CERRE_Digital-Markets-Act_a-first-assessment_January2021.pdf (last accessed: December 30, 2025).

Center on Regulation in Europe/CERRE. (2021b). Making the Digital Markets Act More Resilient and Effective (Recommendations Paper). https://cerre.eu/wp-content/uploads/2021/05/CERRE_-DMA_European-Parliament-Council-recommendations_FULL-PAPER_May-2021.pdf (last accessed: December 30, 2025).

Cohen, A. (2020). Supreme Inequality: The Supreme Court's Fifty-Year Battle for a More Unjust America. New York, Penguin.

Commission 'Competition Law 4.0.' (2019). A New Competition Framework for the Digital Economy. www.bmwi.de/Redaktion/EN/Publikationen/Wirtschaft/a-new-competition-framework-for-the-digital-economy.pdf?__blob=publicationFile&v=3 (last accessed: December 30, 2025).

Competition and Markets Authority (CMA), Australian Competition and Consumer Commission (ACCC), & Bundeskartellamt (2021). Joint Statement on Merger Control Enforcement. www.accc.gov.au/system/files/Joint%20statement%20-%20merger%20control%20enforcement.pdf (last accessed: December 30, 2025).

Corporate Europe Observatory. (2025). Big Tech Lobby Budgets Hit Record Levels. https://corporateeurope.org/en/2025/10/big-tech-lobby-budgets-hit-record-levels (last accessed: December 30, 2025).

Crémer, J., Montjoye, Y., & Schweitzer, H. (2019). Competition Policy for the Digital Era. Final Report. https://ec.europa.eu/competition/publications/reports/kd0419345enn.pdf (last accessed: December 30, 2025).

Crémer, J., Crawford, G., Dinielli, D., Fletcher, A., Heidhues, P., Scott Morton, F., & Seim, K. (2021). Fairness and Contestability in the Digital Markets Act. https://papers.ssrn.com/sol3/papers.cfm?abstract_id=3923599 (last accessed: December 30, 2025).

Department of Justice (DOJ). (2021). Workload Statistics of the Antitrust Division. www.justice.gov/atr/division-operations (last accessed: December 30, 2025).

De Streel, A. & Larouche, P. (2021). The European Digital Markets Act Proposal: How to Improve a Regulatory Revolution. Concurrences 2-2021. 46–63.

Elhauge, E. (2018). Horizontal Shareholding. Harvard Law Review 129. 1267–1317.

Eucken, W. (1946/1999). Über die Verstaatlichung der privaten Banken. In: Eucken, W. Ordnungspolitik. Münster, LIT. 38–58.

Eucken, W. (1952/2004). Grundsätze der Wirtschaftspolitik. Tübingen, Mohr Siebeck.

European Commission. (2017). Google Search (Shopping). https://ec.europa.eu/competition/antitrust/cases/dec_docs/39740/39740_14996_3.pdf (last accessed: December 30, 2025).

European Commission. (2018). Google Android. https://ec.europa.eu/competition/antitrust/cases/dec_docs/40099/40099_9993_3.pdf (last accessed: December 30, 2025).

European Commission. (2019). Google Search (AdSense). https://ec.europa.eu/competition/antitrust/cases/dec_docs/40411/40411_1619_11.pdf (last accessed: December 30, 2025).

European Commission. (2024). Commission Fines Apple Over €1.8 Billion Over Abusive App Store Rules for Music Streaming Providers. https://ec.europa.eu/commission/presscorner/detail/en/ip_24_1161 (last accessed: December 30, 2025).

European Commission. (2025a). Digital Markets Act – Cases. https://digital-markets-act-cases.ec.europa.eu/search (last accessed: December 30, 2025).

European Commission. (2025b). Commission Fines Google €2.95 Billion Over Abusive Practices in Online Advertising Technology. https://ec.europa.eu/commission/presscorner/detail/en/ip_25_1992 (last accessed: December 30, 2025).

European Commission. (2025c). Commission Opens Investigation Into Potential Digital Markets Act Breach By Google in Demoting Media Publishers' Content in Search Results. https://ec.europa.eu/commission/presscorner/detail/en/ip_25_2675 (last accessed: December 30, 2025).

European Parliament & Council of the European Union. (2022). Digital Markets Act. https://eur-lex.europa.eu/legal-content/EN/TXT/PDF/?uri=CELEX:32022R1925 (last accessed: December 30, 2025).

Federal Trade Commission vs. Meta Platforms, Inc. (2025). Case 20-cv-3590-JEB (Filed 11/18/25). https://www.govinfo.gov/content/pkg/USCOURTS-dcd-1_20-cv-03590/pdf/USCOURTS-dcd-1_20-cv-03590-6.pdf (last accessed: December 30, 2025).

Financial Times. (2025). Big Tech Lobbying Surges as Companies Try to Shape Trump's AI Policy. https://www.ft.com/content/df01dcf8-dbc4-4b56-8d8b-67b7e6a83eef (last accessed: December 30, 2025).

Franck, J.-U. & Peitz, M. (2021). How to Challenge Big Tech. In: Richter, H., Straub, M., & Tuchtfeld, E. (eds.). To Break Up or Regulate Big Tech? Avenues to Constrain Private Power in the DSA/DMA Package. Max Planck Institute for Innovation and Competition Research Paper Series 21–25. 84–89.

Frenkel, S. & Kang, C. (2021). An Ugly Truth. Inside Facebook's Battle for Domination. New York, Harper.

Furman, J., Coyle, D., Fletcher, A., Marsden, P. & McAuley, D. (2019). Unlocking Digital Competition: Report of the Digital Competition Expert Panel ('Furman Report'). www.gov.uk/government/publications/unlocking-digital-competition-report-of-the-digital-competition-expert-panel (last accessed: December 30, 2025).

Glick, M., Ruetschlin, C., & Bush, D. (2020). Big Tech's Buying Spree and the Failed Ideology of Competition Law. https://papers.ssrn.com/sol3/papers.cfm?abstract_id=3746728 (last accessed: December 30, 2025).

GovInfo.Gov. (2025). 20-3590 – Federal Trade Commission v. Meta Platforms, Inc. https://www.govinfo.gov/app/details/USCOURTS-dcd-1_20-cv-03590/context (last accessed: December 30, 2025).

Habermas, J. (1983). Moralbewusstsein und kommunikatives Handeln. Frankfurt, Suhrkamp.

Habermas, J. (1991). Erläuterungen zur Diskursethik. Frankfurt, Suhrkamp.

Haidt, J. (2024). The Anxious Generation: How the Great Rewiring of Childhood is Causing an Epidemic of Mental Illness. New York, Penguin Press.

Helbing, D., Frey, B., Gigerenzer, G., Hafen, E., Hagner, M., Hofstetter, Y., Hoven, J., Zicari, R., & Zwitter, A. (2017). Will Democracy Survive Big Data and Artificial Intelligence? www.scientificamerican.com/article/will-democracy-survive-big-data-and-artificial-intelligence/ (last accessed: December 30, 2025).

Hovenkamp, H. (2019). Whatever Did Happen to the Antitrust Movement? Notre Dame Law Review 94(2). 583–638.

Hovenkamp, H. (2021a). The Looming Crisis in Antitrust Economics. Boston University Law Review 101. 489–545.

Hovenkamp, H. (2021b). Antitrust and Platform Monopoly. Yale Law Journal 130. 1901–2001.

Hovenkamp, H. & Scott Morton, F. (2020). Framing the Chicago School of Antitrust Analysis. University of Pennsylvania Law Review 168(7). 1843–1878.

Issue One. (2025). As Big Tech Gears Up for the 2026 Midterms, Its Lobbying Operations Continue Unabated. https://issueone.org/articles/big-tech-lobbying-2025-q3/?ref=dispatch.techoversight.org (last accessed: December 30, 2025).

Khan, L. (2017). Amazon's Antitrust Paradox. Yale Law Journal 126. 710–805.

Khan, L. (2018). The New Brandeis Movement: America's Antimonopoly Debate. Journal of European Competition Law & Practice 9(3). 131–132.

Klobuchar, A. (2021). Antitrust: Taking on Monopoly Power from the Gilded Age to the Digital Age. New York, Knopf.

Klump, R. & Wörsdörfer, M. (2015). Paternalist Economic Policies. Foundations, Implications, and Critical Evaluations. ORDO Yearbook of Economic and Social Order 66. 27–60.

Kornelakis, A. (2021). Digital Markets, Competition Regimes, and Models of Capitalism: A Comparative Institutional Analysis of European and U.S. Responses to Google. Competition & Change (Online First). 1–23.

Kornelakis, A., & Hublart, P. (2022). Digital Markets, Competition Regimes and Models of Capitalism: A Comparative Institutional Analysis of European and US Responses to Google. Competition & Change 26(3–4). 334–356.

Kovacic, W. (2007): The Intellectual DNA of Modern U.S. Competition Law for Dominant Firm Conduct: The Chicago/Harvard Double Helix. Columbia Business Law Review 1. 1–80.

Lanier, J. (2013). Who Owns the Future? New York, Simon & Schuster.

Larouche, P. & de Streel, A. (2021). The European Digital Markets Act: A Revolution Grounded on Traditions. Journal of European Competition Law & Practice 12(7). 542–560.

Leistner, M. (2021). The Commission's Vision for Europe's Digital Future: Proposals for the Data Governance Act, the Digital Markets Act, and the Digital Services Act – A Critical Primer. https://papers.ssrn.com/sol3/papers.cfm?abstract_id=3789041 (last accessed: December 30, 2025).

Meta. (2025). Messaging Interoperability: WhatsApp Enables Third-Party Chats for Users in Europe. https://about.fb.com/news/2025/11/messaging-interoperability-whatsapp-enables-third-party-chats-for-users-in-europe/ (last accessed: December 30, 2025).

Monti, G. (2021). The Digital Markets Act – Institutional Design and Suggestions for Improvement. https://papers.ssrn.com/sol3/papers.cfm?abstract_id=3797730 (last accessed: December 30, 2025).

Muldoon, J., Graham, M., & Cant, C. (2025). Feeding the Machine: The Hidden Human Labor Powering AI. Edinburgh, Canongate.

New York Times. (2025a). Google, Meta, Visa: A Guide to a New Era of U.S. Antitrust Cases. https://www.nytimes.com/interactive/2024/business/antitrust-case-tracker.html (last accessed: December 30, 2025).

New York Times. (2025b). Apple and Meta Are First to Be Hit By E.U. Digital Competition Law. https://www.nytimes.com/2025/04/23/technology/apple-meta-eu-fines-competition-law.html (last accessed: December 30, 2025).

New York Times. (2025c). What a Ruling to Fix Google's Search Monopoly Means for the Company. https://www.nytimes.com/2025/09/02/technology/google-antitrust-case-ruling.html?smid=nytcore-ios-share&referringSource=articleShare (last accessed: December 30, 2025).

New York Times. (2025d). What If Google Just Broke Itself Up? A Tech Insider Makes the Case. https://www.nytimes.com/2025/06/02/technology/google-antitrust-breakup.html (last accessed: December 30, 2025).

O'Neil, C. (2016). Weapons of Math Destruction. How Big Data Increases Inequality and Threatens Democracy. New York, Penguin.

Pariser, E. (2011). The Filter Bubble: How the New Personalized Web is Changing What We Read and How We Think. New York, Penguin.

Petit, N. (2020). Big Tech and the Digital Economy. The Moligopoly Scenario. Oxford, Oxford University Press.

Petit, N. (2021). The Proposed Digital Markets Act (DMA). A Legal and Policy Review. https://papers.ssrn.com/sol3/papers.cfm?abstract_id=3843497 (last accessed: December 30, 2025).

Podszun, R. (2021). Private Enforcement and the Digital Markets Act. In: Richter, H., Straub, M., & Tuchtfeld, E. (eds.). To Break Up or Regulate Big Tech? Avenues to Constrain Private Power in the DSA/DMA Package. Max Planck Institute for Innovation and Competition Research Paper Series 21–25. 92–97.

Putnam, R. (1993a). Making Democracy Work. Princeton, Princeton University Press.

Putnam, R. (1993b). The Prosperous Community – Social Capital and Public Life. American Prospect 13. 35–42.

Putnam, R. (2000). Bowling Alone. The Collapse and Revival of American Community. New York, Simon & Schuster.

Schweitzer, H. (2021). The Art to Make Gatekeeper Positions Contestable and the Challenge to Know What is Fair: A Discussion of the Digital Markets Act Proposal. https://papers.ssrn.com/sol3/papers.cfm?abstract_id=3837341 (last accessed: December 30, 2025).

Scott Morton, F. (2019). Modern U.S. Antitrust Theory and Evidence Amid Rising Concerns of Market Power and Its Effects. An Overview of Recent Academic Literature. https://equitablegrowth.org/research-paper/modern-u-s-antitrust-theory-and-evidence-amid-rising-concerns-of-market-power-and-its-effects/?longform=true (last accessed: December 30, 2025).

Shapiro, C. (2019). Protecting Competition in the American Economy. Merger Control, Tech Titans, Labor Markets. Journal of Economic Perspectives 33(3). 69–93.

Snyder, T. (2017). On Tyranny. Twenty Lessons From the Twentieth Century. New York, Tim Duggan Books.

Srinivasan, D. (2019). The Antitrust Case Against Facebook. A Monopolist's Journey Towards Pervasive Surveillance in Spite of Consumers' Preference for Privacy. Berkeley Business Law Journal 16(1). 39–101.

Statista. (2025a). Google, Amazon, Meta, Apple, and Microsoft (GAMAM) – Statistics & Facts. https://www.statista.com/topics/4213/google-apple-facebook-amazon-and-microsoft-gafam/#topicOverview (last accessed: December 30, 2025).

Statista. (2025b). Leading Lobbying Spenders in the United States in 2024. https://www.statista.com/statistics/257344/top-lobbying-spenders-in-the-us/ (last accessed: December 30, 2025).

Stigler Center for the Study of the Economy and the State. (2019). Report of the Committee for the Study of Digital Platforms. Market Structure and Antitrust Subcommittee ('Stigler Report'). https://research.chicagobooth.edu/-/media/research/stigler/pdfs/market-structure–report-as-of-15-may-2019.pd (last accessed: December 30, 2025).

Subcommittee on Antitrust. (2020). Investigation of Competition in Digital Markets. https://judiciary.house.gov/news/documentsingle.aspx?DocumentID=3429 (last accessed: December 30, 2025).

Taplin, J. (2018). Move Fast and Break Things: How Facebook, Google, and Amazon Cornered Culture and Undermined Democracy. New York, Back Bay Books.

United States vs. Apple Inc. (2024). Case No. 24-cv-4055 (Filed: 03/21/24). https://static01.nyt.com/newsgraphics/documenttools/9765671b79f64ad9/6cfe3c6c-full.pdf (last accessed: December 30, 2025).

United States et al. vs. Google LLC. (2020). Case No. 20-cv-3010 (APM) (Filed: 10/20/20). https://www.courtlistener.com/docket/18552824/1/united-states-of-america-v-google-llc/ (last accessed: December 30, 2025).

United States et al. vs. Google LLC. (2023). Case No. 23-cv-108 (Filed: 01/24/23). https://storage.courtlistener.com/recap/gov.uscourts.vaed.533508/gov.uscourts.vaed.533508.1.0_2.pdf (last accessed: December 30, 2025).

United States et al. vs. Google LLC. (2024). Case No. 20-cv-3010 (APM)/20-cv-3715 (APM) (Filed: 08/05/24). https://static01.nyt.com/newsgraphics/documenttools/f6ab5c368725101c/43d7c2a0-full.pdf (last accessed: December 30, 2025).

United States et al. vs. Google LLC. (2025). Case No. 20-cv-3010 (APM)/20-cv-3715 (APM) (Filed: 09/02/25). https://www.courtlistener.com/docket/18552824/1436/united-states-of-america-v-google-llc/ (last accessed: December 30, 2025).

Washington Post. (2021a). How Big Tech Got So Big: Hundreds of Acquisitions. www.washingtonpost.com/technology/interactive/2021/amazon-apple-facebook-google-acquisitions/ (last accessed: December 30, 2025).

Wörsdörfer, M. (2020). Ordoliberalism 2.0: Towards a New Regulatory Policy for the Digital Age. Philosophy of Management 19(2). 191–215.

Wörsdörfer, M. (2021). Digital Platforms and Competition Policy: A Business-Ethical Assessment. Journal for Markets and Ethics 9(2). 97–119.

Wörsdörfer, M. (2022a). What Happened to 'Big Tech' and Antitrust? And How to Fix Them! Philosophy of Management 21(3). 345–369.

Wörsdörfer, M. (2022b). Big Tech and Antitrust: An Ordoliberal Analysis. Philosophy & Technology 35. Article 85.

Wörsdörfer, M. (2022c). Walter Eucken: Foundations of Economics. In: Biebricher, T., Nedergaard, P., & Bonefeld, W. (eds.). The Oxford Handbook of Ordoliberalism. Oxford, Oxford University Press. 91–107.

Wörsdörfer, M. (2023a). The Digital Markets Act and E.U. Competition Policy: A Critical Ordoliberal Evaluation. Philosophy of Management 22(1). 149–171.

Wörsdörfer, M. (2023b). Brandeis and Eucken – Two Pioneers of the Modern Big Tech and Antitrust Debate. History of Economic Ideas 2023(2). 87–125.

Wörsdörfer, M. (2023c). Louis D. Brandeis and the New Brandeis Movement – Parallels and Differences. The Antitrust Bulletin 68(3). 440–459.

Wörsdörfer, M. (2023d). Louis Brandeis – Father of Modern-Day Antitrust? History of Economic Thought and Policy 1-2023. 5–43.

Wörsdörfer, M. (2024). Apple's Antitrust Paradox. European Competition Journal 20(1). 113–146.

Wörsdörfer, M. (2025). 'Regulating the Undefined: Addressing Systemic Risks in the Digital Services Act (with an Appendix on the AI Act)' – A Commentary. Philosophy & Technology 38. Article 76.

Wu, T. (2003). Network Neutrality, Broadband Discrimination. Journal of Telecommunications and High Technology Law 2. 141–179.

Wu, T. (2011). The Master Switch. The Rise and Fall of Information Empires. New York, Vintage.

Wu, T. (2018). The Curse of Bigness: Antitrust in the New Gilded Age. New York, Columbia Global Reports.

Wu, T. (2025a). The Age of Extraction: How Tech Platforms Conquered the Economy and Threaten Our Future Prosperity. New York, Knopf.

Wu, T. (2025b). The Bad Reasoning in the Meta Antitrust Ruling Isn't Even the Worst Part. https://www.nytimes.com/2025/11/23/opinion/meta-facebook-antitrust-ruling.html?searchResultPosition=1 (last accessed: December 30, 2025).

Zuboff, S. (2019). The Age of Surveillance Capitalism: The Fight for a Human Future at the New Frontier of Power. New York, Public Affairs.

Chapter 7
Final thoughts

7.1 Introduction

Recent developments in the E.U.'s digital regulatory framework have sparked significant debate over the balance between innovation and digital rights. The Commission's proposed *Digital Omnibus package* (Netzpolitik.org, 2025b, 2025c), revealed in November 2025, seeks to revise key pieces of legislation, including the General Data Protection Regulation (GDPR), the AI Act, the ePrivacy rules, and related data-use laws.[1] While the stated aim of the package is to simplify overlapping legal frameworks and reduce compliance burdens – particularly for small and medium-sized enterprises (SMEs) and start-ups – critics warn that it represents more than a 'technical streamlining,' amounting instead to a substantial weakening of Europe's longstanding protections for personal data, privacy, and algorithmic governance (Deutsche Welle, 2025; Netzpolitik.org, 2025a; Politico, 2025).

Among the most consequential proposed changes is a narrowing of the definition of personal data, which could potentially allow pseudonymized or otherwise processed information to fall outside the GDPR's protections. This would grant firms greater latitude to process personal data, particularly for training AI systems, with fewer consent requirements. Consent obligations for cookies and online tracking may also be relaxed, potentially enabling more pervasive data collection by companies or government actors. For AI regulation, the Omnibus package proposes delaying compliance deadlines for high-risk AI systems, such as biometric identification, law enforcement applications, healthcare algorithms, and credit-rating tools, while reducing obligations for registration, transparency, and oversight, and postponing or removing penalties for misuse of potentially harmful systems. Taken together, these reforms risk substantially eroding the E.U.'s regulatory safeguards and increasing the informational and operational power of large technology firms.

The Omnibus reforms have elicited intense criticism from civil society organizations, trade unions, and human rights defenders.[2] Over 120 groups have argued that the proposals would weaken fundamental safeguards that protect individuals from intrusive surveillance, ensure corporate and government accountability, and prevent unchecked AI decision-making. Critics emphasize that the loosening of GDPR protections and ePrivacy rules effectively allows companies to 'mark their own homework'

1 Notably, as of the end of 2025, the E.U.'s Digital Markets Act remains unaffected.

2 Proponents, on the other hand, argue that simplifying regulatory frameworks is necessary to reduce legal fragmentation across E.U. member states, lower barriers to market entry for SMEs and startups, and foster innovation in AI and digital services. While regulatory efficiency is a crucial consideration, the proposed measures underscore the tension between economic objectives and the protection of fundamental digital rights.

 | https://doi.org/10.1515/9783112245958-008

in matters of data handling, undermining transparency, individual autonomy, and platform neutrality – a principle essential to safeguarding the digital rights of consumers, SMEs, and workers. By easing oversight and compliance requirements, the reforms disproportionately benefit large tech platforms, consolidating their economic and political power while exacerbating socio-economic inequality. In effect, the proposed deregulation[3] risks further entrenching a two-class digital economy in which corporate extractors and AI platforms dominate over dependent businesses, consumers, and employees (Amnesty International et al., 2025; Wu, 2025).

The concerns raised by these civil society organizations and human rights defenders align closely with the argument advanced in this book. Building on their critique, these concluding remarks challenge the prevailing 'human rights minimalism' and reliance on corporate voluntarism (Wettstein, 2009b, 2010b), arguing that overcoming this bias is not only ethically necessary but also essential for addressing the socioeconomic and political inequalities amplified by large tech platforms. What is required is an expansion of direct, morally grounded, and positive and leverage-based human rights obligations for corporations, alongside a shift toward more non-voluntary rules that apply to both state and non-state actors. In particular, two arguments support the move toward mandatory, legally binding rules for multinational corporations (MNCs): the quasi-political role and responsibilities (i.e., power) of MNCs and the moral nature of human rights (Wettstein, 2009b, 2010b; Wettstein & Waddock, 2005; Wood, 2011, 2012).

7.2 Political role and responsibilities of multinational corporations

First, contemporary political discourse often views MNCs, including big tech, as private, apolitical entities, consistent with the traditional Westphalian worldview (Kobrin, 2009). Yet the political nature of human rights responsibilities in a post-Westphalian order (Zumbansen, 2010a, 2010b, 2010c) stands in stark contrast to this purportedly apolitical corporate identity (Wettstein, 2012b). Research in political corporate social responsibility (CSR) and transnational legal theory documents the gradual politicization of MNCs and big tech, as well as the transformation of business-government-society relations (Kobrin, 2009). Foucault (2010) and other proponents of governmentality studies describe a 'post-regulatory model' (Conley & Williams, 2011), in which private (soft law) self-regulation increasingly supplements and sometimes substitutes traditional government (hard law) regulation. These emerging (transnational) governance regimes reflect a 'shift from government to governance': state and non-state actors form coalitions and

3 This regulatory push toward deregulation, including weakening the GDPR, revising the Data Act, and delaying enforcement of the AI Act for high-risk systems, reflects a broader global trend, as evidenced by the analysis of Trump-era economic policies discussed earlier.

public-private partnerships, contributing to a 'governmentality regulatory network.' Top-down state regulation is weakened, governmental functions are outsourced to non-state actors (Chan, 2012), and powers, rights, and responsibilities are increasingly diffused. New governance agents – MNCs, nongovernmental organizations (NGOs), and civil society groups – enter the regulatory arena, often acting across borders and using market mechanisms to pursue socio-environmental goals (Conley & Williams, 2011). These 'governance without government' systems (Rosenau & Czempiel, 1992) create a new division of regulatory labor among state, market, and civil society actors.

Within this evolving governance landscape, MNCs, such as big tech, assume roles and functions traditionally associated with nation-states. Most notably, they increasingly engage in the protection, facilitation, and enabling of citizens' rights (Matten & Crane, 2005). In the realm of *social and cultural rights*, corporations act as providers of essential services. With respect to *civil rights*, they serve as enablers, capable of both constraining and empowering individuals. Regarding *political rights*, they serve as channels through which individuals can exercise these rights. Consequently, MNCs, including big tech, now play a pivotal quasi-political role in shaping and facilitating rights linked to citizenship; they are central actors in the domain of political rights. In essence, they operate as de facto rule-makers, standard-setters, and (co-)authors of regulations, exercising functions similar to those of public authorities (Matten & Crane, 2005; Wettstein, 2009a).

This heightened political status justifies and demands expanded moral duties. As power shifts, so too must responsibilities. Political authority entails public responsibilities (Kobrin, 2009), including regulatory and political co-responsibilities (Scherer & Palazzo, 2007; Wettstein, 2010b). These obligations go beyond avoiding harm. MNCs – including major tech companies – must utilize their immense power for the common good, particularly in protecting human rights.[4] The 'argument of symmetry' holds that power, authority, and rights imply corresponding duties, obligations, and liabili-

4 Corporate human rights advocacy (and human rights due diligence) relies on several key strategies to identify, address, and mitigate violations within a company's supply chains. A central element is rigorous supply-chain screening and monitoring, supported by contractual covenants and, when necessary, divestment. One effective way to exert leverage over business partners in global supply chains is through business contracts: companies can embed human rights expectations, such as due diligence processes, impact assessments and action plans, stakeholder engagement, impact-benefit agreements, and grievance and remedy mechanisms, directly into their commercial agreements and supply-chain management systems. When partners violate these clauses, companies may suspend funding, terminate the relationship, or pursue legal action. Divestment provides an additional pressure mechanism. Firms can disengage from entities that repeatedly breach international socio-environmental and human-rights standards. By ending direct or indirect relationships with corporations known for harmful practices, companies signal a clear refusal to tolerate abuse. This 'exit option' helps reinforce accountability and strengthens norms around human-rights compliance in global supply chains. Human-rights lobbyism represents another important dimension of corporate advocacy. Companies can publicly oppose ongoing, systematic, or severe abuses by participating in human-rights discourse and collaborating with NGOs, civil-society groups, and governments in both home and host countries. Through diplomatic engagement and policy dialogue, they can also advocate for stronger industry

ties (Kobrin, 2009). Put differently: leverage – defined in terms of organizational size, operational scale, financial and human resources, strategic network positions, and access to elites (Wood 2011, 2012) – correlates directly with responsibility. The greater the leverage, the greater the responsibility (Kobrin, 2009; Wood, 2011, 2012).

7.3 Moral nature of human rights

Second, the current reliance on voluntarism is incompatible with the moral nature of human rights (Wettstein, 2012b). Human rights are fundamental moral rights inherent to all human beings, expressing their equal moral worth (Fasterling & Demuijnck, 2013; Wettstein, 2009a, 2009b, 2010a, 2010b, 2012a, 2012b). They are grounded in human dignity (Foucault, 2010; Gosepath & Lohmann, 1998/1999; Kobrin, 2009; Wettstein & Waddock, 2005; Wettstein, 2009a) and are essential for autonomous and dignified human life. Because they derive from dignity, they are universal, egalitarian, indivisible, inalienable, undeniable, and unconditional moral rights (Cragg, 2005, 2010/2012; Wettstein, 2009b). Human rights pre-exist the state; while they are codified in laws and constitutions, their moral validity does not depend on legal recognition (Lane, 2005). Thus, the moral obligations they generate exceed legal obligations (Cragg, 2005, 2010/2012, 2012; Sorrell, 2005).

Given their moral status, human rights cannot be subject to arbitrariness, discretion, or voluntariness. They are not matters of charitable choice. Accordingly, MNCs, including big tech companies, have both direct negative (do no harm) and positive (do good) moral obligations to respect, protect, and realize human rights – obligations that apply regardless of national legal requirements (Wettstein & Waddock, 2005). Businesses are direct duty-bearers and should be held directly liable for human rights violations or complicity in them (Kobrin, 2009). States are not the sole bearers of positive human rights obligations. Corporate duties must extend beyond 'do no harm'; they also include protecting and promoting human rights (Murphy & Vives, 2013). These positive duties encompass responsibilities traditionally assigned only to states, including protecting victims of human rights abuses, especially in humanitarian crises; speaking out against abuses; promoting human rights-compatible institutions; and contributing to political and economic reform across the value chain (Fasterling & Demuijnck, 2013).

In summary, as quasi-political authorities, MNCs, such as big tech companies, bear political responsibilities and have direct human rights obligations. They must respect, protect, and realize human rights. The tripartite typology of human rights obligations (Ruggie, 2013; Shue, 1980/1996) therefore applies not only to states but also to non-state actors, and corporations must fulfill both negative and positive duties.

---

rules and governmental standards, ensuring that respect for human rights is embedded across their operations (Wörsdörfer, 2015, 2017).

References

Amnesty International et al. (2025). Joint Statement: The EU Must Uphold Hard-Won Protections for Digital Human Rights. https://www.amnesty.eu/news/eu-must-uphold-protections-for-digital-human-rights/ (last accessed: December 30, 2025).

Chan, M. (2012). What about Psychological Actors? Behavioral Analysis of Equator Principle Adoption and Its Implications. German Law Journal 13(12). 1339–1362.

Conley, J. & Williams, C. (2011): Global Banks as Global Sustainability Regulators? The Equator Principles. Law and Policy 33(4). 542–575.

Cragg, W. (2005). Human Rights, Globalization, and the Modern Shareholder-Owned Corporation. In: Campbell, T. & Miller, S. (eds). Human Rights and the Moral Responsibilities of Corporate and Public Sector Organizations. Dordrecht, Springer. 105–127.

Cragg, W. (2010/2012). Business and Human Rights: A Principle and Value-Based Analysis. In: Brenkert, G. & Beauchamp, T. (eds). The Oxford Handbook of Business Ethics. Oxford, Oxford University Press. 267–304.

Cragg, W. (2012): Ethics, Enlightened Self-Interest, and the Corporate Responsibility to Respect Human Rights: A Critical Look at the Justificatory Foundations of the U.N. Framework. Business Ethics Quarterly 22(1). 9–36.

Deutsche Welle. (2025). EU Plans to Ease GDPR Laws and AI Constraints in Major Shift. https://www.dw.com/en/eu-plans-to-ease-gdpr-laws-and-ai-constraints-in-major-shift/a-74792773 (last accessed: December 30, 2025).

Fasterling, B. & Demuijnck, G. (2013). Human Rights in the Void? Due Diligence in the U.N. Guiding Principles on Business and Human Rights. Journal of Business Ethics 116(4). 799–814.

Foucault, M. (2010). The Birth of Biopolitics: Lectures at the Collège de France, 1978–1979. New York, Picador.

Gosepath, S. & Lohmann, G. (eds.) (1998/1999). Philosophie der Menschenrechte. Frankfurt, Suhrkamp.

Kobrin, S. (2009). Private Political Authority and Public Responsibility: Transnational Politics, Transnational Firms, and Human Rights. Business Ethics Quarterly 19(3). 349–374.

Lane, M. (2005). Autonomy as a Central Human Right and Its Implications for the Moral Responsibilities of Corporations. In: Campbell, T. & Miller, S. (eds). Human Rights and the Moral Responsibilities of Corporate and Public Sector Organizations. Dordrecht, Springer. 145–163.

Matten, D., & Crane, A. (2005). Corporate Citizenship: Toward an Extended Theoretical Conceptualization. Academy of Management 30(1). 166–179.

Murphy, M. & Vives, J. (2013). Perceptions of Justice and the Human Rights Protect, Respect, and Remedy Framework. Journal of Business Ethics 116(4). 781–797.

Netzpolitik.org. (2025a). EU-Kommission will Datenschutzgrundverordnung und KI-Regulierung schleifen. https://netzpolitik.org/2025/digitaler-omnibus-eu-kommission-will-datenschutzgrundverordnung-und-ki-regulierung-schleifen/ (last accessed: December 30, 2025).

Netzpolitik.org. (2025b). Digital Omnibus on AI (Digital Package on Simplification). https://cdn.netzpolitik.org/wp-upload/2025/11/EU-Kommission-Digital-Omnibus-B-KI.pdf (last accessed: December 30, 2025).

Netzpolitik.org. (2025c). Digital Omnibus for the Digital Acquis (Digital Package on Simplification). https://cdn.netzpolitik.org/wp-upload/2025/11/EU-Kommission-Digital-Omnibus-A-Data-Act-und-DSGVO.pdf (last accessed: December 30, 2025).

Politico. (2025). EU Prepares to Delay Landmark AI Rules By One Year. https://www.politico.eu/article/eu-to-propose-delay-of-key-part-of-landmark-ai-law-by-one-year/ (last accessed: December 30, 2025).

Rosenau, J. & Czempiel, E.-O. (eds.) (1992). Governance without Government: Order and Change in World Politics. Cambridge, Cambridge University Press.

Ruggie, J. (2013). Just Business: Multinational Corporations and Human Rights. New York, Norton.

Scherer, A. & Palazzo, G. (2007). Toward a Political Conception of Corporate Responsibility: Business and Society Seen From a Habermasian Perspective. Academy of Management Review 32(4). 1096–1120.
Shue, H. (1980/1996). Basic Rights: Subsistence, Affluence, and U.S. Foreign Policy. Princeton, Princeton University Press.
Sorrell, T. (2005). Business and Human Rights. In: Campbell, T. & Miller, S. (eds). Human Rights and the Moral Responsibilities of Corporate and Public Sector Organizations. Dordrecht, Springer. 129–144.
Wettstein, F. (2009a). Multinational Corporations and Global Justice. Human Rights Obligations of a Quasi-Governmental Institution. Stanford, Stanford University Press.
Wettstein, F. (2009b). Beyond Voluntariness, Beyond CSR: Making a Case for Human Rights and Justice. Business and Society Review 114(1). 125–152.
Wettstein, F. (2010a). The Duty to Protect: Corporate Complicity, Political Responsibility, and Human Rights Advocacy. Journal of Business Ethics 96(1). 33–47.
Wettstein, F. (2010b). For Better or For Worse: Corporate Responsibility Beyond 'Do No Harm.' Business Ethics Quarterly 20(2). 275–283.
Wettstein, F. (2012a). Silence as Complicity: Elements of a Corporate Duty to Speak Out against the Violation of Human Rights. Business Ethics Quarterly 22(1). 37–61.
Wettstein, F. (2012b). CSR and the Debate on Business and Human Rights: Bridging the Great Divide. Business Ethics Quarterly 22(4). 739–770.
Wettstein, F. & Waddock, S. (2005). Voluntary or Mandatory: That is (Not) the Question. Linking Corporate Citizenship to Human Rights Obligations for Business. zfwu 6(3). 304–320.
Wörsdörfer, M. (2015). The Equator Principles and Human Rights Due Diligence – Towards a Positive and Leverage-Based Concept of Corporate Social Responsibility. Philosophy of Management 14(3). 193–218.
Wörsdörfer, M. (2017). The Equator Principles and the Business and Human Rights Debate: Hype or Hope? In: A. de Jonge & R. Tomasic (eds.). Research Handbook on Transnational Corporations. Cheltenham, Elgar. 139–168.
Wood, S. (2011). Four Varieties of Social Responsibility: Making Sense of the 'Sphere of Influence' and 'Leverage' Debate via the Case of ISO 26000. http://papers.ssrn.com/sol3/papers.cfm?abstract_id=1777505 (last accessed: December 30, 2025).
Wood, S. (2012). The Case for Leverage-Based Corporate Human Rights Responsibility. Business Ethics Quarterly 22(1). 63–98.
Wu, T. (2025). The Age of Extraction: How Tech Platforms Conquered the Economy and Threaten Our Future Prosperity. New York, Knopf.
Zumbansen, P. (2010a). Corporate Governance, Capital Market Regulation, and the Challenge of Disembedded Markets. Osgoode CLPE 24/2010.
Zumbansen, P. (2010b). Transnational Legal Pluralism. Transnational Legal Theory 1(2). 141–189.
Zumbansen, P. (2010c). Neither 'Public' nor 'Private,' 'National' nor 'International.' Transnational Corporate Governance from a Legal Pluralist Perspective. Osgoode CLPE 22/2010.

About the author

Dr Wörsdörfer is an associate professor of management and computing ethics at the Maine Business School and the School of Computing and Information Science, and an associate member of the Climate Change Institute and AI Initiative at the University of Maine. Before joining UMaine, he served as a lecturer and research fellow at the Murdough Center for Engineering Professionalism and as a member of the Climate Science Center at Texas Tech University. He was also a postdoctoral research fellow at the Cluster of Excellence *The Formation of Normative Orders* and a member of the Centre for Business Ethics at Goethe University Frankfurt. Additionally, he has held visiting research fellowships at Beijing University, Carnegie Mellon University, the University of Toronto, and York University. Dr Wörsdörfer's research centers on business and human rights, particularly political CSR, and on AI ethics with a focus on big tech and antitrust. His work has been presented at major international conferences, including the annual meetings of the Australasian Business Ethics Network, European Business Ethics Network, International Association for Computing and Philosophy, and the Society for Business Ethics, and published in journals such as *AI and Ethics, Business and Society Review, Digital Society, European Competition Journal, European Journal of the History of Economic Thought, History of Economic Ideas, Journal of Business Ethics, Journal of the History of Economic Thought, Philosophy & Technology, Philosophy of Management, The Antitrust Bulletin*, and *Transnational Legal Theory*.

 | https://doi.org/10.1515/9783112245958-009

Subject index

Name index

 | https://doi.org/10.1515/9783112245958-011

www.ingramcontent.com/pod-product-compliance
Lightning Source LLC
LaVergne TN
LVHW081314110826
845149LV00006B/1506

* 9 7 8 3 1 1 2 2 4 5 9 4 1 *